**An Economic History
of the United States**

# An Economic History of the United States

Martin L. Primack
James F. Willis

The Benjamin/Cummings Publishing Company, Inc.
Menlo Park, California • Reading, Massachusetts
London • Amsterdam • Don Mills, Ontario • Sydney

To my loving wife, Marlene.
M. L. Primack

To my wife, my son, and my mother. In memory of my father,
who loved history and was a teacher for most of his life.
J. F. Willis

AN ECONOMIC HISTORY OF THE UNITED STATES by
Martin L. Primack and James F. Willis.

Copyright © 1980 by The Benjamin/Cummings Publishing Company, Inc. Philippines copyright 1980 by The Benjamin/Cum-
mings Publishing Company, Inc.

Library of Congress Cataloging in Publication Data

Primack, Martin L     1929–
   An economic history of the United States.

   Includes bibliographies and index.
   1. United States—Economic conditions.   I. Willis,
James Frederick, 1932–   joint author.   II. Title.
HC103.P85        330.9'73        79-22731
ISBN 0-8053-8010-8

ABCDEFGHIJ-HA-83210

The Benjamin/Cummings Publishing Company, Inc.
2727 Sand Hill Road
Menlo Park, California 94025

# Contents

# Preface

## Why This Book?

During our many years of teaching U.S. economic history, we searched for a text that would meet the needs of our students. This book is the end result of our efforts to meet those needs.

Our students have been a mixture of those with formal economics training plus those with little such background. We felt that a text was needed, therefore, that was clearly written and that contained enough of a review of economic principles to bolster any lack of training and to recall important concepts where needed. At the same time, we wanted the principles to be optional to the instructor, who would be free to bypass the review for students with more extensive backgrounds in economic theory.

We wanted a text that would meet the following requirements. First, the material should be organized into clearly defined time periods. Second, the materials should include, as much as is practical, a review of the important scholarly contributions to various areas of research in the U.S. economic history. Third, the various areas should be analyzed using concepts of economic theory. Finally, review questions covering basic economic theories should be added to the necessary chapters to facilitate the application of economic theory.

We concluded that not only would such a book meet our teaching needs, but it would also be useful for others. Although designed for junior and senior classes in economic history, this book can be used in lower-division courses in economic history by placing an emphasis on the end-of-chapter reviews of economic concepts. It can also serve as a one-semester principles text. And, if supplemented with additional readings, this book can be used in graduate courses.

## The Approach of the Book

All authors of this subject matter have their own theoretical biases which are compounded by their historical biases. In other words, it is impossible to write a completely "objective" U.S. economic history text. Our goal was to present an eclectic approach, as much as is possible to do so. We have taken considerable pains to examine the various points of view on the many controversial areas of U.S. economic history. For example, in the controversy between Keynesianism and monetarism, we fall on the side of Keynesianism and aggregate demand. However, the role of money and its effects on economic activity have not been neglected.

## The Structure of the Book

This book is divided into chronological segments, each focussing on a particular time period. The models or theories used to explain these periods are presented at the end of each chapter in "A Review of Economic Concepts." Additionally, each chapter contains review questions and glossary terms. For a more in-depth analysis of the structure of this text, please refer to the Introduction.

## Acknowledgments

Perhaps only an author fully understands the dual reality of writing a book. On the one hand is the tremendous debt one owes to others for their assistance, and on the other hand is the sole responsibility for what ends up on the printed page.

What we know and understand about U.S. economic history is, for the most part, the end product of the long and continuing process of research by many scholars in this evolving field. And, in large measure, we are grateful to our teachers, with whom our understanding of this history first began. Martin Primack is indebted to William N. Parker, and James Willis is indebted to J. S. Spratt and Eastin Nelson, among others.

A number of colleagues have given generously of their time, expertise and advice. We owe sincere thanks to Lloyd Mercer of the University of California at Santa Barbara, Barry Poulson of the University of Colorado, Barbara Vatter of Memphis State University, Forrest Hill of the University of Texas, and Robert Francis of DeAnza College. Their efforts have improved this book. The errors that remain may be ascribed to our stubborn pride.

We also wish to thank Mrs. Geri Brandt and Mrs. Sumiko Hoshino for their invaluable assistance in typing the manuscript.

Finally, we deeply appreciate the understanding and patience of our wives, Marlene and Marianna.

# About the Authors

Martin L. Primack received his B.S. in agricultural economics from Pennsylvania State University in 1953, his M.A. from the University of Maryland in 1959, and his Ph.D. in economics from the University of North Carolina in 1963. He has taught at the University of North Carolina, Pennsylvania Military College, the University of Delaware, Bentley College of Boston, Boston University, Northeastern University, and Stanford University. Presently, he is Professor of Economics at San Jose State University, San Jose, California. His primary research was in nineteenth-century agricultural history, and he has written several articles on the subject that appeared in the *Journal of Economic History*. Stuart Bruchy chose Primack's dissertation, "Farm-Formed Capital in American Agriculture 1860 to 1910," for inclusion in the 1977 series, *Dissertations on U.S. Economic History*. Teaching has always been one of his prime concerns, and his text writing has stemmed from an equal concern for more useful teaching materials.

James F. Willis received his B.A. and M.A. degrees in Latin American Studies from the University of Texas. In 1966, he received his Ph.D. degree from Southern Methodist University. Willis has taught at the University of Texas (Austin and Arlington), Southern Methodist University, and San Jose State University. He is presently Professor of Economics and Chairman of the Department of Economics at San Jose State. Most of his research has been in Latin American economic history and development, and he has served as an economic advisor to Latin American nations as well as to the government of the United States. Because of their mutual interests in economic history and development, the authors are presently joined in research on the relationship between debt and credit in the transfer of agricultural resources to industrial uses in the early stages of economic development.

# Introduction

Many people have researched the history of the American economy, and many textbooks have been published on that subject. Each of the latter has its strengths. Some of the texts are very lengthy, containing an almost encyclopedic wealth of information on a variety of historical subjects. Other books are relatively brief, containing less descriptive information but providing excellent, up-to-date summaries of research work in economic history. Some works contain very explicit analytical (theoretical) frameworks; others have a largely implicit framework. As teachers of economic history for many years, we were dissatisfied with the blend of theory and description in existing books and set out (perhaps with excessive immodesty) to write a text that would be a more *flexible* tool for instructors and for students beginning the study of U.S. economic history.

We decided to achieve flexibility by concentrating on those historical topics that, in our judgment, are of most general concern and interest. Admittedly, that involved us in judgments with which some economic historians will disagree. Also, we decided to include very explicit economic principles or introductory economic theory in the book, for the benefit of students who have not studied—or have not recently studied—that subject. In our view, those principles are necessary in order for students to understand the economic focus on American history. Since many students, however, will be familiar with elementary economic theory, we have put the lengthy theory expositions in Reviews of Economic Concepts. These may be bypassed where further exposure to beginning theory is inappropriate.

Because we sought flexibility rather than encyclopedic coverage, most instructors will wish to use this book as a major component of their course. Depending on the emphasis of that course, each will wish to either "flesh out" the theory (for students with very limited exposure to economic principles) or ignore the Reviews of Economic Concepts altogether. All, we assume, will wish to expand on the depth of topical coverage with original source materials, or with some of the excellent, specialized, secondary source materials that are available. Many of both of these are cited in the Suggested Readings sections at the end of each chapter. This will permit instructors to emphasize those topics they prefer.

Finally, to encourage an understanding of our history, or changes in our economy through time, we have written the book and organized its chapters in chronological, rather than topical order. We believe that this arrangement provides greater historical continuity.

## About History

The human events recorded by historians can be interpreted from many different perspectives. An event such as the American Revolution, for example, can be interpreted as military history, diplomatic history, or political history. But a war can also be viewed as economic history, because it results partly from economic causes and has a series of economic consequences.

Scholars rarely interpret the history of human events in purely economic terms. As we shall see in subsequent chapters, a few, such as Charles Beard and Karl Marx (not, necessarily, present-day Marxists), have sought to view history as a progression of events in which people act almost exclusively on the basis of their economic self-interest or through adjusting to the changing economic reality. This notion of **economic determinism** is now almost totally rejected. Today economists are concerned with the interrelationships among political, social, cultural, and economic events. We will see some of these interactions, for example, when we observe how British political policies affected the economic position of the American colonies and how the economic position of the colonies affected their political relationship to Great Britain.

Because such interactions are extremely complex, this introductory section is devoted to explaining some basic ideas about economics and economic history. Most importantly, we'll explain how this book is organized and suggest an effective way to use it as a tool in your studies.

## A Skeletal View of the Book

This book has a structure, an organizational plan, designed to provide maximum benefits to the reader. Each chapter will contain an outline or skeleton on which we'll build the body of American economic history:

1. A clear statement of economic **theory**. In most chapters, we will set forth a theory or **model**. Recall that a model is a set of formal relationships between factors or forces. As such, a model is an abstraction from, or a simplification of, the immensely complex reality of a period. Because economic reality is always too complex to be described fully, we build these abstractions in order to focus on key interrelationships.

2. The **data**. As economic events are recorded, they become data. Economists work with two general classes of data, **time series data** and **cross-sectional data**. Time series data show the occurrence of a particular kind of event at different points in time. The amount of cotton exported during each year between 1815 and 1860 is an example. Cross-sectional data show the occurrence of a particular event in different activities at the same point in time or over the same span of time. The rates of return on investment in agriculture, industry, and commerce in the period from 1900 to 1930 are an example. Throughout this book, you will encounter both kinds of data.

   Of course, in a broader sense the word *data* refers to all events or happenings that are observed and recorded, not simply those that are quantified or quantifiable. Many data, especially those of an institutional nature, are not amenable to either time series or cross-sectional quantification. Bear in mind, though, that when economists talk about data, they generally refer to those quantified phenomena that can be used in testing various hypotheses or arguments within theories or models.

3. An **interpretation**. Theory and the data appropriately suggested by that theory to test hypotheses are the ingredients necessary to interpret and explain historical events and sequences of events. By using the data to test a hypothesis within the framework of a model, economic historians can determine whether to accept or reject that argument. Frequently this method permits the student of history to determine to what extent the occurrence of one event may be explained by the occurrence of another event or of several other events. Such a study might, for example, permit a student of the American colonial period to conclude that per capita income in the colonies would have been only 1% higher in the absence of British economic controls. A reasonable interpretation of this result might be that the British controls had little effect on colonial growth, that the colonies would not have grown appreciably more rapidly in the absence of those controls. A further possible interpretation might be that this indicates an absence of colonial "exploitation."

   Such interpretations are the final products of economic history. You will notice that the interpretations are diverse; even for the same period, the explanation of cause-and-effect relationships will vary, depending on the model of historical assumptions employed and on the data used to test that model. As new interpretations are made, old interpretations are sometimes rejected. The rejection by more recent scholars of Charles Beard's economic interpretation of the formulation and adoption of the federal Constitution is an example.

4. **Glossary**. Economists, including economic historians, have a distinct language in which they communicate among themselves and with others. Terms such as *demand function, aggregate demand,* and *linearly homogeneous production function* have very precise meanings. All students of economics must attribute the same meaning to a term and use it correctly—unlike Humpty Dumpty, who said, "Words mean whatever I say they mean!" To help you learn the economist's vocabulary, we will define each term at the end of the chapter in which it is first used. The same term may be used again many times throughout the book. If you have forgotten the meaning of the term, you can find the definition again easily and quickly in the Glossary at the end of the book.

5. **Questions.** The questions at the end of each chapter provide an opportunity for self-evaluation and call attention to topics the reader should review before going on to the next chapter. When you have answered the questions correctly, you will have summarized the major elements and conclusions of the chapter and strengthened your understanding through effective repetition.

6. **Suggested Readings.** American historians have long said that they suffer from "an embarrassment of riches." The riches are the numerous research studies of virtually every period of our history. Although some unexplored areas remain open for fruitful study, the literature of United States economic history is extensive. Some of the most important studies are listed in the Suggested Readings at the end of each chapter. Citations to those studies are found in the supercript numbers throughout the chapters. For example, a reference within a chapter followed by a supercript[5] means that the citation to that author's work may be found as the fifth item in the Suggested Readings section at the end of the chapter. The list will enable you to read further into the subject area of the chapter and also to begin the reading for a research paper.

Keeping these points and this overview in mind as you read subsequent chapters will enhance the contribution this book can make to your study of economic history.

# Glossary

**Cross-sectional data**   Data that show the occurrence of a particular event in different activities at the same point in time or over the same span of time.

**Data**  The records of economic events; in a broad sense, the word *data* refers to all events or happenings that are observed and recorded, not simply those that are quantified.

**Economic determinism**  In the pure sense, the view that human history is a progression of events in which people act almost exclusively on the basis of their economic self-interest or through adjusting to the changing economic reality.

**Interpretation**  The final product of economic history; the result of drawing historical conclusions by testing hypotheses within the framework of theory.

**Model**  See **Theory.**

**Theory**  A set of formal relationships between forces or factors; a model; an analogy to, or a simplification of, the complex reality of a period.

**Time series data**  Data that show the occurrence of a particular kind of event at different points in time.

# Chapter 1

# The Colonies Before 1763

The expectation of substantially different economic as well as social, political, and religious conditions and opportunities was a strong force in bringing the European colonists to North America. In large measure, those expectations, particularly those regarding changed economic conditions, were fulfilled, although not always in the ways the early colonists expected. From the early seventeenth century to the end of the French and Indian War, we can observe in North America the evolution of an economy that reflects the peculiar economic conditions of the area and the evolution also of a set of economic ties to the European economies that reflects the specialized advantages of the two parts of the world.

What accounts for the relatively rapid growth of the North American colonies even before 1763? What caused the **production possibilities function** of the colonies, the relationship that shows the various combinations of output that the full employment use of a nation's resources (land, labor, capital and entrepreneurship), using the best of current technology, to shift upward? In graphical terms, what caused the **production possibilities curve,** the diagrammatic presentation of the production possibilities function to shift to the right? Were the colonies an "empty land," with few resistances to economic development, and waiting to be developed? The "empty land–staple export–leading sector" hypothesis about colonial growth provides some very useful insights into the reasons for the colony's success. According to this hypothesis, it is the emergence of one or more leading export sectors that provide the stimulus to incorporate more and more of a society's resources into development-oriented uses.

As we shall see in looking at the individual colonies and geographic regions, staple exports played a very important role in colonial growth, especially in providing the funds with which to import scarce resources. The growth of leading sectors benefiting from demand increases clearly offset what might have been a tendency toward the unfavorable terms of trade that some commodity-exporting areas suffer in the early phases of economic development.

## Replacing and Learning from the Indian Economies

A major qualification to the staple theory's usefulness in explaining North America's development lies in its failure to encompass some of the area's peculiar advantages. It is important to remember that the colonists adapted to the resources they encountered and also found in those initial conditions certain favorable elements created by the Indian cultures. North America, thus, was not a completely empty land. Not only did the colonists learn of new crops, especially corn and tobacco, from the Indians, but they also learned much about cultivation, crop rotation (which they frequently ignored), and about agricultural tools and fishing techniques. Economic development is a learning process. The eastern Indian tribes lived well, reflecting a relatively high level of productivity the result of long-term learning. It was no small advantage to the colonists, in offsetting increasing costs, that they were able to avail themselves of the adaptive learning processes of several million indigenous people. The technological superiority of the colonists, especially in the uses of metals, made it possible for them ultimately to supplant the Indians. Ironically, these advantages were few in number but were extremely important in determining which of the two cultures and economies would become dominant in North America. The Europeans' slight technological edge, together with the Indians' lack of immunity to European diseases, virtually dictated the answer, in spite of an amazing adaptation by the North American Indians to European resources (including horses) and economic techniques.

Although with this important qualification, the processes of development described in the model worked generally throughout the colonies, the specifics were different. Also, both the type and size of the spread effects (demand-supply effects on the rest of the economy) differed, not only from one colony to another but also, and more especially, from one area of the colonies to another. What we shall do, therefore, is to look at the colonies separately and then draw the evidence together in order to form some conclusions for the colonies in general.

**Economic growth** may be extensive or intensive. Extensive growth occurs when more resources are used to produce an output unchanged in composition or techniques of production. **Intensive growth** involves increased productivity and involves a changed composition of output and techniques of production. **Economic development** is a long-term process through which per capita output grows and structural changes occur as well. All are processes that involve learning to adapt. This is especially true in an empty land, where precedents for successful and unsuccessful commercial enterprise are lacking. Thus, in the southern colonies, there were various early attempts to adjust to the relative resource endowments of the region by finding a crop structure that would provide not only consumption goods for the colonists but also entry into the large European market. Of course, colonial farmers, who were familiar with small grains, did adapt to the indigenous crops found in North America, especially corn (also squash and beans). Although the Jamestown colony almost failed in its first year for lack of food and because of weather conditions, shortly afterward a remarkably successful export was developed. In 1616, a low-cost process for curing tobacco was developed that permitted shipment to Europe. Although other export staples were developed later, the success of tobacco exports, in spite of the English king's strong feelings against what he regarded as a "noxious weed," is reflected in the growing importation of American tobacco by England from 1620 to 1760 (Table 1-1).

Table 1-1. Imports of American Tobacco by England (including reexports).

| Year | Millions of Pounds | Year | Millions of Pounds |
|------|--------------------|------|--------------------|
| 1620 | 0.1                | 1730 | 41.0               |
| 1630 | 0.5                | 1740 | 41.0               |
| 1640 | 1.3                | 1755 | 64.0               |
| 1672 | 17.6               | 1760 | 85.0               |
| 1708 | 30.0               |      |                    |
| 1722 | 35.0               |      |                    |

*Source:* U.S. Bureau of the Census, *Historical Statistics of the United States, Colonial Times to 1957,* (Washington, D.C.: U.S. Government Printing Office, 1960).

The data indicate that tobacco exports (imports by England for its consumption plus those reexported to the European continent) grew very rapidly (especially from 1640 to 1672); nonetheless, such exports grew over the entire period from 1620 to 1760. Most of the tobacco market was in Europe, which meant, given overland transportation costs, that early tobacco plantations were located near the headwaters of rivers and their tributaries. The supply increases reflected in the data show that the creative entrepreneurship, to use the phrase coined by Joseph Schumpeter, that was required for this staple product expansion was forthcoming.

These data suggest that tobacco, which was the first major export staple from the North American colonies, may well have been the area's first leading sector. Once the institutional incentive restraints on entrepreneurship were relaxed, resources were clearly allocated and reallocated toward growth in the staple export sector.* Still, the growing of tobacco was a very labor-intensive activity (the labor input per acre of land was about one-half a man-year). From early growth in seedbeds through the drying, grading, and packing, much labor was required. Since that was a factor in short supply, relatively high wage rates (reflecting its productivity to employers), were required to attract the immigrants to the South, especially the upper South during the early years of the colonies. The success of the market signal may be seen in the population growth figures in Table 1-2.

Several important facts are reflected in the population growth figures. Note that there was a very high rate of overall population growth. In each 30-year period from 1660 to 1780, colonial population more than doubled.† This was unquestionably one of the highest rates of population growth in the world at that time. In an empty land, it was a decided plus so far as expanding the labor force (extensive growth), restraining wage cost increases, and increasing the size of the market were concerned. It clearly shifted the production possibilities curve of the colonies to the right.

It is important to note that the growth effects of the increase in staple exports were not evenly distributed through the colonies. This is a familiar effect in economic development; some areas or regions are better suited than others to take advantage of the original stimuli that an increase in staple exports creates. We see thus in Table 1-2 that the relative populations (and market sizes) of the colonies changed substantially. Whereas in 1660 the New England colonies contained about 53% of total population (47,000 of 89,000), by 1780 that northernmost region contained only about 26% of the total population (714,000 of 2,726,000). At the same time, we should note that even New England's population grew 15-fold between 1660 and 1780, a growth that seems modest only by comparison with the 30-fold increase for all the colonies and 37-fold increase for the colonies from Delaware south to Georgia.

## The Southern Colonies

By 1720, Virginia was the most populous colony. Its growth depended very heavily on the increasing demand for tobacco, an increase that continued throughout the colonial period. Because tobacco-growing techniques of the period rapidly depleted the soil, plantations after a few years simply moved on, clearing a new region farther inland and beginning the produc-

---

* The principal such restraint was a prohibition against private land ownership and the pooling of output that had existed during the early "starvation years."
† Although it is outside the time dimension of this chapter, 1780 is included here to accommodate the 30-year comparisons.

Table 1-2. Population of the American Colonies, 1630–1780.

| | 1780 | 1750 | 1720 | 1690 | 1660 | 1630 |
|---|---|---|---|---|---|---|
| Maine[a] | 49,000 | — | — | — | — | — |
| New Hampshire | 88,000 | 28,000 | 9,000 | 4,000 | 2,000 | —[b] |
| Vermont | 48,000 | — | — | — | — | — |
| Massachusetts | 269,000 | 188,000 | 91,000 | 57,000 | 35,000 | 1,000 |
| Rhode Island | 53,000 | 33,000 | 12,000 | 4,000 | 2,000 | — |
| Connecticut | 207,000 | 111,000 | 59,000 | 22,000 | 8,000 | — |
| Subtotal | 714,000 | 360,000 | 171,000 | 87,000 | 47,000 | |
| New York | 211,000 | 77,000 | 37,000 | 14,000 | 5,000 | —[b] |
| New Jersey | 140,000 | 71,000 | 30,000 | 8,000 | — | — |
| Pennsylvania | 327,000 | 120,000 | 31,000 | 11,000 | — | — |
| Subtotal | 678,000 | 268,000 | 98,000 | 33,000 | 5,000 | |
| Delaware | 45,000 | 29,000 | 5,000 | 1,000 | —[b] | — |
| Maryland | 245,000 | 141,000 | 66,000 | 24,000 | 8,000 | — |
| Virginia | 538,000 | 231,000 | 88,000 | 53,000 | 27,000 | 3,000 |
| North Carolina | 270,000 | 73,000 | 21,000 | 7,000 | 1,000 | — |
| South Carolina | 180,000 | 64,000 | 17,000 | 4,000 | — | — |
| Georgia | 56,000 | 5,000 | — | — | — | — |
| Subtotal | 1,334,000 | 543,000 | 197,000 | 89,000 | 36,000 | |
| Grand Total | 2,726,000 | 1,171,000 | 466,000 | 209,000 | 89,000 | 5,000 |

a Maine was included in Massachusetts until 1760.
b Less than 1000.
Source: Adapted from U.S. Bureau of the Census. Historical Statistics of the United States, Colonial Times to 1957 (Washington, D.C.: U.S. Government Printing

tion cycle again. Although tobacco was grown commercially even on the frontier, high transportation costs imposed a severe limit on its supply from interior locations. Largely for this reason, the tobacco plantation system, with its spread effects, moved north to Maryland and even south to the Carolinas.

One of the direct growth effects in South Carolina was in the development of a port city and the service industries to facilitate the low-cost export of indigo and rice (see Table 1-3). South Carolina's premier city, Charleston, became the only large urban area in the South during the colonial period. By the time of the American Revolution, Charleston had 10,000 people, making it the fourth largest city in the colonies, after New York (28,000), Philadelphia (22,000), and Boston (15,000).

Table 1-3. Rice Exported from Charleston (five-year averages).

| Years | Barrels |
|---|---|
| 1716–1720 | 9,000 |
| 1721–1725 | 19,000 |
| 1726–1730 | 31,000 |
| 1731–1735 | 41,000 |
| 1736–1740 | 58,000 |
| 1741–1745 | 68,000 |
| 1746–1750 | 51,000 |
| 1751–1755 | 58,000 |
| 1756–1760 | 69,000 |

Source: Lewis Cecil Gray, *History of Agriculture in the Southern United States to 1860,* vol. 1 (Washington, D.C.: Carnegie Institution, 1933).

The very rapid growth of North Carolina's population is more difficult to explain in terms of exporting staples and the growth effects of those activities. Relatively little of the colony was settled before 1700. One may also see that until 1700 little of the area beyond the immediate coast or tidewater had been settled. It is apparent from Figure 1-1 that even by 1775 the colonial economy and society, especially that part engaged in commercial activities, was tied to deep-water shipment, which restricted them from colonizing the far inland areas as a growth effect of staple exports. The tidewater area that was settled and that had been commercialized, was an extension of the rice-growing agriculture to the south and the tobacco-growing agriculture to the north. Throughout the colonial period, North Carolina remained essentially a frontier area. Land availability and soil productivity were sufficiently high to afford a fairly substantial real income to those settlers who were drawn to its piedmont or

Figure 1-1. Colonial Settlement, 1607–1775.

*Source:* Rowland Berthoff, *An Unsettled People: Social Order and Disorder in American History* (New York: Harper & Row, 1971), p. 25.

interior areas (frequently drawn there from Virginia). The high transportation costs of overland shipment of goods placed a major barrier on the commercialization of these frontier areas.

## The Middle Colonies

The middle colonies (those from New York south to Maryland) enjoyed a substantial increase in population from 1660 to 1780. New York, New Jersey, and Pennsylvania (which was the second most populous colony by 1780), with a population of 5000 in 1600 had a combined total of 678,000 inhabitants in 1780. The growth of agricultural exports appears great enough to explain most of that population increase and extensive growth.

The general agricultural advantage of the middle colonies was not merely a large supply of land, for land that is not readily usable for commercial agriculture because of transportation costs is not truly a resource. In the case of the middle colonies, there was a large supply of commercially usable land because of the network of rivers and waterways that laced the area. The combination of the two attracted large numbers of immigrants (including the so-called Scotch-Irish, in the eighteenth century), especially to Pennsylvania.

Farming in the middle colonies was extensive; that is, it was land intensive, with relatively little capital or fertilizer used. This pattern is common to many agricultural areas in the early phases of economic development. Although it often depletes the soil at a rapid rate, it may well be a rational pattern in terms of the size, and growth in size, of the market and the relative prices of land, capital, and fertilizer.

The major exports developed in the middle colonies were wheat and flour (by far the two largest), corn, meat, lumber, flaxseed, and livestock. This pattern of exports became especially pronounced with the increase of exports to the West Indies and reexports of southern tobacco and other products (especially from Philadelphia) to England and the European continent. Philadelphia and New York City also provided an urban market for specialized agricultural goods as well as for the processed goods that urban laborers and merchants demanded.

One interesting question about this area in this era is why so much of the growth and its spread effects were concentrated in Pennsylvania, an area that became known as "the best poor man's country," because it seemed possible to immigrants that even a poor man could do well there. While the concentration was partly due to a different set of restraints, it was basically explained by the availability of land. New York offered limited opportunities in the seventeenth century, because of the large landholdings of the old Dutch patroon system, together with the limits imposed by Indian (Iroquois) control. New Jersey suffered from the political instability engendered by a long-standing dispute over its colonial charter and corresponding problems with land titles. William Penn's colony, however, had a relatively abundant amount of land, good river systems to transport bulky commodities such as wheat at a cost that left a net profit to growers and shippers, a political and religious climate that was favorable to creative enterpreneurship, and highly fertile land near the coast. The combination of these factors is probably enough to explain the relatively greater growth of Pennsylvania than of New York or New Jersey. The combination also probably explains why the spread effects within New York of the growth of its great port city (as noted, the largest in the colonies by the time of the Revolution) were more limited than they might have been with different land availability constraints.

## The New England Colonies

Recall that in 1660, New England (from Maine to Connecticut) contained over half of the population of the colonies. By 1780, the region contained only slightly more than one-fourth of the population. The reason for the *relatively* slower growth is that in the period when intensive growth and development depended so strongly on staple exports New England had no such export commodity.

New England, constrained in its frontier expansion by the lands of the Indian tribes, encountered intermittent conflict throughout the seventeenth century. Even after the end of King Phillip's War in 1678, the conflicts were numerous, the losses high. Only in the eighteenth century did the frontier expansion resume; even then the pace was slow until 1763 and the end of the French and Indian Wars. Nonetheless, the region did have certain natural advantages in terms of its initial resource endowments. The main such endowment was a series of fine natural habors. Fishing, fish-processing, whaling, and shipbuilding became important economic activities. Indeed shipbuilding, a manufacturing activity permitted and even encouraged under England's laws, had become a leading sector. As such, it was an important source of the earnings that permitted the import not only of consumer goods but also of the capital that financed early colonial expansion.

New England's disadvantage in the colonial period was not that it failed to export. It exported fish, lumber, ships, whale oil, and many other products. It simply did not, however, with the possible exception of shipping services, have a single export staple (or combination of staples) whose market(s) grew rapidly due to European taste and preference, or to income growth, or because they complemented the economic expansion of the continent. Even within the region, however, success was relative. Although Boston declined as a port relative to New York and Philadelphia (perhaps even to Charleston), it was a prosperous city. Newport, Rhode Island, also prospered, particularly through export and reexport of goods

An early American port. (Photo no. 30-N-38-840 in the National Archives)

to the West Indies. The important point, again, is that the leading sectors of the colonial economy were largely in the southern and middle colonies rather than in New England. The structure of European demand, the initial endowment of resources, and the relative advantage of the colonies all dictated that, through most of the colonial period, the impetus for intensive growth was strongly concentrated geographically from Pennsylvania to South Carolina.

## The Institutional Background

Although the colonies grew, in real income terms, at a rate that was very rapid for their times, that rate would probably seem modest by more recent American experience. Nonetheless, their emergence as a growing society is unquestionable. In large measure, this ability to take advantage of favorable international market conditions, to supply staple exports to a growing European market, was attributable to favorable political, social, and economic institutions—including indentured servitude and even slavery. No matter how noxious the idea of self-imposed servitude limited in time by contract or of the imposed lifetime service of slavery is to twentieth-century minds and values, in colonial times these institutions provided a labor supply that was important to North America's development. We have already mentioned the early decisions to permit private ownership of land and to permit private appropriation of the profits (and losses) of engaging in economic activity. While it is difficult to quantify the effects of these decisions on economic development, they were undeniably important in terms of reallocating resources and achieving creative entrepreneurship.

However, efforts to inhibit reallocation of resources were undertaken. After the restoration of King Charles II, for example, the proprietors in South Carolina sought to create a feudal economy, with all its obstacles to resource reallocation (including a group of serfs tied to the land). In all instances, these efforts were rejected, a result not surprising among people who fled such restrictions and who, confronted with readily available land (at least initially), refused to be tied to feudal baronies.

## The Marginal Propensity to Import

Little is known in any systematic fashion about the colonists' marginal propensity to import. The production function, especially of the southern colonies, together with the unequal distribution of resource ownership, probably yielded an unequal distribution of income. Also, it appears that in both the middle and New England colonies unequal income distribution did result later in the colonial period and domestically produced goods did increase in supply. Within the limits of the (small) domestic market, home manufacturers complemented the growth of a group of colonial merchants who were very unspecialized. These jacks-of-all-trades entrepreneurs were especially important in advancing credit to farmers, thus providing the financing necessary to ensure increased supplies of agricultural commodities. In some cases, the merchants even financed the manufacture of certain products. Generally, it does not appear that the marginal propensity to import was so high that it imposed a barrier to the diversification of the colonial economy.

## The Colonies: Underdeveloped or Waiting to Be Developed?

The staple theory does provide insights into the development of the North American colonies from the early 1600s to 1763. Yet it is probably not accurate to consider those colonies underdeveloped. In many respects, the physical endowments of the region (the natural resource base) in relation to world market demand made the area not so much an "empty land" as one capable of being developed by a group with an institutional structure that could harness the demand signals, reallocate resources to their most productive uses, and provide staple exports that would provide the income basis for further economic expansion.

---

# Review of Economic Concepts: Some Fundamentals

## Determining Prices

How are prices established in market places? The following statement is familiar to almost everyone: "Prices are determined by supply and demand." The statement is correct; indeed, it is definitional. We can add one stipulation: "So long as competitive conditions exist, the *independent* influences of supply and demand determine price."

Before we go further, we should define the term **competition.** Competition is the market form in which no buyer or seller is able to influence price by his or her own actions. The conditions necessary in a market for competition to exist are:

1. *Absence of collusion.* No buyers and no sellers act together to influence price.
2. *Flexible prices.* Prices determined by supply and demand must be completely free to move up or down to whatever level is market determined.
3. *Free entry and exit.* Buyers and sellers must be free to enter and leave the market without nonmarket restrictions, and the market restrictions must make entry and exit relatively easy.

Finally, in order for supply and demand influences to be independent, the demand for a good must not depend on the incomes that are generated by the production of that good (a condition that would be violated, for example, in a mill town where employees were the principal customers of the mill and whose demand depended on the incomes received from the company).

**What Is Demand?** Since, by assumption, demand and supply are independent of each other in our market pricing model, let us examine each influence in turn before putting them together to form a theory of pricing.

The first fact to remember about demand is that it is a schedule of relationships. Specifically, **demand** is a schedule that indicates the quantity of a good that will be purchased at each of a set of prices in a particular time period.

What will such a schedule look like? Economists expect a picture of a demand schedule usually to look like the demand curve drawn in Figure 1-2. (Note that economists call such relationships *curves* even if they are linear.)

A second thing to remember about demand is the **law of demand,** which states that consumers will buy more at (relatively) low prices than at (relatively) high prices. The downward-sloping demand curve in Figure 1-2 obeys this law. Note that as price falls (for example, from 5 to 4) the quantity of tobacco sold increases (from 9 to 10). The law of demand can be explained in terms of two effects that derive from price changes:

1. The **substitution effect** of a price changes. As the price of a good falls, consumers tend to substitute that relatively cheaper good for other now relatively more expensive goods. In Figure 1-2, as the price of tobacco falls, consumers tend to substitute that good for other (now) relatively more expensive goods (whose prices, by assumption, are unchanged).
2. The **income effect** of a price change. As the price of a good falls, the purchasing power or real income of a consumer is increased, and the consumer tends to buy more of that good. (For the time being, we'll ignore the exceptions to this effect and focus only on normal goods, those whose rate of consumption increases as purchasing power increases.)

Figure 1-2. A Hypothetical Demand Curve for Colonial Tobacco.

**Quantity Demanded and Demand Shifts**     The combination of these two effects, then, ordinarily produces a downward-sloping demand curve such as that shown in Figure 1-2. A demand curve is drawn on the assumption that the price of the good (measured on the vertical axis) is the independent variable, and the resulting quantity demanded (measured on the horizontal axis) is the dependent variable. Thus, we say that—other things being equal—*only* a change in the price of a good can cause a change in the quantity demanded of that good. The qualification that other things must be equal is known as the *ceteris paribus* assumption.

The **ceteris paribus assumption** involves holding constant (a) money income, (b) tastes and preferences, (c) prices of substitutes (goods whose consumption is a substitute for the good in question) and complements (goods consumed in conjunction with the good in question), (d) population, or the number of consumers, and (e) expectations about future prices. A change in any one of these factors (or any combination of them) will tend to cause a change in demand or a shift of the demand curve.

Figure 1-3 is useful for illustrating the difference between changes in demand and changes in quantity demanded. Along Demand Curve $D_1$, for example, changes in price occur from price = 15 to price = 3. Each of these price changes causes a change in quantity demanded (as price decreases, there is an increase in quantity demanded). Changes in quantity de-

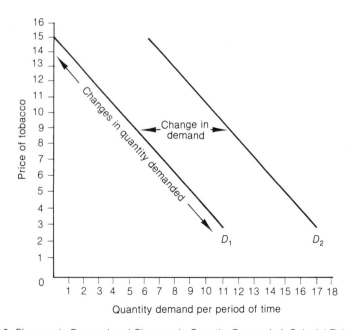

Figure 1-3. Changes in Demand and Changes in Quantity Demanded, Colonial Tobacco.

manded, thus, are the same as movements along a particular demand curve. The movement from Demand Curve $D_1$ to Demand Curve $D_2$, however, is an increase in demand, or a shift of the demand curve. The movement from $D_1$ to $D_2$ may be the result of a change in any of the five shift factors identified earlier (for example, an increase in population).

The hypothetical demand curves in Figures 1-2 and 1-3 are market or industry demand curves; that is, they reflect the total demand for the product portrayed. Underlying any such demand curves are numerous individual demand curves. Market demand curves are the summation or adding up of individual demand curves (assuming no interdependencies among consumers). Since all consumers, by assumption, are affected by income and substitution effects, individual demand curves generally have the same downward-sloping configuration as the market curves we have shown.

**What Is Supply?**   Like demand, supply is a schedule of relationships. **Supply** is defined as the schedule showing the quantity of a good that a firm or various firms will offer for sale at each of a set of prices in a particular period of time.

What will such a schedule or set of relationships look like? Economists expect the picture of a supply curve generally to resemble the supply curve in Figure 1-4. Note that the supply curve slopes up, to the right. The curve, in other words, reflects the **law of supply**—the hypothesis that firms supply more to the market at (relatively) higher prices than at (relatively) lower prices.

Why is the law of supply a generally valid and applicable principle? To answer this question, we must learn what determines supply. Supply basically depends on the costs of production, which, in turn, depend on the prices of resources employed in production and the productivity of those resources. Two market factors may cause the upward-sloping supply curve: (a) as the firm produces more, its costs may increase because it has to pay a higher price for each unit of a resource; (b) as the firm produces more, it will ultimately experience diminishing productivity from the additional resources it hires. This latter effect is known as the **law of diminishing returns:** As a firm hires successive equal increments of a variable resource and uses the resource in conjunction with a fixed resource (or resource), a point will be reached beyond which the additional units of the variable resource add less and less to output. As this happens, each additional unit of output costs more than the previous one (even at a constant resource price).

For either one or both of these reasons, profit-maximizing firms supplying tobacco to the market will supply more only as price rises. Since this is true for each firm, it is true of *all* firms, as the upward-sloping market supply curve in Figure 1-4 shows. Market supply curves, like

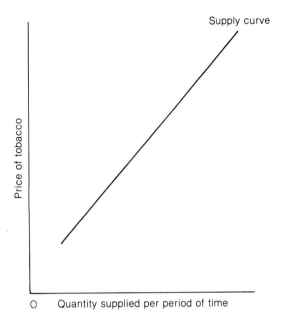

Figure 1-4. Hypothetical Supply Curve, Colonial Tobacco.

market demand curves, are aggregates; they involve adding up the quantities supplied by each firm at each possible price (assuming no collusion or interdependencies between firms).

You have probably noticed the reappearance of the *ceteris paribus* assumption. In Figure 1-4, the only factors that changed were the price of the good (the independent variable) and quantity supplied (the dependent variable). These are the factors held constant: (a) technology or techniques of production; (b) resource prices (if the firm does not buy them at constant prices; that is, as a competitor); (c) prices of other products; (d) firms' expectations about future prices for their product; and (e) the number of firms. Changes in any one of these five factors could cause the change in supply reflected in the shift from $S_1$ to $S_2$ in Figure 1-5. Suppose, for example, that tobacco producers expected tobacco prices to fall in the future. This change in their price expectations might well cause producers to supply more at all prices in the present.

We have shown that the only factor that *can* cause a change in the quantity supplied of a good is a change in that good's price. The factors that can cause a change in supply include changing technology and changed expectations of future prices. The only factor that *cannot* cause a change in the supply of a good is a change in the price of that good.

The supply changes we have looked at were all due to changes in market factors, especially those affecting the costs of firms. Of course, cost changes can be imposed on firms by governments. Taxes, duties, regulations of one sort or another that raise the costs of firms—all can cause a reduced supply. In Figure 1-5, tobacco producers might have been willing to supply $S_2$ tobacco to a free market. If governments imposed import duties on that tobacco, or imposed cost-increasing regulations on the sellers of tobacco, then supply might have shifted to $S_1$.

**Prices:  Putting Supply and Demand Together**      We began this section by saying that prices are determined by supply and demand. Now, let us see just how and why that is so. Figure 1-6 will be helpful in this regard. In the figure, we have drawn the demand curve for colonial tobacco from Figure 1-2 and the supply curve for that same product from Figure 1-4. What price will result, given $D$ and $S$? It will be an **equilibrium price,** the central tendency of this market. Also, it will be a market clearing price, one that eliminates both gluts and shortages.

In this instance, price will tend toward 8.2, where demand equals supply. Why this is so can be made evident by comparing the equilibrium price with disequilibrium prices, both those above 8.2 and those below 8.2. Consider the situation if the price were 10. At that price, consumers want to buy $A$ while suppliers offer to sell $B$. The difference $(AB)$ is excess supply, or surplus or unintended accumulation of tobacco by producers.

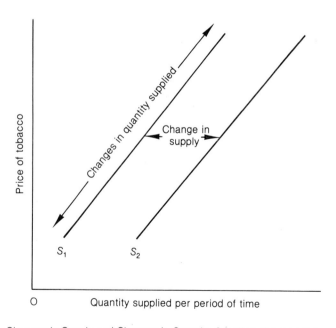

Figure 1-5. Changes in Supply and Changes in Quantity Supplied, Colonial Tobacco.

Since this is a competitive market, the information about excess supply or surplus is readily transmitted, and, in response, sellers offer lower and lower prices to eliminate the glut. Finally, prices will tend toward 8.2, at which point the quantity supplied (offered for sale) equals the quantity demanded.

Next, consider price=6.4. At that price, consumers want to buy $D$ while suppliers only want to offer $C$. The difference, $CD$, is excess demand, or a shortage. Knowing of this shortage and attempting to buy more, consumers begin to offer higher and higher prices. As a result, the price rises toward 8.2, where the shortage or excess demand is eliminated.

**Summing Up**    We conclude that prices in competitive markets are established by the independent influences of supply and demand. These prices are equilibrium prices that tend to clear the markets; that is, they eliminate excess supply and excess demand.

## Growth and Development

**Intensive and Extensive Growth**    There are two dimensions to growth itself. When total output increases due to the use of more resources (land,

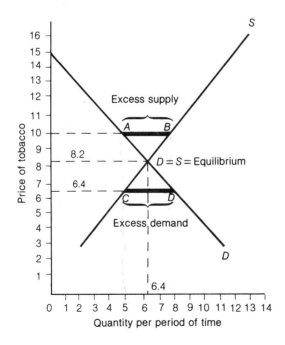

Figure 1-6. Pricing Colonial Tobacco.

labor, capital, and entrepreneurship), **extensive growth** occurs. As land is cleared, as population grows, as more capital instruments are used, output of commodities and services increases. This type of growth tends to occur in almost all societies, although stagnation is possible, as is even decline if less good land is used, if population falls, or the like. Extensive growth usually involves little change in the composition of output; if such a society has been producing basic food staples or textiles, it is likely to demand more of those items. Moreover, from the supply side, it is likely to produce them in the same ways or with the same techniques as previously employed.

On the other hand, intensive growth involves not only significant changes in the composition of output but also increasing output per capita. This means that the composition of output changes (usually to fewer basic agricultural goods and more semiprocessed and processed goods) and that there are more goods of all types available to be consumed. As productivity (output per unit of input) grows from the supply side, the techniques of production change to accommodate the productivity growth that larger demand makes possible.

Finally, economic development is the end product of long-term intensive growth. As per capita income grows and as the mix of goods and services changes, structural change tends to occur. While it is impossible to specify the precise structural changes, a few illustrations will suffice. The distribution of income is likely to change, either because of changes in the pattern of ownership of resources and returns to resource owners or because of changes in public subsidization of activities and because of transfer payments to individuals. Some would argue that population growth is likely to decline (beyond some point), that the age distribution of the population will change, that more social or publicly provided overhead capital will be added. Not all of these changes will necessarily occur in a particular country, but they illustrate the kinds of structural changes that seem likely to accompany intensive growth and transform it into a joint process of economic development.

A useful way to view and summarize both intensive and extensive growth is in terms of the aggregate production function, the function showing the factors that determine output changes.

$$Q = f(L, K, R, T)$$

where $Q$ = output
$L$ = labor
$K$ = capital
$R$ = resources
$T$ = state of technology

Since growth is the change in output, we have

$$d_Q = MP_L \cdot d_L + MP_K \cdot d_K + MP_R \cdot d_R + T'$$

where $d$ = a small change in
$MP_L$ = marginal product of labor
$MP_K$ = marginal product of capital
$MP_R$ = marginal product of resources
$T'$ = the effect of change in technology

In terms of our preceding discussion, then, extensive growth occurs when $d_L$, $d_K$, and $d_R$ are positive. Intensive growth occurs when $MP_L$, $MP_K$, and $MP_R$ are growing and when $T'$, effect of change in technology, make available new techniques of production that, in turn, increase the marginal productivity of labor, capital, and resources.

**Production Possibilities**   A visual representation of intensive and extensive growth may be seen in the **production possibilities curve,** a curve showing the various combinations of output that full employment of a nation's resources, and the best of current technology, can produce. Such a curve is seen in Figure 1-7; *ABC* represents a frontier or the maximum at-

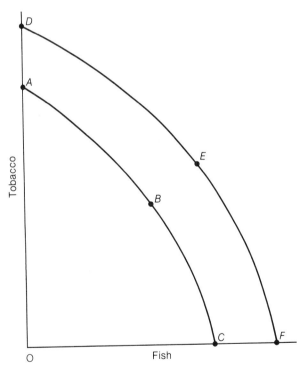

Figure 1-7. Hypothetical Production Possibilities Curves, North American Colony, Tobacco and Fish.

tainable output with full employment of the colony's resources and the best technology at a given time. It is concave to the origin, to reflect **increasing opportunity cost;** that is, as resources are reallocated from the production of one good to production of the other (say, from producing tobacco to catching and processing fish), more and more of the one good (tobacco) must be given up to obtain a constantly increasing amount of the other (fish). This effect is also known as the **law of diminishing returns.** Curve *ABC*, then, is a frontier, the maximum output combination of the two goods attainable with colony's limited resources as the colony attempts to meet the (assumed) unlimited wants of its people or to deal with the problem of scarcity.

Curve *DEF* represents a higher level of attainable combinations of the two goods. What can move a society such as the hypothetical colony from *ABC* to *DEF*? The answer is indicated in the aggregate production function. The shift may result from more resources, labor and capital ($d_R > 0$, $d_L > 0$, $d_K > 0$); if so, it is the result of extensive growth. Alternatively, the shift may result from increasing marginal productivity of resources ($MP_L$, $MP_K$, and $MP_R$ are growing), and this may be the result of a positive $T'$, or improving technology; if so, the shift is the result of intensive growth.

## Economic Institutions

Finally, economic development is the end product, the improvement in human welfare that results from the structural changes that accompany combined extensive and intensive growth. In this regard, it is vitally important to productivity growth that economic institutions, the organizational means through which economic decisions are made and implemented, enhance productivity growth. They may do so by reducing the impediments to an efficient allocation of resources and by exhausting the economies of scale that an evolving technology makes possible. The particular economic institutions established by a society bear directly on the fundamental questions that all economies must answer. If private ownership of the means of production, combined with legal enforcement of market-determined contractual arrangements, is a basic institutional feature, a market system will primarily answer the questions *how* to produce, *what* to produce, *who* will receive the output, and what to provide for the future. A different set of institutional arrangements, such as public ownership and control, would result in other answers.

A society's institutions also affect the efficiency or costs of making economic decisions. One of the basic costs of decisions is information cost, the cost of obtaining the price information and technical information necessary to make rational decisions—those consistent with individual and group objectives. The other basic cost is **transactions cost,** the cost of effectuating exchanges between buyers and sellers. An efficient set of institutions minimizes these two kinds of costs for buyers and sellers. How close a society comes to achieving its greatest output significantly depends on the effectiveness or efficiency of its economic institutions.

## The Staple Theory of Leading Sectors

Several historians have written about the importance to economies, in their early economic development, of the production and export of staple commodities. Perhaps the most important of these scholars is Harold A. Innis,[9, 10] a Canadian economic historian, whose arguments, while limited in his own case to Canada, have broader applicability.

Fundamentally, Innis' staple theory is one of a group of **leading sector** theories, which hypothesize the existence of a sector or sectors of the economy that create effects on intensive growth and development that spread through demand and supply influences to the rest of the economy (hence the term **spread effects**). Such sectors (for example, tobacco exports) literally lead the rest of the economy into processes of intensive growth and of development. The Innis argument clearly and perhaps only applies to "empty lands," those in which a new economy (rather than an evolution from an old economic order) evolves.

The importance of staple exports, then, consists in the diversification effects of the exporting of one or more staple commodities, on the creation and expansion of domestic markets. In turn, this market growth depends on the export-import patterns that exist between the staple-producing area and the rest of the trading world. The supply of staple exports will depend on the initial endowments (relative amounts of land, labor, and capital) and on the technology of producing the staple good or goods.

The combination of two things—initial endowments and the technology of staple production—will determine the input-output combinations, the **production function** of the staple-producing area, and the substitutability of production factors. Given the production function and the size of the market for the staple export, there will be a derived set of demands for the factors of production, land, labor, and capital. Given the supplies of the three resources, this set of demands will determine their market incomes. The resultant pattern of production will create a distribution of market incomes and, thereby, a size and pattern of domestic demand, together with the possibility of processing intermediate goods from the staple commodities.

An example will illustrate how this process tends to work in an "empty land" area. Let us suppose that the staple-producing area begins with certain initial endowments of land, labor, and capital and that there is an initial set of supply-demand relationships for the staple. For the sake of specificity, let us suppose that tobacco is the staple good and that there is an increase in the demand for tobacco. The demand increase will induce an increase in the quantity supplied with immediate spread effects to the resource markets through increases in the demand for land, labor, capital, and entrepreneurship. These increases in demand will increase the incomes of some or all of the resource owners involved, through increasing the quantity of those resources employed, or their prices, or both.

If land is the factor of production in relatively great supply, if that land is highly fertile and if labor and capital can be readily imported (and, of course, if entrepreneurs are forthcoming in the society), then average incomes in the staple export society will rise substantially. The distribution of that income, together with the marginal propensity to import—the amount of increased income spent on imported goods—will determine the amount and the way in which the structure of demand changes. The **production function of the staple,** the function that shows the relationship between resource inputs and staple product output, may be such that the staple is produced on large plantations. If so, and if the incomes flow largely to a small group of people with a high marginal propensity to import, then the increase in demand for domestically produced products will be relatively small. There will be relatively small increases in the size of the domestic market. If the reverse occurs, if the income increase is more widely spread among people with lower marginal propensities to import, the spread effects on the domestic economy will be relatively great.

What will determine the ability of the staple economy to continue the process of growth and diversification? If it begins with a favorable land-labor ratio, it must be able to reallocate its own resources and to import relatively scarce factors, labor, and capital. The **empty land** is not one in which population is pressing on the means of subsistence, but one in which high soil fertility and a large supply of land attract (initially through immigration) a large number of people who anticipate relatively high real incomes. These resource supply factors permit the initial and continuing increases in product supply and counteract the tendency to increasing costs that is built into all production processes. At the same time, the income increases permit an economic diversification that has many benefits, including the relative price and income stability that is lacking in economies tied to a single staple export.

Clearly the entire process just outlined will only succeed in societies that are nontraditional, whose institutional structure permits and encourages entrepreneurs to reallocate resources in favor of productivity-increasing uses. This means that development must be seen not only as possible but also as desirable. "Creative entrepreneurship," to use a phrase of Joseph Schumpeter's, must be allowed to work to allocate the presumably large supplies of the abundant resource(s) and also to allocate the scarce resources presumably available through importation to produce new products, old products in new and more productive ways, to open new markets (including resource markets) or to distribute these products in new ways, or to change the organization of industries.

---

# Glossary

**Aggregate production function**   The function showing the factors that determine changes in output.

**Ceteris paribus**   "Other things being equal"; the assumption that other things relevant to a system of analysis are held constant. For a particular demand curve, only price and quantity can change, while income, tastes and preferences, and other demand-related factors are held constant.

**Competition**   The market form in which no buyer or seller is able to influence price by his or her own actions. Competition requires the following conditions: absence of collusion, flexible prices, and free entry and exit.

**Demand**   A schedule that indicates the quantity of a good that will be purchased at each of a set of prices in a particular time period.

**Economic development**   The-long term process through which per capita output grows and structural changes occur as well.

**Economic institutions**   The organizational means through which economic decisions are made and implemented.

**Empty lands**   Those lands in which a new economy evolves (rather than an evolution from an old economic order).

**Equilibrium price**   Also a market clearing price. The central price tendency of a market or the price that tends to eliminate both gluts and shortages.

**Extensive growth**   The growth that occurs when more resources are used to produce an output unchanged in composition or techniques of production.

**Income effect**   The change in the consumption of a good due to a change in purchasing power resulting from a change in the price of that good.

**Increasing opportunity cost**   Opportunity cost is the combination of other goods given up or foregone in producing something or opting for any economic alternative. When one must give up more and more of one good to get a constant amount of the other, there is increasing opportunity cost.

**Intensive growth**   The growth that involves increased productivity and involves a changed composition of output and techniques of production.

**Law of demand**   The hypothesis that consumers will buy more of a good at (relatively) lower prices than at (relatively) higher prices.

**Law of diminishing returns**   Also known as the law of increasing opportunity cost. The idea that in reallocating resources to produce one good, a society must ultimately give up more and more of another good.

**Law of supply**   The hypothesis that firms supply more to the market at (relatively) higher prices than at (relatively) lower prices.

**Leading sector theories**   Theories which hypothesize the existence of a sector or sectors of the economy that create effects on intensive growth and development that spread through supply and demand influence to the rest of the economy.

**Production function**   The input-output combination of an economy, an industry or a firm.

**Production function of the staple**   The function that shows the relationship between resource input and staple product output.

**Production possibilities curve**   A diagrammatic presentation of a production possibilities function.

**Production possibilities function**   A relationship that shows the various combinations of output that the full employment of a nation's resources (land, labor, capital, and entrepreneurship), using the best of current technology, can produce.

**Spread effects**   See **Leading sector theories.**

**Substitution effect**   The amount by which consumers tend to substitute a good when its price is falling, for other, now relatively more expensive, goods (as implied by the law of demand).

**Supply**   A schedule of the various quantities that sellers are willing and able to sell at various prices during a given time.

**Transactions costs**   The costs of effecting exchanges between buyers and sellers.

# Questions

1. What is the staple theory developed by Harold Innis, and to what type of countries does it apply?
2. What is the production function of a staple-producing area, and how does it relate to the demand for resources and the distribution of market incomes?
3. How does a high marginal propensity to import affect the spread effects of staple exports?
4. What is the importance of immigration to the success of the staple export-producing land? The importance of creative entrepreneurship?

5. In what ways did the southern colonies adapt to the initial resource conditions they encountered? What became the first great staple export of the upper South?

6. Why is it likely that spread effects of staple export increases will not be evenly spread through a nation or region or set of colonies?

7. Why did so many of the spread effects of staple export growth in the colonial period accrue to Virginia?

8. What caused South Carolina's dramatic population growth during the colonial period? What of North Carolina?

9. In what respects did the middle colonies differ in their economic growth from the south? What accounts for the relative concentration of spread effects in Pennsylvania among the middle colonies?

10. What caused New England to grow relatively less rapidly during the colonial period than either the southern or middle colonies? What were the successful aspects of New England's growth?

11. In what respects were the institutional structures of the colonies favorable to staple export-led growth? To what should we attribute this institutional success?

12. Does it appear that the marginal propensity to import was a barrier to the diversification of the colonial economy? If it was not, what *was* the principal barrier?

13. Were the North American colonies an underdeveloped area or an empty land waiting to be developed?

14. What was the importance of the Indian heritage to the economic development of the colonies?

## Suggested Readings

1. Anderson, Terry. "Wealth Estimates for the New England Colonies, 1650–1709." *Explanations in Economic History,* 12 (1975).

2. Baldwin, Robert E. "Patterns of Development in Newly Settled Regions." *Manchester Schools of Economic and Social Studies,* 24 (1956).

3. Bidwell, Percey W., and Falconer, John I. *History of Agriculture in the Northern United States, 1620–1860.* Washington, D.C.: Carnegie Institution, 1925.

4. Bruchey, Stuart. *The Colonial Merchant: Sources and Readings.* New York: Harcourt Brace Jovanovich, 1966.

5. Callender, Guy S. *Selections from the Economic History of the United States, 1765–1860.* Boston: Ginn, 1909.

6. Egnal, Marc. "The Economic Development of the Thirteen Continental

Colonies, 1720 to 1775." *William and Mary Quarterly, 32,* 3rd ser., (1975).

7. Gray, Lewis Cecil. *History of Agriculture in the Southern United States to 1860.* Vol. 1. Washington, D.C.: Carnegie Institution, 1933.

8. Gunderson, Gerald. *A New Economic History of America.* New York: McGraw-Hill, 1976. Chap. Two, pp. 28–68.

9. Innis, Harold A. *The Fur Trade in Canada: An Introduction to Canadian Economic History.* Toronto: University of Toronto Press, 1930.

10. Innis, Harold A. *The Cod Fisheries: The History of an International Economy.* Toronto: University of Toronto Press, 1940.

11. Josephby, Alvin M. *The Indian Heritage of America.* New York: Knopf, 1968.

12. Land, Aubrey C. "The Tobacco Staple and the Planter's Problems: Technology, Labor and Crops." *Agricultural History, 43* (1969).

13. Price, Jacob. "The Economic Growth of America and the European Market, 1697–1775." *Journal of Economic History, 24* (1964).

14. Watkins, M. H. "A Staple Theory of Economic Growth." *The Canadian Journal of Economics and Political Science* (May 1963).

# Chapter 2

---

# The Late Colonial Economy, 1770

To illustrate the late colonial period processes of extensive and intensive economic growth and of economic development in the North American colonies, we shall focus on the year 1770. In the model of this era, we shall attempt to include the appropriate economic relationships between the North American colonies and Great Britain. It is necessary to understand these relationships in order to answer the important question raised in Chapter 3: "What effects did the complex economic controls imposed on the colonies by British mercantile policy have on colonial growth and welfare?"

In the Review of Economic Concepts in Chapter 1, we set forth a very general production possibilities model of economic development based on fully employed resources.* Let us add the following specifications about relationships in the dualistic or two-sector economy of the North American colonies. First, the cash sector of the colonial economy was tied to both internal and foreign trade on a fairly regular basis. But the barter sector was only infrequently and irregularly tied to internal, coastal, or overseas trade.

Second, the production processes of the cash sector involved higher capital-labor ratios than those in the barter sector. The latter were relatively labor and land intensive. Because of this, productivity was higher in the cash sector than in the barter sector.

---

\* The reader who has not studied the principles of economics or who has not done so recently may find it useful to read this Review of Economic Concepts in order to benefit more from this and subsequent chapters.

**33**

Third, while the barter sector might be growing through land clearing, population growth, and even through employment of some capital equipment, intensive growth—the increase in real per capita output—was tied to productivity increase and thus occurred largely in the cash sector. Specifically, the assumption is that as people moved from subsistence activities to urban cash activities, the loss in productivity and real income (for example, to women producing goods on subsistence farms) was more than offset by the increased real goods produced by people working with more capital instruments.

# Specific Factors Affecting Late Colonial Growth

We have assumed that development, the sustained growth in real per capita income and its accompanying structural change, occurs almost exclusively in the "modern" sector of the colonial economy. Now let us add one additional specification for our general model of colonial development: The growth in market size, which is the key to further specialization and productivity growth, may occur either through an increase in internal commerce or through an increase in overseas commerce (exports and imports).

In this chapter, we shall look at the factors affecting both internal and overseas trade. Because the data for internal trade are relatively poor, we will use simple measures of that influence. We will spell out our model of foreign trade influences, however, in order to use the foreign trade data to assess the impact of British colonial policy on the North American colonies.

## A Foreign Trade Model

Owing in part to the relatively low cost of deep-water shipment as opposed to overland shipment, much of the cash sector of the North American colonial economy was closely tied to overseas trade. The colonies were exporters of many kinds of raw materials and some semifinished and finished goods. These were the **visible items of exports.** In addition, the colonies sold services, the **invisible items of exports** (primarily shipping services). Like many other producers of raw materials, the colonies imported both visible items, such as tea, cocoa, clothing, and machinery, and invisible items, such as the services of foreign shippers, insurance companies, and bankers.

Overseas trade, thus, was a very important factor in determining the extensive and intensive growth of the colonies. A key measure of this factor's influence is contained in the terms of trade of the colonies. The **terms**

**of trade** of the colonies refers to the ratio of export prices received to the import prices paid by the colonists. In other words:

$$\text{Terms of trade} = \frac{P_e}{P_i}$$

Where $P_e$ = Prices of exports
$P_i$ = Prices of imports

Of course, both $P_e$ and $P_i$ are indexes composed of many different prices. When export prices rise relative to import prices, it is common to say that the terms of trade have moved in favor of an area. When that area's import prices rise relative to its export prices, however, it is common to say that the terms of trade have moved against it.* Later we will see what happened to the terms of trade of the North American colonies and what influences British colonial policies had on that movement. With this model and these potential trade influences in mind, we shall now turn to an examination of agriculture, manufacturing, and commerce in the late colonial period to assess their structure and the sources of their growth.

## Colonial Agriculture

Agriculture was, by far, the most important sector of the colonial economy. Although urban areas were becoming more important, only about 4% of the people lived in towns in 1770. Thus, it was in agriculture that the vast majority of the population found their employment, income, and living environment around 1770, the period just before the American Revolution.

We have already seen that the production possibilities curve, which identifies the possible combinations of output of an economy, is determined by the supply of factors of production and the state of technology; it is drawn on the assumption that these factors of production are fully employed with the best technology. A fruitful approach to an analysis of colonial agriculture, therefore, is to examine the three factors of production—land, labor, and capital—and to analyze the state of technology with which they were employed. In addition, the production possibility frontier could also be affected by changes in productivity from sources other than technological change, and thus it is appropriate to consider these forms of changing productivity also.

---

* Strictly speaking, this is not necessarily correct. The improvement or deterioration will depend on the quantity of trade at the new prices and also the cause of the change in prices, whether from changes in foreign demand or from changes in domestic supply cost.

## Land

Although land was abundant and almost anyone who wished to farm could buy land on easy terms, land ownership was not evenly divided, and the pattern of land ownership varied from one colony to another. Changes in these patterns involved significant institutional change, although the institutional form differed greatly. In some areas, the family farm became dominant; in other areas, commercial plantations evolved. In New England, agriculture was dominated by small family-size farms concentrating on general-purpose agriculture. This pattern was probably due, at least in part, to the lack of any specific export crop that required larger size to gain **economies of scale** (reduced unit costs of the crop available with higher rates of production).

In New York, there were some large holdings owned by the descendants of the original Dutch settlers of New Amsterdam. When the British conquered this Dutch colony, they reaffirmed the existing ownership.

In Pennslyvania, there were holdings larger than family size in the rich agricultural lands above and to the west of Philadelphia. Because of high land fertility in these areas, specialized wheat export farming was profitable.

In the coastal areas of Maryland and Virginia around Chesapeake Bay, large tobacco plantations were flourishing. These large tobacco plantations in the Piedmont area were based on the export demand for tobacco.

In North Carolina, small, family-size farms were the rule. In South Carolina and Georgia, there were rice plantations along the coast and indigo plantations farther inland. Slaves were used as the labor force, and rice and indigo were important export crops. Rice production required large holdings and considerable capital investment for irrigation structures in order to achieve economies of scale.

In summary, then, there were large landholdings of the Dutch patroons in New York, on the commercial wheat-exporting farms in Bucks and Lancaster counties in Pennsylvania, on the tobacco plantations around Chesapeake Bay in Maryland and Virginia, and on the rice and indigo plantations of South Carolina and Georgia. Other areas in the North American colonies were characterized by relatively small-scale family farms devoted to general agriculture. It is important to remember that, despite the uneven distribution of land ownership, the supply of land was plentiful and in the language of economists, there was relative ease of entry into agriculture during colonial times.

## Labor

On a family-size farm, the family provided its own labor. But on the large commercial farms of Virginia, Maryland, South Carolina, Georgia, and

Pennsylvania, the problem of finding labor was crucial. The relative cheapness of land prevented a large supply of free (nonslave) labor from developing.Why work for someone else when you could farm your own land—unless, of course, you could earn much more as a wage laborer? And this was unlikely, given the high level of labor productivity associated with a nearly free good, land.

Because of the small supply of wage labor, the large commercial farms resorted to unfree labor. At first they used indentured servants, primarily Englishmen, but also including indentured blacks. Indentured servants were sold into servitude for various lengths of time: usually four to seven years. Some whites put themselves into bondage voluntarily to pay the cost of transportation to the New World. Slavery became the other source of unfree labor. By the end of the seventeenth century, slaves brought from the West Indies and Africa, and strictly the property of their owners, to a marked degree had replaced indentured labor in the tobacco areas of Virginia and Maryland and the indigo and rice areas of South Carolina and Georgia.

## Capital

Major forms of capital formation in agriculture were the clearing of land for cultivation, the construction of necessary farm buildings, and, to a lesser degree, the accumulation of farm animals. The most important costs in constructing this capital were the labor costs provided by the farm family itself. Drawn out over a number of years, such labor was extremely costly, even though it did not involve substantial outlays of money. Martin Primack[13] has estimated that the cost of clearing one acre of forest in the eastern United states in 1860 was at least 35 days of labor. It was probably higher in the colonial period.

For small-scale farming, very little cash was necessary, in part because land was cheap and easy terms were available. Much land was obtained through settling towns (as in New England), squatting (for example, in Pennsylvania), and through grants for settling (for example, in Virginia). The few simple tools that were needed were made by the farmer himself or by the local blacksmith. The problem of money capital was much more critical for large-scale commercial agriculture. The amount of funds necessary for purchasing land was much greater. Animals, tools, and buildings required larger cash outlays; and labor costs, especially slave labor costs, were higher.

The three major sources of money capital were funds brought by the commercial settlers themselves on emigration from Great Britain and other European countries, reinvestment of profits, and foreign (British) investment. It should be noted that the third source, British investment, may have been significant for individual investments, but not for total investment. As Shephard,[15] Walton,[16] and Williamson[17] have shown, the balance of trade of the colonies (exports minus imports) was roughly zero. In view of this, there could have been no net foreign investment in the colonies. Many of the plantations of the southern colonies were established by the younger sons of moderately well-to-do families from England. These settlers arrived in the New World with funds and often with grants of land in the colonies. Other plantations were started with meager resources but proved profitable, and some of these profits were reinvested in the plantations. It is impossible to estimate how much was reinvested.

The earliest British investments in the colonies were channeled through special monopoly corporations. These corporations, chartered by the king, had exclusive rights to engage in activities in certain areas. An important example was the Virginia Company, which founded and supported the Jamestown and Virginia settlements. Although their efforts to realize profits for their investors failed uniformly, these companies succeeded in providing the basic support needed by a number of colonies in their early years.

By the mid-seventeenth century, corporate support to the colonies had been replaced by a web of commercial credit extended by British merchants, in exchange for the planters' crops. Such merchants would extend credit to a planter for supplies, equipment, consumer goods, and, especially, slaves. Seldom did a planter find his crop sufficient to repay the debt.

## Agricultural Productivity

The colonial period was spread over 168 years, from the founding of Jamestown in 1607 to the American Revolution in 1775. Most writers assume that there was very little change in agricultural productivity during the period; that is, that output per unit of input did not increase appreciably. If one only looks at the tools and equipment, and techniques used, this would seem to be true. Technological improvement was, in effect, nonexistent. Agricultural innovations developed in Britain in the eighteenth century had not reached the North American continent by 1775. There were, however, three factors that may have contributed to increased productivity between 1607 and 1760: increased knowledge of how to farm in the New World, increasingly favorable land-labor ratios, and opportunities for specialization permitted by increases in market sizes that resulted from increased population and exports.

The advantages of increased knowledge of an agricultural area are obvious. Every geographic area differs in climatic conditions (such as temperature and rainfall), kinds of soil, and soil conditions (drainage and so on). All of these factors create a certain set of optimal agricultural practices because they affect decisions about the kinds of crops grown, planting time, cultivation, and harvesting time. Farmers developing a new agricultural area up to its highest productive potential need time to acquire this knowledge. The rate of increase in output through increased knowledge diminished as farmers approached the optimum set of agricultural product mix and practices, but as new areas were settled this learning process was repeated.

Increases in productivity through more favorable land-labor ratios are more complex. For a given technology, there is a certain combination of land and labor that will produce the lowest cost per unit of agricultural output. In the colonies, land (other than cleared land taken from the Indians) had to be cleared of trees. Therefore, the settler started with an amount of cleared or improved land that was too small to produce lowest costs. As more land was cleared, the land-labor ratio moved toward the optimal (low-cost) ratio, and the productivity increase resulted in decreased costs.

But once again, in the more settled areas, this source of productivity increase diminished as a more efficient combination of land and labor was achieved. As settlers moved into the frontier, the process was repeated. We assume that increases in productivity in the new areas were more than enough to offset the losses in productivity caused by losses in soil fertility in the settled areas.

As our model concluded, it is the size of the market that determines the degree to which any producer can specialize his labor. The greater the opportunity for specialization, the higher the potential for increased productivity. Therefore, as urban population slowly increased, demand increased for agricultural products around these small but growing urban areas. Farmers specialized more in dairy products, vegetable crops, poultry, and other animal products. International trade also stimulated specialization. Therefore, specialized areas appeared for tobacco in Virginia and Maryland, for indigo and rice in South Carolina and Georgia, and for grain in eastern Pennsylvania.

To summarize briefly, productivity increases in colonial agriculture were not obtained primarily through technological development or through new crops. Rather, productivity increased through the dynamics of a developing economy with a growing supply of land.

## Self-Sufficiency

We have said that high internal transportation costs and other factors limited the amount of internal commerce. Nonetheless, internal trade was important in the colonies because very few farms—only those in the most inaccessible frontier areas—were completely self-sufficient. Prior to 1770, most settlements were located along river systems leading to the sea. Maintaining a settlement far from these rivers was made difficult by high transportation costs. A system of general stores that sprang up on the frontiers connected frontier agriculture to the port cities by rivers. Even the more remote settlers were served by wandering peddlers who traded with the general store.

Besides articles of consumption, farmers needed gunpowder, iron, and iron products. In exchange, farmers sold crops, livestock, and, in frontier areas, furs. After clearing land, farmers reduced the trees to pearl and potash for sale. Despite commercial contact, however, a substantial amount of home manufacturing provided a degree of self-sufficiency on even the largest and most accessible plantations.

The commercial nexus was obvious in the grain farms of Pennsylvania, in the tobacco plantations of Virginia and Maryland, and in the indigo and rice plantations of South Carolina and Georgia. But even here self-sufficiency and its corollary, home manufacture, were highly developed. Corn, wheat, vegetables, and animal products were produced to feed both the slave population and the owner and his family. Clothing, furniture, and farm tools also were widely produced on the plantation.

In brief, both the totally commercial farm and the totally self-sufficient farm were rare. In terms of dualism, few of the colonists (except those on the isolated frontier) were totally within the noncash economy, and few were totally within the cash economy. The substantial majority were, with varying degrees of intensity, producing within both the cash and noncash economies.

# Colonial Manufacturing

Before 1770, manufacturing for sale in the North American colonies was rudimentary and employed only a small percentage of the total labor force. Industry was severely hampered by two main factors: relative factor endowments, especially scarce and therefore costly labor, and, second, the limited demand that resulted from a small market constrained by high internal transportation costs.

First, the easy availability of land continually siphoned off the potential wage-earning labor force from manufacturing. This short supply of labor resulted in high wages and, thus, high production costs. The colonies' comparative advantage, thus, rested largely in land intensive (agricultural) activities rather than in relatively capital- and labor-intensive (manufacturing) activities.

A characteristic, if not a limiting, factor in the development of manufacturing was the relatively inexperienced management and simplistic technology in the colonies. The industrial labor force consisted primarily of artisans working with simple tools in small establishments. They had little experience with the processes and industries that were developing in the home country. Although the industrial revolution had barely begun in England by 1770, England had undergone a process of quickening development in a wide variety of industries over the preceding 200 years. These developments had not yet reached the colonies. But, if colonial technology was not as productive as England's, it was nevertheless appropriate to the demands created by a much smaller market. One should not, therefore, consider the relatively unsophisticated colonial technology as an important limiting factor in manufacturing development.

The most severe limitation on manufacturing development was simply the size of markets. The colonies had few manufacturing export markets because there were few goods in which the colonies enjoyed a comparative manufacturing advantage over the British manufacturers.

It is not surprising that those few were goods that drew on forest products and iron—resources in abundance in the colonies. Shipbuilding, an industry of substantial importance in New England by the late colonial period, was an important example. Some manufactured export goods that drew on abundant colonial resources were severely restricted also by British efforts to limit certain American markets for themselves. Shipbuilding was an activity the British needed and in which they had no comparative advantage (after depleting their own stands of timber, that is). Beginning in 1699, though, and continuing through 1750, a series of laws made it illegal, first, to export colonial wool, woolen yarn, and wool products; then, to export hats made from beaver fur; and, finally, in 1750, to export finished iron products (although pig and bar iron were allowed duty-free entry). The overall impact of these restrictions was to limit foreign markets for certain goods and thereby to limit the combined domestic and foreign market.

Again, however, it was the high cost of transportation beyond the sea coast and the tributary river systems that limited the domestic market. The colonists were few in number (although growing rapidly) and also were widely scattered. Home manufacturing and family self-sufficiency further reduced both the demand for manufactured goods and the money income of potential consumers. Low demand and small market size prevented the specialization of labor that might have reduced costs to levels more nearly equal to those of Britain. Specialization of labor was low within enterprises, and specialization of the enterprises themselves was prevented.

Around 1770, the generalizations we have made about colonial manufacturers became less valid. As the population increased, growing cities and towns provided a local market for small-scale craft-oriented enterprises, and a labor force of skilled craftsmen developed. By 1770, a small, locally oriented system of small-scale manufacturers had developed to meet the need for simple manufactures. The most significant form of local manufactures took place within the blacksmith shop, where the blacksmith made to order and repaired the simple tools of the farmer.

Skills were transmitted from one generation to the next through the apprentice system. An average manufacturing enterprise was composed of the master employer, a few journeymen working for wages, and a few apprentices learning the trade. Under this system, significant improvements in technology were unlikely.

After the initial settlement of the coastal areas, some increases in productivity probably were achieved by growth of market demand and by improvements in knowledge gained through experience, which led to greater ability and proficiency in serving developing markets and utilizing local materials. These productivity-increasing factors were small, however, and the manufacturing sector itself was small. Therefore, increases in manufacturing productivity had little impact on the economy as a whole.

# Colonial Commerce

Colonial commerce consisted of exchanges of commodities and services not only within colonies and between colonies but also with Great Britain and—through Britain—with western Europe.

Intracolonial trade, or trade within a particular colony, grew more slowly than other forms of trade. A major reason for the relatively slow growth of internal markets was the cost of overland transportation. The building of roads and canals progressed slowly because the colonies had made only small investments in **social overhead capital,** those forms of capital available for use or consumption by the public. Intracolonial trade was confined to localized activities, such as the milling of grain for farm families in a small market area. The cost of marketing increased rapidly when goods were moved over longer distances. These high transportation costs encouraged relative self-sufficiency in the interiors of the colonies.

Although precise data on intracolonial trade are lacking, we can draw four inferences based on our knowledge of that trade and our model of development: (a) barriers to integration of resource usage were high; (b) the opportunity costs of self-sufficiency were low; (c) the degree of specialization and division of labor and capital was relatively low; and (d) productivity, output per hour of labor employed, was lower than in other areas of commerce.

Trade between the North American colonies, which we shall call *intercolonial trade,* was more significant.* Intercolonial coastal trade was subject to substantial growth because ocean transportation costs were

---

* Although trade with the West Indies was literally *intercolonial,* we shall treat those exchanges as part of overseas trade and use the term *intercolonial* to refer to exchanges between the North American colonies.

much lower than overland costs. Deep-water shipping was then and is even now the cheapest means of transporting bulky (high weight-price ratio) goods. Many of the goods that moved in intercolonial trade, such as grains and sugar, benefited from this low transportation cost. In this trade, some social overhead capital, such as port facilities, reduced the costs to colonial merchants.

James Shepherd and Samuel Williamson[16] estimated that coastal exports amounted to an annual average of £7,676,000 sterling in the period from 1768 to 1772. Of course, no data exist for gross product for the North American colonies. If, however, we consider a range of £20 million to £30 million as representing the estimates of various scholars, then coastal trade made up about 2% to 4% of that product. According to recent studies by David Klingaman,[11] coastal trade was growing in the late colonial period; moreover, it was growing in per capita terms, at least as far as Virginia, the most populous of the colonies (after 1730), was concerned.

If we consider that, in spite of high costs, there was a modest amount of trading between colonies by land routes, then the sum of both overland trade and the coastal trade probably amounted to not more than 4% to 5% of colonial gross product even at the end of the colonial period. In terms of our model, however, the cost advantages of coastal trade were such that productivity, related to specialization of resources, was probably growing with a growing market size in the coastal activity of the cash economy.

Did the North American colonies trade according to the principle of comparative advantage? Basically, the answer is yes. The answer is clearly yes insofar as the coastal trade between the colonies is concerned. Indeed, the scenario was very similar to the hypothetical one presented in the Review of Economic Concepts later in this chapter. Virginia shipped large quantities of corn to Massachusetts and wheat to New York and other northern colonial areas. In turn, Virginia received shipments from those areas (often reexports) of sugar, rum, molasses, fish, and salt. Where the earnings from these commodity exports (visible items) were inadequate to pay for the imports, the northern colonies earned the difference through shipping services, financial services, and the like.

## The Overseas Trade

Specialization and comparative advantage trade tended also to dominate the overseas exchanges of the colonies. The New England colonies exported such things as dried fish, naval stores, and whale oil to Britain and the West Indies, as well as to southern European countries. The southern colonies developed comparative advantage agricultural exports. Maryland and Virginia primarily exported tobacco, a crop whose demand grew throughout the colonial period. The Carolinas found specialized advantages in two exports, rice and indigo.

The middle colonies (Pennsylvania, Delaware, New Jersey, and New York) specialized in wheat and wheat products, such as biscuits, together with the reexport business (reshipping to the West Indies and England). This is why, as Boston declined in relative shipping importance, Philadelphia and then New York grew.

By the end of the colonial period, both exports and imports were remarkably concentrated according to comparative advantage. Eight commodities accounted for over four-fifths of exports in 1770. In order of importance, the commodities that dominated exports were tobacco, grains and flour, fish, livestock and meat, naval stores, furs and deerskins, indigo, and extracted products.

Manufactured goods dominated the commodity imports from Europe. There was a substantial trade with the West Indies in rum, molasses, and sugar (mostly reexported from the middle colonies to northern and southern colonies). Of course, comparative advantage was dominant in the import pattern, but it was not always a market-determined advantage in either exports or imports. The case of indigo exports is a classic example. Because British textile manufacturers needed indigo to dye their products, the industry was heavily subsidized in the southern colonies and elsewhere in the British Empire. The subsidy shifted the cost advantage in favor of indigo, which made up slightly less than 4% of colonial exports in 1770.

Slaves were a major import of the colonies, especially after 1680. Slave importation occurred primarily in the southern colonies, but it occurred in the middle and northern colonies as well. The black (mostly slave) population of the colonies grew from about 16,000 in 1690 to about 500,000 at the time of the revolution.

The colonies benefited from a commodity **trade surplus** (exports greater than imports) with southern Europe; but 75% to 80% of their trade was with Britain and represented **trade deficits** (imports greater than exports). As we see from Table 2-1, the commodity trade deficit was financed primarily by selling the shipping and other services of the colonists and by the administrative and military expenditures of the British. Overall, as Shepherd and Williamson have shown,[16] the colonial trade relationship was balanced.

## Money and Trade

A supply of money was needed to accommodate both foreign and intercolonial trade. A commercial British model was probably impractical, because of the small size of the market. Since money is anything commonly accepted as a medium of exchange, various commodities, including tobacco, were used for that purpose. Barter had been employed early in the colonial trade, especially in the triangular trade with Britain and the

Table 2-1. Colonial Balance of Payments 1770 (thousands of pounds sterling).

| Item | Credit | Debit |
|---|---|---|
| Commodity exports | 3023 | — |
| Commodities imports | — | 3961 |
| Slave imports | — | 108 |
| Imports of indentured servants | — | 75 |
| Total balance, visible items | | 1121 |
| Shipping and other services | 845 | — |
| British expenditures on colonial government services | 400 | — |
| Total balance, invisible items | 1245 | |
| Total balance of payments (visible and invisible items) | 124 | |

Source: Adapted from James F. Shepherd and Gary M. Walton, "Estimates of 'Invisible' Earnings in the Balance of Payments of the British North American Colonies, 1768–1772," *Journal of Economic History,* June 1969; also Ralph Gray and John M. Peterson, *Economic Development of the United States* (Homewood, Ill.: Irwin, 1974).

West Indies. Because of bulkiness, deterioration, and other factors, however, commodities proved to be a high-cost means of financing exchanges, and as a result the colonial merchants turned increasingly to currency and coin.

Even though the volume of commercial transactions was increasing, the growth of the money supply was subject to severe restrictions. The English government restricted the minting of coins and closed down the mint established by Massachusetts. Colonial currency, or paper money, was sometimes issued in such large quantities that both colonial and British merchants refused to accept it at par (face value). The reduced acceptability of currency called into effect **Gresham's law**—(relatively) overvalued or "cheap" money drives out (relatively) undervalued or "dear" money. Merchants tended to hoard the coin and use the paper money, thus further reducing velocity and the growth of the effective money supply. Overall, there were inflationary pressures on colonial prices, especially the prices at which goods were exchanged either at home or abroad in depreciated paper money.

Most students of the colonial period have concluded that, although the money supply problems raised the costs of trading (both information and transactions costs), the opportunity cost of creating a commercial banking system in the small colonial market would have been high even if the institutional restraints of British mercantile policy had permitted or encouraged such a development.

# Wealth and Growth in the Colonies

Some people have viewed the colonies as a frontier society in which wealth was distributed fairly equally. The data, including recent important research of Alice Hanson Jones,[10] suggest that wealth inequality was great and actually increased during the colonial period. James Henretta[9] came to the same conclusion about wealth ownership in Boston, where the propertyless group doubled from 14% to 29% of the population between the 1680s and the 1770s. Jones suggests that wealth inequality probably increased in the eighteenth century compared to a century earlier.

Wealth almost certainly was unequally distributed at the outset of the colonial period (reflecting different endowments of land, financial capital, and skills and abilities). Also, there was no governmental policy, such as progressive taxes, designed to reduce inequality of wealth ownership. But some students of economics believe that growing inequality of income and wealth are not only inevitable but also necessary if savings and investments are to occur on a scale that guarantees ongoing economic development in the early years of development.

Growth of the colonial economy was assured by increasing trade and by an eightfold increase in population between 1700 and 1770 (from about 250,000 to just over 2 million). But scholars disagree about the extent of development, or change in per capita income.

George Taylor[20] argues that per capita growth was very slow before 1710, rapid from 1710 to 1775, then slow or zero from 1775 to 1840. Taylor suggests that between 1710 and 1775 per capita output grew from $45 to $90, a substantial increase that, if translated roughly into present-day dollars, amounts to about $500 in 1710 and $1000 in 1775. These per capita output figures compare favorably with those of all but the very well-developed nations of the 1970s.

Later scholars have questioned Taylor's figures. Robert Gallman[5] believes per capita income may have been as high as $60 as early as 1710. Based on Alice Jones's[10] research of wealth data (developed from probate records, which were among the few good nonexport-import data), a figure of $60 to $70 seems reasonable. If so, it appears that slow steady growth of per capita output occurred in the 1710–1775 period. The growth rate was perhaps 0.5% per year, which is significant for that period (perhaps among the highest in the world), although much less than the 2.1% per year in the United States since the late nineteenth century.

# Review of Economic Concepts: Development

## A Classical View

The two objectives of rising output per capita and decreasing dualism approximate the process of development. Development results when a nation chooses more future goods; that is, when it saves and invests, creates more capital goods, and increases its capacity to produce while it undergoes the structural change necessary to accommodate this process. The rate at which it develops depends on how large a part of current output is saved and invested and on the power of compound interest. The production possibilities model, however, does not give us the insights we need concerning the underlying causes of development and the factors that constrain it for economies in general and for colonial economies in particular.

A very general and widely accepted view of the causes and limitations of economic development is the **classical view** set forth in one form or another by economists beginning with Adam Smith (1723–1790) in the late eighteenth and early nineteenth centuries. Despite its relative antiquity, the classical view is still valid today and applies to all economies, colonial or noncolonial, integrated or dualistic, agricultural or industrial, high income or low income.

According to this classical view, intensive growth and economic development are virtually synonymous with productivity growth. Basically, productivity growth is determined by the degree of specialization and division of labor and capital in production processes. Adam Smith pointed out that, as both people and machines took on more and more specialized tasks, their productivity grew very rapidly. Smith observed this growth, for example, in the operation of an eighteenth-century pin factory where the number of pins produced per worker grew very quickly with specialized labor tasks and with specialized machines.

What determines the extent of, or the limits to, specialization and division of labor and capital? According to the classical economists, it is the size of the market. As the size of the market grows it becomes feasible for people to specialize and to employ specialized kinds of capital. The size of markets depends on both demand and supply. Any of the factors that may cause demand to grow (population and income growth, for instance) or supply to grow (reduced transportation cost, for instance) will increase the size of markets. As Smith noted:[18] "When the market is very small, no person can have any encouragement to dedicate himself entirely to one employment, for want of power to exchange all that surplus part of the produce of his own labor, which is over and above his own consumption, for such parts of the produce of other men's labor as he has occasion for."

Classical economists generally felt that the size of the market depended on the amount or stock of capital and the pattern of institutions.

According to Smith, "No regulation of commerce can increase the quantity of industry in any society beyond what its capital can maintain." In other words, greater specialization of labor—a condition for productivity growth— must be preceded by an increased stock of capital. The second factor influencing the size of the market was the pattern of economic institutions and institutional regulations. The classical economists argued that the optimal set of institutions was that which permitted and enforced competition for those harnessed the self-interests of individuals to increase the goods and services available to a society through what Smith referred to as the influence of the "invisible hand."

With the exception of Smith, the classical economists were pessimistic about the ability of economies to continue to experience intensive growth and to develop indefinitely. Others saw an early upper limit to real per capita output, a stationary state as shown in Figure 2-1. At first, growth occurs rapidly. Then the rate of growth diminishes, for a variety of reasons, including a limited supply of land, a diminishing growth of productivity of capital, the use of technology from a fixed menu of choices that adds less and less to output, a falling rate of profit, or a population growth that outstrips output gains. Finally these resistances grow strong enough to offset any tendencies to increasing real per capital output, and the economy reaches its stationary state. Among the classical group, only Smith thought this stationary state could occur at a very high level of real output or income.

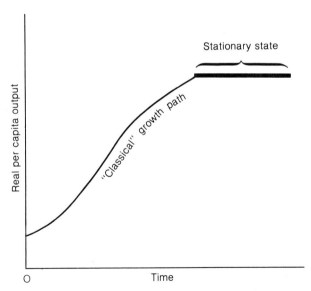

Figure 2-1. A Classical Growth Path.

## Comparative Advantage: Why People Trade

When market exchanges occur, it is because buyers and sellers expect to improve their respective positions. A common explanation for this disposition to trade is based on the **principle of comparative advantage.** According to this principle, resources are relatively more productive in some uses than in others. Thus, an area, region, or nation (including a colony) can have a greater volume of commodities and services for consumption if it specializes in producing those goods in which it has its greatest relative efficiency or productivity and then trades some of its output to import goods produced by other areas or nations producing according to their own greatest relative efficiency or productivity. This is true for any nation or area, even though it may produce each good it consumes with an **absolute advantage,** with fewer real resources per unit of output than any other nation or area with which it trades.

Assume, for example, that both Massachusetts and Virginia could produce grain, make flour, and catch and process fish. Acording to the principle of comparative advantage, each should specialize in producing the thing(s) in which it is relatively more efficient. Perhaps Massachusetts should specialize in its fisheries industry, since its soil is relatively poor, and Virginia should specialize in its grain and flour industry, since its soil is relatively rich.

The gains from this trade are illustrated in Figure 2-2, which shows the relationship between the production possibilities curve of each colony before trade and the consumption possibilities curve of each after trade.

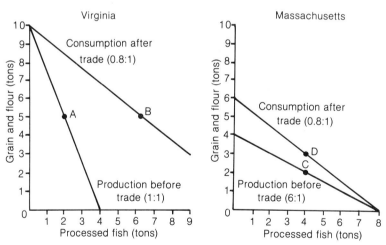

Figure 2-2. Hypothetical Production and Consumption Possibilities for Virginia and Massachusetts.

## The Gains from Trade

Each of the hypothetical production-before-trade (production possibilities) curves in Figure 2-2 represents the various combinations of grain and flour and processed fish that Virginia or Massachusetts could produce at a given time with full employment of resources and use of the best technology. Each is drawn as a straight line to reflect a simplifying assumption of no specialization of resources, or a constant rate of real cost (constant rather than diminishing returns). Notice also that the internal rate of exchange, the rate at which either colony must give up one commodity to get more of the other, is different in the two colonies. In Virginia, the rate of exchange is approximately 1:1 (1 ton of grain and flour for 1 ton of processed fish). In Massachusetts, however, the ratio is about 0.45:1. Massachusetts must give up 0.45 tons of grain and flour to obtain a ton of processed fish. Virginia, thus, has a comparative advantage in producing grain and flour, and Massachusetts has a comparative advantage in producing processed fish.

If both colonies specialize and if each exports to the other part of its output of the comparative advantage good, both can have more goods for consumption (indicated in the consumption-after-trade curves for each colony) than would be available without trade. The rate at which Virginia's grain and flour exchange for Massachusetts' fish depends on the structure of their two markets.

Suppose, for the sake of illustration, that the exchange rate becomes 0.8:1 (0.8 ton of Virginia grain for 1 ton of Massachusetts fish). Compare Points C and D; if Massachusetts produces only fish (8 tons) but exchanges 4 tons with Virginia, it can obtain 3.2 ($4 \times 0.8$) tons of grain. Thus, it can consume 4 tons of fish and 3.2 tons of grain and flour with trade, whereas it could consume only 4 tons of fish and 2 tons of grain and flour without trade (Point C). The additional 1.2 tons of grain and flour is a gain from trade. Likewise, if Virginia produces only grain and flour (10 tons) and, for example, exchanges 5 tons of those commodities with Massachusetts, it can obtain 6.25 tons of fish ($5 \times 1\frac{1}{8} = 6.25$). Thus, with trade, Virginia can consume 5 tons of grain and flour plus 6.25 tons of fish, more than the 5 tons of grain and flour and 2 tons of fish available without trade. Again, the additional 4.25 tons of fish is a gain from trade.

Although the gains from trade in this example accrue primarily to one colony, Virginia, there are gains to both trading partners. Allowing for increasing costs (concave production-before-trade curves), specialization will not be complete; both trading partners will reach a point at which they will produce *some* of both products.

# Glossary

**Absolute advantage**   The advantage that occurs when a nation or area is more efficient in producing a good or all goods than any other nation from which it might import that good or those goods.

**Classical view**   A view of economic development set forth in various forms during the late eighteenth and early nineteenth centuries by the classical economists, beginning with Adam Smith. Economic development is regarded as productivity growth, which is obtained through specialization and division of labor and capital, which in turn depend on the size of the market, the stock of capital, and economic institutions.

**Economies of scale**   In agriculture, the reduced unit costs of the crop available with higher rates of production.

**Gresham's law**   The rule that relatively overvalued or "cheap" money drives relatively undervalued or "dear" money out of circulation.

**Invisible items of exports**   Services, such as shipping, that can be exchanged in trade.

**Principle of comparative advantage**   The advantage that a nation or area derives from specializing in producing those goods in which it is relatively most efficient and importing from other nations the goods that they produce with relatively greater efficiency.

**Social overhead capital**   Forms of capital available for use or consumption by the public (such as roads, canals, railroads, and educational facilities).

**Terms of trade**   The ratio of export prices received to import prices paid (stated in the form of indices).

**Trade deficit**   A deficit that occurs when imports exceed exports.

**Trade surplus**   A surplus that occurs when exports exceed imports.

**Visible items of export**   Commodities, such as tobacco, that can be exchanged in trade.

# Questions

1. What are the major economic differences between a cash economy and a barter economy?
2. According to the classical economists, what causes economic development to occur? What determines the rate at which development occurs? How did Adam Smith differ from other classical economists in describing the possible *level* of economic well-being at the stationary state?

3. Why are the terms of trade so important to an economy?
4. What is the difference between absolute advantage and comparative advantage? What are the sources of the gains from trade that comparative advantage exchanges make possible?
5. Was the distribution of colonial land ownership relatively even? What were the obstacles to land ownership? How was a labor force provided for the family-size farm? For the commercial farm?
6. What was the main process of capital formation in the family-size farm? What were the main sources of financial capital for the commercial farms?
7. What were the basic factors causing productivity increases in colonial agriculture? Explain.
8. Evaluate the statement, "The totally self-sufficient colonial farm was rare, as was the totally commercial farm."
9. Why was the level of productivity increase so low in colonial manufacturing?
10. Why are the British restrictions on colonial banking and paper money considered to have been of little burden to the colonial economy?
11. What were the major obstacles to development of internal markets in the North American colonies?
12. Did coastal trade grow during the colonial period? Why?
13. Did the North American colonies engage in comparative advantage trade? What was the pattern of overseas trade by the colonies?
14. What happened to the trade balance of the colonies in the eighteenth century?
15. What were the problems associated with financing colonial trade? What is Gresham's law? How does it apply to the colonial trade?
16. What changes occurred in the distribution of wealth in the North American colonies? Were any changes in this distribution favorable to economic development? Why?
17. What are the views about the level and rate of growth of per capita income in the colonies?

# Suggested Readings

1. Bidwell, Percy W., and Falconer, John I. *History of Agriculture in the Northern United States, 1620–1860.* Washington, D.C.: Carnegie Institution of Washington, 1925.
2. Bridenbaugh, Carl. *The Colonial Craftsman.* New York: New York University Press, 1950.

3. Bruchey, Stuart. *The Roots of American Economic Growth, 1607–1861.* New York: Harper & Row, 1968. Pp. 23–41.

4. Ferguson, E. James. "Currency Finance: An Interpretation of Colonial Monetary Practices." In *Issues in American Economic History,* ed. Gerald D. Nash. Lexington, Mass.: Heath, 1972.

5. Gallman, Robert. "The Pace and Pattern of American Economic Growth." In *American Economic Growth,* ed. L. Davis, R. Easterlin, and W. Parker. New York: Harper & Row, 1972.

6. Gray, Lewis C. *History of Agriculture in the Southern States to 1860.* Vol. 1. Washington, D.C.: Carnegie Institute of Washington, 1933.

7. Harper, Lawrence. "The Burden of the Navigation Acts on the Thirteen Colonies." In *United States Economic History,* ed. Harry B. Scheiber. New York: Knopf, 1964.

8. Harris, Marshall. *Origin of the Land Tenure System in the United States.* Ames: University of Iowa, 1953.

9. Henretta, James A. "Economic Development and Social Structure in Colonial Boston." *William and Mary Quarterly* (January 1965).

10. Jones, Alice Hanson. "Wealth Estimates of the New England Colonies about 1770." *Journal of Economic History, 33* (March 1972).

11. Klingaman, David C. "Food Surpluses and Deficits in the American Colonies, 1768–1772." *Journal of Economic History, 36* (September 1975).

12. Loehr, Rodney C. "Self-Sufficiency of the Farm." *Agricultural History, 26* (April 1952).

13. Primack, Martin L. "Land Clearing Under Nineteenth-Century Techniques: Some Preliminary Calculations." *Journal of Economic History, 23* (December 1962).

14. Sacks, William. "Agricultural Conditions in the Northern Colonies Before the Revolution." *Journal of Economic History, 13* (Summer 1953): 274–290.

15. Shepherd, James F., and Walton, Gary M. "Trade, Distribution and Economic Growth in Colonial America." *Journal of Economic History* (March 1972).

16. Shepherd, James F., and Williamson, Samuel. "The Coastal Trade of British North American Colonies, 1768–1772." *Journal of Economic History, 33* (December 1972).

17. Smith, Abbott E. *Colonists in Bondage: White Servitude and Convict Labor In America, 1607–1776.* Chapel Hill, N.C.: University of North Carolina Press, 1947.

18. Smith, Adam. *An Enquiry Into the Causes of the Wealth of the Nation.* New York: The Modern Library, 1937.

19. Stampp, Kenneth M. *The Peculiar Institution: Slavery in the Ante-Bellum South*. New York: Alfred A. Knopf, 1956.

20. Taylor, George Rogers. "American Economic Growth Before 1840: An Exploratory Essay." *Journal of Economic History, 25* (December 1964).

21. Tryon, Rolla M. *Household Manufacturers in the United States, 1640–1860*. Chicago, 1917.

22. Turner, Frederick Jackson. *The Frontier in American History*. New York: Holt, Rinehart and Winston, 1962.

23. Weiss, Roger W. "The Issue of Paper Money in the American Colonies, 1720–1774." *Journal of Economic History, 30* (December 1970).

# Chapter 3

---

# Motivations, Mercantilism, and the Revolution

In this chapter, we shall analyze the psychological and institutional character of the colonial economy; specifically, we are concerned with factors determining the motivations of the colonists and the economic effects of government policy both within the colonies themselves and between the colonists and the government of England. In large part, our objective is to understand how these processes contributed to the causes of the American Revolution.

## Economic Motivations and the Colonial Mind

Many people feel intuitively that attitudes toward economic activity seriously affect economic development. People are surely more capable of taking advantage of opportunities for economic development if they are motivated to work hard, willing to try improved techniques, and willing to save and invest capital to increase output. Such people seem better prepared for development than those who are more traditionally oriented, satisfied with what is, and reluctant to try to develop new, more productive methods. But, while we understand intuitively the importance of attitudes about economic activity, it is difficult to construct theories about them and their effects on economic development.

Now, what factors molded the American colonists' attitudes toward economic activity? First, the settlers had been conditioned by the religious doctrines of Luther and Calvin, summarized in the **Weber Thesis** (described in the following section). Second, the political and economic philosophy of John Locke had a profound effect especially on the Founding Fathers of the United States. Third, the colonists were affected by being within a frontier environment. Finally, the southern colonies were also affected by the institution of slavery.

## The Weber Thesis

Max Weber,[18] a German sociologist writing in the early twentieth century, concluded that the theology of the sixteenth- and seventeenth-century Reformation period influenced human behavior in ways that were beneficial to economic development. Weber was concerned with the psychological conditioning that resulted from the theological positions of the Protestant reformers, especially Luther and Calvin.

Luther and Calvin continued to maintain the Catholic position that economic effort was an area of personal activity subject to the moral judgments of religious prescriptions. These Protestant reformers considered usury and violations of "just price" (fair price) as improper conduct. They condemned high interest rates and unjust prices (high prices from a short supply) as exploitive economic practices.

Both Luther and Calvin placed great importance on the concept of the "calling" (one's earthly occupation) and on the obligation to work hard and diligently. Calvin added that a person is obligated to choose the best "calling" he or she is capable of performing. This ideal was coupled with the belief that, since all wealth belongs to God, each person is God's earthly steward over his or her own share of wealth. One should not spend God's wealth foolishly; frugality and saving are virtues, and each person is required to invest wisely in order to increase God's wealth. This commandment leads to investments oriented toward increases in output.

According to Weber, the Calvinist concept of predestination supports this system of hard work, frugality, savings, and productive investment and leads to increased output. Calvin said that God ordained at the beginning of time who would be saved and who would be condemned to the fires of hell. There was nothing an individual could do to change that outcome. There also was a way to tell if a person was one of the elect, one of those who would be saved. The individual must live the proper life, and even more important, must believe in being saved; any element of doubt about one's own election for salvation was ultimate proof against election. The doctrine of predestination adds an inner discipline to a concept of the "proper life" that includes hard work, rational selection of a calling to maximize income, and frugality and savings so as not to waste God's wealth. All these psychological characteristics are excellently suited to produce a population that strives toward economic development.

A secular manifestation of this Protestant ethic can be found in sayings of Ben Franklin from *Poor Richard*, for example, "A penny saved is a

John Hancock (left), and Samuel Adams, colonial merchants and revolutionary leaders. (Photo nos. 59-LP-12 and 148-GW-811 in the National Archives)

penny earned," "God helps them who help themselves," and "Early to bed and early to rise makes a man healthy, wealthy, and wise." Note that Franklin was a product of Calvinist Boston.

Weber and many other writers emphasize that the Protestant ethic cannot be attributed exclusively to the Puritans of New England. Most of the colonies were settled originally by groups with a strong religious background, and all but the Catholics of Maryland were of Calvinist origin. New York was first settled by the Calvinistic Dutch. In Pennsylvania, the Quaker followers of William Penn and the German Moravians were both Calvinist. New Jersey had the Calvinist Swedes, while Virginia had the Scottish Presbyterians—again, Calvinist. Perhaps even the Catholics of Maryland should not be left out, for many of Weber's critics have pointed out that Protestant ethic elements emerged in Catholic thought during the sixteenth and seventeenth centuries.

Some writers, including Stuart Bruchey,[2] argue that the Protestant ethic was irrelevant to the American colonial economy. These authors stress the conflict between capitalist activity and religious prescriptions forbidding the taking of interest and insisting on "just price." These critics are right in the sense that religion limited profit-seeking activity dealing with consumer leading and taking advantage of limited-supply conditions. But, with such activities banned as immoral behavior, colonists conditioned by the new theology channeled their efforts into production.

Patrick Henry. (Photo no. 148-GW-129A in the National Archives)

## The Philosophy of John Locke

The Founding Fathers of the United States were undoubtedly influenced by John Locke, the seventeenth-century political philosopher to whom the sanctity of private property was the central justification for government. According to Locke, the best method of producing the goods society needs is through private ownership of the tools of production and of output. In a society without government, however, all would war against each other, and the strong would take from the weak. To protect private property, the many should combine, form a social contract, and create a government; thus, the main function of government is to protect private property, which is the best institution to ensure economic production.

In the Declaration of Independence, Jefferson paraphrased Locke, who would have said "Life, liberty and the pursuit of property." The popular ideology of colonial times gave a central place to individual private property rights. But Locke himself was influenced by the Protestant religious ethic, and implicit in the rights of private property was the obligation to utilize that property for rational investment and production.

## The Frontier

From the beginning of settlement in 1607, the frontier nature of the colonies reinforced habits and attitudes that proved conducive to economic

development: individual initiative; economic optimism, with its characteristic high level of effort; and a willingness to enter into cooperative effort
when necessary.

Individual effort was needed first to survive and then to obtain com-
forts. This initiative reinforced a sense of individuality and at the same
time proved that economic gains could be made through individual effort.
Because labor was scarce and raw materials were abundant, labor was
conserved, and resources such as trees and fertile soil were used freely in a
manner that many today would consider wasteful and ecologically damaging. During the frontier era, however, this manner of using resources
saved labor and allowed for rapid increases in output. When the frontier
people faced tasks that were too difficult for individual effort, they
cooperated to achieve desired ends. With the abundant resources of the
frontier, economic and social mobility was greater in the colonies than in
Europe, and this factor retarded the development of an entrenched class
structure.

## Slavery and the South

During the colonial period, another factor was introduced that had a
special effect for the South, namely, the factor of slavery and the plantation system. Settlers in the plantation areas of Maryland, Virginia, the
Carolinas, and Georgia were generally conditioned by the same factors
that affected the population of the rest of the colonies, namely, the
religious work ethic, the philosophy of John Locke, and frontier conditions. However, slavery and the plantation system created a new and
peculiar set of conditions. The institution of slavery created new social
relations and attitudes that tended to affect mobility of resources. Slavery
enabled larger units (plantations) to be formed and increased the political,
social, and economic influence of the plantation owners. Whites dominated blacks, and one race became set against another.

## McClelland and the Achieving Society

The first three factors just described seem to contribute to attitudes conducive to economic development. A present-day theory concerned with
atittudes and economic development is the one developed by David C. Mc-
Clelland.[11] It will be useful to review his theory here, keeping in mind
how the conditions just described foster the attitudes that McClelland considers beneficial to economic development.

McClelland, a psychologist, "invaded" the domain of the economist
with his book *The Achieving Society* (1961). McClelland maintained that
one specific motive, the need for achievement (n-achievement, or n-ach) is
essential for high degrees of entrepreneurship. In brief, n-achievement

stimulates entrepreneurship, which in turn stimulates economic development. McClelland feels that differences in degree of n-achievement significantly explain why some groups and countries take advantage of developmental situations while other groups and countries do not. The important
advantage of the n-achievement concept, according to McClelland, is that
it can be measured with an index and related to the level of economic activity.

Some characteristics of high n-achievers are the following: They are
more interested in a job well done than in the more mundane rewards of
money or prestige. They can work in groups as well as alone. They have a
rational framework for decision-making. Although they are willing to risk
failure in seeking achievement, they carefully evaluate realistic probabil-
ities for success by distinguishing factors that are susceptible to control
from those that depend on chance. High n-achievers have a greater future
time sense. They are willing to forego immediate gratification to obtain
future rewards. They are more inclined to use their own carefully rea-
soned judgment, after obtaining information about an investment, than to
be overwhelmed by the prevailing opinion of others; that is, they are more
independent and less susceptible to social pressure. In brief, high
n-achievers make rational decisions after careful reasoning on the
evidence; they are more independent, more willing to take reasonable
risks, more willing to plan ahead and await future rewards, and more concerned with accomplishment than with power.

The American colonists seem to fit in large measure McClelland's
description of high n-achievers. This in part may have been due to the
selective biases that operated in terms of who chose to come to the colonies. Perhaps the rigors of immigrating and its challenges biased this
selection to the more daring, vigorous, healthy, youthful, and so on. Also
in part, high n-achievers amongst the colonists may have been due to the
specific qualities of those imbued with the Protestant ethic.

## Government and the Colonies

The economist must look at the effect of government activities on the
economic development of the American colonies at two levels. We must
look at both the activities of the government residing within the thirteen
colonies and, more importantly, at the activities (laws and enforcement) of
the government in England as they related to the American colonies.

The American Revolution was an outgrowth of conflict between the
colonists and the government in England. Can one explain in economic
terms the conflicts that ended in the revolution? Was England exercising
control to exploit the colonies for the home country's benefit, or was its
mercantilist policy used to maximize economic benefits for both the col-

onial and English economies? Is there a reasonable economic explanation for the American Revolution?

By the beginning of the eighteenth century, the British government had increased its control of the governing of the colonies. In doing so, it had replaced private control by the separate proprietors with royal appointment of governors; it also had reduced the power of the local assemblies. Market economies had developed enough so that the royal governments now had some impact on the economy. Their effects were small but noticeable and were manifested mostly in the area of patronage. Government had enough demand for goods that it could give out some contracts, almost all of which went to the favorites of the governors. In this way, a small group of colonial merchants obtained a somewhat special advantage in economic activity, and a small class of favored merchants had a special interest in protecting royal control over the colonies.

At the same time, the self-governing institutions of the colonies intervened widely, developing their own local mercantilism. They attempted to stimulate desired kinds of enterprises and regulated significant aspects of the economy, at times including prices and interest rates. Some faced the conflict either of defending royal control out of self-interest from special treatment or of defending local self-rule and its local mercantilism.

## Mercantilism and the American Colonies

**Mercantilism** was a system of practical European economic policies dominant in the seventeenth and eighteenth centuries. Although the recommendations and policies varied from one country to another and from one period of time to another, some common theories provided threads binding mercantilist thought and practice.

The basic motivation of mercantilist policy was to maximize the economic power of the nation. To accomplish this, the national government had to become involved in all facets of economic activity. A mercantilist economy was a "managed" economy.

Our concern here is with only one aspect of mercantilism, that concerned with international trade and colony–home country relations. The volume of international trade was regarded as fixed. If France's exports increased, some other countries' exports would have to decrease. The aim of a single country, thus, was to increase its **favorable balance of trade** (the excess of exports over imports). A country with a favorable balance of trade would receive an inflow of money (gold and silver) in payment for its excess of exports. As its supply of gold and silver increased, the wealth and power of the nation would increase.

The accumulation of gold and silver was more important in France than in England, where greater emphasis was placed on maximizing output, profits, and employment. Also, primary emphasis was placed on international trade in England, but not in France where greater emphasis was placed on internal affairs.

The function of colonies was to help in this economic objective. Mercantilists viewed the home country and colonies as one entity, each with a different role. The colonies were to provide the raw materials needed by the home country and thus to reduce the need to import such raw materials. In turn, the colonies would provide a market for the manufactured goods of the home country. In this way, the empire would become more self-sufficient and reduce the need for imports from outside.

As developed by the major imperial powers—England, France, Holland, and Spain—during the sixteenth, seventeenth, and eighteenth centuries, mercantile policy aimed at implementing these approaches. Each nation passed laws restricting their colonies' trade with other nations. Subsidies and other forms of help were extended to colonies to facilitate production of desired raw materials, but the colonies were restricted in their right to produce manufactured goods in competition with the home country.

The goal was to create a separate, self-contained economic world within each empire. Economic benefits generated by this interrelationship would arise through specialization of functions and through cooperation between the two parts—not through exploitation of the colonies by the home country. In the British mind, at least, both home country and colonies would benefit economically. A major question for us, then, is "Was English mercantile policy beneficial to the North American colonists?"

Beyond the question of the economic effects of mercantilist laws, one must ask whether the colonies were benefited or hurt by membership in the British Empire, with all of its privileges and burdens. The answer to that question is not simple, and, as is the case with all complex situations, historians disagree on the relative importance of different factors. Some historians condemn the British for blatantly exploiting the colonies (Harper[8] and Aptheker[1], for example), and others conclude that the colonies received marked net benefits from their relationship with Britain (Dickerson[4], for example), while still others take an intermediate position (Nettels[13] and Thomas[16]). It is difficult to quantify all the complex interrelationships and give a definitive answer. The various elements of British mercantilist policy are summarized in Table 3-1.

An important regulation in the **Navigation Acts** was the restriction that trade within the empire could be carried on only by British ships. Because the colonists were considered citizens of the empire, their ships were not excluded. This policy established a common market of considerable size. The elimination of foreign competition, especially from Dutch and French shipping, was an advantage to colonial shipping interests, although it reduced competition and in turn increased shipping rates for colonial products. By the end of the colonial period, the advan-

Table 3-1. Selected Acts of Parliament and the King that Affected the American Colonies.

| Year | Description |
|------|-------------|
| 1651 | *Navigation Acts.* Required that ships flying the merchant flag of England must be of |
| 1660 | English or colonial construction and must be owned and manned by citizens of the |
| 1696 | British Empire. All enumerated articles exported from the colonies had to be sent to |
|      | Britain. Also, imports into the colonies coming from Europe and the Far East had to go |
|      | through Britain. Only British Empire vessels could engage in the colonial British trade. |
| 1699 | *Woolen Act.* Prohibited export of wool and woolen products from the colonies. |
| 1732 | *Hat Act.* Forbade the export of beaver hats from the colonies. |
| 1733 | *Molasses Act.* Was considered the "old sugar act." Among other things, all molasses not produced in the British West Indies was taxed 6 pence per gallon. Considerable smuggling occurred to avoid this law. |
| 1750 | *Iron Act.* Placed restrictions on manufacturing of iron products and encouraged production of pig and bar iron. |
| 1751 | *Paper Money Act.* Regulated the issues of paper money in New England by requiring that provision be made for redemption within five years. |
| 1763 | *Proclamation of 1763.* Created the Indian country west of the Appalachian Mountains and restricted western expansion. |
| 1764 | *Revenue Act of 1764.* Was generally known as the Sugar Act. It was designed in part to pay for British troops employed in America to control the Indians and the conquered French. It amended the 1733 Sugar Act by reducing the tax on foreign-produced molasses to 3 pence per gallon. |
| 1764 | *Stamp Act.* Levied taxes to obtain stamps on official and business documents. Opposition was so well organized and effective that the act was voided by 1766. |
| 1767 | *Revenue Act of 1767 or the Townshend Act.* Levied import duties on glass, paper, paint, and tea imported into the colonies. Resistance by the colonists was strong; the act was repealed in 1770. |
| 1773 | *Tea Act.* Placed import taxes on tea and gave a monopoly on tea to the East India Company by allowing the company to ship tea directly to the colonies, eliminating the cost of shipment to England. Very strong resistance included the Boston Tea Party. |
| 1774 | *Quebec Act of 1774.* Among other things, extended the territory of Quebec to the south, limiting expansion of settlement beyond Pennsylvania. |

tages and disadvantages of the elimination of foreign shipping competition were probably of little importance. The colonists held a cost advantage in the coastal and West Indies trade because of geographic proximity and raw material advantages in the construction of ships. At this time, transatlantic shipping was dominated by English interests, and here the English held the advantage over the colonists because of their geographic proximity to the European continent. The French and Dutch found it hard to compete in either the coastal or transatlantic trade.

It must be kept in mind that all the colonial powers had similar mercantile regulations. It was illegal for American colonial ships to trade with the colonies of France, Spain, and Holland in the West Indies, although significant amounts of illegal traffic did occur. If the American colonies had been outside of the British empire after 1763, they would have been legally excluded from their lucrative trade with the British West Indies. Also, keep in mind that the discussion about the cost of being outside the British Empire just made is separate from the general argument about the cost to the colonists of the Navigation Acts themselves.

Given the political structure of the world trading community, the imperial requirement that only British ships could trade within the empire was a benefit to the prerevolutionary colonial economy. The disadvantage to the colonist from higher shipping cost for their exports and imports was not large, because foreign shippers were unable to compete against the comparative advantage of colonial and British shipping.

A second set of regulations within the Navigation Acts was perhaps of greater importance in its effects on the American colonial economy. These regulations required that colonial exports, enumerated by various Acts of Parliament, should be shipped first to England and that colonial imports should be shipped through England, regardless of their origin. British West Indies trade, however, was exempt from this requirement to use England as the **entrepot** for both imports and exports. Another exemption allowed the colonists to ship agricultural provisions directly to Spain south of Cape Finisterre and in the southern Mediterranean.

For the colonies, the shipping, handling, storage, and middleman costs of both imports and exports were increased by this requirement to ship exports ultimately destined for non-British Europe to Britain and to obtain imports produced on the continent by way of Britain. Furthermore, banning direct trade with the European continent north of Cape Finisterre restricted the area of economic activity of colonial merchants and shippers. Some argue that these restrictions in effect created a monopoly by British mercantile interests of colonial trade destined for and originating in continental Europe. Lawrence Harper[8] concludes that the economic costs of these restrictions were substantial: at least $5 million to $7.5 million a year toward the end of the colonial period. This total, he maintains, was greater than federal expenditures per year during Washington's presidency.

Robert Thomas[16] presents a hypothetical example of the burden of requiring that the enumerated exports of the colonies first be shipped to Britain (Figure 3-1). The price would be $P_2$, and the quantity $Q_2$, if there were no restrictions.

As Thomas expresses it, "The additional transport costs borne by enumerated goods upon their reexport has the effect of lowering the prices received by the colonial producer and depressing the quantity exported." In economic terms, the world market price shown in Figure 3-1 would, in

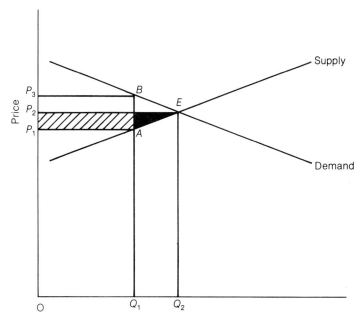

Figure 3-1. Hypothetical Supply and Demand for Colonial Enumerated Product.

*Source:* Robert P. Thomas, "A Quantitative Approach to the Study of the Effects of British Imperial Policy upon Colonial Welfare: Some Preliminary Findings," *Journal of Economic History, 25* (4), (December 1965), 622, 623. © Economic History Association.

the absence of regulation, be $P_2$ and exports would be $Q_2$. The effect of the additional cost of shipment through England is to raise the price to the consumer to $P_3$. Colonial exports, consequently, are reduced to $Q_1$; therefore, both consumers and producers suffer from the enumeration of colonial exports whose final destination is not England.

The measure of the burden to the colonial exports is the shaded triangle between $P_1$ and $P_2$ (indirect burden of foreign revenue) plus the crosshatched rectangle $(P_2 - P_1 \times Q_1)$, the direct burden or revenue loss at the prevailing quantity and price.

Thomas concludes, then, that the requirement to ship enumerated products first to England did lower prices to the colonists and raise prices to the ultimate European consumer. However, Thomas estimates that the burden was modest, with the total burden of British mercantile policy amounting to $905,000 in 1770 or about $.42 per colonist. Gary M. Walton[17] substantially agreed with Thomas' general conclusions but showed that Thomas' estimates were about 100% too high.

Stuart Bruchey[2] also maintains that the additional costs of shipment first to Britain were not as high as Harper estimated. Bruchey points out that merchants in England performed a number of functions that would have been performed by colonial merchants if the use of England had been avoided. These English merchants, for example, graded, repacked, and sorted tobacco and had contacts on the continent from which to obtain necessary information about where, when, and how much to ship. The costs of performing these marketing services must be subtracted from Harper's estimates of additional costs incurred because of the requirement to ship first to Britain. Oliver Dickerson[4] maintains that the decline of total tobacco exports after the revolution can be explained, at least in part, by the loss of these British marketing services. These kinds of services were performed for other exports from the colonies as well.

The transatlantic crossing had to be carried by larger ships than the coastal trade, and these larger ships had higher total operating costs. Significant losses of efficiency would result if the storage holds of these ships were not fully used. They therefore had to be able to pick up and deliver cargo to one place or only a few places. Sufficient cargo had to be concentrated at one place so that all cargo space would be used. British ports served as collection points for European cargo and added to it the substantial addition of British exports. In other words, the need to pick up and deliver cargo at specific places in order to operate transatlantic ships most efficiently could have prevented significant direct trade with the continent. Tobacco might have been shipped directly to France, but it is unlikely that sufficient return cargo could have been found at prices competitive with British manufacturing prices. The potential gains from direct trade would have been smaller than some have presumed.

Furthermore, if direct trade with the continent of Europe had been permitted, resources of the colonies would have been diverted from existing uses. Were the opportunity costs of direct trade high enough to justify shifting shipping from the coastal and West Indies trade? Transatlantic direct trade would have had to yield higher returns than coastal West Indies trade to move these resources to direct trade. One might ask, "Why didn't the colonists build more ships?" If full employment existed—and there is little evidence to show that this was not the case—to build more ships would have required that resources be moved out of their uses. If resources would have been shifted, then the opportunity costs in those uses would have to be taken into account. These factors seem to justify accepting Walton's lower estimate over that of Thomas.

It seems that the colonies' costs were increased and economic opportunities restricted by the need to ship enumerated exports to England and to import goods from England, but costs and restricted opportunities were decreased by these factors: British merchants performed valuable services of grading, sorting, and packaging; of concentrating export cargo to the colonies; of dispersing import cargo from the colonies; and of maintaining the commercial contacts necessary to time the distribution of cargo from the colonies. Even without the Navigation Acts, the need to concentrate cargo to use storage space efficiently would have led to much trade being concentrated through Britain. Finally, the opportunity cost (the revenue earned in occupations that would have to be given up as resources move from what they were doing to the activities involved in direct trade) of direct continental trade might not have been much higher than the income earned in indirect trade.

A third set of mercantile laws involved restrictions on colonial industrial production in competition with British manufacturing. These restrictions were used against colonial production of such goods as hats, textiles, and iron products. Even Harper admits that manufacturing restrictions had little effect on the colonial economy, which was not suited to the production of manufactured items for sale. Competition with Britain was prevented in the colonies by the scarcity and consequent high costs of labor and capital, the low level of technical skills and knowledge, and the limited size of the colonial market, which reduced the economies of specialization and size. One industry in which the colonies could compete was shipbuilding. Another industry in which the colonist excelled was the production of pig iron, most of it exported to England duty-free. The colonies provided about one-seventh of world pig iron production. The main advantage of the colonists in these two areas was an abundance of raw material—wood and iron ore deposits. When opportunities looked profitable, the colonies often violated the restrictions of the mercantile laws.

Other mercantile laws involved bounties and subsidies supporting export sectors of the colonial economy. Bounties and subsidies for the timber industry of northern New England were intended to encourage the export of trees for use in constructing ships for the British navy. Naval stores such as tar and pitch from the pine forests of North Carolina were subsidized. South Carolina and Georgia received subsidies for the growing and exporting of indigo, a dye used in British textiles. Such subsidies increased the cash income of the colonial economy.

An additional question to that of the economic effects of the British mercantile system, one must remember that all colonial empires were run on the basis of mercantile philosophy. If the American colonies had not been part of a colonial empire, they would have been excluded from legal trade with all of Europe and its colonies. Would this exclusion have been even more economically damaging than membership in an empire? Perhaps the most relevant question to ask is not whether one mercantile law or another was a net benefit to the colonial economy, but, rather, was membership in the British Empire with all of its obligations and privileges economically beneficial to the colonial economy?

## Taxes and More Taxes?

Every analysis of the events leading up to the American Revolution has stressed the role of taxes levied on the American colonies by Britain. Our concern is for the economic importance of these taxes, not their political and philosophical implications. How heavy was taxation? Why was it imposed?

Statistics from the eighteenth century are subject to question, but even so, the data in Table 3-2 reflect striking differences in taxation. Whatever adjustments one might make to Table 3-2, the conclusion is unchanged. Considering that per capita income was probably higher in the colonies than in Britain, the tax burden on the colonists was relatively low. It was the British, not the colonists, who paid most of the direct costs of the French and Indian War, which ended in 1763 and removed the very real threat of France on the colonial frontier.

Table 3-2. Total Taxes per Capita—
Britain and the Colonies, 1765.

|  | *Taxes per capita* |
|---|---|
| Great Britain | $5.79 |
| Massachusetts | 0.22 |
| Pennsylvania | 0.22 |
| Maryland | 0.22 |
| New York | 0.15 |
| Connecticut | 0.13 |
| Virginia | 0.10 |

*Source:* R. R. Palmer, *The Age of Democratic Revolution: A Political History of Europe and America 1760–1800,* Vol. 1: *The Challenge* (Princeton, N.J.: University Press, 1969), p. 155. In Gerald Gunderson, *A New Economic History of America* (New York: McGraw-Hill, 1976), p. 89.

The effort to increase colonial taxes, through various tax laws enacted from 1764 to 1775, would have resulted in an increase in revenues to Britain of approximately £120,000, or about £.10 per capita, in the colonies. Only a small fraction of this increase was realized, an amount hardly large enough to justify a charge of massive increase in colonial taxes. The question was not the size of the tax, for that was indeed moderate, but the manner in which tax laws were passed. Perhaps, however, the colonists had the expectation that the tax burden would be raised to that of Great Britain, and this expectation may have been an economic factor in the buildup to the revolution.

Remember, whether taxes are a burden depends on the services that are received in return. If more is paid in taxes than is received in services, taxes may be considered a burden. A British army was maintained in the colonies to protect the settlers from the Indians at least until the 1770s, when the army was increasingly used against the colonists themselves. The cost of maintaining the army in the colonies, almost £370,000 in 1764, was far more than the amount received from taxation. Even more important was protection afforded by the British navy to the commercial activities of the colonists. The navy provided protection from pirates for colonial ships trading with the West Indies, Africa, and Spain, as well as protection during time of war. The diplomatic strength of the British government was used to the colonists' advantage; for example, in obtaining from Spain the right for the colonists to use the port of New Orleans. This privilege enabled the colonists to ship western agricultural products down tributaries to the Mississippi River and on to New Orleans and the Gulf of Mexico. The benefits obtained from the British government far exceeded the tax cost to the colonists.

The Sugar Tax of 1764 actually lowered the tax on molasses imported from the French West Indies. After smuggling and laxness in enforcement had reduced the old Sugar Tax of 1733 to a dead letter, the British lowered the tax rate on imported molasses and were determined to enforce the new tax. Since taxes were not collected on the old act, even the lower rate meant a higher real tax burden and, therefore, reduced the profits and the prosperity of the smuggling trade with the French West Indies. The British were angered by the smuggling activities of the colonists, especially by the illegal trade with the enemy during the French and Indian War. Enforcement involved not only catching the smugglers but also convicting them. A jury of colonial peers would not convict. Therefore, smugglers were removed from the jurisdiction of the colonial courts to the admiralty courts, where there was no jury trial. Conflict was stimulated not only by economic motivations but also by contending political philosophies.

Even the infamous Tea Tax of 1773 seemed moderate; but the outcry, especially from colonial merchants, was huge. The British East India Company was given the right to directly ship tea to the colonies without going through England. This reduced the cost of tea below that of tea smuggled in by colonial merchants. The British East India Company could now undersell colonial merchants.

In the Proclamation of 1763, further westward movement into the frontier was forbidden. Explanations for this prohibition vary from concern to prevent future Indian wars, to the fear that competition with British manufacturing would develop in isolated settlements. Perhaps a more important explanation was that the British wanted to protect the western fur trade for the Hudson Bay Company, operating out of Canada. This restriction alienated western settlers and also those living farther east who were heavily involved in western land speculation inside the prohibited area. It seems that many of the Virginia-Maryland plantation owners were involved in this speculation.

When the advantages of being part of a colonial empire are weighed carefully, it is not at all clear that British economic policy had a net detrimental effect on the colonies. The various costs and benefits are difficult to measure, and the casual interrelationships are complex. The debate about whether membership in the British Empire was a burden to the colonists will not be resolved here, but will continue to fascinate historians and economists.

# An Economic Justification of the American Revolution?

If, on balance, it is not at all clear that membership in the British Empire in 1770 was harmful to the colonial economy as a whole, what kind of economic explanation can be offered for the American Revolution?

One explanation is that various aspects of British economic policy had alienated one group or another, regardless of that policy's overall benefit. What may have been important was the distribution of the burdens of British economic policy among specific groups that held political power. Furthermore, certain groups, especially the wealthier members of colonial society, may have developed expectations about the direction of post-1763 British policy and their expected impact on their economic position. Consider the following:

1. Both the western pioneer and the eastern land speculator were alienated by the Proclamation of 1763 forbidding western settlement. For example, Patrick Henry may have been thus alienated.
2. Colonial merchants excluded from patronage may have wished either to eliminate special privileges or to replace those obtaining this patronage. John Hancock or Samuel Adams of Boston may have had such motives.
3. Plantation owners may have considered that the monopoly of British merchants in marketing and financing the tobacco crop constituted an unfair burden on Virginia and Maryland. George Washington and Thomas Jefferson may be examples.
4. Colonial merchants, after experiencing the tea tax and privileges granted to the East India Company to their own disadvantage, might have feared further discriminatory legislation that would benefit British capital at the expense of the colonial economy.
5. Other merchants and shipowners may have felt restive under British restrictions on direct trade outside the empire.

Another explanation, or partial explanation, concerns the expulsion of the French from Canada at the end of the French and Indian Wars. The American colonists had diverged in character and sentiment from the people of Britain. A society devoid of many of the social and economic restriction of the Old World and separated from it by 3000 miles of ocean and months of travel, the frontier produced a unique society with a sense of its own distinctiveness. The existence of the French on the northern frontier presented a threat that tied the colonies to Britain. With the British capture of Canada, both the threat and the dependence were eliminated.

Yet economic causes of the American Revolution were not the only causes. Although economic reasons no doubt contributed to the conflict, a complete picture would include analysis of differences in philosophical, political, and social conditions between the colonies and Britain. Economic analysis is helpful, but not sufficient, for an understanding of the causes of the American Revolution. In this particular case, economic determinism does not work too well. Economic factors became only a part of broader social and political considerations.

# Glossary

**Entrepot trade**   Trade that enters a country and then is transhipped to another country without changing the form of the original import.

**Favorable balance of trade**   The condition in which exports exceed imports.

**Mercantilism**   A system of practical economic policy, dominant in the seventeenth and eighteenth centuries, giving rise to "managed" economies with extensive government involvement. Each government aimed to maximize the economic power of the nation by creating a favorable balance of trade resulting in an inflow of gold.

**Navigation Acts**   A series of acts by which the British Parliament regulated trade during the colonial period. Among other regulations, the acts restricted trade within the empire to ships of the British Empire and enumerated exports that had to be shipped directly to Britain, regardless of their ultimate destination.

**Weber Thesis**   Max Weber's argument that Protestant theological ideas of the Reformation period influenced the behavior of people in ways that were beneficial to rapid economic development. Weber said that psychological conditioning was induced by the theological positions of religious leaders, especially Luther and Calvin.

# Questions

1. Describe the main elements of mercantilist theory. How was mercantilism used in the colonial policy of the home country?

2. Describe religious and philosophical factors affecting colonial attitudes toward economic development. Which were conducive to economic development? Why? Which were not? Why?

3. Describe the chief regulations of British mercantile policy. Did these regulations restrict colonial economic development?

4. What was the role of the West Indies in the economic relationships between the colonies and England? How did British mercantilism affect this role?

5. Were the taxes that the British government tried to levy on the American colonies from 1764 to 1775 an "unjust" burden on the colonial economy?

6. On balance, was membership in the British Empire an economic burden to the American colonies up to 1775?

7. Present your analysis of the economic causes of the American Revolution.

8. What was the special economic situation of New England in regard to the causes of the revolution?

# Suggested Readings

1. Aptheker, Herbert. *The American Revolution, 1763–1783.* New York: International Publishers, 1960. Chaps. 1 and 2.

2. Bruchey, Stuart. *The Roots of American Economic Growth, 1607–1861.* New York: Harper & Row, 1968. Pp. 42–48.

3. Clough, Shepard B. *European Economic History: The Economic Development of Western Civilization.* New York: McGraw-Hill 1968. Chap. 11.

4. Dickerson, Oliver M. *The Navigation Acts and the American Revolution.* New York: Barnes, 1963.

5. Dorfman, Joseph. *The Economic Mind in American Civilization, 1606–1865.* Vol. 1. New York: Viking, 1959.

6. Gipson, Lawrence H. *The Coming of the Revolution, 1763–1775.* New York: Harper & Row, 1954.

7. Green, Robert W., ed. *Protestantism, Capitalism and Social Science.* Lexington, Mass.: Heath, 1973.

8. Harper, Lawrence A. "Mercantilism and the American Revolution." *Canadian Historical Review, 23* (March 1942).

9. Hofstadter, Richard, and Lipset, Seymour M., eds. *Turner and the Sociology of the Frontier.* New York: Basic Books, 1968.

10. Johnson, A. J. "The Economic Philosophy of John Winthrop." In *Issues*

*in American Economic History,* ed. Gerald D. Nash. Lexington, Mass.: Heath, 1972.

11. McClelland, David C., and Winter, David G. *Motivating Economic Achievement.* New York: Free Press, 1969.

12. McClelland, Peter D. "The Cost to America of British Imperial Policy." *American Economic Review, 59* (May 1969).

13. Nettels, Curtis P. "British Mercantilism and the Economic Development of the Thirteen Colonies." *Journal of Economic History, 12* (Spring 1952).

14. Reid, Joseph. "On Navigating the Navigation Acts with Peter O. McClelland: Comment." *American Economic Review, 10* (December 1920).

15. Tawney, R. H. *Religion and the Rise of Capitalism.* New York: New American Library, 1954.

16. Thomas, Robert Paul. "A Quantitative Approach to the Study of the Effects of British Imperial Policy upon Colonial Welfare: Some Preliminary Findings." *Journal of Economic History, 25* (December 1965).

17. Walton, Gary M. "The New Economic History and the Burdens of the Navigation Act." *Economic History Review, 24* (November 1971).

18. Weber, Max. *The Protestant Ethic and the Spirit of Capitalism.* New York: Scribner's, 1958.

# Chapter 4

---

# The Revolution and the Economic Effects of the Break with England, 1776-1789

The major economic problem of the young United States from the time of the Declaration of Independence (1776) to the adoption of the Constitution (1789) was to accommodate the American economy to the break with the British Empire. The colonial economy had been dependent on and tied to the rest of the British Empire not only by the system of mercantile laws and regulations that had grown up over the first 170 years of the colonies' life, but also by a system of economic relationships that surprisingly were substantially based on comparative advantage. But the international economic community was primarily based on imperial mercantile relationships; each empire had its own mercantile relationships. Could the young United States achieve both political and economic independence?

This revolutionary bid for economic independence created difficulties. In part, these difficulties involved the sharp increase in the money supply during the revolution, followed by a reduction in the money supply after independence was achieved in the 1780s. In addition, the break with Britain created problems concerning new sources of exports to replace those lost by withdrawal from the British Empire. These two problems—variations in the supply of money and the need for alternative sources of foreign markets—are important themes affecting economic processes from 1776 to 1789.

Included in the Review of Economic Concepts in this chapter is a brief presentation of the equation of exchange and the demand for money approach to explain the effects on prices of variations in the supply of money. Also included is a short discussion of the effect of variations of prices on debtors and creditors.

# The Revolution and the Economy

At the beginning of his excellent history, *The Emergence of a National Economy, 1775–1815,* Curtis Nettels[7] wrote, "During the forty years after 1775 the American people brought forth not only a new nation, but also a national economy. The Revolution began a process of change that modified nearly every phase of American life." By necessity, our treatment of that process will be restricted to two areas: (a) the responses of the American economy to the absence of commercial trade with Britain during the war and (b) the economic effects of efforts to finance the revolution.

## Commercial Independence

Even before declaring political independence from Great Britain, the Continental Congress had made a declaration of economic independence from the British Empire. On October 20, 1774, the First Continental Congress formed the Continental Association and declared a boycott against all British Empire goods. On September 10, 1775, an embargo, or a ban, was declared on exports from America to Britain, the British West Indies, or Ireland. On April 6, 1776, Congress opened American ports to all foreign ships, except those of the citizens of Great Britain. The Congress sent representatives to European countries, especially to France, to negotiate economic assistance.

The British in turn passed the Prohibitory Act of December 22, 1775, which prohibited vessels from trading with the 13 colonies and authorized seizures of vessels that violated the act. Although the British launched a blockade in an effort to prevent trade with the 13 colonies, they had neither the ships nor the bases to make the blockade effective.

## Substitutes for British Trade

Before the revolution, the American colonies were economically bound to Britain. In all practical terms, the British Empire was both their source of manufactured goods and their primary export market. Where would the former colonists get their manufactured goods, and where would they sell their surplus output? The new nation increased commercial trade with European nations other than Britain, expanded domestic manufactures, and tried to meet the demands of the revolutionary armies. Also, privateering became an important source of money and goods.

At that time, governments often granted commissions making it legal for privately owned sea raiders to capture enemy merchant vessels, sell them, and distribute the proceeds among the owners and the crew. Congress gave commissions to 1,697 privateers, and the state of Massachusetts commissioned an additional 958 vessels. About 10,000 seamen served on these vessels. According to Nettels, the British lost 2,000 vessels, 12,000 sailors and £18 million, mostly through the actions of the privateers.

These privateers brought in significant quantities of military and civilian supplies for the new nation, plus needed hard currency from selling their prizes in Europe. Substantial losses to British mercantile enterprise resulted in some bankruptcies. Privateering provided employment in American shipbuilding, substitute employment for sailors from fishing, and commerce—all industries severely restricted by the outbreak of the revolution.

With the stoppage of legal trade with the empire, the Americans were successful in establishing extensive direct trade with other European nations, especially France, Holland, and Spain, and also with their colonies in the West Indies. There was even a roundabout trade with Britain itself. British goods were imported into Holland and reexported to the United States; in payment, American goods were imported into Holland, repacked and relettered, and shipped to Britain. Imports were paid for in part by loans from France, Holland, and Spain but mostly through exports of U.S. products, especially tobacco. Major imports included all kinds of military supplies, from gunpowder to army uniforms.

Although imports from non-British sources and goods seized by privateers were important, they were not adequate to meet the needs of both the civilian population and the military. These insufficiencies, plus the British blockade, stimulated an increase in demand for the domestic economy's output. Needs of the military severely strained the simple economy of the time.

Agents of the Congress set up a system of procurement throughout the country to provide supplies for the army. These activities not only increased market production but also called for improved roads and gave many people experience in organizing economic activity on a large scale.

The colonial economy was essentially a dual economy: One was a money exchange economy and the other a nonmoney economy with large amounts of home-produced and -consumed production, or production locally bartered in exchange. On balance whether or not the revolution was "beneficial" is hard to determine and depends on the time frame within which benefits are measured. The increased needs of the military, American, British, or—at the end—French, drew more of the nonexchange economy into a money exchange system. The foreign export-oriented sections of the colonial economy, such as tobacco and indigo, were seriously disrupted by wartime interferences of their normal export markets. The war disruptions created tendencies that expanded and also contracted money exchange activities.

Thus, economic needs created by the revolution led to a number of significant changes. American merchants learned to trade with the world trading community, not merely with Britain, and these wider contacts were maintained after the war. Within the new nation, experience was obtained in handling large economic transactions, which included working with larger manufacturing enterprises. Major expansion of foreign trade did not occur until after 1792, and sustained manufacturing expansion did not occur until 1815; but the training and experience in these areas gained during the revolutionary period were important prerequisites for future development.

## Financing the Revolution

Financing military operations of the war was a vexing problem for the Continental Congress. Various solutions were considered. The Congress could tax, issue paper currency without gold or silver backing, borrow from the American public through interest-bearing bills of credit, or finally, borrow from foreign countries. At one time or another, the Continental Congress used each of the four methods to finance the Revolutionary War.

The Continental Congress lacked a major prerequisite of sovereignty, because the authority to tax resided solely in the states. Although Congress could request funds from the states and could request that the states approve a tax to be levied and collected by Congress, unanimous approval of all the states was needed to allow Congress to levy a specific tax. As part of a wider effort to reform its finances, the Congress tried to get approval of a 5% federal tax on imports. Rhode Island remained the lone holdout, thus preventing implementation of the tax.

Because taxes were never a realistic solution, the Congress early issued paper currency not redeemable in specie. The idea was that if each state would tax and accept the continental currency, the total amount could be kept within reasonable bounds. However, not only were the states reluctant to tax, but many issued their own paper currency. By 1783, state-issued currency amounted to about $200 million.

The first issue of continental currency occurred in June 1775 in the amount of $2 million. Because of increased issues and the lack of taxes by the states to withdraw this currency from circulation, the total amount of continental currency increased to a high point of $191.5 million by 1780. The amounts issued each year were $6 million in 1775, $19 million in 1776, $13 million in 1777, $63.5 million in 1778, and $90 million in 1779.

As the amounts in circulation increased, currency depreciated rapidly in comparison with gold or silver coins. In December 1776, the rate was $1.00 in coin to $1.50 in currency. By the end of 1779, the ratio was 1 to 42.2, and by 1781 it was $1.00 in coin to $147.97 in currency. This depreciation obviously meant that prices, in terms of continental currency, rose rapidly. Toward the end of the revolution, people were even reluctant to accept this currency in payment for goods. By 1783, the currency had been removed from circulation, an act accomplished in part by its conversion to long-term debt of the central government and in part by withdrawal through payment of state taxes.

Here we see the workings of the equation of exchange: $MV = PQ$. The supply of money ($M$) was increasingly rapidly with the successive increases in continental currency. The velocity of exchange ($V$), the number of times that supply of money changes hands, probably also increased as, even with slow communications, transportation, and almost nonexistent banking systems, people tried to pass on the rapidly depreciating paper currency. With $MV$ increasing, $P$ (prices) and $Q$ (output) had to increase. Output ($Q$) increased to some extent as the nonexchange economy experienced some shift to the exchange economy. But the bulk of the impact of increases in $MV$ caused increases in prices ($P$). This disastrous experience in uncontrolled increase in the supply of money was matched, in American experience, only by the issuance of Confederate currency during the Civil War.

Early in the revolution, the Continental Congress tried with little success to sell long-term interest-bearing debt. The lack of sufficient domestic wealth and the uncertainty of the outcome of the revolution worked against efforts to persuade Americans to lend money to fight the war. Toward the end, after substantial funds lent by France, Holland, and Spain had provided gold and silver to pay interest on domestic loans, these efforts were more successful. The central government, especially aided by Robert Morris, was able to raise about $11.5 million in domestic loans—a small part of the total required to run the war. Robert Morris, like others, was willing to loan money to the central government once interest payments were made in gold and silver.

A much-needed source of gold and silver came from $7.8 million in foreign loans. Most of the loans were obtained from France ($6.4 million), but private loans were obtained in Holland for $1.3 million, and $174,017 was borrowed from Spain. Most of the proceeds of the loans were spent in Europe for desperately needed military supplies.

Hession and Sardy[4] sum up the results of the financial costs of the revolution as follows: "In summation, it may be noted that the direct money cost of the Revolution is estimated in specie to have been $135 million. Against this total we may place the federal debt which stood at $42,413,000, and state debts which aggregated $18,271,786. The difference between the total direct costs as stated and the total debts of over $60 million may be considered as paid for by taxation, depreciated paper money, and other sources of revenue." The bulk of this $75 million was paid by people holding depreciating continental currency. When a farmer was paid in currency for supplies sold to Washington's army, he lost by the amount that the currency depreciated while he had it.

# The Postwar Economy

## Imports After the Revolution

During the revolution, manufactured goods imported from France and Holland and goods brought in by privateers (from captured British vessels) amounted to a small fraction of the prewar imports from England. Under the protection of the price stimulus created by the British wartime blockade, domestic manufactures increased, and some goods were newly manufactured in North America. This increased output was negligible in amount and variety, however, and products were of poor quality. In 1783, inventories of consumer goods were very low in the new nation, the United States, and the demand for manufactured imports was very high among Americans long deprived of many kinds of manufactured goods.

British merchants regained their former dominance in the American market. French and Dutch merchants could not compete in price, variety, and quality and, perhaps most important, were not willing to extend credit. Furthermore, American merchants preferred to deal with British merchants because of their common language, similarity in culture and customs, renewal of old contracts, and familiarity with business practices and products. From 1784 to 1786, Americans imported almost $7.6 million worth of manufactured goods of all descriptions, from cotton cloth to playing cards. These imports were obtained on credit, and that credit was extended throughout the economy. British exporters sold to American importers on credit; importers sold to wholesalers on credit, who sold to retailers on credit, who finally sold to consumers on credit. The problem was how to pay for these imports.

## Exports After the Revolution

Normally, imports are paid for by the claims to money obtained from exports. In the 1780s, however, the United States had just made its break from the British Empire, and exports suffered during the period of adjustment. From 1784 to 1786, the United States exported goods worth only $1.26 million per year, one-third of its imports for the same time period. In brief, the young country had a substantial **deficit in its balance of trade.** That deficit can be defined simply as the excess of its payments for imports of goods and services over its earnings from the export of goods and services.

In 1763, tobacco exports from Maryland and Virginia had comprised 44% of all exports by value from the American colonies. By the end of the revolution, the Chesapeake area had suffered serious damage. Virginia's labor force was depleted by the loss of 30,000 slaves, mostly through transfer of slaves by the British to the West Indies. In comparison to 1774, Virginia's output was 18% less in 1783–1784 and 7% less in 1784–1785. Loss in output, though, was not the most serious problem; the relatively low prices of 1783 to 1786 were of greater importance.

Since the American colonies were no longer in the British Empire, Britain placed a tax of 15 pence per hundred weight on tobacco imported into Britain. This tax decreased the quantity of American tobacco demanded by the British. France, which was the major ultimate market for American tobacco, created the Farmers General, a monopsony (only one buyer) importing agent for American tobacco in France. Thomas Jefferson maintained that this monopsony purchasing agent forced prices down by 50% from 1785 to 1787. No doubt, part of this decrease in price realized by Virginia and Maryland planters was due to the fact that British merchants were no longer performing such functions as repacking, grading, sorting, and managing an efficient flow of tobacco to the European market, as they had before the revolution.

A second major export crop was rice produced in South Carolina. Because of physical destruction during the revolution and the loss of possibly as many as 20,000 slaves, rice production fell by 46% of the 1770–1773 average during 1783–1786. But, despite falling supply, prices received by farmers fell. Britain placed high import duties on rice imported into the British West Indies and into Britain itself. Harassment by pirates from the Barbary States of North Africa reduced exports of rice into the Mediterranean. Other markets could not be found quickly enough to prevent a collapse of prices between 1783 and 1786.

Prior to the revolution, naval stores from North Carolina, timber from New England, and indigo from South Carolina received bounties from Britain. With independence, these bounties disappeared. The British maintained a preference for output from their remaining colonies. The French, applying mercantile concepts, also favored their own colonists over America. Export earnings therefore dropped drastically for these products; for naval stores, earnings dropped to less than a third of the prewar level.

Before the revolution, agricultural products of the northern states, including wheat and flour, animal products, and corn, had been exported to the British West Indies and, under British protection, to Spain and the Mediterranean area. After the revolution, these sources of foreign exchange were drastically reduced. No longer part of the British Empire, America could not legally trade with the British West Indies. In the Mediterranean, the Barbary States of Algeria, Tripoli, and Morocco demanded tribute from the United States. Congress could neither raise the money for tribute nor finance a navy to protect U.S. ships.

And the story goes on and on: One area after another of export earnings was reduced as the United States had to stand alone. Potential fur exports from the frontier were reduced as Britain refused to vacate the frontier forts. Agricultural exports from the frontier settlements west of the mountains were interfered with as Spain refused to allow the frontiersmen the use of New Orleans, the terminal of the river route to markets. New England found it difficult to compete in sale of ships to Britain as restrictions were placed on U.S. sales after independence. Demand for the output of U.S. fisheries fell off as the French West Indies failed to replace lost markets in England and the British West Indies, and as the Barbary states interfered in southern Europe.

In brief, then, the deficit in the balance of trade during 1784 and 1785 was directly due to the severance of ties that placed the United States outside the mercantile system of Great Britain. The former colonies could not engage in free trade, since every other country had a mercantile relationship with its colonies. Restrictions were placed on U.S. trade with most major areas. The French, for instance, allowed the United States to trade with their colonies in the West Indies, but prohibited the sale of U.S. wheat and flour there. Furthermore, the U.S. government, under the Articles of Confederation, lacked the economic, diplomatic, or military power to force concessions from anyone.

## The Depression of 1785-1786

With foreign exchange earned by exports only about one-third the value of imports, the only other source of repayment, specie (gold and silver) exports, was also inadequate to solve the problem without crisis. Despite the large amounts of gold and silver in the economy in 1782, largely from the proceeds of loans from Holland and France during the revolution and from spending by French and English troops in the colonies, after 1783 the drain of gold and silver from the United States to Britain to service this rapidly expanded commercial debt was too great for economic stability. One estimate of the flow of gold and silver to Britain between 1784 and 1786 was $1.6 million, an amount large enough to reduce the supply of money seriously, although it was not large enough to finance the imbalance of trade, the excess of imports over exports. That remaining imbalance was financed primarily by British short-term commercial credit and long-term investments.

This drastic decline in the supply of money had two major economic effects that began to be felt by the end of 1784. First, the reduced supply of money decreased prices. Remember the equation of exchange: $MV = PQ$. Now the supply of money ($M$) is decreasing while velocity ($V$) is constant, then $P$, the price level, must fall. This assumes that output ($Q$) is constant or also falling. Remember, too, that debtors are hurt by a deflation (a decline in prices), because they must repay their loans with money that has higher purchasing power than that which they borrowed. Also, if prices are falling, debtors have to sell more of whatever they produce to earn the quantity of dollars needed to pay their debts. The second effect of a constricted money supply was the scarcity of actual coin to pay debts. The supply of money became so reduced that in a number of rural areas people were forced out of money exchange relationships. The general effect of this drastic cut in the supply of money was to make it difficult for debtors to pay their debts. These economic effects only applied to the money exchange sectors of the economy. The nonmoney exchange sector comprised a great deal of the economy and was insulated from these processes.

Since the system of debt relationships was so pervasive, the commercial economy shook like a house of cards. Consumers couldn't pay retailers, who couldn't pay wholesalers, who couldn't pay importers, who couldn't pay British exporters. Not coincidentally, the number of commercial bankruptcies was significant in the United States in 1785 and 1786, and a few prominent ones occurred in England. Nettels[7] provides a number of examples: "Some fairly substantial merchants failed—among them Clement Biddle of Baltimore and Samuel A. Otis of Boston. Other prominent merchants, including George Meade, Haym Solomon, and Robert Morris in Philadelphia, the Purviance brothers in Baltimore, and Jackson and Higginson in Boston found themselves hard pressed for funds. Ruin befell many small inexperienced traders who, unable to collect money from their debtors, lost their assets through forced sales for the benefit of their creditors."

Because the economy was primarily agricultural and because agriculture was still significantly self-sufficient (much of its output and consumption was not within the cash economy), the depression of the mid-1780s was primarily a commercial and financial one. However, the slow recovery of the agricultural export market, and high levels of debt within agriculture in general, caused economic hardship in that whole sector, especially on the part of those producers who were in debt. Exacerbating the situation were high levels of government debt, especially those of the various states, incurred primarily during the revolution. Any effort of the states to meet their debt obligations only added to the repayment problems of the economy.

# The Search for Solutions

In summary, the economic difficulties facing the young nation resulted from these factors: High import levels from 1783 to 1785 were financed primarily by the extension of credit by British merchants. The inability of the economy to export enough to pay for the high levels of imports caused a flow of specie to Britain, which in turn caused a reduction in the supply of money. This forced prices down. A need arose for additions to the supply of money not only to stem falling prices but also to provide needed means of internal and international payments. Insufficient means of payments to carry on economic transactions were responsible for increased use of barter in many areas outside the major cities. The result was not only higher transaction costs but also significant commercial failures in the cities.

The search for solutions led to two major conclusions: The United States had to reduce the excess of imports over exports and had to increase its supply of money.

## Efforts to Increase Exports

Attempts to increase U.S. exports involved reducing the various economic and political obstacles to trade. These problems could be solved only through international diplomacy. The central government, under the Articles of Confederation, sent various diplomatic missions to a number of countries in efforts to enlarge foreign markets. These missions uniformly failed.

John Adams was sent to England to negotiate both a commercial treaty and an evacuation of the forts held by Britain on American soil. When Adams failed, Congress lacked the power to retaliate against the British. The English thought that the Americans would continue to buy British goods because they were cheaper than domestic manufactures. Congress did not have the funds to pay the remaining prewar commercial debts and reimbursements to the loyalists for seized property, the major points of British contention.

The U.S. mission to the Barbary States of North Africa failed in its efforts to end attacks against American ships in the Mediterranean and, thereby, to open up trade with southern Europe. Congress had neither the money to buy off the pirates nor the navy to fight them.

American diplomats tried unsuccessfully to gain further commercial access for U.S. exports to the markets of Spain and its colonies and to obtain access through the Mississippi River systems and New Orleans for the shipment of the products of western farmers. Efforts to gain more liberal commercial access to France and French colonial markets also failed.

These diplomatic efforts to increase U.S. exports were unsuccessful, in large measure because Congress, under the Articles of Confederation, had no powers that could be used in negotiations with foreign governments. These attempts to negotiate only emphasized the need for a stronger union.

## Efforts to Decrease Imports

The inability of the central government to reduce through diplomatic means the large deficit in the balance of trade shifted responsibility for solutions to the states. A number of states tried to use tariffs to protect their domestic industries and to reduce imports. During the mid-1780s, New York, Pennsylvania, Rhode Island, Massachusetts, and New Hampshire enacted tariff laws. These experiments showed that tariff laws, to be effective, had to be instituted by the central government.

Through larger enterprises and the increased use of machinery, many industries were able to produce goods for several states. One state could not provide tariff protection for a market larger than one state. And, because tariff protection was completely absent in the South, northern manufacturers could not compete there against British products. Finally, it was feared that individual states would begin to raise tariffs against movement of goods from one state to another. Such tariffs would, in effect, destroy any union among the states and would create 13 independent economies.

## Manufacturing in the United States

One alternative to imports was domestic manufacturing. The high cost of U.S. manufactures prevented their effectively substituting for British imports; yet it is informative to look at manufacturing in the United States during this period.

Under the stimulus of the revolution and efforts to counter the depression, a number of enterprises, in such industries as metal working and gun and textile manufacture, grew larger than the typical master-journeyman-apprentice firm and produced for a wider market. Some of these firms benefited from state tariffs and were able to survive renewed trade with Britain. These few enterprises and their small output promised little potential for the future because they were operated with low efficiency and high costs. Labor costs were high, capital was scarce, interest rates were high, and technological knowledge was scanty.

Internal markets were small and fragmented by the lack of a unified transportation system. With such small markets, there was little opportunity for specialization and increases in productivity. In 1786, it seemed unlikely that these conditions would change enough in the near future to enable domestic manufactures to compete with imports.

With all of these limitations, however, the manufacturing development of this period provided an advantage that was indispensable to subsequent industrialization: Larger firms were valuable training grounds for management. By operating on a larger scale, a few firms accumulated personnel with experience in managing labor and in managing the organizational problems of material sources, production, and sale, with the corollary problems of capital supply and technological development. To a limited extent, the necessary learning process began during these early years of independence.

# The Supply of Money

Between 1784 and 1786, as the excess of imports over exports continued to result in an outflow of gold and silver, a great controversy arose about how to increase the supply of money in the United States. We have already seen how decreases in the supply of money reduced prices and output and increased the burden on those in debt: Debtors, who had borrowed money that had low purchasing power, had to repay their loans with money that had high purchasing power; meanwhile, they had to accept lower prices for the products that they sold. As the supply of money fell, neither individuals nor governments could find enough money to provide for economic transactions, including the payment of debts. The overall financial burden was increased by any effort to raise taxes to pay the government debt and its interest cost.

The controversy focused on three ways to increase the supply of money and thus to increase prices. Currency could be issued by merchant banks. Currency could be issued through what were called *land banks*. State and national governments could print money.

# Merchant Banks

By 1786, three **merchant banks** had been chartered by state governments with the power to issue currency backed by specie (gold and silver). One such bank was located in each of three cities: Philadelphia, New York, and Boston. Their ability to expand the supply of money by issuing currency was limited by the faith of the public in the bank's ability to pay specie on demand for currency or in the reserves held in the form of specie, and by the amount of demand for specie. The issuance of paper currency was then restricted by this factor to some ratio of the amount of specie held by the banks.

Since not everyone who had a bank's currency would want specie at the same time, the bank could have more currency in circulation than specie in the vaults of the bank. In that situation, banks turned to the practice of holding **fractional reserves;** the reserves were equal to only a fraction of their currency in circulation plus demand deposits (checking accounts).

Merchant banks, then, provided a specie-backed money supply in the major commercial centers, in addition to credit facilities for the holding of demand deposits. These banks were extremely conservative in that they extended predominantly short-term credit and generally demanded prompt repayment.

Opposition to these banks was widespread. Some critics charged that they favored only a small group of merchants in the towns where the banks were located. The short-term credit they extended did not help the farmers, who needed long-term credit. The currency they issued circulated in the towns where the banks were located and did not benefit the entire state.

## Land Banks and State Issuance of Paper Currency

Major opposition to the merchant banks came from the farmers, who needed long-term loans and an increase in the supply of money both to pay debts and taxes and to increase prices. They proposed the establishment of **land banks,** which would issue paper currency backed only by loans on land. South Carolina, New Jersey, New York, and Rhode Island established land banks and issued currency backed by mortgages on land. Georgia, North Carolina, and Pennsylvania issued paper currency, without specie backing, directly through the state governments.

Merchants and creditors strongly opposed this issuance of "unbacked" currency from land banks and state governments. These merchants owed money to the British exporter and had to pay in gold or silver. Since they in turn were owed money for products that they sold, they were afraid they would be paid in depreciated currency that could not be used to pay the British merchants. Creditors generally wanted to be paid in hard money (gold and silver), while the debt-ridden farmers wanted inflated currency that would increase prices and their ability to repay debts. It was the eternal battle between creditors and debtors, in all its economic and political complexity.

The conflict was bitter throughout the 13 states. In Georgia, South Carolina, and North Carolina, paper currency depreciated rapidly. In Pennsylvania, the conflict was extreme and centered around the activity of the Bank of North America in Philadelphia. In Rhode Island, laws were passed to enforce acceptance of the paper currency at par with gold. The conflict that ensued stopped just short of armed clashes. In New Hampshire, there was armed conflict, and there was Shays's Rebellion in Massachusetts.

## A Conclusion

By 1787, it seemed obvious to many that the central government under the Articles of Confederation did *not* have the power to deal with the international commercial problems of the United States or to provide a stable monetary system. Also, it was clear to wide segments of the population, not only to the creditor groups, that individual states could not by themselves solve the many economic problems created by independence. The young nation needed greater unity to survive not only politically but also economically in a world based on mercantilist policy. Prior to the revolution, colonists had been limited by British mercantilism, but they had also been protected by being a part of it.

Not until the Napoleonic wars was this mercantile system weakened and then destroyed. Only then did the United States gain the opportunity for less restricted trade with the whole world. But before that happened the new nation had changed its system of government and introduced a new set of political institutions that were extremely favorable to the economic development of the United States.

## Controversy Continues

Beginning in the 1950s, a number of historians began to dissent from the position that the 1783–1789 period was critical in U.S. economic history and that the inadequacies of political structure contributed to economic problems. Merrill Jensen[5] viewed the 1780s as a period of "extraordinary economic growth" based on expanding exports, growth of manufacturing, and the recovery of the South. The majority view, however, seems to be substantiated by the evidence, although proof is mixed, and Jensen's claim of economic growth lacks widespread support.

One factor of the 1780s that contributed to the recovery of the U.S. economy was the increasingly favorable terms of trade. Remember that a movement toward more favorable terms of trade occurs when the index of export prices increases relative to the index of import prices. A given amount of physical exports buys more imports. Gordon C. Bjork[1] points out that these relative export-import prices (the terms of trade) were favorable to the United States in the 1780s. In the 1770s, before the revolution (see column 3 in Table 4-1), the index of the terms of trade was mostly in the 60s; in the 1780s, it was mostly in the 90s and 100s. Bjork seems to prefer to consider the glass half full, rather than half empty; he comments that one should not be surprised that exports were so low in the 1780s but should be pleased that they were so high.

The favorable terms of trade in the 1780s are generally attributed to the increased efficiency of foreign trade that resulted from the freedom the United States now enjoyed. No longer restricted by Britain, Americans could now import from the cheapest source; for example, they could import sugar or molasses from the French West Indies rather than the British West Indies. However, it should be noted that export prices fell between 1784 and 1789, while import prices remained constant. The terms of trade, although higher than before the revolution, fell from 112 in 1784 to 88 in 1789.

Bjork, who points out that eighteenth-century statistics should be approached with a great deal of caution, considers his own results preliminary. But, although the reliability and representativeness of the data

Table 4-1. Import-Export Prices and the Terms of Trade.

|  | 1 Index of Export Prices (1790 = 100) | 2 Index of Import Prices (1790 = 100) | 3 Terms of Trade (1) ÷ (2) |
|---|---|---|---|
| 1770 | 69 | 110 | 63 |
| 1771 | 75 | 104 | 72 |
| 1772 | 83 | 102 | 81 |
| 1773 | 78 | 109 | 72 |
| 1774 | 73 | 108 | 68 |
| 1775 | 70 | 109 | 64 |
| 1784 | 115 | 103 | 112 |
| 1785 | 106 | ·101 | 105 |
| 1786 | 97 | 101 | 96 |
| 1787 | 92 | 101 | 91 |
| 1788 | 87 | 99 | 88 |
| 1789 | 87 | 99 | 88 |
| 1790 | 100 | 100 | 100 |

*Source:* Gordon C. Bjork, "The Weaning of the American Economy: Independence, Market Changes, and Economic Development," *Journal of Economic History, 24* (December 1964), 554.

are open to question, the trends indicated by the data seem reliable.

The controversy continues, but it seems clear that the economic problems of the 1780s, whether a matter of rolling adjustment to the end of war or a critical situation demanding immediate drastic remedies, provided a strong motivation to a complete contemporary reevaluation of the political system of the United States. The result was the Constitution of 1789.

# Review of Economic Concepts: Theory of Money and Prices

## The Equation of Exchange

The quantity theory of money, based on the equation of exchange, is a simple model that explores the effect of variations of the supply of money on prices and output. **The equation of exchange** is stated as $MV = PQ$. $M$ represents the supply of money, $V$ the velocity of exchange, $P$ the price level, and $Q$ the output in physical terms.

During the revolution, from 1775 to 1781, large amounts of paper money, unbacked by gold and silver, were issued by the Continental Congress and the various states, supplementing the gold and silver components of the supply of money ($M$). During the 1780s, the supply of money

(M) in the young United States consisted mainly of gold and silver coins. **The velocity of exchange** (V) is the number of times the supply of money changes hands during a particular period of time. The kinds of purchases that cause money to change may be defined in a number of ways. The simplest (and the one to be used here) is that V, or the changing of money from one person to another, is for final goods and services. Velocity depends on the habits and customs of the people and, perhaps more significantly, on the degree of development of the financial institutions of the economy. Since the financial institutions of the economy were rudimentary and communication was slow from 1775 to 1789, it seems reasonable to assume that velocity (V) was constant. Velocity varies as people respond to unusual circumstances. Velocity can increase when people spend depreciating currency (for example, during the revolution) more quickly. Velocity can decrease as people hold on to a scarce money supply (1784–1786) as the money supply decreases still further.

If the supply of money increases, while velocity is constant, PQ must increase. As long as there are unemployed resources, output (Q) of final goods and services can increase. As the economy approaches full employment, however, prices (P) must increase, and at full employment only prices (P) can increase.

If the supply of money (M) decreases, while velocity (V) is constant, prices (P) must decrease, and output (Q) may decrease as well. But the proportion of total output sold within markets was small in the United States from 1775 to 1789 because many products were produced and consumed at home. Thus the main effect of a decrease in the supply of money was to reduce prices.

## The Demand for Money

Three basic motives explain why a person desires to hold a certain amount of money at any point in time:

1. The **transactions motive.** Because the receipt of money through wages or gifts is not perfectly timed with the desire to purchase goods, a person must keep some money to pay for all purchases made until the next payday.
2. The **precautionary motive.** People hold money against unforeseen happenings. If an illness should occur, for example, money will be needed to buy medicine and pay the doctor or hospital.
3. The **speculative motive.** Holding money is an advantage when a person encounters an opportunity to make a good investment.

What determines the specific amount of money that a person wishes to hold? The answer includes a number of factors, such as habits and customs, the level of income generated in the economy, the inventory of consumer goods that the individual holds, and the amount of assets that can be converted into money. Although individuals vary, each person wishes to hold a certain amount of money. When changes in the supply of money change the amounts that individuals actually hold, people react in ways that restore an equilibrium.

If the supply of money is increased, people find that they hold more money than wanted and, as a result, attempt to convert this money into consumer or investment goods. If such goods are in short supply, prices will increase. However, if the supply of money is decreased, people have less money than they want and, as a result, attempt to increase their holdings of money by reducing purchases of consumer or investment goods. The resulting decrease in demand decreases prices.

Whether we use the equation of exchange or the demand for money as our model, the results are the same. If the economy is at full employment, an increase in the supply of money increases prices, while a decrease in the supply of money decreases prices.

## Price Changes: Debtors and Creditors

When prices increase, debtors benefit at the expense of creditors. Since the purchasing power of money decreases as prices increase, debtors borrow money that has higher purchasing power when prices are lower and pay back money that has lower purchasing power when prices rise. Creditors suffer because they loan money with higher purchasing power and are repaid in money with lower purchasing power. When prices fall, the reverse occurs: Debtors suffer, and creditors gain. In addition, if no change occurs in the quantity of output, money incomes fall as prices fall, and the debtor has less money income to pay back the loan. (These generalizations ignore the possible effects of changes in price expectations. If borrower and lenders have anticipated future price changes correctly, prices already reflect those expectations).

Variations in prices create conflict between debtors and creditors about government policies. It is in the debtors' self-interest to encourage policies that are inflationary (that increase prices) but it is in the creditors' self-interest to oppose price-increasing policies.

---

# Glossary

**Deficit in the balance of trade**  A deficit that results when a country imports more goods and services than it exports.

**Equation of exchange** $(MV = PQ)$  A definitional relationship that states that the supply of money times the velocity of exchange equals prices times output.

**Fractional reserves** In colonial times, refers to the need of a merchant bank to keep reserves in the form of gold or silver that are a fraction (smaller than 100%) of the currency in circulation. This is because not everyone holding currency comes into the bank and wants gold or silver for the currency.

**Land banks** Banks, established by a number of states in the 1780s, that could issue paper currency backed only by mortgages on land.

**Merchant banks** (1780s) Banks chartered by state governments with the power to issue currency backed by gold and silver. Their loans were primarily commercial.

**Precautionary motive for holding money** Holding money for protection against unforeseen happenings that require spending.

**Speculative motive for holding money** Holding money in order to make investments when opportunities arise.

**Transactions motive for holding money** Holding money to buy things between paydays.

**Velocity of exchange** (V) The number of times the supply of money changes hands in a given time period. The assumption, here, is that money is spent only for final goods and services.

# Questions

1. How did the Continental Congress declare economic independence from Britain?

2. In what ways did the American economy adjust to the loss of Britain as a source of manufactured goods and a market for American exports during the revolution?

3. What were the problems facing the Continental Congress in financing the American Revolution? How did the Congress attempt to meet these problems?

4. Why were U.S. exports restricted after the revolution? What were the specific restrictions placed on some major American exports?

5. What caused the depression of 1785–1786? Describe in detail the role of the supply of money in that depression.

6. How did the Continental Congress attempt to expand U.S. exports? Was the attempt successful? Why?

7. How did the state governments attempt to constrict imports? Were they successful? Why?

8. Explain the three means that were available to increase the supply of money in the 1780s. What were the controversies surrounding each approach?

9. If you were a debtor in 1786, which approach to the supply of money would you have favored? Why? If you were a creditor, which one would you have favored? Why?

10. Some authors dissent from the position that the 1780s were a crucial economic period. What points do they make to support their argument?

# Suggested Readings

1. Bjork, Gordon C. "The Weaning of the American Economy: Independence, Market Changes and Economic Development." *Journal of Economic History*, 24 (December 1964).

2. Ferguson, E. James. *The Power of the Purse: A History of American Public Finance 1776–1790*. Chapel Hill: University of North Carolina Press, 1961.

3. Hammond, Bray. *Banks and Politics in America, from the Revolution to the Civil War*. Princeton, N.J.: Princeton University Press, 1957.

4. Hession, Charles H., and Sardy, Hyman. *Ascent to Affluence*. Boston: Allyn & Bacon, 1969. Pp. 48–56.

5. Jensen, Merrill E. *The New Nation: A History of the United States During the Confederation, 1787–1789*. New York: Knopf, 1950.

6. Nash, Gerald D., ed. *Issues in American Economic History*. Lexington, Mass.: Heath, 1972. Chap. 7.

7. Nettels, Curtis P. *The Emergence of a National Economy, 1775–1815*. New York: Harper & Row, 1969.

8. Willis, James F., and Primack, Martin L. *Explorations in Economics*. Boston: Houghton Mifflin, 1977. Pp. 144–145, 269–273.

9. Wright, Esmond, ed. *Causes and Consequences of the American Revolution*. New York: Quadrangle, 1966.

# Chapter 5

---

# The Constitution and the Federalist Program, 1787-1792

The United States was now independent. But the political processes were not complete, for the political revolution that overthrew the Articles of Confederation was yet to come. The adoption of the Constitution was to complete the political transformation of the new country. The formulation and adoption of the Constitution had its economic causes. As we have seen, these economic factors were in large measure caused by the inability of either the state or central governments to solve the deficit of trade and by the drain on the money supply in the mid-1780s. Thus, the major economic problems of the U.S. economy after the revolution stemmed from difficulties in the foreign trade sector. In the Review of Economic Concepts in this chapter is a simple model of how comparative advantage works in international trade. This import substitution model should be kept in mind as the chapter reviews the foreign trade problems of the 1780s and outlines the economic implications of the Constitution. The comparative advantage model will also be helpful in understanding some implications of the Federalist program in the new government's early years under the Constitution of 1789.

## A Recap

After the revolution, the United States imported about three times the value of the goods it exported. The inadequate level of exports meant that these imports were paid for by exporting gold and silver. The major difficulty in balancing the excess imports through trade was that the United

States, as an independent nation, was outside the mercantilist systems of the world trading communities. These communities did not allow trade based on comparative advantage and maintained discriminatory systems favorable to their own colonies. The United States had lost the essentially comparative advantage trade that the colonies had enjoyed within the protective trading system of the British Empire. Imports remained high as the United States found it very difficult to maintain a self-contained economy without trade, as depicted in Figure 5-1 in the Review of Economic Concepts.

We have seen what happened to the United States as a result of the outflow of gold and silver: The domestic supply of money declined substantially, prices fell, and debtors unable to pay their debts were forced into bankruptcies. The outcome was the depression of 1785–1786. The individual states could not resolve these problems, and under the Articles of Confederation Congress failed to deal with any of these problems successfully.

# Inadequacies of the Articles of Confederation

The depression of 1785–1786 seemed to reveal inadequacies of the American political system under the Articles of Confederation. These inadequacies can be seen within three categories.

First, the central government was not strong enough to negotiate concessions from the major colonial powers, Great Britain, France, and Spain. The Congress had no power to tax and thus provide a treasury for the maintenance of military forces. This lack of power doomed to failure efforts of the Congress to obtain favorable trade access to the European countries or their colonies. Comparative advantage trade could not be achieved through negotiations.

Second, the central government did not have the power to control entry of foreign goods (imports) into the United States. The efforts of individual states to impose controls on imports through tariffs proved ineffective and raised the specter of tariff discrimination between states. The American economy was unable to retreat to a no-trade or less-trade position that would have offered increased self-sufficiency.

Third, the central government could not protect against threats to property and contracts. Examples of these threats include Shays's Rebellion, debt moratorium laws by the states, inflationary monetary policy, and widespread "leveler" sentiment.

And, finally, the central government did not have the power to establish and control the money supply and to create a sound credit and banking system.

Monied and commercial groups wanted a revision of the Articles of

Confederation to provide a system capable of protecting property and creating situations where profit could be more easily obtained. They wanted to reverse the trend of the debtor classes, who had gained control over state legislatures and, as they saw it, expropriated property by creating an inflated, unbacked currency. (Remember that increases in prices transfer real wealth from creditors to debtors, because the debtors pay back loans with money that has lower purchasing power than the money they borrowed.)

A new constitutional convention was called in 1787 to formulate changes in the Articles of Confederation. What emerged, of course, was a completely new system of government based on the present Constitution of the United States. Although it appears that the creditor groups controlled this constitutional convention, and that small farm owners and others in society had little representation, many groups in the United States supported the adoption of the Constitution. The Constitution held the promise of reviving economic conditions and of creating greater economic stability. In examining the powers given to the federal government under the new Constitution and how these powers were used in the Federalist program, we must carefully note how the rights of property were strengthened and a more favorable environment for obtaining property was created.

Obviously, all economic activity takes place within a set of institutions. Institutions define not only specifics—for example, a specific type of banking system that establishes conditions under which money and credit function—but also the ideological system, that system of beliefs about how economic activity *should* take place. The Constitution of the United States recommended in 1788 set the basic legal framework within which economic activity has taken place ever since. In a similar sense, the Constitution *ratified* a huge amount of legal powers that were worked out through *state* constitutions and laws.

## Economic Changes of the Constitution

The Constitution achieved three main economic objectives. First, it created the political environment for a single free-trade area within the United States. Second, it made the central government a potentially effective instrument of foreign economic policy. Third, it firmly recognized the primacy of property rights and the freedom of individuals to acquire and transfer property.

The Constitution created the potential for a common market area within the United States by granting the following important powers to the federal government. First, the federal government had the exclusive power to regulate both foreign and interstate trade (trade between states). Interstate and foreign trade would be subject to a single set of uniform laws and a single set of uniform taxes. These regulations prevented individual states from creating barriers to the movement of goods between states and, from the political point of view, created the possibility of one large common market area within the United States. Federal control made possible a unified economic policy toward international trade.

Second, the federal government had the power to define, create, and regulate the supply of money. State governments were prohibited from issuing money directly but were permitted to charter banks that could issue currency. This power enabled the federal government ultimately to create a unified monetary system and to remove the specter of state-issued, unbacked, inflationary currency that haunted the creditor classes.

Third, the federal government had the power to make uniform rules governing naturalization of immigrants. Because immigrants were given greater freedom to choose their place of residence within the United States, the mobility of labor was increased, and a unified labor market was ensured for the entire country.

Fourth, the states were prohibited from enacting laws interfering with the obligations of contract. No state could interfere with the carrying out of contractual obligations, either interstate or intrastate (within the state itself). This guarantee helped to remove barriers between the states and promoted nationwide economic activity.

Fifth, the federal government became responsible for setting up a single postal service and common standards of weights and measures. Also, the federal government could grant patents and copyrights that applied to the entire country. These last two powers again reinforced the freedom of economic activity between the various states.

Sixth, various powers granted to the federal government under the Constitution made it a more effective instrument for foreign economic policy. The federal government had the power to make treaties; these treaties were the law of the land and held precedence over state law. And now, at last, the central government had the power to tax. This power enabled the federal government to control imports and to finance an army and a navy, in addition to a central bureaucracy. The central government now had effective bargaining instruments in foreign negotiations and could exert greater power in international economic relations.

It would be inappropriate to argue that these powers were unambiguously net benefits. Some economists have argued that the use of some of these powers has proved detrimental to economic activity. An example often cited is the rise of public regulation at the end of the nineteenth century. Later in this book, we will consider both the advantages and disadvantages of regulation.

The strengthening of property rights promoted private enterprise. No one could impede the enforcement of private contracts. These provisions were essential for releasing the energies of individuals to pursue personal gain and, as Adam Smith put it, for maximizing the public good through economic activity and economic development.

## Beard's Interpretation of the Constitution

What we have set forth is an economic interpretation of the origins of the Constitution: that it grew out of the inability of the Articles of Confederation to deal with the many economic problems generated by independence. The idea of an economic interpretation of the Constitution was first associated, however, with Charles Beard[1] through his path-breaking book, *An Economic Interpretation of the Constitution of the United States.* His interpretation differs substantially from the one just given.

As a result of his research, Beard concluded that the framers of the constitution were motivated by personal self-interest and that the small farmer, the mechanic, and the poorer classes were not represented at the Constitutional Convention of 1788. Beard attributed to the 54 delegates the following distribution of economic interests:

40 holders of continental and state debt
24 money lenders
15 southern slaveholders
14 involved in land speculation
11 involved in manufacturing, commerce, and shipping

Beard maintained that, "The overwhelming majority of members, at least five-sixths, were immediately, directly, and personally interested in the outcome of their labors at Philadelphia, and were to a greater or lesser extent economic beneficiaries from the adoption of the Constitution."

Furthermore, Beard concluded that the same interests provided the dynamic element both in formulating the Constitution and in moving its adoption by the various states. He maintained that the leading supporters of the movement to adopt the Constitution were those who had personal property interests embodied primarily in speculation in continental and state debt.

Beard, who broke new ground in the analysis of the motives involved in the formulation and adoption of the Constitution, hoped that his scanty research would encourage further investigation. His hope was realized. Although at first there was widespread agreement with his formulation, in time critics appeared. One of the most compelling of these critics was Forrest McDonald,[4] who published *We the People: The Economic Origins of the Constitution* in 1958.

McDonald maintained that Beard's analysis was an oversimplification because the motivations concerning both formulation and adoption of the Constitution were more complex than Beard realized. He argued also that these motivations varied from one section of the country to another. McDonald concluded that it was not at all apparent that personal property interest represented in ownership of revolutionary debt was the primary element in pushing for the Constitution. Seven of the delegates opposed to the Constitution had more than twice the per capita holdings of revolutionary debt of those who supported the Constitution.

McDonald found that the most common property interest of the delegates was ownership of agricultural land. Beard had implied that, in the campaign over the ratification of the Constitution, farmers were opposed to the Constitution and the holders of revolutionary debt were in favor of adoption. This contention does not seem to be supported by the facts. The Constitution was easily passed in the primarily agricultural states of Connecticut, New Jersey, Delaware, Maryland, and Georgia. McDonald concluded from his own analysis of the votes on ratification that in some states security holders were a small minority of the supporters of the Constitution; in others, security holders were a larger percentage of those opposed than of those in favor of ratification; in many states, there was no correlation between security holdings and positions on ratification. It seems that as many security holders were opposed to ratification as were for it.

Although Beard's argument has been weakened by the subsequent research that he stimulated, Beard is recognized as a pioneer who opened a new territory of study and analysis.

# The Federalist Program

Although the discussion that follows concentrates on the federal level, one should not overlook the importance of state governments in economic development. State constitutions were already in place, dealing with property rights, corporations, banks, common carriers, and so forth. State programs to stimulate internal development were widespread. However, lack of space here restricts the discussion to the federal level.

Although the Constitution laid down the general framework of political institutions within which economic activity was to take place, how this framework would work in practice depended on the policies of the political parties in control of the government after 1789. The political party that controlled decision-making in the formative years of the new government was the Federalist party. The Federalists maintained control through the two administrations of George Washington and one of John Adams; that is, the 12 years from 1789 to 1801. The most important economic spokesman for the Federalists was Alexander Hamilton.

Hamilton's primary concern was to foster the development within the United States of a strong manufacturing sector. His *Report on Manufactures* called for high protective tariffs and used an "infant industries" argument to justify them. That his program as adopted did not achieve this objective was due in large measure to the lack of a comparative advantage in manufacturing, not to a lack of favorable political policies. The immediate effect of the Hamilton (Federalist) program was to stimulate commercial advancement. In time, when the basic economic conditions for industrial development appeared, the political structure was there to assist it.

The first Federalist measure was the Tariff Act of 1789, a declaration of commercial independence from Britain. Hamilton's *Report on Manufactures* called for high protective tariffs to protect the infant manufacturing industries of the United States. Also, it had a strong "mercantilist" flavor, urging a strong program of internal improvements. The north wanted protection from British imports for its manufacturing industries. The south, basically an importer of manufactured goods, opposed the Tariff Act because tariffs would increase the price of these imports. The comparative advantage of the south was in agricultural exports, primarily tobacco (and later cotton). Because of southern opposition, the tariff passed in 1789 was a compromise and therefore basically moderate. It provided some protection for the north's infant industries, and the proceeds of the tariff provided needed revenues for the Federalist government.

Another measure in the Federalist program was the Tonnage Act of 1789, which raised additional revenues for the federal government and provided aid to the northern shipping interests. Foreign-built and -owned ships had to pay 50 cents a ton on their cargo on entering U.S. ports. United States-built but foreign-owned ships had to pay 30 cents a ton, while domestic-owned and -built ships paid only 6 cents a ton. The difference in tonnage fees gave an advantage to U.S. shipping and also offered inducements to foreign shipping interests to buy vessels manufactured in the United States. Again opposition came from southern states, especially Georgia and South Carolina. The Tonnage Act increased prices to the south through higher shipping charges.

The intent of the Hamiltonian programs, as mirrored in both the Tariff and Tonnage Acts, was to interfere in the workings of comparative advantage for the benefit of specific interest groups, namely northern manufacturing and shipping.

Hamilton's plan for the public debt was detailed in his *Report on the Public Credit*. He wanted the federal government to assume all the debts of the states and refund the old federal and state debt at face value, issuing new debt at 6% interest payable in coin. Hamilton argued that this funding of the old federal and state debt would restore international confidence in both the public and private credit of the United States and would encourage commerce. Because of the restoration of confidence, the new debt would extend, augment, and complement the supply of money and raise prices. Allowing the interest rate on federal debt to decline significantly to 6% would lower general interest rates, which would tend to encourage economic growth. Furthermore, the public debt would encourage thrift (savings), growth of capital markets, and attitudes of investing in securities (including corporate securities).

Vigorous opposition to this refunding proposal was led by Thomas Jefferson and was especially strong in the South. The criticisms were based primarily on two arguments. First, many of the original purchasers of both the federal and state revolutionary debt, those who had actually supported the revolution financially, had sold their debt at very large discounts. Therefore, the speculators who had purchased this debt would make large gains when the debt was refunded at par, its original issue price. Second, opponents objected that the assumption of state debts by the federal government would increase the power of a remote central government at the expense of the states and home rule.

In the end, Jefferson supported the funding act in exchange for placing the capital on the Potomac River between Virginia and Maryland. Hamilton's *Report on Public Credit* provided the basis for the Funding Act of 1790. This act, however, increased the need for new taxes to pay the interest. One of them was the tax on whiskey, which sparked the Whiskey Rebellion of 1794 in western Pennsylvania.

Hamilton's 1790 *Report on a National Bank* was embodied in the 1791 act that established the First Bank of the United States with a 20-year federal charter. The bank had $10 million in capital stock, of which $6 million was in securities of the U.S. government. The bank could issue up to $10 million in currency, which was to be acceptable in all payments; that is, currency of the bank was declared **legal tender,** money that by law must be accepted in payment for all debts both public and private. The home office was in Philadelphia, and by 1805 it had eight branches throughout the United States.

The bank was conservative, and as a private profit-making enterprise it was successful. It could keep the issuance of currency by other banks under strong limitations. All currency received in the bank from its customers and the government could quickly be presented to the issuing bank for payment in gold and silver. This practice could keep currency close to the holdings of gold and silver by the banks and provided a secure but restricted currency supply. Although the Bank of the United States had the power to restrict currency issues, most observers conclude that it did not do so to its maximum potential. The Bank of the United States made primarily commercial and short-term loans.

Hamilton and other Federalists opposed westward expansion. They argued that the movement to the west drew part of the labor supply from the east, raised eastern wages, and hindered the development of eastern manufacturing. Therefore, to stimulate manufacturing the westward movement had to be slowed. The 1784 act that had required a minimum purchase of 640 acres in the western territories, at $1 an acre for cash, was changed in 1796, when Congress set a price of $2 an acre. At a cost of $1280, the minimum purchase was beyond the means of most small farmers.

Alexander Hamilton, advocate of manufacturing and shipping (left), and Thomas Jefferson, advocate of farmers and laborers. (Photo nos. 148-GW-734 and 148-GW-910C in the National Archives)

## Economic Effects of the Federalist Program

The immediate result of the Federalist program was a vast increase in the paper wealth of the country through the refunding of old federal and state debt and the capital stock and currency of the Bank of the United States, among others. The increased credit resources and currency for business had a marked inflationary effect. (Remember the equation of exchange.) Prices rose from an index of 78 in March 1789 to 100 by June 1790, a rise of 22% in just over one year.

Federalist measures succeeded in fostering a lively interest in manufacturing in the northern states. Town societies to promote manufacturing sprang up, and new enterprises were established. Domestic prices rose rapidly as a result of the financial expansion. But because experienced managers, skilled workers, and up-to-date machinery were lacking, domestic manufactures could not compete with imports. When international trade was restored, much domestic industry, even that protected by the tariff of 1789, could not survive. The manufacturing expansion collapsed in 1792.

Hamilton's program primarily benefited the commercial northeast. The Funding Act and the creation of the Bank of the United States established U.S. international credit, expanded commercial credit domestically, and generated a sounder monetary system. The Tonnage Act fostered northeastern shipping interests. The increased authority of the federal government contributed to the effectiveness of the United States in negotiations with foreign governments.

The Hamilton program was aimed at interfering with the workings of comparative advantage in international trade, primarily through the Tariff and Funding Acts. Hamilton's intent was to provide protection for northern industries until they became efficient enough to compete with foreign manufacturers. In effect, then, he was attempting to change the comparative advantage situation over time through government action. One result of this effort was the intensification of conflict between the South, which suffered from higher prices for its imports, and the North, which obtained protection for its industries.

## The Republican Opposition

Opposition to the Federalist program enabled the Republican Party (the Democratic Party of today) to elect Thomas Jefferson in 1802. Gathering strength on the frontier and among the debt-ridden farmers and laborers, the Republicans charged that the Federalists had created inequities that favored manufacturers and speculators. Led by Jefferson and Madison, the Republicans made the following charges.

Federalist financial policies had benefited a northeastern area with a seaboard-European nexus and retarded development of the West. The Funding Act had stripped the poor to enrich the wealthy; speculators had made huge capital gains. The Bank of the United States was an engine of monopoly and privilege that concentrated banking capital in the urban, commercial seaboard area. The whiskey tax was cited as another example of discrimination; the tax was used to finance the Funding Act and develop a navy to further commercial diplomacy; but it oppressed the farmers, who could market whiskey more easily than corn. The tariff and the tonnage acts increased prices to the agricultural sectors and favored the commercial, shipping, and manufacturing sectors of the northeast.

Although the Republican criticisms of Federalist programs were substantially correct, the Federalists had maintained control of the government for 12 years, as a result of the widespread desire for economic and political stability and general economic development in the United States. But one should not conclude that the Republican opposition was totally unsuccessful during those 12 years. They were able to moderate much of Hamilton's promanufacturing program, especially in the area of tariffs. However, when Jeffersonian Republicans came to power in 1802 the Hamiltonian program remained basically unchanged.

# Review of Economic Concepts: A Model of Import Substitution Effects

Nations trade commodities and services with each other because such trade is to their mutual advantage. When one nation produces those goods in which it has a comparative advantage and imports the goods in which another nation has such an advantage, both countries are better off; each has more to consume than it would have had in the absence of trade.

Now, what happens in an economy that has attained a comparative advantage trade equilibrium if that equilibrium is severely disrupted by war, a decision to forego international trade, a change in trading relationships with other nations, or any other set of events?

Figure 5-1, which represents hypothetical production and consumption possibilities of a colony or nation with and without trade, is useful as a means of visualizing the kinds of relationships set in motion by such a trade disequilibrium. Shown in Figure 5-1(a) are the domestic production possibilities curve of an agricultural economy and that economy's consumption possibilities curve when it engages in trade with another nation

(a) Domestic production without trade and consumption with trade

(b) Domestic pricing of manufactured goods, with and without imports

Figure 5-1. Hypothetical Production-Possibilities and Consumption-Possibilities Curves. Domestic Pricing of Manufactured Goods (with and without Imports).

that has a comparative advantage in producing manufactured goods. For simplicity's sake, both "curves" are drawn as straight lines, to reflect an assumption of no specialization of resources and a constant rate at which one good must be given up in order to produce the other. Let's take Point R ($A_0$ of agricultural goods and $M_0$ of manufactured goods) as a reference point. Since Point R lies on the economy's production possibilities curve, it is a possible equilibrium without trade; in fact, we shall suppose (arbitrarily) that R is the initial equilibrium. At Point R, $A_0$ of agricultural goods and $M_0$ of manufactured goods are available for consumption.

Turning to Figure 5-1(b), $S_d$ is the domestic supply of manufactured goods, while $D$ is the nation's demand for manufactured goods. Supply ($S_d$) and demand are equal at Price $P_0$. Now what is its gain if the agricultural nation engaged in bilateral trade with the other nation? Point R', while not unique, illustrates that gain. By exporting some of the agricultural goods in which it has a comparative advantage to the other nation and importing some of that country's comparative advantage manufactured goods, our hypothetical nation can reach Point R' on its consumption possibilities curve. Point R' represents $A_0$ of agricultural goods and $M_0'$ $M_0$; therefore, is a gain from trade. Now look again at Figure 5-1(b). The increase in the supply of manufactured goods through trade ($M_0' - M_0$) causes the supply curve of such goods to increase, to shift to $S_{d+f}$ (domestic and foreign). As a result, the price of manufactured goods falls to $P_1$.

What happens now if international trade is disrupted? For example, what happens if war breaks out between the two nations who had been exchanging agricultural and manufactured goods? For simplicity's sake, let us assume that there is a total cessation of trade (no blockade runners or other illegal trade). Initially, the domestic supply of manufactured goods returns to $S_d$, and the society tends to return to Point R (with $A_0$ of agricultural goods and $M_0$ of manufactured goods). But suppose that the society whose imports of manufactured goods have ceased decides to produce more of those goods itself; in other words, it decides it must turn inward and substitute its own products for those it has previously imported.

In turning inward, the nation denied trade is constrained—even at full employment—to the choices along its domestic production possibilities curve. Since we are assuming that the nation wants to produce more manufactured goods (to prosecute the war or for whatever reason), it will move down that curve (to the right of Point R). The higher prices of manufactured goods (such as $P_0$ with domestically produced supply $S_d$) will act as incentives to domestic producers or would-be domestic producers to expand or create manufacturing enterprises.

We have been assuming in this chapter that the PP curve was a straight line. Now we will use concave PP curves. Remember, though, that in moving down the now concave curve, the nation faces an increasingly unfavorable tradeoff: It foregoes more and more agricultural goods to get each increment in manufactured goods. The nation may, as the former North American colonies did, successfully create a gunpowder and munitions industry, but that industry will probably produce goods less efficiently than foreign producers.

Let's suppose that ultimately our hypothetical nation reaches Point S, at which it is producing $A_1$ of agricultural goods and $M_2$ of manufactured goods. In turn—look at Figure 5-1(b) again—domestic supply of manufactured goods increases to $S_d'$ and price falls to $P_2$, still far above the price with trade, $P_1$.

Throughout this discussion, we have assumed a constant demand for manufactured goods. If, as seems likely, that demand increases during the cessation of trade (from new military supplies plus some of the old civilian demand), prices will be greater than they would have been otherwise (above $P_2$), and the stimulus to manufacturing enterprise will be further enhanced.

## Restoration of Trade

Let's suppose now that the war or other event that caused the cessation of trade is ended and that trade is restored on the old terms. Assume that there has been no change in either country's comparative advantage. Equilibrium trading relationships now exist all along the consumption-possibilities-with-trade curve of the nation represented in Figure 5-1(a). In other words, the other country's comparative advantage (cheaper) manufactured goods can now enter our hypothetical nation. Let us suppose (again, arbitrarily) that Point R' is restored as the consumption possibilities equilibrium. If we assume that there are some minor barriers to complete specialization (in which our hypothetical country would produce only agricultural goods and the other country only manufactured goods) domestic supply becomes $S_d$ and total supply (domestic plus foreign) becomes $S_{d+f}$. Manufactured goods' prices fall to $P_1$.

The model shows that nations (or nations and their colonies) can have more to consume if they trade with each other on the basis of comparative advantage. A nation that "turns inward" (creates infant industries) may successfully produce goods that are not in its comparative advantage so long as trade is blocked, as occurred during the revolution. When trade is restored, however, the price stimulus will be removed, and prices of goods traded on a comparative-advantage basis will fall. Domestic industries created during the hiatus in trade will find themselves at a disadvantage, and some, if not all, will find it unprofitable to continue producing the good(s) that are not in the country's comparative advantage.

## Glossary

**Legal tender**   Money that must, by law, be accepted in payment for all debts, public or private.

## Questions

1. What were the major economic difficulties facing the United States in the 1780s? What efforts were made to deal with these problems prior to the Constitution of 1789? Were these efforts successful?
2. Why was Congress unable to solve the economic problems of the 1780s under the Articles of Confederation?
3. What is the authors' view of the economic factors that fostered the development of the Constitution?
4. What was Beard's economic interpretation of the Constitution? Do you think he was correct? Why?
5. What economic changes were made possible by the Constitution?
6. What were the main objectives of the Federalist program? How did the Federalists try to implement their goals?
7. What were the main economic effects of the Federalist program? What were the criticisms of this program?
8. Do you favor Hamilton's view or Jefferson's view of economic policy in the early years of the United States? Explain your choice.

## Suggested Readings

1. Beard, Charles A. *An Economic Interpretation of the Constitution of the United States.* New York: Macmillan, 1913.
2. Brown, R. E. *Charles Beard and the Constitution.* Princeton, N.J.: Princeton University Press, 1956.
3. Ferguson, E. James. "The Nationalists of 1781–1783 and the Economic Interpretation of the Constitution." *Journal of American History,* 56 (1969).
4. McDonald, Forrest. *We the People: The Economic Origins of the Constitution.* Chicago: University of Chicago Press, 1958.
5. Nettels, C. P. *The Emergence of a National Economy, 1775–1815.* New York: Holt, Rinehart and Winston, 1962.

# Chapter **6**

# The Napoleonic Wars and U.S. Commercial Expansion, 1793-1815

In 1790, the prospects for rapid economic development of the American economy seemed dim. However, in the next 25 years, just such a period of expansion occurred. What factors could cause such a dramatic turnabout? The answer is wars—but not ones directly involving the United States; rather, wars in which the United States is the most prominent neutral.

This chapter continues the economic history from 1790 through the Napoleonic Wars and the U.S. War of 1812 (1812–1815). The single most important economic factor in this period was the very substantial increase in U.S. commodity exports and shipping earnings. Thus the foreign trade sector of the U.S. economy played the crucial role in economic development during these 25 years. The Review of Economic Concepts in this chapter contains a simple model of export-led development that will prove useful in understanding this period.

## The U.S. Economy in 1790

The classical theory of economic development emphasizes the importance of the size of markets and the level of technology. Market size was the factor limiting specialization and division of labor. With a given technology, as specialization and division of labor increases, productivity (output per unit of labor input) increases and intensive growth (increasing real per capita output) occurs. The size of markets then is a determining factor in economic development, and to understand the potential for economic development in the United States in 1790, we must concentrate on an analysis of the potential for growth of markets.

Douglass C. North[4] in his excellent study, *The Economic Growth of the United States 1790–1860,* draws the following conclusion: "By 1790 the political crises had been resolved and the economy enjoyed a measure of prosperity. Given political stability, an energetic populace, and an abundance of resources, the country's long-run economic growth would appear assured. Yet there was little prospect of rapid growth on the horizon, and available information about the economy from 1789 through 1792 provides incomplete but convincing evidence that the prospects of the economy in the foreseeable future were limited by the size of the domestic market and an inability to expand the foreign market." In brief, while the Constitution plus the economic ideology of the American people created a favorable political, social, and psychological environment for development, potential development was severely limited by size of internal and foreign markets.

## Limits of the Internal Market

Although the population of the United States in 1790 was almost 4 million, and in real terms, not money income, the per capita real income was substantially higher than in England, only a small part of the output resulted in market demand. There were almost 700,000 slaves in the South and 200,000 settlers west of the Appalachian Mountains, and the frontier was primarily self-sufficient. The rest of the rural population, 2.8 million, maintained market relationships of varying degrees. Even the 200,000 people in urban centers produced a significant amount of home manufactures, thus reducing the size of the cash market. Although few people were completely self-sufficient (completely within the noncash economy), most had varying degrees of self-sufficiency (varying degrees of noncash involvement).

The primary factor restricting the spread of the market was the high cost of transportation other than by rivers and by sea. Most agricultural products are high bulk and low value; land transportation for such products was restricted to short distances. It is hard, then to find fault with North's conclusion: "Whatever proportion of the rural population is assumed to have been part of the domestic market, it is impossible to escape the conclusion that this market was small and not heavily concentrated." In other words, the cash economy was small and not heavily concentrated.

## Limits of the Export Market

The restrictions of the export market are, by now, familiar to you. When the United States was part of the British Empire, it received all the economic privileges of mercantilist relationships. After the revolution, the United States lost its favored treatment from Britain. Indeed, it then faced unfavorable, discriminatory treatment from most western European countries. Not only was direct trade with the colonies of European countries severely restricted, but restrictions were also applied in many areas to the home countries themselves. These restrictions included prohibition of trade with certain colonies, prohibition of import of certain goods, import taxes on certain goods, and taxes levied against foreign ships (including U.S. ships) engaged in direct trade with certain countries.

These restrictions on U.S. foreign trade limited its ability to increase exports and restricted the further expansion of the American carrying trade. In 1790, only 58.6% of the foreign trade of the United States was carried in U.S. ships.

In 1790, the prospects seemed to be the following: Internal trade was relatively low and unlikely to increase because of high transportation costs. External trade was limited because of mercantilist trade restrictions employed by the European powers. With such an abundance of land and with labor and capital costs relatively high in manufacturing, the American economy was at a comparative disadvantage with Europe in manufactured goods. The prospects for rapid economic growth by increases in the size of the market seemed very dim in 1790.

# Economic Expansion, 1793–1815

Now, let us examine the experience of the United States from 1793 to 1815. Although prospects for a period of substantial economic development in the United States in 1790 seemed dim, external events changed that picture and initiated just such a period between 1793 and 1815. The leading sectors in this expansion were the shipping and export industries, the latter including both reexports of foreign products and exports of American products. The reexports came primarily from the colonies of the belligerents in the Napoleonic Wars in the West Indies. These exports could not be carried directly from the West Indies colonies to the home country—for example, from French colonies to France—because they would be seized (by England) as contraband. Therefore, a legal fiction was created by these exports being carried to U.S. ports and reexported as U.S. goods. The British Essex decision in 1805 sought to restrict neutrals to the trade they had carried before the war. Napoleon's Milan decree destroyed this legal fiction concerning reexports and declared a blockade of Britain. Both, along with the British Orders in Council in 1807 laid U.S. ships carrying reexports from the West Indies open to seizure by the British or French navies.

Every turn in this expansion of the American economy was deter-

mined by economic and military policies connected with intermittent warfare between Britain and France from 1793 to 1812. There was a mild
break in this expansion in 1797 as France accelerated its capture of U.S.
merchant vessels and as there was some talk of peace. There was a sharp
break in 1801 and 1802 while an unstable peace existed between France
and Britain. Resumption of war in Europe in 1803, however, marked a
renewal of expansion in American trade. In response to seizures of U.S.
ships by both Britain and France (528 ships by Britain and 389 by France,
due to the British Essex decision and Napoleon's Milan decree), President
Jefferson enforced, over the violent opposition of the shippers themselves,
the **Embargo of December 1807,** an embargo that was replaced by the
**Nonintercourse Act of 1809.** After the latter date, trade slowly resumed
with the European continent, excluding Britain. In 1812, a second war between the United States and Great Britain brought an end to the era.

What caused such a large expansion of the carrying trade and of reexports? Largely, the disappearance of many merchant ships of the
belligerents, France, Holland, and Spain. The vast colonial trade of
Europe was placed in the hands of neutrals, and the neutral nation most
capable of handling this trade was the United States. Even Britain found it
advisable temporarily to open the British West Indies to U.S. ships. The
Napoleonic Wars thus substantially, if temporarily, broke down the mercantilist system that had restricted the ability of the United States to expand foreign markets. When war gave the United States an opportunity to
expand, United States merchants and shippers took full advantage of it.

Part of what happened is illustrated in the Review of Economic Concepts, especially in Figure 6-2. Demand for U.S. exports and the services of
U.S. ships through the reexport trade increased. Prices of exports and fees
for U.S. shipping increased, shifting resources from the noncash economy
and from the nonexport-oriented cash economy into the export-oriented
cash economy. Productivity increased as these resources flowed from
lower productivity activities and as the size of the market in export-
oriented activities increased, stimulating specialization and division of
labor.

## The Carrying Trade

British-French conflict created an opportunity for U.S. ships to trade with
both the colonies and the home countries of the European empires. As a
result, from 1790 to 1807 earnings of U.S. ships increased 700%. Net earnings (total receipts minus costs) for the carrying trade rose from $5.9
million in 1790 to $42.1 million in 1807 (see Table 6-1). This increase was
due, in significant measure, not only to increases in ocean freight rates but
also to increased efficiency in the utilization of ships and especially to a
doubling in the total tonnage of American shipping.

Table 6-1. Exports, Reexports, Imports, and Earnings of the Carrying Trade (in Millions of Dollars).

| Year | Exports | Reexports | Imports for Domestic Use | Net Freight Earnings |
|------|---------|-----------|--------------------------|----------------------|
| 1790 | 20.2 | 0.3 | 23.5 | 5.9 |
| 1791 | 19.0 | 0.5 | 30.0 | 6.2 |
| 1792 | 20.8 | 1.0 | 31.5 | 7.4 |
| 1793 | 26.1 | 1.8 | 30.8 | 11.9 |
| 1794 | 33.0 | 6.5 | 29.5 | 15.5 |
| 1795 | 48.0 | 8.3 | 63.0 | 19.0 |
| 1796 | 67.1 | 26.3 | 56.6 | 21.6 |
| 1797 | 56.9 | 27.0 | 50.4 | 17.1 |
| 1798 | 61.5 | 33.0 | 37.6 | 16.6 |
| 1799 | 78.7 | 45.5 | 35.5 | 24.2 |
| 1800 | 71.0 | 49.1 | 44.1 | 26.2 |
| 1801 | 94.1 | 46.6 | 66.7 | 31.0 |
| 1802 | 72.5 | 35.8 | 42.6 | 18.2 |
| 1803 | 55.8 | 13.6 | 52.1 | 23.7 |
| 1804 | 71.7 | 36.2 | 50.8 | 26.9 |
| 1805 | 95.6 | 53.8 | 72.3 | 29.7 |
| 1806 | 101.5 | 60.3 | 76.3 | 34.6 |
| 1807 | 108.3 | 59.6 | 85.1 | 42.1 |
| 1808 | 22.4 | 13.0 | 45.1 | 23.0 |
| 1809 | 52.2 | 20.8 | 40.2 | 26.2 |
| 1810 | 66.8 | 24.4 | 65.0 | 39.5 |
| 1811 | 61.3 | 16.0 | 41.9 | 40.8 |
| 1812 | 38.5 | 8.5 | 70.3 | 29.6 |
| 1813 | 27.9 | 2.8 | 19.3 | 10.2 |
| 1814 | 6.9 | 0.1 | 12.8 | 2.6 |
| 1815 | 52.6 | 6.6 | 78.8 | 20.6 |

*Source:* Douglass C. North, "The United States Balance of Payments, 1790–1860," *Trends in the American Economy in the Nineteenth Century,* Studies in Income and Wealth of the National Bureau of Economic Research, Vol. 24 (Princeton, N.J.: Princeton University Press, 1960), pp. 591–592, 595.

Another sign of the expansion of American shipping, as the British-French wars drove belligerent merchant vessels from the seas, was the dramatic increase in the use of U.S. ships for transporting U.S. exports and imports. U.S. shipping had carried only about 59% of its foreign trade in 1790, but it increased to 90% by 1807. The increase was concentrated primarily in the Northeast, especially in the three large port cities of Boston, New York, and Philadelphia.

## Exports and Reexports

This remarkable increase in the earnings from shipping was accompanied by increases in exports, both exports of American-produced commodities and reexports. **Reexports** were commodities produced outside of the United States, shipped to a U.S. port, temporarily stored in warehouses, and reshipped without being changed in form. Important examples of such reexports were the sugar and molasses produced in the West Indies sugar islands of Britain, France, and Spain. The Napoleonic Wars restricted the ability of vessels from these countries to carry the sugar, leaving the trade primarily to the United States. U.S. merchants' efforts to find new markets resulted in the reexporting of tea from China.

American-produced exports were primarily agricultural commodities, led by southern staples. Cotton, which dominated the expansion of domestic exports, accounted for half of the increase. Next in importance was tobacco, and then general agricultural output from the North, consisting of wheat, flour, and animal products.

From 1790 to the peak year of 1807, total exports rose from $20.2 million to $108.3 million—an impressive fivefold increase (Table 6-1). Expansion of the reexport trade was the major factor in this increase. Reexports, $0.3 million in 1790, increased to $59.6 million in 1807, while domestic exports rose from $19.9 million to $58.5 million.

## Imports, Terms of Trade, and the Balance of Payments

Imports for domestic use increased from $23.5 million in 1790 to $81.8 million in 1807—almost a fourfold increase. Reexports have been separated from the import and export data in Table 6-1 because they increase imports when they come into the United States and increase exports when they leave. When imports for domestic use are compared to exports, we see an import surplus (imports exceed exports) in every year from 1790 through 1814 except 1811 and 1813. This commodity import surplus was more than made up by earning from the carrying trade. For example, in 1807 imports for domestic use were $81.8 million, while exports were $58.5 million, an import surplus of $23.3 million. Earnings of the carrying trade in 1807 were $42.1 million, more than enough to cover that import surplus.

The analysis of the simple export-led model indicated that this surge in export demand should lead to increases in prices. Increased demand for imports would indicate also an increase in import prices. These increases in prices had a marked effect on both imports and exports. A useful measure to compare relative changes in export-import prices is the terms of trade—the index that measures how much a dollar's worth of exports could buy of imports. Table 4-1 gives the terms of trade index to 1790, and Table 6-2 continues the index to 1815. Using 1790 as 100, the terms of trade fell to about 70 for 1792, rose to a high of 161 in 1798 and 1799, then fell to a low of 85 in 1808. During the period of 1792 to 1807, the terms of trade were favorable to the United States. This means not only that there was substantial expansion in U.S. exports, reexports, and earnings on the carrying trade but also that export prices rose more rapidly than import prices. On the whole, U.S. imports became cheaper, relative to U.S. exports.

These favorable terms of trade meant that each physical unit of exports could purchase a larger physical amount of imports. The results could lead to combinations of the following. It could mean that more imports of consumption goods could be obtained, thus increasing total consumption. Also it could mean that increases in imports of capital goods could be obtained, increasing the productive capacity of the American economy. Finally, it meant that resources within the U.S. economy could be shifted into alternative uses, and imports could replace the output lost by this shift. All three possibilities combined to increase U.S. per capita income.

## Internal and Coastal Trade

Internal trade was primarily local, extending out from the seaports into the surrounding areas (their hinterland). Towns farther away were usually connected to the coastal cities by rivers. There was some increase in the geographic as well as economic (demand-supply determined) size of these local markets because of the expansion of turnpikes (roads). But the economic effects of road expansion were minimal, and cost of land transportation was still high.

After 1792, along with the expansion of domestic exports and imports, coastal trade expanded rapidly. Trade in the West expanded after New Orleans was opened to U.S. commerce in 1793; New Orleans was closed again, however, in 1802. Finally, the Louisiana Purchase by President Jefferson brought New Orleans under U.S. control. Western trade (from Ohio, Kentucky, Tennessee, Indiana, and Illinois) on the Mississippi was primarily one-way down the river. Agricultural products moved downstream on flatboats, and even the flatboats themselves were sold in New Orleans. Most of the goods shipped north were carried on horseback or muleback, which was cheaper than poling upstream.

## The Foreign Sector's Impact on the Economy

The leading sectors pacing the rapid economic growth from 1793 to 1807 included domestic exports, reexports, and the carrying trade—all ex-

Table 6-2. Index of Export and Import Prices
and the Terms of Trade 1700–1815
(1790 = 100).

| Year | Exports | Imports | Terms of Trade |
|------|---------|---------|----------------|
| 1790 | 100.0 | 100.0 | 100.0 |
| 1791 | 85.8 | 109.8 | 78.1 |
| 1792 | 81.7 | 118.8 | 68.8 |
| 1793 | 97.8 | 108.4 | 90.2 |
| 1794 | 103.6 | 129.2 | 80.2 |
| 1795 | 153.6 | 124.3 | 123.6 |
| 1796 | 172.6 | 132.8 | 130.0 |
| 1797 | 174.8 | 139.9 | 124.9 |
| 1798 | 207.4 | 127.6 | 162.5 |
| 1799 | 220.3 | 135.5 | 162.6 |
| 1800 | 145.9 | 124.6 | 117.1 |
| 1801 | 154.1 | 119.9 | 128.5 |
| 1802 | 131.6 | 111.8 | 117.7 |
| 1803 | 132.8 | 118.0 | 112.5 |
| 1804 | 147.7 | 134.7 | 109.7 |
| 1805 | 156.4 | 139.5 | 112.1 |
| 1806 | 142.0 | 129.8 | 109.4 |
| 1807 | 136.2 | 124.7 | 109.2 |
| 1808 | 115.3 | 124.3 | 92.8 |
| 1809 | 116.2 | 129.1 | 90.0 |
| 1810 | 128.6 | 129.8 | 99.1 |
| 1811 | 128.6 | 121.1 | 106.2 |
| 1812 | 127.1 | 131.7 | 96.5 |
| 1813 | 126.5 | 179.7 | 70.4 |
| 1814 | 127.3 | 232.3 | 54.8 |
| 1815 | 182.9 | 191.3 | 95.6 |

Source: Douglass C. North, *The Economic Growth of the United States 1790–1860* (New York: Norton, 1966), pp. 221, 229.

panded by the opportunities created by British-French conflict—in addition to the economic effects from raising export prices and fees for shipping and the economic effects of the favorable terms of trade already mentioned. This expansion had substantial impact on the growth of urban areas. The carrying and reexport trade was primarily concentrated in the Northeast and was strongly mirrored in the growth of the four major port cities of Philadelphia, New York, Boston, and Baltimore. Each of these cities (Table 6-3) doubled in population, and New York and Baltimore almost tripled from 1790 to 1810. Increase in domestic exports was especially strong in the South, where the export of short-staple cotton caused growth in Charleston, South Carolina. Urbanization increased from 5.1% of the population in 1790 to 7.3% in 1810.

Table 6-3. Population of the Four Major Cities, 1790–1810.

| City | 1790 | 1800 | 1810 |
|------|------|------|------|
| Baltimore | 13,503 | 26,114 | 35,583 |
| Boston | 18,038 | 24,937 | 33,250 |
| New York | 33,131 | 60,489 | 96,373 |
| Philadelphia | 42,520 | 69,403 | 91,874 |

Source: U.S. Census Bureau, *Compendium of the Seventh Census* (Washington, D.C.: Senate Printer, 1854), p. 192.

A growing export activity encouraged growth in what Douglass North[4] called "subsidiary, complementary, and residentiary types of economic activities" and was confined primarily to the Northeast. A **subsidiary industry** is one that is needed so that another industry can function. Most important as a subsidiary industry, one directly created by export activity, was shipbuilding, which more than doubled in terms of merchant ship tonnage. Various shipfitting industries developed around shipbuilding.

Examples of **complementary industries** were commission merchants, brokers and others who implement trade, marine insurance, banks, and facilities for warehouses and docking. These complementary industries were originally created to service the export sector but, once created, were available to help expand internal trade. Growth in these industries was substantial and provided a basis for further growth after 1815.

Increasing urbanization tied to increased export trade stimulated a variety of locally oriented manufactures and services designed to meet the needs of a growing urban population. Such industries are called **residentiary industries.** The widening urban markets exerted pressure to improve local transportation through turnpike construction to bring in needed agricultural supplies for the maintenance of this increased population. Thus, this growth stimulated increased market relationships into the hinterland around the port cities.

# Agriculture, 1790–1815

Three distinct agricultural regions appeared in the United States during the years 1790–1815: the North included New England, New York, Pennsylvania, and New Jersey; the South included the states along the Atlantic south of Pennsylvania, the middle states of Kentucky and Tennessee, and the "New South" of Arkansas, Alabama, Louisiana, and Mississippi; the West included Ohio, Indiana, and Illinois.

## The South

As may be seen in Figure 6-1, by 1815, the "Old South," those southern states along the Atlantic, had no discernible frontier as the frontier moved westward, while the middle states of Kentucky and Tennessee were rapidly reaching that same position. The frontier was a so-called New South, consisting of Louisiana, Mississippi, Arkansas, and Alabama.

A significant shift occurred in the relative importance and location of southern staple crops. Tobacco had shifted from the Virginia-Maryland piedmont to North Carolina, Kentucky, and Tennessee. Soil erosion, a problem common to agriculture in the early development of many nations, was the primary reason for the shift from tobacco to wheat in the piedmont of Virginia and Maryland. Rice was still grown along the coast of Georgia and South Carolina, where ocean tides were used to flood the rice fields. A new staple, sugar, developed along the coast of Louisiana. In the rest of the South, cotton was "king" and had replaced tobacco as the region's most important staple.

The revolution in textile production in England, starting in the 1760s, greatly increased world demand for raw cotton. In the United States in 1790, a few islands off the Atlantic coast could grow what was called *Sea Island* or *long-staple* cotton, a variety in which removal of cotton seed was simple and required little labor. On the mainland, though, only short-staple cotton could be grown. Labor cost involved in removing short-staple cotton seed was very high and severely limited the spread of its cultivation. Eli Whitney, while visiting the South in 1793, invented the cotton gin, which greatly reduced the labor cost of removing the seed from short-staple cotton. This machine was a simple one and so easy to produce that Whitney decided not to bother with patenting it. This invention dramatically increased productivity, reduced the cost of cleaning (removing the seed), and made short-staple cotton a very profitable crop. As a result, the crop spread rapidly throughout the South; by 1815, cotton was "king." From 1800 to 1860, cotton accounted for more than half the exports from the United States.

Reviving southern staple crops, especially the introduction and expansion of cotton, revalidated the economic advantages of slavery, and that "peculiar institution" showed new vigor. From 1790 to 1810, the rate of growth of the slave population was twice that of the previous 15 years. This growth came primarily from natural increase, not slave importation. Legal importation of slaves was forbidden in 1807. We shall reserve a

Figure 6-1. Extent of Settlements, 1775 to 1820.

*Source:* R. R. Palmer, ed., *Historical Atlas of the World* (New York: Rand McNally, 1965), p. 20. Copyright © 1970 by Rand McNally and Company, Chicago, and reprinted by permission of Rand McNally College Publishing Company.

detailed analysis of the economic importance of slavery for later chapters dealing with the period from 1815 to 1860.

## The North

In this period, 1790 to 1815, there was little technological change in agriculture and therefore little increase in productivity. The composition of output, thus, was little changed. The major exports of the north were still wheat and some animal products. Around the growing urban areas, there was increased specialization in dairying and vegetable farming. Dynamic increases in agricultural productivity were yet to come.

After the revolution, the states renounced their claims to the north-western territories, which were turned over to the federal government. (Western land policy under the Federalists was discussed in Chapter 5). States, however, held title to large tracts of unoccupied land within their respective borders. Generally, these were sold in large blocks to speculators, especially in New York. These speculators tried to hold the land until values went up, but the economic difficulties of 1783–1792 bankrupted many of them, including Robert Morris, the "financier" of the revolution. The interior of New York was not completely settled until the opening of the Erie Canal in the 1820s.

## The West

Until 1815, the western frontier consisted of the "old northwest" of Ohio, Indiana, and Illinois (see Figure 6-1). As in the east, settlement took place along the river systems that in the West fed into the Mississippi system. With the opening of New Orleans after 1795, the agricultural output, such as wheat, corn, oats, and animal products, traveled downstream by flat-boat to New Orleans and from there on to the northeast and Europe. As mentioned earlier, upstream trade of manufactured consumer products was transported mostly by horses or mules, and transportation costs were much higher than downstream. This transportation problem was the major obstacle to western development. The beginning of a solution was on the scene by 1815 with the appearance of the early steamboats on the Mississippi. Completion of transportation development, however, occurred during the next time period we shall examine, 1815 to 1860.

# Industry, 1790-1815

Various stages of industrial development existed side by side. First, home manufacture continued at a high level, as rural families still made most of the manufactured items that they used. Second, the **putting-out system of manufactures** was being used primarily in New England, at least in the production of shoes and woolen textiles. A merchant manufacturer would provide raw materials and at times simple tools and machines to workers who worked in their own homes, doing one or more operations. The merchant manufacturer would pick up the finished goods and take them to the worker who would do the next operation, and so on, until the commodity was finished; the merchant would then sell the commodity. The workers, usually farmers and their families, worked on these manufactures in their spare time.

Third, there was the small-scale independent master craftsmen serving a limited market. The major limitation on the size of these small-scale enterprises was the lack of a large market that resulted from inadequate and costly transportation. In 1815, firms hiring 15 or more workers were exceptions.

Finally, larger enterprises, using power-driven machinery—mostly water power, although the steam engine was beginning to be used—were being formed. The period of greatest growth in these larger enterprises was from 1807 to 1815, from the embargo through the War of 1812. The decline in U.S. international trade after 1807 caused capital to shift in part from trade into manufacturing. But even more important in stimulating manufactures in the United States was the complete prohibition or severe restriction placed on imports of manufactured products especially from England by the Embargo of 1807, the Nonintercourse Act of 1809, and finally the War of 1812 itself. Shortages of manufactured imports increased prices, causing resources to shift to manufacturing within the United States.

## Larger-Scale Enterprises

Before 1815, the larger firms, called *mills,* produced iron, flour, lumber, and textiles. Location was determined by a combination of availability of raw material, water power, and centers of demand.

Iron smelting and the production of iron products were widespread because iron deposits were abundant and widespread. Water for power was readily available, and fuel in the form of charcoal was obtained from surrounding forests; iron smelting was located near iron ore deposits. It was not until coal was used as a fuel in the form of coke that the smelting industry became concentrated. Iron was used mostly in small, widely scattered blacksmith shops located near the farmers who used the output of the shops. Because not enough iron was produced to meet the needs of the economy, about one-fourth of the iron used was imported.

Flour mills made notable progress after 1790, and an increased percentage of wheat was exported in the form of flour. Mills catering to the internal market were decentralized, located near the scattered centers of internal demand. Those catering to exports were concentrated around Philadelphia to draw on the wheat produced in fertile Bucks and Lancaster counties of Pennsylvania and around Richmond to draw on the wheat produced in the Virginia-Maryland piedmont. Water power, wheat supplies, and access to the sea were all close by. Larger mills were developed, machinery was improved, and after 1800 steam power was applied. As an example of this developing technology, in 1803 Oliver Evans of Philadelphia built his automated mill, the most advanced flour mill of the day.

Lumber mills were widely scattered, since supplies of the forest were readily available throughout the country and demand was widely scattered. Water, the primary source of power, was widely available. Lumber mills catered primarily to the local market.

In 1787, the first cotton textile mill that used the spinning jenny was built in Beverly, Massachusetts. Samuel Slater introduced the water frame, another spinning machine, in 1790. Francis Cabot Lowell of Boston added the power loom for the weaving of cotton cloth to his spinning mills in Waltham, Massachusetts, in 1813. The Embargo of 1807 and the War of 1812 diverted considerable commercial capital to manufacturing, especially to cotton textiles. By 1809, over 5000 people were employed in cotton mills centered mostly in New England.

From 1790 to 1815 was a period of stirrings and beginnings rather than one of pervasive changes. Many of the manufacturing beginnings, especially in textiles, were wiped out by imports of British-manufactured products at the end of the War of 1812. But the beginnings had been made. Experience had been gained in handling the many problems of production on a larger scale. Managers had learned how to handle a larger labor force, new technology, need for larger sources of supply, and the need to sell the larger output. The beginnings had been made in preparation for more rapid growth after 1815.

## Banking and Finance, 1790-1815

From 1781 to 1798, 22 banks were established. These were conservative and dealt mainly with mercantile activities involved in foreign trade. Of these banks, 12 were located in New England. From 1798 to 1816, 65 more banks were established. Although these banks were more conservative than those of the post-Jackson period after 1832, they were less conservative than those of the earlier period. More liberal state laws were enacted in regard to bank notes and specie (gold and silver) reserves and thus increased the currency in circulation. The kinds of loans increased in variety.

The First Bank of the United States could serve as a regulator of and a check on the state banks in regard to their issue of currency. The federal government would deposit all the state bank notes into the First Bank of the United States, which in turn could present them to the banks for specie payment. Through this practice, the Bank of the United States restrained the issuance of currency by merchant banking. However, one should not overestimate this practice and its effects on the supply of money. It was not used consistently, and the Bank of the United States did not interfere with its own profit-seeking activities to ensure currency restraint in the banking system. The Jeffersonian Republicans refused to recharter the First Bank of the United States in 1810.

Under the impact of expanding trade after 1792, insurance companies developed. The first incorporated in Philadelphia in 1794, and by 1800, 33 active companies provided sources of investment funds. The activities of the banks and insurance companies were primarily in commerce. Only the barest beginning of a noncommercial capital market had been laid by 1815.

# Review of Economic Concepts: A Simple Model of Export-Led Development

Most economies in the early phase of economic development are tied to foreign trade and its vagaries. To provide a framework for understanding the developmental forces at work in the American economy during the 25 years from 1790 to 1815, we shall build a simple model that shows how foreign trade *may* become a positive influence on that course of development.

Let us make the following assumptions about the economy in question:

1. Two separable economies exist. One is a noncash economy which is generally agricultural and has a low **capital-labor ratio.** The other is a cash economy with a relatively high capital-labor ratio.
2. Because of the disparity in the capital-labor ratios and because larger market sizes permit greater specialization and division of labor and capital, productivity is higher in the cash economy than in the noncash economy and, for the same reasons, higher in the export activities than in the domestic market activities of the cash economy.
3. A significant proportion of the resources of the cash economy is employed in the foreign trade sector to produce commodities and services connected with exports and imports.

Suppose that our hypothetical economy is initially in equilibrium, allocating its resources according to comparative advantage uses given the tastes and preferences of its citizens. Let us also suppose that the terms of trade are, in some sense, "neutral," equal to 100, which means that export prices (an index) are equal to import prices (an index). We can see this initial relationship in Figure 6-2. With demand for imports $D_0$ and supply of imports $S_0$, import prices are $P_i$. It is apparent that (arbitrarily) $P_e = P_i$ or terms of trade are equal to 100.

Now we want to isolate the effects of changes in the nation's export markets. To do so, we hold demand and supply constant in its import markets. Suppose that initially there is an increase in the demand for that nation's exports of both commodities and services. Perhaps there is an industry in another country that requires more of the export commodity as an input or that the invisible items of the nation's trade (its financial services, its merchant fleet services, and the like) are more in demand. If we look at Figure 6-2(a), we see that an increase in export demand to $D_1$ will bid up export prices to $P_e'$. The terms of trade would become $P_e' \div P_i$ which *is greater than* $P_e \div P_i$, or greater than 100. Terms of trade have moved "in favor" of the exporting nation. In other words, it takes a smaller quantity of its exports or real resources to buy a particular amount of imports.

Put in another way, the nation's export earnings $(P_e' \times Q_e')$ have risen (are greater than $P_e \times Q_e$). The additional foreign exchange can be used to import not only consumer goods but also capital, technology, and the like. Or, the domestic resource that would have been used to produce the exports necessary to finance a given level of imports can, instead, be

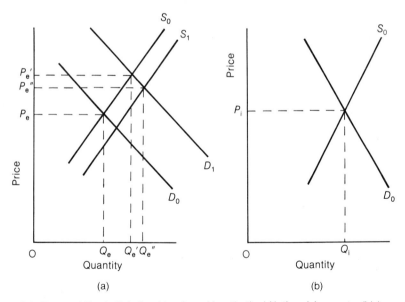

Figure 6-2. Terms of Trade Relationships for a Hypothetical Nation: (a) exports, (b) imports.

employed to produce commodities and services for the domestic market.

Since export prices have risen, resource allocation may be changed in two ways. The opportunity cost of using resources (including one's own labor time) in the noncash economy is raised; as a result, resources are bid into the cash economy, where with more capital and a larger market size, productivity is greater. Also, since prices of exports have risen, resources within the cash economy are bid into export industries where, with higher capital-labor ratios and larger market sizes, greater specialization ensues and productivity increases. As productivity rises, output and income per capita rise; development is the result.

To this point, we have seen how a nation may benefit from increases in demand for its exports. Of course, the supply side of its export market may change as well. Let's suppose there is some cost-reducing technological innovation in a principal export industry and that this technology, in turn, results in an increase in the supply of exports. We see this effect in Figure 6-2(a). Export supply increases from $S_0$ to $S_1$. As a result, export prices fall from $P_e'$ (the price resulting from the demand increase). If supply continues to increase, it will tend back toward $P_e$ if, at that earlier price, resources were being paid for according to their opportunity cost.

What do the price-quantity relationships in Figure 6-2(a) mean to our hypothetical country? They represent its foreign exchange earnings, its command over foreign goods and services. Thus, as the combination of demand and supply changes cause $P \times Q$ to grow larger, the nation can import more, not only of consumer goods but also of financial and physical capital, technological improvements, labor skills in short supply, or whatever is required to expand its leading industries.

Throughout this discussion, we have assumed supply and demand in Figure 6-2(b), our nation's import market, to be constant. This assumption was for convenience, not description. Ultimately, the hypothetical country enjoying the benefits of supply-demand changes in its export market will, and indeed *must*, import more. Almost all countries in an early phase of economic development require imports that are not readily supplied by domestic industry. It must import more because its imports give foreigners claim to its currency, claims that they must have in order to buy exports of the country represented in Figure 6-2.

---

# Glossary

**Capital-labor ratio**   The number of dollars of capital (invested in machines, buildings, and so on) used per unit of labor.

**Complementary industries**   Industries that serve a number of different industries, although they may have been created to service only one.

**Embargo of December 1807**   Congress gave President Jefferson the power to forbid the import or export of goods from and to Britain and France in retaliation for their seizure of U.S. commercial vessels from 1792 to 1807.

**Nonintercourse Act of 1809**   Act of Congress that would allow trade with Britain or France if they stopped seizure of U.S. ships. In 1809, trade was allowed to resume with France.

**Putting-out system of manufactures**   Home industries using materials supplied by merchant manufacturers. The merchant would then pick up these finished or semifinished products from the workers' homes and pay them.

**Reexports**   Foreign imports that are exported again without any change in form.

**Residentiary industries**   Industries that provide goods and services needed by residents of a particular area.

**Subsidiary industries**   Industries needed to allow another industry to function. In the leading sector of 1792–1815, foreign trade, shipbuilding and shipfitting were subsidiary.

# Questions

1. How does an increase in exports affect prices and economic development?
2. Why was it predictable that development would be low in 1790? Was growth likely to occur in the internal market? The external market? Why?
3. How does growth in markets stimulate economic growth?
4. What caused the economy to change after 1792? How did expansion in exports, imports, and shipping affect economic development?
5. Describe the agricultural economy of 1815.
6. Was manufacturing important to the American economy between 1790 and 1815? Why?
7. Could the American economy have grown without the Napoleonic Wars? Explain your answer.

# Suggested Readings

1. Bruchey, Stuart. *The Roots of American Economic Growth, 1607–1861.* New York: Harper & Row, 1965.
2. Clark, V. S. *History of Manufactures in the United States.* 3 vols. New York: McGraw-Hill, 1929.
3. Nettels, Curtis P. *The Emergence of a National Economy, 1775–1815.* New York: Harper & Row, 1962.
4. North, Douglass C. *The Economic Growth of the United States 1790–1860.* New York: Norton, 1966. Pp. 1–60.
5. North, Douglass C. "The United States Balance of Payments, 1790–1860." *Trends in the American Economy in the Nineteenth Century.* Studies in Income and Wealth of the National Bureau of Economic Research, Vol. 24. Princeton, N.J.: Princeton University Press, 1960.

# Chapter 7

---

# The Transportation Revolution and Regional Integration

As we have seen in earlier chapters, major barriers existed to the growth of the internal market system first of the colonies and then of the independent American states. Among the most important of such obstacles was the high cost of overland movement of goods and resources over long distances. In the colonial period, consequently, growth and development were tied to coastal trade and, more importantly, to overseas trade. In the early years of independence (1783–1815), this pattern continued.

Many remarkable changes occurred in the American economy between 1815 and 1860. As we shall see, there are disagreements among scholars about the cause-and-effect relationships involved in these changes. Included in these disagreements are the quantitative and qualitative effects of a changing transportation system on the rapid development pace of the nation, especially the pace from 1840 to 1860. Those who have studied the era agree, however, that a significant set of such effects took place. It is this subject, including those disagreements, that we want to examine in this chapter.

## A Simple Model of Transportation Costs and Integration

How are transportation costs related to market size, specialization and division of resources, and **economic integration**? Are product and resource markets tied together in such a way that resources are allocated to their most efficient uses? To answer these questions fully, we need first to repeat some assumptions about market behavior. First, we have assumed that people make market (supply-demand) decisions because of the anticipation that those decisions are in their own self-interest and, therefore, that market exchanges reflect anticipated mutual advantages to buyers and sellers. Second, suppliers seek their advantage through maximizing profit, the difference between total revenue and total cost (where cost includes an opportunity cost payment to capital and entrepreneurship). Transportation cost is, of course, a part of total cost—often an important part. The higher is transportation cost, the shorter is the distance it is profitable to ship goods (or to move resources).

In Figure 7-1, three cities are represented: New York, Albany, and Chicago. The arrows connecting them represent the transportation systems existing between them at some particular time, and the dollar figures ($6, $2) above these arrows, the cost per ton-mile of moving goods between the cities. Below the arrows are numbers ( − $3, $1) that represent the unit profit of shipping between the cities. With the existing mode(s) of transportation (perhaps barges or flat bottom river boats), it is profitable to ship between New York and Albany ($1). As a consequence, both cities are within the same market system, and whatever economies of specialization exist in that market are available to both. Note, however, that between Albany and Chicago transportation costs ($6) are higher, and unit profit is negative ( − $3). As a result, those two cities are not part of the same market system. Indeed, unless Chicago is profitably tied by existing transportation means to other cities (or market areas), it is outside the regional or national market system and is denied whatever economies of specialization are available within that system.

Figure 7-1. Hypothetical Effects of Transportation Costs on Regional Integration.

$6                        $2

Chicago ⟷ Albany ⟷ New York

( − $3)                    ($1)

The general, if simple, principle that we are setting forth here is the following: The lower transportation costs are, the greater is the distance over which trade may profitably take place. As this distance increases, resources are bid into market production, market sizes increase, and economies of specialization increase.

## Cost Externalities, Profits, and Rents

As a new transportation system is introduced or an old system extended or improved, the reduced transportation costs available to firms using that transportation system may become **cost externalities.** Such externalities

The Erie Canal, 1825. (Photo no. 119-M-1A-12 in the National Archives)

are reduced average unit costs to firms that result from actions taken out-side of those firms. Clearly, the building of a turnpike, canal, or railroad tends to have such effects.

As cost externalities accrue to firms and industries, the profit margin shifts; that is, previously marginal firms with lowered costs now become profitable firms. Of course, over long periods of time, all firms must cover the opportunity costs of using resources, must pay those resources at least what they can earn in alternative uses, in order to bid successfully for their use. One such cost is the opportunity cost of **entrepreneurship:** the organiz-ing skill and abilities necessary to combine other resources into produc-ing activities. This payment, the opportunity cost of entrepreneurship, is called **normal profit.**

Lower costs of production and distribution, along with enlarged markets that are associated with improved transportation systems tend, however, to produce **economic profits** or **economic rents:** payments to en-trepreneurship in excess of what it can earn in alternative uses. Whether such economic profits or rents can be maintained depends primarily on whether the industries in which they exist exhibit free entry. At any rate, to know the total profitability or return on investment in different trans-portation systems, we must include not only the normal and economic profit of the transportation enterprises themselves but also the profits that accrue to other enterprises as a result of cost externalities.

# Early Land Transportation

There is no single input or factor whose provision is a sufficient condition for economic development to occur. Among those generally considered necessary, however, are (a) a transportation system that permits tying together of markets and (b) the efficiencies made possible by up-to-date technology and specialization in the uses of resources.

Early forms of overland transportation were rather primitive and high in cost. Throughout its colonial period and up to approximately 1815, the American cash economy was largely confined to the coastal areas, primarily because coastal shipping was much less expensive than land shipping. According to George Taylor,[19] it was cheaper to ship grain 300 miles from Northhampton to Boston by water than to ship it 100 miles by road between those two points. Indeed, it cost twice as much to transport grain the first 36 miles by road as to move it 250 miles by deep-water shipment.

References to the transportation "revolution" are misleading if the word *revolution* is associated with "coup d'etat." In this chapter, we are examining changes in transportation technology that evolved over at least half a century. The changes occurred in an evolutionary way but combined to produce revolutionary effects.

## Roads and Turnpikes

Nothing illustrates better the evolutionary nature of changes in transportation technology than the evolving technology of road building. Throughout the colonial period, even up to the early 1790s, roads were poorly constructed and expensive to maintain. Describing the short trip from Baltimore to Washington, a traveler reported in 1795 that "the roads are so exceedingly bad that a carriage will sometimes sink so deeply as to defy the utmost exertion of the strongest horse to draw it forwards. . . . Bridges built across are equally perilous, being formed of a few loose boards that totter while a carriage passes over them."

Road-building technology began to progress in the 1790s, when private companies began building turnpikes. Turnpikes were usually built with rock foundations and were better graded than earlier roads. Because of these improvements and also because permanent bridges were built along them, the turnpikes were used throughout the year. These improvements not only made possible heavier horse-drawn loads and faster speeds but also assured year-round supplies of lower-cost commodities and services between the markets thus connected. Like other transportation facilities, the turnpikes had a very high ratio of fixed to variable costs; as the seasonal variations on the use of improved roads were reduced, the costs of their operation were reduced. Not surprisingly, as costs fell and

An early turnpike, c. 1830. (Photo no. 30-N-39-14 in the National Archives)

demand increased with larger, more continuous markets, the most efficient turnpikes were profitable. The Lancaster-Philadelphia Turnpike, completed in 1794, was such a success that Pennsylvania alone chartered 86 turnpike companies during the next 30 years. Few, however, were as well built as the Lancaster turnpike, and few connected such large commodity and consumer goods markets. One exception was the National Pike, or Cumberland Road, built by the federal government between 1811 and 1838 to connect Maryland and Illinois. East-west travel time and cost were greatly reduced.

A final set of improvements in antebellum road-building technology came along in the 1830s. These were the plank roads called "farmer's railroads" because they were widely used in areas not reached by rail. Constructed of heavy planks tied together by parallel stringers, they permitted horses to pull heavier loads at faster speeds than were possible on the macadamized turnpikes. Although cheaper to construct than first-rate turnpikes ($1200 to $1500 per mile versus $5000 to $7000 per mile), they were costly to maintain. As with other roads, building them was a capital-intensive activity.

Because of the high price of capital and its high opportunity costs (in terms of returns in agriculture and manufacturing), no true "national system" of roads had been built either by private enterprise or by government even as late as the 1850s. Indeed, further major improvements in American roads were to wait until the twentieth century, when automobiles and trucks created demand and the relative price of capital declined.

A summary point that deserves emphasis is that as early as 1820 the United States had a system of relatively good roads that connected its major cities for north-south travel. That system, together with some east-west roads, continued to evolve in the succeeding three decades but did not lead to significant regional integration or to the building of a national system of integrated internal markets. Again, the main reason quite simply was the relatively high unit cost of shipping goods over those roads with horse-drawn vehicles, compared with the unit costs of deep-water (coastal and foreign) shipment.

## Steamboats

Early in the nineteenth century, two new transportation systems began to evolve. Both were to have a significant, although unequal, impact on lowering internal transportation costs and integrating the market systems of the United States.

The first commercial application of the steam engine to transportation occurred in 1807 when Robert Fulton's steamboat went from New York to Albany. As Eric Haites and James Mak[5, 6] have shown, steamboat traffic grew very rapidly, particularly on western rivers such as the Ohio and Mississippi. This growth can be seen in Table 7-1. As you can see, the growth of steamboating continued up to the time of the Civil War. Although it declined relative to the railroads in the 1850s, it remained a thriving, growing industry throughout the antebellum period.

Table 7-1. Tonnage of Steamboats on the Western Rivers of the United States, 1814–1860.

| Years | Net New Construction[a] | Average Total Tonnage in Operation |
|---|---|---|
| 1814–1816 | 629 | 1,490 |
| 1824–1826 | 1,599 | 13,429 |
| 1834–1836 | 6,845 | 49,504 |
| 1844–1846 | 8,809 | 97,603 |
| 1854–1856 | 6,296 | 176,617 |
| 1858–1860 | − 1,516 | 194,738 |

[a]Per year, in tons; net represents new construction less depreciation.
*Source:* Eric Haites and James Mak, "The Decline of Steamboating on the Antebellum Western Rivers: New Evidence and an Alternatitive Hypothesis," *Explorations in Economic History* (Fall 1973).

What were the great cost advantages of the steamboats? Speed was one: The time to travel from New York to Albany was cut from about three days to about eight hours. Steamboats, as a result, permitted firms to ship over long distances and function with less working capital. In addition, steamboats could navigate upstream as well as downstream; upstream travel was uneconomical for the old flatboats.

Mak and Walton have shown that productivity grew rapidly in the steamboat industry. Although most of the productivity increase occurred before 1850, it averaged almost 5% a year between 1815 and 1850. Mak and Walton[8] believe that this productivity increase was greater than that of any other form of transportation during any 35-year period of the nineteenth century. Rapid productivity growth, together with substantial competitiveness in the steamboat industry, caused steamboat freight rates to fall greatly. Haites and Mak show, for instance, that in the important trans-Mississippi traffic between Louisville and New Orleans, the per ton rate fell from $20 between 1810 and 1819 to $6 in 1849.

Productivity growth in steamboating was due primarily to improvements in steamboat construction and to greater year-round utilization of the boats. Competitiveness was enhanced through constitutional interpretation. In 1824, in *Gibbons v. Ogden,* the Supreme Court ruled that states could not grant monopoly rights to navigation of their waterways. As a result, interstate commerce, including that by steamboats, became easier to enter as it fell under the exclusive jurisdiction of the federal government. As we shall see in subsequent chapters, federal control over interstate commerce has led to reduced competitiveness in some instances; in steamboating, however, there is no doubt that it enhanced competitiveness. Lower rates, greater traffic, and increasing regional integration were the results. It is startling to remember that in 1803 Thomas Jefferson said it would be a thousand years before the area east of the Mississippi could be fully settled. A combination of river steamboats, barge canal traffic, and trans-Appalachian railroad construction reduced that period dramatically, as we shall see.

## Canal Building

Only five years after Fulton's first steamboat trip, a new mode of shipping goods over long distances began evolving. Canals, man-made waterways, frequently connecting natural bodies of water and employing a series of locks to adjust for differences in level, became popular and were constructed in three waves between 1812 and 1860 (see Figure 7-2). Unlike turnpikes and steamboats, which were the subject of large private investments, the canals were heavily subsidized by state and local governments and to a much smaller extent by the federal government. Carter Goodrich[4] has estimated that government undertook about 70% of total

Figure 7-2. Principal Canals of the Ante Bellum Period, 1800–1860.

Source: Carter Goodrich, ed., Canals and American Economic Development (New York: Columbia University Press, 1961).

canal expenditures between 1815 and 1860. Private investment was limited, primarily because canals were relatively expensive projects that proposed to push into sparsely settled areas. (The Erie Canal alone represented an investment of more than $10 million.)

Another reason for public participation in canal building was that potential benefits were reaped by others besides the canal builders. In other words, cost externalities were significant. As an example, the opening of the very successful Erie Canal reduced freight rates from 20 cents to 2 cents per ton-mile. The 134-mile Erie Canal connected Albany on the Hudson River with Buffalo on the Great Lakes. Because of the waterway that now extended from New York to Cleveland and Toledo, costs were reduced dramatically for firms from the eastern seaboard to the old northwest.

In terms of our original model, the most successful canals generated economic profits or rents, revenues in excess of costs, though, reducing costs and creating cost externalities. Thus, even if a canal was not privately profitable (and, according to Roger Ransom, many were not)[14, 15, 16] it might well have been socially beneficial and properly the object of public subsidy.

Ransom, the most prolific writer on canals, has estimated the externalities associated with the canal system through estimating economic rents. A wheat farmer in eastern Ohio, for example, earns a rent (economic profit) of $2 a ton because he can ship over the Erie Canal to eastern markets. A farmer farther away—in Indiana, for example—has higher costs and presumably will not transport his wheat to market unless he can cover all his costs. The farmer will not use the canal if the resulting costs cannot be covered out of revenue. If $2 per ton is maximum rent earned in this activity, then no farmer will ship his goods over the canal who cannot at least cover costs. All who can and who can earn some of the $2 per ton rent will engage in market exchange; others, who cannot, will use their resources some other way, including not shipping to market at all but engaging in subsistence agriculture instead.

Ransom's estimates, based on the Ohio and Erie Canal and others, indicate that of the $102 million expended on canals up to 1860, only $31 million was invested successfully in terms of the alternative uses of those resources. Indeed, he believes that other forms of capital investment might have been wiser and that "The role of the canals in contributing toward the economic growth of the United States is far from obvious." Competition from the railroads was a chief cause of declining canal profits during the 1840s and 1850s. According to Ransom, the rate of return on investment in the very successful Ohio and Erie Canal fell from 15.4% per annum in 1851 to 2.7% between 1854 and 1856. Because of a high ratio of total fixed costs to total variable costs, the canals faced sharply higher average fixed and average total costs as they produced for smaller markets.

A debate that continues is whether the canal system encouraged a more specialized use of resources by encouraging interregional trade. Albert Niemi[10] concludes that the canals stimulated regional diversification—production of a wide range of goods—rather than specialization or production of a smaller range of goods. Ransom draws a contrary conclusion, arguing that in both East and West specialization took the form of developing industries specialized to the comparative advantage uses of resources. The growth of manufacturing along and near canals indicates to Ransom that the agricultural goods moving over the canals were being transformed into semimanufactured and manufactured goods according to comparative advantage. On balance, we believe that the comparative advantage specialization argument is the more reasonable one.

In summary, the canals appear to have made a significant but mixed contribution to our economic development and to the integration of this country's economic regions. Some, such as the Erie and Ohio, were very successful. Others, such as the Philadelphia and Pittsburgh, were much less successful. What is clear is that by the 1850s the canal era was ending, although a few canals continued to operate profitably. It was the building of railroads in the 1840s and 1850s that virtually brought the canal era to a close.

## Railroads

Perhaps no change in transportation technology has occasioned so much research, debate, or disagreement as the railroads. Let us begin with some of the undisputed facts about the railroads before turning to more troublesome issues.

Rail transportation, of course, depended on another application of the steam engine. In 1830, the Baltimore and Ohio opened for business. As the data in Table 7-2 indicate, the railway system grew rapidly prior to 1860.

Table 7-2. Railway Mileage, 1830–1860.

| Years | Net Additions of Track in Miles | Total Miles of Track at End of Period |
|---|---|---|
| 1830–1839 | 2,302 | 2,302 |
| 1840–1849 | 5,063 | 7,365 |
| 1850–1859 | 21,424 | 28,789 |

Source: U.S. Bureau of the Census, *Historical Statistics, Colonial Times to 1957* (Washington, D.C.: U.S. Government Printing Office, 1960).

During the 1840s and 1850s, the system was extended across the Appalachian Mountains and then into the present-day Midwest. By 1860, the rails had pushed west to St. Joseph, Missouri, and south to New Orleans (Figure 7-3). Throughout the period, railroad technology improved. Replacing iron-capped wooden rails, the iron rails of the 1840s permitted faster, cheaper movement. Further improvements in boiler locomotive and freight car construction, together with a movement toward uniform-gauge rails, also lowered transportation costs. We should remember, however, that rail transportation was not cheap. A hundred-mile railway trip cost a month's wages for a typical American in the 1830s and two to three weeks' wages in the 1850s. Nonetheless, over the period from 1815 to 1860, railways were becoming increasingly price competitive with canals and turnpikes, as we see in Table 7-3.

Table 7-3. Average Freight Rate, Different Transportation Forms, 1816, 1853, 1860.

| Transport Form | 1816 (dollars)[a] | 1853 (dollars)[a] | 1860 (dollars)[a] |
|---|---|---|---|
| Turnpikes | 30.00 | 15.00 | 15.00 |
| Missouri-Ohio River, upstream | 5.80 | — | 0.37 |
| Erie Canal | — | 1.10 | 0.99 |
| Pennsylvania, Main Line Canal | — | 2.40 | — |
| New York Central Railroad | — | 3.40 | 2.06 |
| Pennsylvania Railroad | — | 3.50 | 1.96 |
| Erie Railroad | — | 2.40 | 1.84 |
| Western Lakes, short voyage | — | 0.10 | — |

[a]Dollars or cents per ton-mile.
*Source:* George Rogers Taylor, *The Transportation Revolution, 1815–1860* (New York: Holt, Rinehart and Winston, 1966).

Although railway freight rates came down in the 1850s, even in 1860, canal shipment ($.99 on the Erie Canal) was less expensive per mile than rail shipment ($1.84 on the Erie Railroad). The data also illustrate the great disparity between either canal or rail shipment and shipping goods over the turnpikes ($15.00, even in 1860). Considering the cost disadvantage of railroads in shipping, why did their demand grow so rapidly? The railroads quickly became the major transportation source for moving goods and people because speed and year-round operation meant lowered annual costs to businesses and individuals in spite of the *apparently* high (unit) costs. Robert Fogel[3] points out the major reason. Although the costs of rail transport were reflected in direct payments to railway carriers, that was not true in the case of water carriers. The important costs not covered

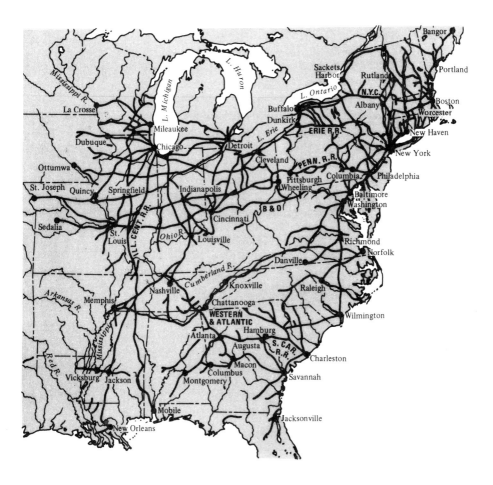

Figure 7-3. Railroads in 1860.

*Source:* George Rogers Taylor, *The Transportation Revolution, 1815–1860.* Copyright 1951 by George Rogers Taylor. Reprinted by permission of George Rogers Taylor.

in the latter industry were cargo losses in transit, transhipment costs, wagon haulage costs from water points to secondary markets not on waterways, capital costs not reflected in water rates, costs caused by the time lost in using a (relatively) slow means of transportation, and the costs of not being able to use the waterways for five months out the year. When these are included, Fogel concludes that the costs of interregional shipments by rail were lower than those by water shipment. In other words, there was a "social savings" attached to the railroads. In addition, productivity grew very rapidly in railroads. Albert Fishlow[1] has shown that productivity throughout a dynamic phase of the railroads (1839–1910) grew almost three times as rapidly as productivity for the economy as a whole. In turn, this growth permitted freight and passenger fares to fall.

## Railroads and American Economic Development

Now let us turn to the most controversial arguments surrounding the railroads. What did they contribute to the economic development of the United States, and were they, in fact, indispensable to its pace of development?

Almost no student of American history has sought to dismiss the railroads or to deny their importance. In terms of what may be called the "modern" position on the railroads, there is general agreement that they played a very important role in our history. Leland Jenks[7] strongly argued that position, within the view that economic development occurs fundamentally as the result of **innovation,** the introduction of new products and processes into an economy. Such innovation is the work of entrepreneur-innovators. Jenks says the railroads must be viewed in three phases: as ideas, as construction enterprises, and, finally, as sellers of transportation services. Jenks argues from the economic development framework of Joseph Schumpeter that productivity increasing innovations cause economic development. Such innovations occur irregularly or in swarms, and the railroads are a classic example, according to Jenks. As an idea, railroads created economic activity through land speculation, urban relocation, and other activities along their right-of-ways. As construction enterprises, railroads also created direct demand for factors of production, labor, land, and capital. Finally, railroads reduced shipping costs, thereby creating external economies and encouraging the growth of other industries.

Since 1960, arguments have arisen that railroads were the indispensable leading sector in this country's economic development. Walt Rostow[17] advanced the view that the railroads moved the United States from its "preconditions for growth" into its "takeoff" stage of development. Since the **takeoff** in Rostow's stage theory of development, is that great "watershed" or turning point in which development becomes the normal condition for a society, and since Rostow says the railroads between 1843 and 1860 were responsible in the "most direct possible way" for the takeoff, his argument for the indispensability of railroads seems clear.

Important studies of the railroads were made in the 1960s by Albert Fishlow[1] and Robert Fogel.[2] As part of his study, Fogel undertook an empirical test of Rostow's takeoff hypothesis. To estimate the effects of the railroads on the "decisive structural change" that Rostow believes took place in the United States between 1840 and 1860, Fogel examined data on changes in the sectoral composition of output. To estimate the "most direct possible" effects of railroad construction during that period, Fogel calculated the direct demand of the railroads for the output of (supposed) major supplying industries, such as iron, coal, and transportation equipment. Fogel concluded that the evidence regarding decisive structural change in the 1840s and 1850s was inconclusive. He believes that if pre-1840 data were available they would show that there was no abrupt increase in the rate of change in sectoral output after 1840. With respect to the direct demand effects, Fogel concludes that "In the absence of the railroads, demand for manufactured commodities would still have resulted in a 230% rise in the output of manufacturing over the years from 1840 to 1859—as opposed to an increase of 240% with the railroads." Fogel, thus, rejects the Rostow argument that ties the American industrial revolution to a 20-year period of railroad building, or to any single industry in any period. Perhaps Fogel has contributed the "bottom line" to the takeoff debate and its bearing on the American industrial revolution in saying, "One should not, however, require a revolution to have the swiftness of a coup d'etat. . . . One need not arbitrarily abstract 18 years out of a continuum to uphold the use of a venerable term."

Is it useful and valid to argue that industrialization requires a leading sector, as Rostow believes and Fogel doubts? If so, were the railroads the leading sector in the American case? The answers remain in doubt. What has become generally apparent is that the impact of the railroads on U.S. economic development must be studied over a time period longer than two decades. Fogel and others have done much work in that direction. In Chapter 12, we shall look at their efforts to measure long-term effects, including those in the post-Civil War era.

# Communications Improvements

In our model, we dealt with the result of improved transportation in lowering **transactions costs,** expanding the market, creating external economies, and promoting development. In the pre-Civil War era, parallel improvements in an evolving technology of communication were reducing **information costs,** the costs to buyers and sellers of obtaining the price and technical information necessary to make rational choices. Clearly, lowering the average cost of securing the price and other information needed to make effective market decisions increases the supply of goods and thereby the size of markets. Thus, lowering information costs also leads to market integration.

Perhaps the most important advance in communications technology in the United States prior to 1860 was the telegraph. Samuel F. B. Morse obtained a grant from Congress in 1843 to establish a line between Baltimore and Washington. The practicality of the telegraph was so obvious by 1860 that 50,000 miles of telegraph lines connected every major city in the country. By 1861, even the West Coast and San Francisco were included. The swiftness and reliability of this communication system greatly reduced the cost of decision-making, especially by providing information about market conditions in different parts of the country. Thus, the tandem improvement of information flows and reduction of transportation time and cost reinforced each other in tying together or integrating markets.

Other improvements in communication at least deserve mention. The U.S. postal system was greatly expanded, its services improved, and the cost of obtaining information through it reduced over the period from 1816 to 1860. Indeed, between 1791 and 1859, the number of post offices increased from 89 to 27,977, and service miles went from about 800,000 to about 86 million. In 1816, it cost 50 cents to send a two-sheet letter 400 miles. In 1850, a flat rate of 3 cents for all letters was introduced. The cost externalities involved in this communication alone (apart from other social benefits) probably justified large public subsidies.

Finally, in the pre-Civil War era, there was a huge increase in newspaper circulation and readership after the development of the cylinder press in 1846 permitted the mass production of inexpensive newspapers. By 1860, there were 10 million copies of daily, weekly, biweekly, and monthly newspapers in circulation in a nation with a population of about 31.5 million.

## Summing Up

The period from 1800 to 1860 saw dramatic, although fairly continual changes and improvements in transportation and communications technology. No single change in that technology, not even the railroad, appears to be significant enough to explain the rapid pace of development in the United States over that period. Taken together, however, they made available very great reductions in transactions and information costs for internal trade and created very large external cost economies to firms. Thus, these changes undoubtedly enhanced the integration of the nation's domestic market system and reduced its dependence on foreign trade as the major source of impetus for its economic development.

# Glossary

**Cost externalities**   Reductions in the average costs of a firm that result from actions taken outside of the firm.

**Economic integration**   The tying together of product and resource markets in such a way that resources are allocated to their most efficient uses.

**Economic profit (rent)**   A payment to a factor of production greater than that necessary to bid for its use or greater than its opportunity costs.

**Economic rent**   See **Economic profit.**

**Entrepreneurship**   The function of organizing resources in such a way that economic production occurs.

**Information costs**   The costs to buyers and sellers of obtaining the price and technical information necessary to make rational choices.

**Innovation**   The introduction of new products and processes into an economy.

**Normal profit**   A payment to entrepreneurship equal to its opportunity costs.

**Takeoff**   In the economic development theory of Walt Rostow, the stage in which economic development becomes the normal and ongoing condition of society.

# Questions

1. In general, why were transportation-related transactions costs and communications-related information costs such significant barriers to developing an integrated internal market system in the United States in 1800?
2. How are reductions in transportation costs related to increasing market sizes and market integration?
3. Trace the evolution of road and turnpike technology over the period from 1800 to 1860. Explain why, even at the end of that period, roads and turnpikes did not integrate the regional markets of the United States.
4. What were the major contributions of the steamboats to integrating internal markets and commerce in the United States?
5. What does *Gibbons* v. *Ogden* illustrate about the relation between the legal structure and constraints on economic development?
6. Why was the canal building era one of widely mixed successes and failures? In what sense and in what ways did the canals generate cost externalities?

7. Does it seem to you that using the concept of economic rent is an appropriate way to assess the externalities of a transportation system? Why?
8. Do you think the canals encouraged regional specialization or diversification? Why?
9. Trace the evolution of railway technology over the period from 1830 to 1860. What were the effects of these changes on transportation costs in the United States?
10. What is Rostow's argument about the relation between railway building and the American takeoff? What is Fogel's conclusion about the validity of the Rostow argument?
11. What were major communications improvements between 1800 and 1860? What were their effects on information costs and economic integration?

# Suggested Readings

1. Fishlow, Albert. *American Railroads and the Transformation of the Antebellum Economy.* Cambridge, Mass.: Harvard University Press, 1965.
2. Fogel, Robert W. "Railroads and the 'Take-off' Thesis: The American Case." In *Railroads and American Economic Growth: Essays in Econometric History.* Baltimore: Johns Hopkins University Press, 1964.
3. Fogel, Robert W. "Railroads and American Economic Growth." In *The Reinterpretation of American Economic History,* Robert W. Fogel and Stanley L. Engerman, eds. New York: Harper & Row, 1971.
4. Goodrich, Carter, ed. *Canals and American Economic Development.* New York: Columbia University Press, 1961.
5. Haites, Erik F., and Mak, James. "Ohio and Mississippi River Transportation, 1800–1860." *Explorations in Economic History* (Winter 1970–1971).
6. Haites, Erik F., and Mak, James. "The Decline of Steamboating on the Antebellum Western Rivers: Some New Evidence and an Alternative Hypothesis. *Explorations in Economic History* (Fall 1973).
7. Jenks, Leland. "Railroads as an Economic Force in American Development." *Journal of Economic History,* 4 (March 1944).
8. Mak, James, and Walton, Gary. "Steamboats and the Great Productivity Surge in River Transportation." *Journal of Economic History, 32* (September 1972).
9. McClelland, Peter. "Railroads, American Growth and the New Economic History: A Critique." *Journal of Economic History, 28* (March 1968).

10. Nerlove, Marc. "Railroads and American Economic Growth." *Journal of Economic History, 26* (March 1966).

11. Niemi, Albert W., Jr. "A Further Look at Interregional Canals and Economic Specialization, 1820–1840." *Explorations in Economic History* (Summer 1970).

12. North, Douglass C. *The Economic Growth of the United States, 1790–1860.* New York: Norton, 1966. Chap. 9.

13. Parker, William N. "From Northwest to Midwest: Social Bases of a Regional History." In *Essays in Nineteenth-Century Economic History,* ed. D. C. Klingaman and R. K. Vedder. Athens: Ohio University Press, 1975.

14. Ransom, Roger. "Canals and Development: A Discussion of the Issues." *American Economic Review* (May 1964).

15. Ransom, Roger. "Social Returns from Public Transport Investment: A Case Study of the Ohio Canal." *Journal of Political Economy* (September-October 1976).

16. Ransom, Roger. "Public Canal Investment and the Opening of the Old Northwest." In *Essays in Nineteenth-Century Economic History,* ed. D. C. Klingaman and R. K. Vedders. Athens: Ohio University Press, 1975.

17. Rostow, Walt W. *The Stages of Economic Growth.* 2d ed. Cambridge, England: Cambridge University Press, 1971.

18. Segal, Harvey. "Cycles of Canal Construction." In *Canals and American Economic Development,* ed. Carter Goodrich. New York: Columbia University Press, 1961.

19. Taylor, George Rogers. *The Transportation Revolution, 1815–1860.* New York: Holt, Rinehart and Winston, 1966.

# Chapter 8

---

# Regional Integration and Specialization to 1860

In Chapter 7, we examined the process through which transportation changes and the extension of low-cost transportation systems drew more and more of the United States into a single market system. That process undoubtedly meant that an increasing part of the nation's resources, including its labor force, was involved in the cash economy. In turn, more and more people were receiving cash incomes and spending those incomes on goods and services produced for the market. The slave population of the South remained an important exception to this pattern of increasing monetization.

In this chapter, we are going to explore the particular and, in many respects, very specialized patterns of development that emerged in each of the three great regions of the United States between 1815 and 1860. The patterns that emerged in the Northeast, the South, and the West were ones of considerable specialization and involved increasing ties to a national as well as an international system of markets. As we shall see, the regional specialization that evolved was far from complete. Nonetheless, two of the broadest economic themes of the era are production for a *national system* of markets and increasing specialization within that pattern of production.

## Foreign and Domestic Trade

This model involves trade among the three geographic regions of the United States. It does not slight or neglect trade between the United States and other nations. Rather, we shall take that trade and the factors that determined it as exogenous to (determined outside of) our internal trade model. While that assumption ignores the interdependence that existed between foreign and domestic trade, particularly their joint efforts on market size, it permits us to focus attention on the elements that caused a very rapid growth of internal trade in the 45 years between 1815 and 1860. Indeed, that growth appears to have been even more rapid than the growth in foreign trade.

## A Model of Interregional Trade

Basically, we still seek to interpret trade by the Northeast, South, and West in terms of their changing patterns of comparative advantage. Initially, as we have seen, these regions in 1815 were very largely independent of each other. Their initial endowments of resources (land, labor, capital, and entrepreneurship) were quite different. The Northeast had the initial advantages of good natural harbors, stands of well-situated timber, and relatively good sources of iron ore and water power or kinetic energy. The South was endowed with richer soil and milder climatic conditions and longer growing seasons. The West had mainly potential resources, primarily in the form of rich soil and timber and furs. As we have seen, the principal constraint on trade both within and between the regions was the lack of low-cost transportation. As that barrier came down, the conditions necessary for specialized comparative advantage trade between the regions began to fall into place.

We examined the theory of comparative advantage in Chapter 2. We saw that nations find it to their mutual advantage to exchange goods and services produced on the basis of the comparative advantages of each because, as a result, each can have more to consume after trade than before trade. This is so because trade permits each to use fewer resources to produce (or import) the goods it finally consumes. We also saw that increasing opportunity cost tends to cause the degree of specialization to be incomplete. Those same principles can be employed to understand movement of goods, services, and resources within a nation.

## Triangular Trade

Successful and growing specialized trade depends on the following:

1. The existence of comparative advantages between the regions
2. Transportation costs that permit the profitable movement over long distances of the comparative advantage-produced goods
3. Growing productivity and incomes that enlarge the size of cash markets
4. More rapid productivity growth in cash income activities than in sub-

sistence income activities (an increase in the opportunity cost of subsistence-oriented economic activities)
5. The existence of a legal, institutional, and social framework that will not only permit but will even encourage the harnessing of the foregoing signals to specialized activities

If all these conditions are fulfilled and if three regions exist, what may emerge is a pattern of bilateral trade such as that shown in Figure 8-1 or even triangular flows among the three regions.

The development scenario suggested in Figure 8-1 is the following: With the differing initial endowments and conditions indicated in the legend, as transportation costs fall, resources in each region will be reallocated to produce those goods in which each region has its comparative advantage(s). Region A will tend to reallocate resources from agriculture to specialize in producing manufactured goods and financial services for Regions B and C. As its industries produce for a larger market, Region B will tend to reallocate its largely agricultural resources to specialize in producing a smaller number of agricultural commodities, for example, cotton and sugar. It avails itself in the long run of **internal and external economies of scale**—lowered production costs that will further enhance the industrial comparative advantage of the region. As new technology develops, whole new manufacturing industries develop, broadening the region's manufacturing base and accentuating its industrial and financial characteristics. Its comparative advantage increasingly shifts. The economy of Region B tends to become **monocultural;** that

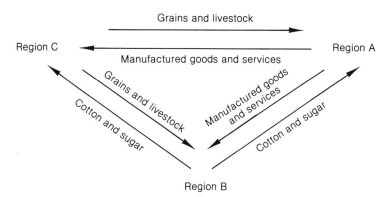

Region A: Waterpower, urban-industrial labor, timber, financial institutions, industrial economies of scale.
Region B: High soil fertility, mild climate, extensive internal river system, agricultural economies of scale.
Region C: High soil fertility, educated farm population, few agricultural economies of scale.
Figure 8-1. Triangular Trade Between Regions.

is, to specialize in and depend on one or a few basic commodities. Region C tends to reallocate its resources in favor of cash crops that are more diversified than those in Region B. This is due to the lack of economies of scale in Region C.

If our model, then, is one of a system of markets without institutional or individual barriers, Region A will specialize in manufacturing and will "export" its goods and financial services to Regions B and C. Region B will specialize in a few basic agricultural commodities and will "export" those to Regions A and C. Region C will specialize in the production of a more diversified mix of agricultural goods, such as grains or livestock produced on relatively smaller scales, and will "export" those to Regions A and B.

## Incomplete Specialization

Recall that, in this model, as in other international trade models of which this is a variant, we assume that as resources are reallocated to different uses, increasing opportunity cost or diminishing productivity ultimately is encountered. As a result, specialization in each region will be incomplete. The sooner encountered and the stronger the increasing cost is, the less will be the degree of specialization. This will be true even if there are no political or other barriers to interregional trade.

## Resource Allocation and Pricing

Specialization within regions requires a means to reallocate resources to their changing most productive uses. For the most part, market signals in the form of relative wage rates, relative rates of return on investment, and other relative prices served that function in the antebellum period. We shall now examine some very fundamental principles that suggest not only how resource prices are determined but also the amount of those resources that are likely to be employed in particular uses.

The resource allocation and pricing model we shall use is one of market equilibrium. It assumes that supply and demand are brought into equilibrium by competitive bidding and that resource markets are thereby cleared of shortages or surpluses. In these respects, equilibrium in a labor market, for instance, is similar to equilibrium in a product market. However, a basic difference exists between product markets and resource or factor markets. Demand for a resource such as labor is a **derived demand**—a demand that is brought about by the demand for the product or service that the resource is employed to produce. Thus, in the period under consideration, the demand for slaves on southern cotton plantations was a function of (depended on) the demand for cotton. As the demand for cotton increased, the derived demand for slaves increased.

The supply of a resource will ordinarily conform to the **law of sup-**

**ply**—that is, that more will be supplied to the markets at relatively higher prices than at relatively lower prices. Fundamentally, this is because an increase in the price of the resource in a particular use causes that resource to be bid away from other now relatively less well-paid uses. These additional amounts of the resource will be successfully obtained by individual firms or regions even if the total supply of that resource, such as slaves, does not change or changes very little with higher prices in the short run, with larger quantities supplied.

Demand for a resource will ordinarily conform to the **law of demand:** More will be demanded at (relatively) lower prices than at (relatively) higher prices. This is fundamentally so for several reasons. A firm hires enough of a resource at any given resource price to maximize its profitable use, to make that resource's contribution to the firm's marginal revenue equal to its contribution to marginal cost. For firms buying resources competitively, factor price is a given; thus factor price becomes the **marginal factor cost:** the cost of hiring an additional unit of the resource. The rule for most profitable use of a resource, then, is that enough is hired to make that resource's contribution to marginal revenue. The latter we call **marginal revenue product** (MRP): the marginal physical product (additional product output of an additional unit of resource) multiplied by the marginal revenue of the firm. We assume that the marginal physical product of any labor ultimately diminishes in the short run or actual production period. Thus, the marginal revenue product schedule, the firm's demand curve for labor, slopes downward.

We see in Figure 8-2 how competitive factor prices are determined and, in turn, how individual firms respond to those price signals in bidding resources into particular uses. Figure 8-2(a) represents the determination of a competitive factor price. For the sake of illustration, assume that the marginal factor price (MFC) determined in Figure 8-2(a) is that of a slave, a prime field hand in 1850. The equilibrium price of the slave, $P_e$, is determined by the competitive bidding (at slave auctions such as in St. Louis) of buyers and sellers. Once established, that price tendency becomes marginal factor cost, the cost of buying an additional slave, to the potential slave owner. Since buying a slave was akin to buying a capital instrument, slave buyers would calculate the expected net revenue flow from a slave and compare that with alternative forms of investment. Suppose that such a slave is expected to produce $50 of net revenue over his lifetime. Ignoring other factors such as aging, if the rate of return on other investments (real estate, crop advances, and the like) is 6%, then an individual slaveowner will buy slaves at any price up to $833.50, which represents the capitalized value of a 6% return on $50, and in Figure 8-2(b) the individual slaveowner will buy enough slaves to make the competitive price equal to the marginal revenue product (MRP) of such slaves. Remember that the MRP schedule slopes downward because of the assumption of diminishing marginal productivity.

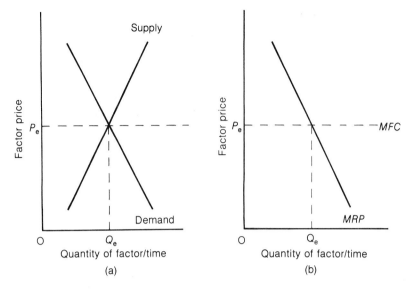

Figure 8-2. Competitive Factor Pricing and Factor Usage by a Single Firm: (a) Competitive factor pricing; (b) Factor use by the firm.

We shall return to the economics of slavery later in the chapter. Slave prices here are taken only as an illustration to show factor pricing and the demand for factors by individual firms.

## The Evidence and the Conclusions

In the remaining parts of this chapter, we are going to look at some of the evidence regarding the patterns of development that emerged in the Northeast, the South, and the West from 1815 to 1860. That will enable us to determine whether the trade model we have outlined gives a good approximation to those patterns. Finally, we are going to look at the overall evidence regarding the bilateral or even trilateral ties among the three regions to determine whether, as the model concludes, those ties emerged and became increasingly strong or whether interferences of one sort or another prevented the development of strong three-way trade patterns.

## The South

It is probably clear to you that Region B in our model comes very close to fitting the basic economic conditions of the South before the Civil War. It was definitely a region with high soil fertility, mild climate, extensive internal river systems, and a comparative advantage in producing a few agricultural crops. Some students of the South have argued that those crops were also subject to greater economies of scale than existed else-where in the United States, but agreement on that is not universal.

These general statements are inadequate to describe completely the antebellum southern economy. Two important specifications must be added to the general framework. From an agricultural and economic point of view, there was not truly one South; rather, there were two. The first South was the "Old South," consisting of a belt of states from Virginia through South Carolina and Georgia. These states, among the original col-onies, had formed an early pattern of extensive agriculture built primarily around tobacco and rice. They failed to form a pattern of soil conserva-tion, which meant that by the second quarter of the nineteenth century, soil fertility in the Old South was seriously diminished.

The second South was the "New South," that area encompassing pri-marily Alabama, Mississippi, Louisiana, Arkansas, Tennessee, and east-ern Texas. This area, well served by river transportation systems and en-joying the great fertility of alluvial soils, experienced extremely high yields per acre in cotton and sugar production. Moreover, in the New South, especially in the trans-Mississippi area, there may have been significant economies of scale (falling production costs per unit of cotton or sugar with larger-sized plantations) or at least few diseconomies of scale (rising unit costs with larger-sized plantations). Thus, in Mississippi and Loui-siana, efficient plantations might consist of several thousand acres, com-pared to much smaller farms in the rest of the nation.

## Slavery: The Peculiar Institution

At the outset of the 45-year period we are examining, most of the South's population and other resources were in the Old South. What mechanisms facilitated the movement of much of that region's resources into the New South? The question cannot be answered without bringing into considera-tion slavery, the second basic characteristic of the South's economic so-ciety. Slavery had existed since early colonial times. Over time, the "peculiar institution," as Kenneth Stampp[25] has called it, became concen-trated almost exclusively in the South. This happened in part because the owner's enforcement of his property rights in slaves became more and more costly in northern (and certain border) states whose populations regarded slavery as socially noxious. Some of these states imposed a ban on slavery, a ban that went beyond the constitutional ban on importing further slaves into the United States after 1808.

After 1815, then, and in the face of a constitutionally restricted sup-ply, purchases of slaves became a major form of capital investment in the South. Only about 25% of the adult male white population owned slaves. Among slaveholders, ownership was concentrated: A fifth of the slave-owners had only one slave. Forming the new, large plantations, then, in-

A southern mansion, with slave quarters in the foreground. (Photo no. 16-G-246 in the National Archives)

volved moving slaves (and other resources) into the new areas of the South.

Was slavery essentially burdensome to the southern economy? Did it hinder resource transfer and the other developmental processes of the region? Few questions in our economic history have been so controversial or so thoroughly researched. Until recent years, the preponderant opinion seemed to be yes. This involved a view of slavery often associated with, among others, Ulrich Phillips, a professor of history at Yale University. In a famous article written in 1905, Phillips[20] argued that slavery was burdensome to the South. In his view, this was so for a variety of reasons, including the "unwillingness of slaves to work hard" (low marginal productivity) or to reproduce and increase their supply. Most importantly, he argued that, especially after 1815, in the face of an increasingly inelastic supply (and a slowly growing supply), slave prices rose to reflect large **quasi-rents** (payments due to the relative inelasticity of supply) to slave sellers but that these higher prices did not reflect growing productivity. Phillips believed that a profit squeeze on cotton growers resulted, especially because cotton prices, he thought, were falling. The profit squeeze would have ultimately forced the abandonment of slavery. Slavery, in other words, would have toppled of its own weight. The Civil War was an unnecessary bloodbath to the extent that it was fought over the issue of slavery.

Beginning especially in the 1930s, various scholars sought to answer the question about the profitability of slavery. Much painstaking examination of plantation records was undertaken. One of the foremost scholars of American agricultural history, Lewis C. Gray,[15] concluded that slavery *was* profitable, that slaveowners earned rates of return comparable to investment returns elsewhere in the economy. Gray, however, was almost alone in that view. A study in 1929 by Charles Ramsdell[21] had argued that slavery would have become unprofitable because the highly productive lands of the New South, especially in Texas, would have increased the supply of cotton relative to its demand, depressing cotton prices and making the crop unprofitable. Although the Ramsdell argument has been disproved in various ways (especially by showing that the price of cotton was *not* falling over time), it was one of many arguments that caused students of antebellum history to conclude that prior to 1860 slavery was already doomed as an institution.

Debates about the profitability of slavery and whether the institution caused the southern economy to stagnate have continued up until recent years. There have been some notable arguments challenging the orthodox view that slavery was deleterious to the southern economy. An example of these is contained in *The Peculiar Institution* by Kenneth Stampp.[25] In 1958, however, a pathbreaking article, "The Economics of Slavery in the Ante-Bellum South" by Alfred Conrad and John Meyer,[4] was published in the *Journal of Political Economy*. In a sense, the "new economic history," employing explicit economic theory and modern quantitative techniques to investigate historical hypotheses, began with this article.

Postulating two production functions, one for the production of slaves, the principal intermediate good, and the other for cotton itself, Conrad and Meyer came to the conclusion that a person purchasing slaves in 1846–1850 could expect, based on recent experience, to earn a rate of return comparable to long-term investments elsewhere in the antebellum economy. Conrad and Meyer found that this was made possible by a well-functioning set of factor markets that transferred slaves from the Old South to the New South, as well as by a well-functioning commodity market for cotton. In other words, slave prices were determined by market forces. Such prices tended to reflect the marginal productivity of slaves, and rising slave prices reflected a growing productivity. The study seems to have laid to rest the Phillips argument about wildly inflated slave prices that reflected conspicuous consumption by planters and the inelastic supplies of slaves.

Although later work by Edward Saraydar[23] reduced the Conrad and Meyer estimates of returns on slaveholding, their basic conclusion still holds; slave buyers in the last half of the 1840s were not, in the main, irrational or given to conspicuous consumption or cavalier reasons for purchasing slaves. Furthermore, a study by Robert Evans, Jr.,[5] broadened the Conrad and Meyer conclusions to the entire period from 1830 to 1860.

## "Time on the Cross"

In 1974, Robert Fogel and Stanley Engerman, two of the best-known "new economic historians," published *Time on the Cross: The Economics of American Negro Slavery,* one of the most controversial and widely read of modern works in economic history.[11] Among other things, Fogel and Engerman have done much to dispel any remaining notions that slavery was an uneconomic or dying institution. They concluded that slaveowners were not cavaliers but were concerned about slave productivity. Slaves were relocated primarily from the Old South to the New South, not as individuals but as families, or as entire plantation labor forces, to avoid diminishing their productivity. From a productivity viewpoint, then, it seems unlikely that the slaveowner engaged in *widespread* disrupting of slave families and beating of slaves. No doubt such incidents occurred as a matter of discipline, but the notion that the practice was widespread has been discredited by virtually all economic historians. Slavery was an economic institution.

Fogel and Engerman's *Time on the Cross* contains many specific profiles of slave prices correlated with particular attributes of slaves. Those attributes include age, sex, and specific skills or disabilities. In the case of each of these profiles, it appears that expectations about relative marginal revenue productivities dictated the demand for slaves and thereby helped determine their prices. Highly skilled slaves such as carpenters and wheelwrights brought prices half again above those for semiskilled slaves. Younger slaves (of productive age) brought higher prices than older slaves, although the prices of skilled slaves peaked at older ages than those of less skilled slaves, reflecting the later payout on investment in their education. All in all, the evidence presented by Fogel and Engerman presents a remarkable demonstration both of the workings of an efficient resource market such as we saw in Figure 8-2 and also of human capital theory. In many instances, Southerners bought slaves, invested in their training, and "rented" them out to others in the obvious expectation that the investment would yield a rate of return higher than that in alternative investments.

## Could Southern Slavery Have Continued?

It appears that widespread nineteenth-century and almost universal twentieth-century moral repugnance for an instutition permitting human beings to own other human beings has clouded our view of the rational economic workings of that institution. If so, has that repugnance also biased our view of the ability of slavery to continue as a means of economic organization? Again, the antebellum South is almost unique as a laboratory to explore that question.

It appears that, for the immediate term beyond 1860 and in the absence of the Civil War, slavery could have continued as a viable economic institution. In an important study, Yasukichi Yasuba[28] investigated the impact of expected *future* earnings from slaves, in order to determine not only the viability of slavery but also to measure the hopeful view of the future of slaveowners. By calculating the cost of producing slaves and comparing that cost from 1820 to 1860 with the market price of such slaves, Yasuba found that slaveowners received a capitalized rent that was never less than 50% of the market price of slaves. Generally, also, these rents moved upward during the period. Yasuba's conclusions reinforce and broaden the Conrad and Meyer conclusions and show that the tripling of slave prices between 1815 and 1860 not only was indeed based on productivity growth (increasing marginal revenue productivity) but also that in 1860 slaveowners had good reason to be sanguine about the immediate future of cotton plantation slavery. These conclusions should not be surprising, since Fogel and Engerman have shown that the demand for cotton was growing more rapidly than its supply in the years preceding the Civil War. We can see the movement of cotton prices in current and real terms in Table 8-1.

Table 8-1. The Price of Raw Cotton (in Cents per Pound), Current Price and Real Price.

| Three-Year Period | Current Price | Real Price[a] |
|---|---|---|
| 1840–1842 | 8.7 | 7.9 |
| 1843–1845 | 6.8 | 7.4 |
| 1846–1848 | 9.0 | 8.9 |
| 1849–1851 | 10.7 | 10.8 |
| 1852–1854 | 10.5 | 9.3 |
| 1855–1857 | 11.4 | 8.8 |
| 1858–1860 | 11.8 | 10.3 |

[a]Deflated, using the Warren-Pearson Index and with 1850 as the base year.

Source: Adapted from Robert W. Fogel and Stanley L. Engerman, "The Economics of Slavery," in *The Reinterpretation of American Economic History*, ed. Robert W. Fogel and Stanley L. Engerman (New York: Harper & Row, 1971), p. 316.

The Phillips, Ramsdell, and other similar arguments that declining cotton prices spelled doom for slavery are not substantiated by the data in

Table 8-1. Current cotton prices were rising from 1843 on and, even in real terms, rose in the period just prior to the Civil War; furthermore, cotton prices never fell back to the lows of the early 1840s (when slavery was considered thriving) in the remaining years before the opening of the Civil War.

## Slavery and Economic Development

To this point, we have seen that the southern slave economy was viable, able to effectively reallocate slave and nonslave resources to their most efficient uses (as revenue productivity alternatives changed) and apparently hopeful about its future. Two further questions arise, however: If the Civil War had not occurred, might slavery have been abandoned because it retarded the absolute and relative growth of per capita income of the South? Also, were the rates of saving, investment, and consumer expenditure affected by slavery in such a way that the South's future economic development would have been inhibited by slavery?

Answering the first question requires a look at the per capita income position of the South in the period prior to 1860. Fogel and Engerman, expanding on the important work of Richard Easterlin, have provided a clear picture of regional per capita income trends from 1840 to 1860. Those results may be seen in Table 8-2.

Table 8-2. Per Capita Income by Region 1840 and 1860 (in 1860 prices).

|  | Total Population | | Free Population | |
|---|---|---|---|---|
|  | *1840* | *1860* | *1840* | *1860* |
| National Average | $ 96 | $128 | $109 | $144 |
| North | 109 | 141 | 110 | 142 |
| Northeast | 129 | 181 | 130 | 183 |
| North Central | 65 | 89 | 66 | 90 |
| South | 74 | 103 | 105 | 150 |
| South Atlantic | 66 | 84 | 96 | 124 |
| East South Central | 69 | 89 | 92 | 124 |
| West South Central | 151 | 184 | 218 | 274 |

*Source:* Robert W. Fogel and Stanley L. Engerman, "The Economics of Slavery," in *The Reinterpretation of American Economic History,* ed. Robert W. Fogel and Stanley L. Engerman (New York: Harper & Row, 1971), p. 335.

The picture that emerges from these data is one of substantial growth in per capita income in both North and South between 1840 and 1860. Nationally, average per capita income grew by one-third in that period. In the

North, per capita income for the total population grew by about 30% and by slightly more than that amount for the free population. The slight difference reflects the fact that few slaves lived in the North. Clearly, free population per capita income growth within the North was somewhat disproportionate, with the Northeast growing by 41% and the North Central states by 36%. We shall return to a discussion of the North's growth in a subsequent section of this chapter.

In the South, a pace and pattern of per capita income growth arose that virtually eliminates any arguments about slavery causing stagnation. For the total population, per capita income grew by about 40% (versus 33% in the North); for the free population, the growth was approximately 43%. Within the South, for the free population, the pace was faster in the South Atlantic and East South Central areas than in the West South Central. Nonetheless, the "New South" had a level of income more than twice that of the "Old South" and almost twice that of the North.

## Development and the Continuation of Slavery

From the foregoing, we might conclude that slavery—whatever may be its social, political, and moral aspects—is capable of being dynamically oriented toward economic development. Before we conclude this section on slavery, however, let us mention some major reservations that have been expressed in that regard.

Some of the arguments advanced for the ultimate decline of slavery are variants of the "natural limits" arguments about slavery. According to one such variant, slavery would ultimately have become uneconomic because of the rise in slave population relative to the geographic limits of slave plantation land. In its simplest and least acceptable form, this argument supposes that slaves could only be employed in cotton production (although only about 55 to 60% were; perhaps 15 to 20% were employed in commerce and industry, with the remainder employed as domestic servants) and that slave prices would have declined. In testing this argument, Fogel and Engerman conclude the contrary, that slave prices in 1860 dollars would have risen by 66% between 1860 and 1890. Moreover, they conclude that cotton demand increased slightly more rapidly than supply up to 1914 and that the amount of land devoted to cotton doubled between 1860 and 1890 and at least doubled again between 1890 and 1925.

In a recent study, Roger Ransom and Richard Sutch question the Fogel and Engerman conclusion. They conclude that cotton prices, especially prices relative to overall wholesale prices, fell from 1869 to 1877, rose in the 1880s, turned down after 1890, and rose again after 1898. Still, say Ransom and Sutch, the relative instability of cotton prices was not the major developmental problem associated with "King Cotton." Rather, they say, it was the lack of diversification and even more importantly, the lack of industrialization in the South that was the main negative legacy of the region's great comparative advantage in growing cotton. Ransom and Sutch say that "There can be little hope for sustained economic growth in an exclusively agricultural society."[22] Admitting that productivity growth in southern agriculture might have lead ultimately to industrialization, the two conclude that imperfections in southern capital markets resulted in very high interest rates that discouraged productivity-increasing investments.

A related argument about stagnation of a slave economy is that the terms of trade (Chapter 2) ultimately turn against a region (or nation) that specializes in the production and export of one or a few basic agricultural staples. As we have seen, the *terms of trade** (for the South, the ratio of cotton prices to overall wholesale prices) were very changeable. An important form of this argument rests on the **income elasticity of demand** for such staples, the rate at which their demand grows with income growth in the areas or nations to which the staple (cotton, here) is exported. According to a frequent assertion, the income elasticity of demand for the staple export ultimately becomes low relative to the income elasticity of demand of the staple-producing area for the semimanufactured and manufactured goods of the areas with which it trades. According to this argument, the South would have faced a declining cotton price relative to the prices of the goods it "imported" from the North, the West, and abroad. It would have been "squeezed" by having to use more and more of its specialized resources to buy a given amount of goods imported from elsewhere in the United States as well as from abroad.

Evidence is mixed about the validity of this terms-of-trade argument with respect to twentieth-century economies. The argument is controversial. In the case of the South, its validity is arguable. Prices in the United States generally declined from 1875 to 1900. Relative cotton prices, on the other hand, rose and fell. As indicated earlier, the terms of trade probably would have moved in favor of the South at some times and against it at others.

A third stagnation, or antidevelopment, argument is one that links slavery with the slow development or nondevelopment of commercial capitalism and its supposed requisite, an urban commercial middle class producing from residentiary industries and selling for cash to a broadly based group of consumers who receive cash income. Eugene Genovese has advanced an argument of this sort about the American South. According to Genovese, the income distribution of the South was so skewed (toward upper income earners in particular and toward whites in general) that there was not sufficient cash demand to cause the widespread development of urban, residentiary industry. Slaves, of course, received little or

---

*See Chapter 2 for a more detailed discussion of this concept.

no cash income. Many white Southerners were outside the cotton plantation economy and also received little cash income.[14] Even by Genovese's estimates, however, southern cash expenditures ($125 per person in Mississippi in 1860) were sufficient, according to Fogel and Engerman, to have provided the base for supporting "over fifty cotton textile plants and more than two hundred boot and shoe establishments of Massachusetts size."[10]

The skewness of the southern income distribution is still in debate. It bears repeating that the primary reason the South lagged seriously in industrialization was that its comparative advantage lay strongly in agriculture and especially with "King Cotton." As Douglass North and others have shown, the region did lag badly in **human capital formation,** the investment in education that results in improved human skills or increased marginal physical productivity of labor. According to North, the ratio of pupils to white population in 1840 was 5.72 in slaveholding states compared to 18.41 in nonslaveholding states.[18] Illiteracy among whites was 2.13% in nonslaveholding states and 7.46% in slaveholding states. It has yet to be shown, however, that this impeded productivity growth in the antebellum South or that such improved skills were necessary to expand the output of cotton plantation agriculture. Also, it does not follow that the relatively high rates of return on human capital formation available in twentieth-century societies employing twentieth-century industrial technology were available to a nineteenth-century agricultural society with its own far less complex technology. Indeed, a better analogy to the antebellum South's experience might be various contemporary agricultural export economies that produce basic commodities; many of these have probably overinvested in human capital formation in terms of the returns available on other investments, including physical capital formation.

## Slavery: A Final Note

From the recent research done on southern slavery, it appears safe to conclude that slavery is not an economic system with a built-in self-destruct mechanism. Still, we are entitled to a bit of historical speculation about the *very* long-term viability of such a system. Would the slave South ultimately have begun to create and expand industries built on its agricultural base (textiles, iron, coal, steel, shoes, and the like)? If so, would this not have created an urbanization of southern slaves, a need to invest in social overhead capital, and a need to increase investments in human capital to complement the new physical capital? Would the enforcement costs of maintaining an urban, better-educated slave population have ultimately outweighed the benefits of slavery?

The answer to all such speculative questions is, of course, "perhaps, perhaps not." Much research remains to be done about the economics of slavery. At this point in our examination, the bottom line is that southern slavery was not in or apparently near its decline at the time of the Civil War. Again, to the extent that this nation's greatest conflict was fought over elimination of slavery, that conflict was *not* an unnecessary bloodbath.

# The West

The western United States evolved a pattern of economic organization similar to that of the South in some ways and remarkably different in others. In 1815, little of the area west of the Appalachians and extending to the Kansas and Nebraska territories had been brought into the commercial economy on a regular basis. As you can see in Figure 8-3, by 1860 that region had become a major wheat-, corn-, and tobacco-growing area, just as the South had become a major cotton-, rice-, tobacco-, and sugar cane-producing area.

The movement westward was, as we have seen, greatly facilitated by improvements in transportation, beginning with steamboats and continuing through the canals and the railroads. That is, the reduced transport costs of western staples increased their supply, not only to the rest of the nation but also to foreign markets. According to Douglass North, though, the growth and settlement of the West would have been much slower if it had depended primarily on these cost reductions to increase the profitability of supplying western goods to other regional and international markets.[18] In addition, the demand for western wheat and corn grew substantially, beginning as early as the late 1820s. As we see in Figure 8-4, land sales, which probably reflect expectations of future profits, paralleled the movements of both wheat prices and corn prices. As wheat and corn prices rose, land prices were bid up in an area; this was followed by a longer-term movement further into the West with the consequent opening up of new lands and the creation of new capacity, awaiting further increases in the demand for those basic staples. Demand, at least in the East and in Europe, was growing with population and income growth. This, together with increasing urbanization and exogenous factors, such as the potato famine in Ireland in the 1840s, were enlarging the market for wheat and corn. The pattern of short-term price increases inducing a movement into new lands was not dissimilar to the pattern of the South, as we have seen.

There were, however, some basic differences in the economic patterns established by the West and the South. Land tenancy in the West involved smaller, family-owned farms, as compared with the larger, southern cotton plantations, especially in the New South. Differences in economies of scale and generally easier entry conditions in western agriculture may

Figure 8-3. Areas of Agricultural Specialization, 1815–1860.

*Source:* Paul Gates, *The Farmer's Age: Agriculture, 1815–1860* (New York: Harper & Row, 1960), frontispiece. By permission of Harper & Row, Publishers, Inc.

Figure 8-4. Land Sales in Seven Western States: 1815–1860 (Ohio, Illinois, Indiana, Michigan, Iowa, Wisconsin, Missouri).

*Source;* Arthur H. Cole, "Cyclical and Seasonal Variations in the Sale of Public Lands, 1816–60," *Review of Economics and Statistics, 9* (1) (January 1927), 50. Reprinted in Douglass C. North, *The Economic Growth of the United States, 1790–1860* (New York: Norton, 1966), p. 137.

have contributed to creating a western distribution of income less skewed toward upper-income groups than some scholars conclude existed in the South.

Western agriculture was less monocultural (less based on a single crop); not even wheat or corn dominated the West as did cotton the South. As a result, the West, although still basically agricultural, developed a broader base than the South, including not only the raising of wheat and corn but also the building of extractive industries for such resources as iron ore, copper, and lead. As North points out, the combination of reduced transportation costs, diversified agriculture, an elastic supply of labor, and a less skewed income distribution created profit possibilities for some intermediate urban industries in the West such as had not developed in the South.[18] An important reason why industries designed to process agricultural commodities grew much more in the West than in the South was found in the weight reduction achieved in processing such goods. Wheat, corn, and livestock were commodities that were dramatically reduced in weight through intermediate processing. The accompanying reduction in unit transportation costs of interregional trade further enhanced such trade and interregional integration. Urban centers, including Louisville, Cincinnati, Pittsburgh, and St. Louis, grew up either as transportation and distribution entrepots or as centers of manufacturing based on capturing more of the value added in agricultural processing or transforming of agricultural commodities into intermediate or final consumer goods. Louisville became a center for the tobacco and whiskey industries. So did Cincinnati, which also added the hog-processing and soap industries. Chicago, of course, became both a transportation center and, later, the center of the meat-packing industry (a development that accelerated with the introduction of refrigerated shipment). Beyond the great river cities, many smaller but growing towns and cities sprang up along the railways in the 1840s and 1850s. These reflected not only land speculation but a demand by farms for the output of residentiary industries (dry goods, seeds, and the like). In the terms of Eugene Genovese,[14] the West was pushed more rapidly by its diversification and income distribution into commercial capitalism than was the South. It is no mere accident that the first national catalog sales organizations, such as Sears and Roebuck, originated in the Midwest.

Productivity grew rapidly in western farming. As with the South and the cotton gin, this productivity growth was often a reaction to the incentives to technological change that profit opportunities posed. A major case in point in the West may be seen with the movement onto the prairies in the 1830s and 1840s. Unlike the forested land left behind, the prairies were frequently covered with thick turf and high grass. Even iron-tipped plows were ineffective in cultivating such soils. With a growing demand for wheat and corn and the high price of land further east, though, human ingenuity came to the fore. A series of technological improvements, beginning with the large breaking plows and extending through steel plows, greatly increased output per unit of labor input.

In general, the terms of trade, according to Thomas Berry,[1] moved in favor of the West. This ability of the West to "import" more goods (both capital and consumer goods), with the use of a given amount of its own resources, almost certainly enhanced the capital accumulation necessary to expand industry. As compared with the South, western firms and farms benefited disproportionately from two major external economies. The first was the relatively heavy investments in social overhead capital, especially in transportation (rails and canals), storage (warehouses), and the urban facilities necessary to serve an increasingly urban population. A second was the relatively heavy western investments in human capital, especially in education and training. Whether measured in terms of literacy, whites in school, or numbers of libraries, the West led the South by a substantial margin. With many family farms and a growing need for an urban skilled labor force, the marginal revenue productivity advantages of investment in human capital were much clearer (and probably much greater) to the West than to the South.

# The Northeast

The great theme between 1815 and 1860 in the New England and Middle Atlantic states (which we shall call the Northeast) was industrialization.

In 1860, the Northeast, with 34% of the U.S. population, contained 67% of manufacturing employment. The lack of industrialization in the South and the relative industrialization of the West are shown by their percentages, 13% and 20%, respectively. (See Table 8-3.)

Table 8-3. Manufacturing Employment, by Regions, 1860.

| Region | Percent of Total Population | Percent of Manufacturing Employment in United States |
|---|---|---|
| East | 34 | 67 |
| West | 31 | 20 |
| South | 35 | 13 |

*Source:* Eighth Census of the United States, *Manufacturers of the United States in 1860* (Washington, D.C.: U.S. Government Printing Office, 1865).

It would be a mistake to equate manufacturing with industrialization. The former had thrived in the United States for many years before 1815. A system of home manufactures had particularly characterized isolated towns and communities since colonial times. Industrialization, however, was a combination of two things: (a) the factory system with its interchangeable parts, assembly line, and specialization and (b) the development of production for a national rather than a local or regional market. The latter, necessary to avail firms of a demand great enough to exhaust economies of scale, was again greatly facilitated by the external economies of improved transportation.

Localized, often home industries (such as the colonial flour mill) are usually tied to a resource subject to diminishing returns, exist primarily because of a particular locational advantage (such as being close to a source of kinetic energy), and generate very small stimuli for the development of other industries. The great industries developing in the Northeast between 1815 and 1860 did not suffer from these disadvantages.

The first great industry in the Northeast indeed, the first to produce for a national market was the cotton textile industry. This industry, using power looms, underwent two dramatic expansions. One occurred in the period of the second war with Britain (1812–1815) and the other after 1817. The growth of the industry can be seen in Table 8-4.

Table 8-4. New England Cotton Industry Output, 1805–1860.

| Year | Yards of cloth (000's) | Value added ($000's) Cloth |
|------|------------------------|----------------------------|
| 1805 | 46 | 2 |
| 1810 | 648 | 34 |
| 1815 | 2,358 | 124 |
| 1820 | 13,874 | 728 |
| 1825 | 69,667 | 3,658 |
| 1830 | 141,616 | 7,435 |
| 1835 | 250,773 | 13,166 |
| 1840 | 323,000 | 16,958 |
| 1845 | 395,762 | 20,778 |
| 1850 | 596,867 | 31,336 |
| 1855 | 634,200 | 33,296 |
| 1860 | 857,225 | 45,004 |

*Source:* Adapted from Robert B. Zevin, "The Growth of Cotton Textile Production After 1815," in *The Reinterpretation of American Economic History*, ed. Robert W. Fogel and Stanley Engerman (New York: Harper & Row, 1971).

According to Robert Zevin,[29] the principal reason for the rapid expansion of the cotton textile industry from 1815 to 1833 was the suitability of mass-produced power loom cloth (called *sheeting*) to meet the demands of the growing western population. After the mid-1830s, the industry grew at a declining rate, although it was still the most important single commodity-producing industry at the time of the Civil War.

Some other parts of the textile industry grew rapidly after 1830, though. Woolen textiles grew slowly, because of the competition of cotton textiles. But mixtures of cotton and wool (called *shoddy*) were produced, and the manufacture of lace, silk, linen, and felt was expanded.

A second industry to develop rapidly in the Northeast was the iron industry, heavily concentrated in Pennsylvania. This industry, like the textile industry (both cotton and woolen textiles) was heavily concentrated in the Northeast. The industry was slow in adopting the "best" (English) iron-making technology due to the bituminous coal available in the East with its high sulfur content which made coking impossible. The iron industry, nonetheless, grew rapidly in spite of its inability to use a coking process—using instead charcoal, in plentiful supply in Pennsylvania—and achieved significant economies of scale in the 1850s and 1860s. Indeed, the industry probably experienced productivity growth equal to that of other industries of the period.

## Secondary and Tertiary Industries

In a real sense, the maxim "Nothing succeeds like success" applies to the Northeast. As the textile and iron industries grew, subsidiary industries grew up around them. The machine goods industry expanded to supply the needs of the textile and iron industries, as well as to supply steamboat engines and, later, the railway industry. In other words, as the scale of established industries grew, this generated external economies for new or would-be industries. Textile factories become more specialized and no longer produced their own machines. Around the manufacturing industries grew up a financial industry in the Northeast. Banks, insurance companies, brokerage houses, and stock exchanges all became much more heavily concentrated in the Northeast than in the South or even in the West.

The growth of basic industries, such as iron, and of satellite industries, such as finance, created external economies for consumer goods industries. A good example is the stove industry. Cast-iron stoves were a major consumer good. The industry, concentrated in New England, produced a value of almost $11 million in 1860. In terms of our model, external economies reduced costs, increased supply, and increased the marginal revenue productivity of labor and other resources. In turn, this increased the derived demand for labor, an increase that resulted in greater immigration and urbanization.

## The Northeast: Summing Up

Clearly, the Northeast became the country's manufacturing center, the hub of industrialization, between 1815 and 1860. Probably the greatest factor that permitted this was the growth in the size of the market. Population growth, growing per capita incomes, increasing urbanization and its corollary, reduced self-sufficiency, created larger and larger markets for both producer and consumer goods. Combined with falling transportation costs, these factors permitted greater specialization and growth of the sizes of firms and industries. The first such firms (textiles, clothing, shoes, boots, stoves, and the like) to produce for a national United States market were heavily concentrated in the Northeast.

A question that remains is why the Northeast became the region that enjoyed so many of the benefits of the initial process of industrialization. One explanation often advanced is that the initial (pre-1815) conditions were differentially favorable to the region. Although its soil and climate had never given it a strong comparative advantage in agriculture (with a few exceptions in areas of the Mid-Atlantic states), its ready source of water power gave it an advantage in manufacturing, at least until steam boilers and electricity freed industries from dependence on kinetic energy.

The Northeast accrued most of the manufacturing stimulus of the 1790–1815 period (the Napoleonic era). Earlier, the country's only large-scale nonagricultural industry, shipbuilding, had located by the timber stands of the New England coast. The best seaports were in the region during the era in which foreign trade dominated the economy; thus, business experience with large-scale enterprises (especially export-import businesses) was concentrated there. In other words, the pattern after 1815 or 1820 merely continued a pattern already established.

In terms of the supply of labor and the marginal revenue productivity of labor, the Northeast attracted most of the arriving immigrants. The region also was the first committed to widespread, if not universal, literacy. The region led the United States in literacy rates, whites in schools, libraries, and the other indices that reflected investment in human capital.

## Specialization: The Model and the Evidence

In an important article written in 1902, Guy Callender[2] set out the argument for the trilateral pattern of trade we saw in Figure 8-1. In that article, Callender stated that early frontier settlement had little to do with economic development in the sense of specialization and tying together of a nation's resources on the basis of comparative advantage uses. The reason, according to Callender, was that incomes (especially cash incomes) were low and transportation costs high. He went on to state that two events changed this pattern. "The first was the introduction of the steamboat; the second was the extension of the cotton culture into the Southwest." According to the argument, the "prosperity which it (these two things) brought to the whole southern and western population increased their ability to purchase such manufactures as they required and thus provided eastern manufacturers with rapidly expanding markets."

From what we have already seen, the broad outlines of the Callender argument are persuasive. The growth of trade over the Erie Canal, the growth of trade at New Orleans, which in value terms increased 20-fold between 1816 and 1858, the manufacturing growth in the Northeast—all these things testify to the growth of a national market system in the 45-year period we are studying.

A later study by Louis Schmidt (1939)[24] seriously questioned the extent of the trilateral trade pattern. According to Schmidt, a triangular or circular pattern of internal trade was replaced by a more direct exchange of commodities between the agrarian South and West and the increasingly industrial East. Still, Douglass North argues that the trilateral pattern was important, that the South produced a few staple goods on its plantation while depending on the East for most of its manufactured goods, and, finally, that the West had a surplus of grain and livestock, supplying the increasing deficits of the South and the East.

The most definitive effort to assess these arguments and measure interregional trade flows has been undertaken by Albert Fishlow.[6] He sets out to show that "interregional exchange was a prominent feature of American antebellum development, but not as a result of interdependence among all regions."

Fishlow's general results may be seen in Table 8-5.

We can see that between 1839 and 1860 interregional trade grew greatly (from a total gross flow of $178 million in 1839 to $657.1 million in 1860). What appears to develop, though, is a pattern not of trilateral trade but of bilateral trade. As Fishlow says, "The clear picture that emerges is one of tenuous linkage between the two regions. To the West, the South was a minor matter for its own demands." In 1860, the North sold $164.3 million to the West and bought $146.5 million from that region. The North sold $213.8 million to the South, and the South sold $69.4 million to the North. Trade between the South and the West was relatively small, however ($20.3 million sold by the South to the West, $42.8 million sold by the West to the South).

Clearly, by 1860 the North was selling its manufactured goods and financial services to both the West and South. In turn, they were selling agricultural goods (and, in the case of the West, some semimanufactured goods) to the North. The weak West-South tie appears to be due to the fact that the South was highly self-sufficient in foodstuffs.* Also, the South was, even in 1860, more heavily dependent on foreign markets than was the West. Although Fishlow's data have been challenged by Robert Fogel,[9] his basic conclusion about bilateral trade stands. Perhaps, in final comment, it is not surprising that two agricultural regions did not develop strong export ties with each other; rather, those regions sought markets, whether domestic or foreign, in which their produce was an input needed in industry or to sustain an urban interdependent labor force.

---

* Plantation records of the period indicate a high degree of self-sufficiency (foods, basic clothing, and the like) throughout much of the region.

Table 8-5. Interregional Merchandise Trade Flows (millions of current dollars).

| Year | Originating Region | North | West | South |
|------|--------------------|-------|------|-------|
| 1839 | North | — | 19.7 | 85.6 |
|      | West | 11.8 | — | 14.9 |
|      |      | 7.1 | — | 5.5 |
|      | South | 39.7 | 6.3 | — |
|      |      | 15.1 | 2.2 | — |
|      |      |      |      |      |
| 1844 | North | — | 25.2 | 73.2 |
|      | West | 20.1 | — | 19.9 |
|      |      | 14.5 | — | 7.6 |
|      | South | 32.4 | 6.2 | — |
|      |      | 11.6 | 3.5 | — |
|      |      |      |      |      |
| 1849 | North | — | 41.4 | 80.0 |
|      | West | 36.8 | — | 36.1 |
|      |      | 24.2 | — | 10.5 |
|      | South | 32.0 | 8.1 | — |
|      |      | 18.9 | 4.8 | — |
|      |      |      |      |      |
| 1853 | North | — | 94.5 | 147.1 |
|      | West | 63.2 | — | 36.9 |
|      |      | 47.9 | — | 19.2 |
|      | South | 61.9 | 17.2 | — |
|      |      | 33.0 | 11.9 | — |
|      |      |      |      |      |
| 1857 | North | — | 163.1 | 165.7 |
|      | West | 96.9 | — | 49.1 |
|      |      | 45.8 | — | 25.5 |
|      | South | 71.1 | 13.2 | — |
|      |      | 38.0 | 5.5 | — |
|      |      |      |      |      |
| 1860 | North | — | 164.3 | 213.8 |
|      | West | 146.5 | — | 42.8 |
|      |      | 107.6 | — | 36.4 |
|      | South | 69.4 | 20.3 | — |
|      |      | 44.6 | 13.6 | — |

*Note:* Uppermost (larger) figure refers to gross flow whether for consumption or reexport; bottom (lower) figure is estimated consumption. In the case of the South-North entry, this is limited to Northern purchases of Southern cotton and molasses.

*Source:* Albert A. Fishlow, "Antebellum Interregional Trade Reconsidered," *American Economic Review*, May 1964.

# Glossary

**Derived demand**   Demand for a resource that is brought about by the demand for a product or service produced by that resource.

**Human capital formation**   The investment in education that results in improved human skills or increased marginal physical productivity.

**Income elasticity of demand**   The rate at which the demand for a commodity grows as incomes grow.

**Internal and external economies of scale**   Lowered unit costs of production associated with larger-scale activity. Such lowered costs are internal if they result from increased scale by the individual firm; they are external if they result from actions taken outside of the individual firm.

**Law of demand**   More will be demanded at relatively lower prices than at relatively higher prices.

**Law of supply**   More of a good or service will be supplied at relatively higher prices than at relatively lower prices.

**Marginal factor cost**   The cost of hiring an additional unit of a resource.

**Marginal revenue product**   The change in total revenue associated with hiring an additional unit of a resource. It is determined by multiplying the marginal physical product of the resource by the marginal revenue of the firm.

**Monocultural**   In reference to a region, monoculturalism refers to specialization in producing one or a very few basic commodities.

**Quasi-rents**   Payments to a resource owner due to the inelasticity of supply of that resource.

# Questions

1. What were two of the broadest economic themes of the period of U.S. development between 1815 and 1860?
2. What determined the basic comparative advantages of the South, the West, and the Northeast?
3. What conditions are necessary for successful and growing specialized trade between regions?
4. In the three-region model of Chapter 8, what were the basic economic characteristics of each region?
5. What determines the supply of a resource? Its demand? Why are the general laws of supply and demand observed in resource pricing as well as product pricing?

6. Why was there a "New South" and an "Old South"? How did they differ economically?

7. Explain the Phillips argument about the ultimate demise of slavery. What were the viewpoints of Lewis Gray and Charles Ramsdell concerning the economics of slavery?

8. What were Conrad and Meyer's conclusions about the profitability of slavery?

9. What do Fogel and Engerman conclude about the rationality of slave prices?

10. What important addition to the study of the economics of slavery did Yasuba contribute?

11. What happened to the price of cotton between 1840 and 1860? What caused this?

12. Did slavery retard the per capita income growth of the South? What are some other possible arguments linking slavery to nondevelopment of the South? Could slavery have remained a viable economic system in the United States beyond 1860?

13. What were the basic similarities and differences between the patterns of economic development of the South and the West?

14. What roles did short-term and long-term agricultural prices play in the settlement of the West? How did changing geographic conditions in the West beget profit incentive for technological change?

15. What happened to the terms of trade of the West between 1815 and 1860? How did external economies affect those terms?

16. What was the great theme of development in the Northeast between 1815 and 1860? How did manufacturing change into a process of industrialization in the Northeast?

17. What were the major industries in the Northeast in the period from 1815 to 1860? What caused these industries to grow rapidly? How did secondary and tertiary industries become established in the Northeast?

18. What is the explanation for the fact that the Northeast became the first great manufacturing center and industrial region of the United States?

19. What was Guy Callender's argument about trilateral trade among the regions of the United States? What are Albert Fishlow's conclusions about the validity of that argument?

# Suggested Readings

1.  Berry, Thomas S. *Western Prices Before 1861, a Study of the Cincinnati Market.* Harvard Economic Studies. Cambridge, Mass.: Harvard University Press, 1943.
2.  Callender, Guy S. "The Early Transportation and Banking Enterprises of the States in Relation to the Growth of Corporations." *Quarterly Journal of Economics* (November 1902).
3.  Cole, Arthur H. "Cyclical and Seasonal Variations in the Sale of Public Lands, 1816–1860." *Review of Economics and Statistics* 9(1), (January 1927).
4.  Conrad, Alfred H., and Meyer, John R. "The Economics of Slavery in the Ante-Bellum South." *Journal of Political Economy,* 66 (April 1958).
5.  Evans, Robert, Jr. "The Economics of American Negro Slavery." Universities–National Bureau Committee for Economic Research, *Aspects of Labor Economics.* Princeton, N.J.: Princeton University Press, 1962.
6.  Fishlow, Albert. "Antebellum Interregional Trade Reconsidered." *American Economic Review,* 54 (May 1964).
7.  Fishlow, Albert. *American Railroads and the Transformation of the Antebellum Economy.* Cambridge, Mass.: Harvard University Press, 1965.
8.  Fogel, Robert W. "Discussion." *American Economic Review,* 54 (May 1964).
9.  Fogel, Robert W. "American Interregional Trade in the Nineteenth Century." In *New Views on American Economic Development,* ed. Ralph Andreano. Cambridge, Mass.: Shenckman, 1965.
10. Fogel, Robert W., and Engerman, Stanley L., eds. *The Reinterpretation of American Economic History.* New York: Harper & Row, 1971.
11. Fogel, Robert W., and Engerman, Stanley L. *Time on the Cross: The Economics of American Negro Slavery* and *Time on the Cross: Evidence and Methods: A Supplement.* Boston: Little, Brown, 1974.
12. Gallman, Robert. "Self-Sufficiency in the Cotton Economy of the Antebellum South." *Agricultural History* (January 1970).
13. Gates, Paul. *The Farmer's Age: Agriculture 1815–1860.* New York: Harper & Row, 1960.
14. Genovese, Eugene D. *The Political Economy of Slavery.* New York: Pantheon Books, 1965.
15. Gray, Lewis C. *History of Agriculture in the Southern United States to 1860.* Gloucester, Mass.: Peter Smith, 1958.
16. Hutchinson, William K., and Williamson, Samuel H. "The Self-Sufficiency of the Antebellum South: Estimates of the Food Supply." *Journal of Economic History,* 31 (September 1971).

17. Johnson, Emory R. *History of Domestic and Foreign Commerce in the United States.* Washington, D.C.: Carnegie Institution of Washington, 1915.
18. North, Douglass C. *The Economic Growth of the United States.* New York: Norton, 1966.
19. Parker, William N., ed. *The Structure of the Cotton Economy of the Antebellum South.* Washington, D.C.: Agriculture History Society, 1970.
20. Phillips, Ulrich B. "The Economic Cost of Slaveholding in the Cotton Belt." *Political Science Quarterly, 20* (June 1905).
21. Ramsdell, Charles W. "The Natural Limits of Slavery Expansion." *The Mississippi Valley Historical Review, 16* (September 1929).
22. Ransom, Roger L., and Sutch, Richard. *One Kind of Freedom.* Cambridge, England: Cambridge University Press, 1977.
23. Saraydar, Edward. "A Note on the Profitability of Antebellum Slavery." *The Southern Economic Journal, 30* (April 1964).
24. Schmidt, Louis B. "Internal Commerce and the Development of National Economy Before 1860." *Journal of Political Economy, 47* (December 1939).
25. Stampp, Kenneth. *The Peculiar Institution: Slavery in the Antebellum South.* New York: Knopf, 1956.
26. Strorolin, Robert S. *Industrial Slavery in the Old South.* New York: Oxford Press, 1970.
27. Eighth Census of the United States. *Manufacturing of the United States in 1860.* Washington, D.C.: U.S. Government Printing Office, 1865.
28. Yasuba, Yasukichi. "The Profitability and Viability of Plantation Slavery in the United States." *The Economic Studies Quarterly, 12* (September 1961).
29. Zevin, Robert B. "The Growth of Cotton Textile Production After 1815." In *The Reinterpretation of American Economic History,* eds. Robert W. Fogel and Stanley L. Engerman. New York: Harper & Row, 1971.

# Chapter 9

---

# Industry, Agriculture, and Finance

As we have seen in Chapter 8, the antebellum period witnessed a process of regional specialization and substantial economic development. Out of that process arose some basic changes not only in the size but also in the organizational structure of American industry, agriculture, and finance.

A key feature to the changes in all three sectors was a growing specialization of economic activities and, within those activities, an increased specialization of labor and capital. Recall, from our earlier discussion of the classical model of economic development, that such specialization is the very source of productivity growth. For the sake of brevity, we shall not repeat that model. Remember, however, that the amount or degree of specialization of activities or of resources within activities is limited by the size of the market (demand) and by a society's economic institutions, which do more or less to encourage productivity growth.

Finally, as a *non*classical addendum to these thoughts on what determines productivity growth, let us add in the familiar element of technological change. In the classical view, technology was a fixed menu of choices about how to organize resources and produce goods and services. Modern thought suggests, though, that the technological menu improves almost continuously in developing societies and thereby makes possible an increase in the productivity of some or all of those societies' resources.

Our major task in this chapter is to assess, for industry and agriculture, how productivity growth was influenced by changing market size and its corollary specialization, as well as by changes in technology. Finally, we shall look at evolving institutions, especially financial institutions and see how they influenced that growth.

# Industry

Evidences of industrial formation in the United States go back at least to the 1790s and the early factories of men such as Samuel Slater and Moses Brown and somewhat later textile factories such as that of Francis C. Lowell. Particularly in the 45 years from 1815 to 1860, however, the United States experienced a process of sustained industrialization. While some have argued that industrialization is the cause of economic development, that view seems excessive and unsupported by the experience of the United States. As we shall see, there was a set of factors influencing the rapid economic development of America before the Civil War. While industrialization was an important member of that set, it is far from influential enough to explain the whole development process.

Let us begin by asking the following question: "What were the basic characteristics of the industrial processes that were either begun or expanded in the period from 1815 to 1860?" In answer, we shall look at the creation of the factory system and at its corollary, the specialization of labor and capital, particularly the assembly line and the use of interchangeable parts. In doing so, we shall concentrate on certain industries whose growth and structural change were prominent in the antebellum period, particularly in the rapid development period from 1840 to 1860.

The factory system involved a significant change from the home manufacturing system of a much more self-sufficient early America. While hand-driven machinery was used in the homes, the machines were usually simple. The factories involved concentrating relatively large, specialized, and expensive power-driven machines in central locations to which a substantial number of laborers were brought. It is worth noting that the factory's specialized functions actually required fewer skills on the part of the laborers and therefore increased the supply of industrial labor by bringing substantial numbers of noncraftsmen into the labor force. In most instances, these new members of the labor force had been in self-sufficient, subsistence-oriented economic activities. In the case of girls and young women, many were able to work for cash income for the first time. This is an early example of how technological and organizational change may increase labor force participation. Furthermore, by increasing the supply of labor, wages were kept down, thereby reducing production costs and encouraging investment and industrial growth. Of course, wages for particular types of labor differed widely at any given time, depending on the locational scarcity of the labor. As we see in Table 9-1, the variation could be very great. According to the data, the weekly wage for a given occupation in 1853 was commonly three times as great in San Francisco, where its supply was relatively scarce, as in New York, where its supply was relatively less scarce. This explanation for *relative* wage differences is valid even if labor was generally scarce in the United States and had been made less scarce in manufacturing by the expansion of the factory system.

Table 9-1. Weekly Wages in San Francisco and New York, 1853.

| Occupation | San Francisco | New York |
|---|---|---|
| Carpenters | $42 | $15 |
| Coopers | 24–36 | 12 |
| Bricklayers | 48–60 | 15 |
| Shipwrights | 42 | 18 |
| Shoemakers | 24 | 16 |
| House painters | 30 | 15 |

*Source:* Data from John R. Commons, *History of Labor in the United States,* Vol. 1 (New York: Macmillan, 1918), pp. 610–611.

A second component of the growth of manufacturing and the factory system during the period under view was the standardization of manufacturing components, which permitted the use of interchangeable parts and very great reductions in the cost of producing goods ranging from such things as firearms to clocks. The implementation of interchangeable parts is popularly ascribed to Eli Whitney, although Robert Woodbury[26] has seriously questioned whether so much of the "American system of manufacturing" can be traced to any individual. According to Woodbury, this system was the "culmination of a number of economic, social and technical forces brought to bear on manufacturing by several men of genius, of whom Whitney can only be said to have been *perhaps* one."

Whatever group of individuals may have been responsible is not important here because we are advancing no "great man" theory of history. Rather, there was a collection of entrepreneur-innovators at work in the period taking advantage of the various opportunities afforded for profitable implementation of new products and processes made possible by a variety of favorable growth factors. Continuous production processes, standardized products with interchangeable components, and the formation of factories, all were parts of the American system. An amusing illustration of just how American this system was is contained in the story of a New England clockmaker who, in 1840, devised a method to produce one-day brass clocks with interchangeable parts for less than fifty cents. This was a dramatic reduction in cost from the largely handmade clocks of the time. When the enterprising manufacturer sent a shipment to England and valued them at 50 cents apiece, English custom officials, convinced the clocks were undervalued, exercised their right to buy them for the declared value. The American clockmaker then sent a larger second batch, which the English also bought up. Presumably delighted with such a growing, low-selling-cost market, a third, even larger shipment was made. Finally convinced of the genuineness of the valuation, the British let the third shipment of clocks into the country.

The American system depended on continuous production, interchangeable parts, factories, and non-labor intensive production processes. Some early attempts at its establishment were unsuccessful; for example, the attempt of Slater in the 1790s, whose original textile mill was largely a copy of its labor intensive English counterparts. Even in textiles, which were perhaps America's earliest "growth sector," the first clearly successful factory was not founded until 1814. Ironically, both Slater and Francis C. Lowell, the founder of the 1814 textile factory, got their original ideas from copying machines and organizational practices observed in Great Britain. By the 1840s, however, it was evident even to the British that continuous production and interchangeable parts had produced a truly American version of the factory system originated in England.

## The Growth of the Manufacturing Sector

The American system clearly reflected a substantial displacement of home manufactures. It meant that the comparative advantage of factories was so great, and the opportunity cost of home manufacture so high, that labor and other resources could be bid into the manufacturing sector. There are some significant data problems with determining just how rapidly this happened before 1840. Nonetheless, the very important studies of Robert Martin (see Figure 9–1) provide some insights for the entire period from 1800 to 1860.

While the data in Figure 9–1 do not directly show the decline of home manufactures, we may infer much from them about that subject. Since

Figure 9-1. Rising Importance of Manufacturing.

*Note:* Commodity output is treated here as half of GNP.

*Source:* R. F. Martin, *National Income in the United States, 1799–1938* (National Industrial Conference Board, 1939); and R. E. Gallman, "Commodity Output, 1839–1899," *Trends in the American Economy in the Nineteenth Century*, Conference on Research in Income and Wealth (Princeton, N.J.: Princeton University Press, 1960).

manufacturing's share of commodity output approximately doubled between 1820 and 1860, that sector's commodity output rose much more rapidly than commodity output in general. Accomplishing this rise required bidding resources into the sector and away from other activities. Available evidence suggests that while some of these resources attracted into manufacturing came from non-market oriented uses, many of them came from home manufactures.

Figure 9–1 directly shows the percent of the total that manufacturing had in workers, income (at current prices), and real commodity output between 1800 and 1860. Bear in mind that the data before 1840 are fragmentary and inadequate. Actually, only the 1850 and 1860 censuses provided data comparable to later periods. According to Martin, the share of income originating in manufacturing rose from about 5 % in 1800 to about 7 ½ % in 1820. Also as the figure indicates, about 7 ½ % of workers were in manufacturing in 1820. By 1860, manufacturing's share of workers had risen to 12 % and its share of income to slightly less than that.

The problem with respect to interpreting the dramatic post-1840 increase in the share of real commodity output attributable to manufacturing is the paucity of pre-1840 data. If the data are accepted, that share rose from about 8 % in 1840 to about 16 % in 1860. While that is a dramatic increase, the percentage increase in manufacturing's share of income is about the same. In terms of both income and real commodity output, though, manufacturing was increasing its size relative to the rest of the economy.

## Some Major Industries

As we have already noted, there is widespread agreement that the textile industry, especially cotton textiles, was the first American manufacturing growth industry to emerge in the nineteenth century. Like many industries, it suffered from some false starts and difficult problems of adaptation. Slater's early effort in the 1790s was not very successful, even though it replaced the spinning jenny with more productive machines, especially Arkwright's water frame and Crompton's mule, because it sought to transplant English technology, with its labor intensive methods, to a labor-scarce America. The cost disadvantage of the American mills served as an incentive to devise an "American technology" suited to the new nation's resource endowments. This incentive became especially strong during the second war with Great Britain.

The Boston Manufacturing Company, established in 1813 by Lowell, was a major response to this cost incentive. Lowell's mill was notable not only for its capitalization ($300,000), which was very large for that day, but also for its integration of production processes, its hiring of young girls rather than children as operators, and for the famous power loom created by Lowell's chief mechanic, Paul Moody. Other American textile producers rapidly adopted the *Waltham Plan,* a system of integrating spinning and weaving power machinery within the same plant.

After the end of the second war with Great Britain, American textile manufacturers found it difficult to compete with the reintroduced British textiles. The adoption of the cost-cutting Waltham plan was part of their reaction. Also, they pressed Congress for tariff protection. As a result, the Tariff Act of 1816 was passed. Although this protective tariff had most of its effect between 1816 and 1824, it nonetheless helped to create a home market for American textiles.

Under these various stimuli, the cotton textile industry grew very rapidly. Research by Robert Zevin[27] has shown just how fast that growth was as well as what were its various causes.

The early growth of the textile industry was reflected in the sixtyfold increase in value added between 1805 and 1815, which we saw in Chapter 8 (Table 8–4). Those were the years of the Napoleonic wars and of the embargo whose influences we have already examined. After the end of the war in 1815, the nation was flooded with British textiles and value added fell from $124,000 in 1815 to $44,000 in 1816. According to Zevin, after 1826 imports of cloth remained fairly steady while domestic production soared.

The relative importance of the cotton goods industry continued to grow through much of the antebellum period. By 1860, it had become the largest manufacturing industry in the United States in terms of value added and the second largest in terms of employment. Those relationships may be seen in Table 9–2.

## What Caused the Industry's Growth

Until recently, it was traditional to ascribe much, if not most, of the growth in America's first industrial growth sector to technological advance. After all, it was clear that new machines, larger machines, more integrated production processes, more specialized inputs (including a separate, specialized machine goods industry), and the interchangeable parts which expedited maintenance and repair, all lowered costs and increased supply. The huge increases in production seem to bear out that kind of analysis.

Robert Zevin posed the question: Since market clearing (equilibrium) output is determined by supply *and* demand, what part did each play in the growth of the textile industry? Zevin's study is a fascinating exercise that classically illustrates the problems of separating supply and demand changes in the history of an industry's market. The supply growth of the textile industry has been well recorded and is shown in our earlier discussion. Zevin was faced with the problem of estimating the **price elasticity of demand for cotton textiles,** the responsiveness of quantity demanded to changes in their price. This estimate was necessary in order to separate the changes in quantities supplied (primarily the technologically derived out-

Table 9-2. Ten Leading Manufacturing Industries 1860.

| Industry | Value added (Millions) | Employees (Thousands) |
|---|---|---|
| 1. Cotton Goods | $ 54.7 | 115.0 |
| 2. Lumber | 53.6 | 75.6 |
| 3. Boots and Shoes | 49.2 | 123.0 |
| 4. Flour and meal | 40.1 | 27.7 |
| 5. Men's clothing | 36.7 | 114.8 |
| 6. Iron products | 35.7 | 49.0 |
| 7. Machinery | 32.6 | 41.2 |
| 8. Woolen goods | 25.0 | 40.6 |
| 9. Carriages, wagons, carts | 23.7 | 37.1 |
| 10. Leather | 22.8 | 22.7 |
| 11. All Manufacturing | 815.0 | 1474.0 |

Source: *Eighth Census of the United States,* Vol. 3 (Washington, D.C.: U.S. Government Printing Office, 1861).

put change) from the change in demand. Zevin knew that five factors might have caused a growth in demand and must have done so unless demand was very price elastic. The five demand-changing factors were

1. *Population growth,* which was about 3% per annum during the period. Of the 16% annual growth rate in output, therefore, 3% came from population growth and not more than 13% from falling cotton prices.
2. *Tariff protection.* Zevin found that by 1820, the steep tariff had reserved most of the American market for domestic producers.
3. *Transportation network improvements.* Even without a change in technology, lower transport costs would have reduced retail prices, quantity demanded would have grown, and output would have increased.
4. *Income growth.* Lack of data for income changes between 1815 and 1820 clouds the question, but Zevin concludes that the growth of income did cause a growth in demand.
5. *Changes in tastes.* Although it is difficult to separate changes in quantity demanded due to price changes in taste in favor of cotton goods (brighter colors, washable, lighter weight, and so on), there may have been such shifts.

Zevin's rather surprising conclusion is that a large increase in cotton textile output would have occurred because of demand changes even if there had been no improvements in technology. The most important point to remember here is that investors, inventors, and entrepreneur-innovators all look at both sides of a market in making supply decisions. Investment and invention both may be, at least in part, a set of responses to actual or anticipated changes in demand for products or processes.

## Noncotton Textiles

Before the 1830s, cloth was a fairly homogeneous product; wool cloth was wool, cotton cloth was cotton, and so on. With the introduction of power machinery, fabrics could be mixed, short- and long-staple cotton could be mixed, even cotton waste could be introduced into the production process. In the 1830s, cotton and hemp were mixed to produce shoddy (as noted in Chapter 8, a cheap cloth of great durability used for basic clothing, especially that of the slaves). In the 1850s, cotton and flax were mixed to produce a kind of imitation linen.

The wool industry in the United States lagged behind the cotton industry in terms of technological innovation. This may have been due in part to the *expectation* of a slower rate of growth in demand for its output. Nonetheless, innovations both in technology such as the Goulding condenser in 1820s, in automatized cording, in transfer to spinning equipment, and in organization (continuous production) caused cost reductions to follow. Between the 1830s and the 1850s, the price of wool cloth fell by more than 50 percent. Even so, it lost part of its share of the market to cotton cloth, whose relative price continued to decline.

Power weaving and knitting were applied to the entire cloth industry. By the 1850s, the sewing machine was in widespread use as a device to save on scarce labor. The resulting greatly reduced price of clothing had an interesting real income effect on Americans. Not only did fewer and fewer American households produce their own clothing (the simple and usually uncolorful homespun), but they also bought more and more diversified clothing. Rotary printing machinery beginning in the 1830s permitted multicolors, and clothing became more specialized (Sunday-go-to-meeting clothes as opposed to work clothes). Laces and ribbons were factory produced. In all these respects, technological change permitted supply increases. Demand growth and increases in quantity demanded probably diminished toward the end of the period as people became somewhat satiated with new clothing. Falling textile prices tell us that supply was growing more rapidly than demand. The result of the whole process, however, was not only lower prices but also a more colorful and enriched society.

## Other Industries

Traditionally, iron and textiles have been viewed as the two key sectors in nineteenth-century industrialization. Two closely related industries, production of coal and of steam engines, are usually included in the complex of sectors considered to have either led or dominated early industrial growth. If this was so, then there is something very peculiar about the early American iron industry. It is true that the industry grew in the 40 or

50 years preceding the Civil War. Total iron output grew 20-fold in that period or at a rate of about 4% per capita.

Yet the impressionistic sense remains among some that the industry was somehow backward, especially in a technological sense. This pejorative judgment is usually traceable to the fact that Americans continued to use charcoal (wood-derived) rather than coke (made from coal) and also used the hammer and reheating method rather than puddling and rolling method (which heated and shaped pig iron without direct contact with the fuel).

At first, it appeared to many investigators that charcoal was preferred because it was cheaper than coke. This turned out not to be true, however, because charcoal production is very labor intensive, and labor was exactly the scarcest factor in America. Around 1830, the English discovered the "hot blast" furnace, replacing the old bellows. The hotter, fuel-saving furnace meant that hard coal (anthracite), which was located in the eastern United States, could be used as a fuel in iron ore production. After 1833, iron ore production in America began more and more to resemble that of Britain.

Why the "backwardness" in reheating and hammering pig iron? Again, Peter Temin[22] has observed, because of the American raw materials to be used in the fuel-consuming furnaces existing prior to the hot blast types, America simply did not have as a resource the bituminous coal that could be "coked." Also much of the iron used in the United States in the early nineteenth century was for stoves, tools, building hardware, and, generally, for items in which iron was not the major component but in which high-quality iron was important. Since wrought (hammered) iron was superior to that produced by puddling, it was reasonable to continue the old method.

Between 1830 and 1860, however, the new furnaces as well as the growing demand for iron caused a concentration of the industry in the eastern areas, particularly in the areas that joined the Great Lakes. Iron ore locations with anthracite (containing neither gas nor sulfur) especially meant concentrations along the Ohio River (such as at Pittsburgh) and along other eastern rivers such as the Delaware (for example, at Philadelphia). In sum, it appears that there was a large increase in the demand for iron, especially wrought iron during the pre-Civil War period. There was only a small increase in supply; that increase, however, prevented larger price increases from occurring.

## Sources of Demand for Iron

It is common to associate the demand for iron products before 1860 with the railroads and their major construction phases in the 1840s and 1850s. There is considerable defensibility in the association for the 1850s when, according to Robert Fogel,[8] about 22% of all domestic crude iron output was consumed by railroad construction and maintenance. Nonetheless, prior to 1840, both stoves and steamboats consumed more iron than did railroads, even if their engines were called "iron horses."

Early urbanization brought forth substantial demand for wrought iron. This was especially the case with "Franklin" stoves, which saved fuel over fireplaces, with water and sewer pipe, lamp posts, and many of the other appurtenances of an increasingly urban society. Although it was many years before America's urban population exceeded its rural population, cities were growing, actually at the fastest *rate* in our history. By 1860, New York had a population in excess of one million, and wrought iron railings had become the major decoration of northern homes.

At least as important as urbanization in the growing demand for iron ore were successive waves of iron-using transportation innovations. The first of these was the steamboat, whose history we traced earlier. With huge iron engine blocks, gears, boilers, mountings, and shafts, it is not surprising that far more iron went into steam engines in 1840 than into railways, including locomotives (which, as Fogel has noted, used primarily wooden rails until the 1840s).

Apart from steam engines in transport, Americans did not use the new power source as extensively as the British. After all, New England, clearly the natural manufacturing center of the period, had a comparative advantage in water power, using either the water wheel or the water turbine—both illustrating the cheapness of kinetic energy. That steam engines were not so widely adapted to industrial uses in the United States as in Britain is another evidence that Americans were not technologically backward; rather, they were adapting to the comparative advantages dictated by their resource endowments.

## Railway Demand

If the "iron horse" itself did not create a dominant demand for iron, what about the railway system, especially its demand for iron rails? It appears that even in this overall sense, railway demand, although very important, can easily be overstated as a source of the growth of the iron industry. The reasons for this have mainly to do with the timing of railroad building and with the relative disadvantages of American iron makers in supplying iron rails.

The first major wave of railroad building occurred in the mid-1840s. It was not until that time that the railroads, which had experimented with many types of rails, settled on the T-shaped iron rail as their standard. Thus, it was not until the mid-1840s that large-scale production of such rails took place in America. Unlike the textile factories, there appear to have been few economies of scale in iron rail production. Indeed, the larger plants were no more productive than smaller ones—simply *larger.* Also the quality (especially the durability) of American-made rails left much to be desired. While all iron rails were generally unsuited to long-term use, as they tended to be bent out of shape and periodically had to be reshaped, American iron rails were more prone to this than those produced by the more mature British industry. In the textile industry, this kind of relative British advantage was quickly overcome. In the case of the iron industry, however, the disadvantage was overcome more slowly; even in the late 1850s a significant part of iron rails used in America were imported from Britain.

## The Machine Tool Industry

No clearer example exists of classical growth stimuli than the American machine tool industry between 1800 and 1860. Until the early 1800s, mill and factory owners such as Samuel Slater were forced to produce their own tools and machinery. In effect, there was a machine and tool shop which was a subdivision of each mill or factory. As the market grew, however, and the complexity and size of machines increased, separate machine shops began to be established. One of the earliest was established in 1810 near Philadelphia by David Wilkinson, who had helped Slater build several mills. American machine builders adapted and improved on many English machine tools such as the slide lathe, the milling machine, and gear cutters.

In the process just described, we see strong growth influences at work. As the textile and iron industries grew, the market for machine tools increased, as well as the profitability of establishing independent and specialized firms. As machine shops grew in number and size, they developed inventions, improvements, and innovations. The Blanchard shaper, the turret lathe, the Verier caliper, to name a few, reduced the costs of industries using such tools. Increasing the profitable supply of goods from those industries was a clear growth stimulus.

In sum, the machine tool industry grew out of the firearms industry and had grown to a major, highly specialized industry by 1860. It served both to create and transmit technical improvements throughout the American economy and to enhance the basic growth industries of the period.

# Agriculture

Because we have dealt extensively with southern and western agriculture in the previous chapter, our treatment of agriculture as a sector of the economy here will be brief. To begin, let us see what happened to agriculture's relative share of output in the American economy. As with so many other indices of nineteenth century economic activity, reliable series date from about 1840. Table 9-3, which is reported by Robert Fogel[8] and based on the work of Robert Gallman[10] provides an overview in constant dollars of the change in percentage distribution of value added in commodity production between 1839 and 1859.

Table 9-3. Percentage Distribution of Value Added in Commodity Production (Gallman's Constant Dollar Series).

| Year | Agriculture | Mining | Manufacturing | Construction |
|------|-------------|--------|---------------|--------------|
| 1839 | 71.9 | 0.7 | 17.4 | 10.1 |
| 1844 | 68.7 | 1.0 | 21.1 | 9.2 |
| 1849 | 59.7 | 1.1 | 29.5 | 9.8 |
| 1854 | 56.8 | 1.1 | 29.2 | 12.9 |
| 1859 | 55.5 | 1.2 | 32.2 | 11.2 |

*Source:* Robert W. Fogel, *Railroads and American Economic Growth: Essays in Econometric History* (Baltimore: Johns Hopkins University Press, 1964).

Clearly the relative shares of the sectors in the commodity output of the nation changed dramatically in the last 20 years of the pre-Civil War era. This is especially so in the 1839–1849 period when agriculture's share fell from 71.9 % to 59.7 % while manufacturing's share rose from 17.4 % to 29.5 %.

Was agriculture then a "declining sector"? In a relative output sense, yes. Two things are apparent in this respect for the entire period from 1800 to 1860. First, agriculture's share declined over that entire period. Assuming proportionality between the percentage of the population engaged in the activities of a sector and that sector's share of commodity output, agriculture probably had declined from about 90% in 1800 to about 55% in 1860. Correspondingly, manufacturing's share had probably risen from about 5% in 1800 to about 33% in 1860.

Second, we should not be surprised at these relative sectoral changes. As we have seen, industrialization was successfully underway in the United States, at least by the 1820s. A successful industrial movement implies a change in the relative position of industry if for no other reason than that, to be successful, it must have a productivity edge over agriculture great enough to warrant resource payments high enough to bid resources out of agriculture. The growth of industrial cities and urban industrial employment reflect that success and that productivity differential.

There is no conflict between viewing agriculture as a declining sector before the Civil War and the evidence we have seen in Chapter 8 of a productive and profitable plantation agriculture in the South (especially the

New South) and an increasingly successful multicrop agriculture in the West. What this sectoral decline means is that agriculture as a set of national economic activities was not growing in the value of its output nearly as rapidly as was manufacturing. It does not mean that agricultural productivity was declining.

There are many reasons why we should expect relative agricultural decline to be associated with the economic development that occurs in a period of industrialization. One of the most important is associated with the **income elasticity of demand***—responsiveness of the demand for agricultural products to changes in income. This elasticity tends to diminish as incomes grow for primary commodities. The demand for secondary and tertiary commodities such as fine clothing and better-quality foods may grow rapidly with income growth (may be income elastic). Demand for other basic agricultural commodities such as coarse clothing and bulky foods, however, may actually decline with income growth (may be income inelastic). The experience of the United States appears to confirm this.

## Success in a Declining Agriculture

A major part of the relative decline of agriculture could be witnessed in the Northeast. It is well known that the period saw a major decline in the role of agriculture in that area. Indeed, the Northeast, as we have seen, became a net importer of agricultural foodstuffs and agricultural raw materials. At the same time, even that area of the nation had some significant agricultural success stories. The growth of the factory system and its corollary, urbanization, produced a substantially different set of demands for foodstuffs in the Northeast. Urban families are, of course, much less self-sufficient than their rural counterparts. New York City, with its late 1850s population of over one million, had to be supplied with dairy products and with fresh vegetables and fruits. Not only did these products have high ratios of price to weight but also the lack of refrigerated means of shipment precluded many of them from being brought from distant areas. As Paul Gates[11] has shown, specialized farms were thriving in the Northeast by the 1830s. According to the records of the period, a surprising variety of fresh fruits and vegetables was available around all urban areas by the 1840s.

Not only was the Northeast, then, shifting from a comparative advantage in agriculture to one in industry and finance, but also, within agriculture, its advantage was in labor and capital intensive crops rather than in land-intensive crops. The fundamental reasons for the shift were previously recorded changes in transportation costs. The canals, steam-

---

*See the Review of Economic Concepts in Chapter 11 for a more detailed discussion of this concept.

boats, and railroads made possible the relatively inexpensive shipment of commodities with high ratios of weight to price over very long distances. Ultimately, they made possible the shipment of corn, wheat and other extensively produced crops from the West to the Northeast.

## Technological Change in Agriculture

Technological change, as we have seen in the case of manufacturing, is an important contributor to productivity growth. It shifts the production function of an industry; that is, it makes all inputs more productive. Although the opening up of a highly elastic supply of fertile farm land contributed to antebellum productivity increase, technical improvements did likewise. Some illustrations will suffice to make the point clear.

In the early 1800s, a farmer typically had little physical capital, a few hand tools, an all-purpose plow, hoes, and simple items of that sort. Given the scarcity of labor, complementary capital that increased the productivity of farm labor was highly desirable. Improvements in plowing and harvesting equipment are illustrative of the incentives that existed to make improvements in equipment.

The simple all-purpose wooden plow showed evolutionary changes over several decades that improved the casting process, reduced breakage, and improved the design and shape of the moldboard. Also, the design of interchangeable parts permitted different plow heads to be used for different purposes. In 1817, Jethro Wood culminated these efforts with the cast iron plow. Although wooden plows were cheaper and easier to obtain (iron plows were produced in factories, wooden ones by local craftsmen), the iron plow became cheaper and dominant even in eastern agriculture by the 1830s. In 1837, John Deere introduced the steel plow, which was to become dominant in the heavy wet soils especially of the West. Changes in steel technology, however, did not cause that to happen rapidly until after the Civil War.

Improvements on plows gradually removed a seasonal supply bottleneck. However, especially with grain crops, one remained, that of quickly harvesting the mature crop. Wheat and hay, among other crops, lose much of their value if not harvested soon after maturity or if allowed to become wet. Here too, there was an evolutionary process at work in the solution of the problem. The horse rake introduced in the 1820s could perform the work of 8 to 10 men; the revolving hay rake in the mid-1850s was a similar improvement. What were also needed were horse-driven machines to cut grain and finally to thresh the crops. The reaper, attributed to Obed Hussy and Cyrus McCormick greatly increased the speed with which grain crops could be harvested. Because the reaper was not well adapted for the efficient (very near the ground) cutting of grass, a separate hay mower was being developed as well. The superiority of the American machines in this respect was demonstrated at the International Exhibition of 1855. In a contest of reaping and mowing machines, a French machine cut an acre in 71 minutes; an English machine in 66 minutes; and an American machine in 22 minutes.

Down to 1830, most grain in the United States was either threshed by wooden flail or trod on earthen floors by oxen or horses. The grain was separated from the chaff by simply tossing it in the air and letting the wind blow away the chaff. Although the fanning mill was an improvement, experimentation continued to develop a threshing machine. Many were developed, but the most efficient was that of Hiram and John Pitt in 1836. Its relative productivity was demonstrated at the Paris Exhibition of 1855. In that demonstration, six men threshed with flails while four different machines did likewise. The results were as follows:

|  | *Liters of Wheat* |
|---|---|
| Six threshers with flails | 36 |
| Threshing Machine |  |
|   Belgian | 150 |
|   French | 250 |
|   English | 410 |
|   American | 740 |

There were two amazing demonstrations. The least efficient machine was over four times as productive as six hand threshers, and the product of the "American system" was three-fourths again as productive as its nearest rival and over 20 times as productive as the six hand threshers. Clearly, this suggests that agriculture's decline was only in relative size; the sector was very vigorous in terms of productivity growth.

The American system of continuous production found its way into agriculture partly in the food-processing industry. The meat-packing industry is illustrative, especially the pork-packing industry centered around Cincinnati and later in Chicago. Hog breeding dramatically changed the quality of swine. With highly specialized meat cutters operating on an automated line, the hogs moved through a highly efficient butchering process. Indeed, it was said that "Everything in the hog was utilized but the oink." In that light, it is not surprising that other related industries soon developed, a lard industry, a hide industry, and a soap industry.

# Finance

An important corollary of the increasingly exchange-oriented economy whose development we have traced from 1815 to 1860 was the development of a financial system, especially a set of institutions to provide the supply of money needed to accommodate market (nonbarter) exchanges. In this area, too, the principle of specialization soon took hold. Whereas until the revolution there were no banks in the colonies, these specialized institutions soon began to develop and paralleled the growth of commerce and industry. The development of banking was anything but smooth, however, since there were great debates in the nation over where control of the banking system should lie as well as broader disputes over the relation between the banking industry and the American political system. Before getting into those disputes and the history of banking in the period, let us recall briefly why the supply of money is so important a concern to an economy.

## The Role(s) of Money

As we have seen, money is any item that is generally accepted in exchange for goods and services. In colonial times, many things ranging from conventional silver coins to unconventional things such as tobacco leaves had served that purpose. Money is necessary for many reasons in an exchange economy. The most important role it plays—whatever form it may take— is that of a medium of exchange. In an economy of increasing specialization, individuals are less and less self-sufficient. They must sell the resources they own and obtain from others the goods and services they need and want. By the same token, firms, as we have seen, become more and more specialized; they must obtain a more and more varied mix of inputs and sell their increasingly specialized output to other specialized firms as well as final consumers. Money's principal role, then, is to be the common denominator through which the absolute and relative values of all these goods and services may be established and, thus, the values at which they exchange for each other.

Money plays other roles as well. Economic development and productivity growth require that there be net investment (current investment > current depreciation) in a society. Investment, of course, requires savings. Savings must be priced in order to establish the tradeoffs between present consumption and future consumption. Money's role as a store of value fulfills this purpose: It permits individuals and firms to establish the present value of a future stream of (interest) returns on savings and investment.

Finally, money has an important aggregate or overall effect on the economy. Since it is money that is the common denominator that permits establishing the individual prices of goods and services, it is not surprising that the supply of money has a direct role to play in establishing overall prices and overall economic activity. We have seen this relationship before in the form of the equation of exchange: $MV = PQ$. Remember that

*M* is the stock of money, *V* is the income velocity, *P* is the price level, and *Q* is the number of (final) goods and services produced. Thus, if *V* and *Q* are constant, a change in *M* produces a proportionate change in *P*. A change in *M*, in other words, must lead to a changed money gross national product (*PQ*) or to a lower velocity. A higher *PQ* does not necessarily reflect more real goods and services; it may simply reflect higher prices for a given amount of real goods and services or may reflect a combination of higher prices and more real goods and services.

## Money in the Antebellum Economy

Early in its history, under the urging of Alexander Hamilton, a *bimetallic standard*, one in which the dollar was valued in terms of two metals, gold and silver, and the two metals valued in terms of each other, was established. Since the government ratio between the two metals, the *mint ratio* was often different from the market valuation of the two, the *market ratio*, problems were created. Whenever the mint ratio overvalued either gold or silver in terms of their market exchange rates, the undervalued metal would be hoarded, often shipped abroad for use in foreign trade, and the overvalued one used in domestic trade. Early in our history, gold was hoarded and silver circulated. Later, after the California gold discovery, the reverse happened, as the relative price of gold fell. Although this deprived the nation of the domestic use of some of its specie, it apparently did not create any serious problems.

## Banks

The main reason why the bimetallic standard had no serious consequences for this country's economy was that coins were not the major form of money in the early nineteenth century. The growth of banks and the various forms of money in the early years of the century can be seen in Table 9-4.

The rapid growth of banking can be readily seen. Authorized capital stock increased more than sixfold in the 15 years, notes in circulation twelvefold, and individual deposits more than sevenfold to 1815 though falling from 1815–1818.

Although most early banks maintained large reserves (gold, silver, coins, and certificates), called **high-powered money,** the conservatism declined rapidly. The ratio of specie to deposits and notes fell from 34.7% in 1803 to 18.8% in 1818.

Banks continued their growth. Although many early banks had been simply extensions or subdivisions of large mercantile operations, by the 1820s, they were highly specialized separate financial institutions. Their continued growth and influence on the supply of money may be seen in Table 9-5.

Table 9-4. Banks in the Early Nineteenth Century, 1803–1818.

| Year | State-Chartered Banks | Authorized Capital Stock[a] | Notes in Circulation[a][b] | Individual Deposits[a] |
|------|------|------|------|------|
| 1803 | 53  | 24,900  | 1,565  | 1,522  |
| 1806 | 78  | 41,340  | 2,849  | 2,638  |
| 1809 | 92  | 45,190  | 3,804  | 2,905  |
| 1812 | 143 | 84,485  | 6,385  | 7,248  |
| 1815 | 212 | 115,232 | 19,907 | 11,672 |
| 1818 | 338 | 160,390 | 18,072 | 9,647  |

[a] Thousands of dollars.
[b] Data available only for the number of banks indicated.
*Source:* J. Van Fenstermaker, "The Statistics of American Commercial Banking, 1782–1818," *Journal of Economic History* (September 1965).

Table 9-5. Banks and Bank Money, 1830–1860.

| Year | Number of Banks | Deposits[a] | Notes[a] |
|------|------|------|------|
| 1834 | 506   | 102 | 95  |
| 1837 | 788   | 190 | 149 |
| 1840 | 901   | 120 | 107 |
| 1843 | 691   | 78  | 59  |
| 1846 | 707   | 125 | 106 |
| 1849 | 782   | 121 | 115 |
| 1852 | 913   | 182 | 161 |
| 1855 | 1,307 | 236 | 187 |
| 1858 | 1,422 | 237 | 155 |
| 1860 | 1,562 | 310 | 207 |

[a] In millions of dollars.
*Source: Historical Statistics, Colonial Times to 1957* (Washington, D.C.: U.S. Department of Commerce).

Although the banking system was not growing as rapidly as in 1803–1818 period, the number of banks nonetheless tripled from 1834 to 1860, as did bank deposits. Notes more than doubled.

## Determining the Supply of Money

In the antebellum period (indeed, as we will see later, up to the early twentieth century), three things determined the American money supply. One was people's preferences for different types of money. If the people wanted to hold specie in gold or silver coins, for example, that reduced the amount of high powered money or reserves available to the banks and reduced the supply of bank money. If people's confidence in banks was threatened, they would convert deposits and notes into specie, reducing the supply of money. This happened several times between 1815 and 1860 and contributed to worsening several financial panics. A second factor affecting the supply of money was the **reserve ratio,** the ratio of reserves to deposits and notes under which banks operated, usually within some form of governmental regulation. The lower was the reserve ratio, the greater was the ability of banks operating within a fractional reserve system to expand the supply of money (mainly demand deposits)—the larger was the **deposit multiplier,** in other words.

Of course, the fractional reserve principle is based on the idea that not all depositors will show up at the same time to demand specie payment for their notes and deposits. While this assumption was generally warranted, it was severely tested during several financial panics. Finally, the supply of money was determined by the amount of specie and thereby the amount of high-powered money in the United States. Inflows or outflows of specie—for example, from international trade—could heavily influence and rapidly cause changes in the amount of high-powered money and in the bank-determined money supply.

## Organization and Regulation of Banks

By 1800, there were banks operating in nearly every state. As we have seen in Tables 9-4 and 9-5, their number, capital, and money supply contribution continued to grow up to 1860. Still, there were problems associated with the growth of the system and its effect on the economy. There was widespread mistrust of banks and recurrent efforts to impose various kinds of controls over the system.

Almost all banks were chartered by the states. Ease of entry into banking, therefore, varied widely from one state to another. So did the controls within which the banks operated. Some states, especially in the old Northwest, at times prohibited banking. Ironically, the West, whose demand for money was growing rapidly, needed a highly interest-elastic supply of money and credit to profitably finance its growing commercialization of agriculture and its agricultural processing industry. Although historians have generally attributed these regional and interstate differences in attitude toward bank chartering and regulation to philosophical differences, Gerald Gunderson[13] believes that it was ultimately the very real differences in need for money and credit to finance development that explained the differences. The West, the area with the greatest need for a highly interest-elastic money supply, was most liberal in granting charters and generally least rigorous in regulation. According to Gunderson, those states that were already settled and stable, such as Louisiana, were the strictest about chartering and regulations.

Areas that were less strict not only had more banks in proportion to population but also had problems with redemption of notes. In some states, after 1836, there were so-called wildcat banks. It was said that to redeem their notes one had to travel to areas habitable only by wildcats. It would be easy to overdraw and overemphasize this aspect of American banking and to conclude that the whole antebellum era was one of chaos and instability in banking. Such was not the case. While there was considerable variation from one region to another, even from one bank to another, the number of banks, at least late in the period, was large enough to offer individual and firm customers banking alternatives. Truly dishonest and corrupt practices by individual banks would have led to a rapid loss of demand for the services of such banks.

Nevertheless, there was an early and persistent feeling in the United States that some kind of regulation and control over the banking system was needed. This was deemed necessary to ensure not only a supply of money adequate to finance a growing value of economic transactions but also a stability in the supply of that money. An adequate and stable supply would prevent both wild variations in economic activity and the depressions or panics so feared, as well as an overconcentration of economic power.

Although most of the regulation or control of banking emanated from state and federal activities, one private effort to provide some qualitative control over bank notes was the "Suffolk System," named after the Suffolk Bank of Boston. Because the country (non-Boston) banks' notes were accepted only at discount by merchants (reflecting both the cost of obtaining specie from afar and also doubt about specie redeemability), people in Boston used the country notes. This confirms **Gresham's law,** that relatively overvalued money drives out undervalued money. In order to get common acceptability of Boston bank notes and country notes, the Suffolk Bank offered to redeem country notes if the country banks maintained deposits at the Boston bank. Since the country banks would have faced a massive presentation of their notes by the Suffolk bank for specie redemption if they refused, they generally complied. Competition between the Boston banks caused the discount on country notes to fall to zero; the notes were redeemed at par. In a sense, then, the Suffolk Bank began to operate like a central bank, maintaining its own reserves, forcing other banks to maintain adequate reserves and acting as a **clearinghouse** for the notes of other banks. All of these relationships along with an expanded system of correspondent banking relationships were to be reinforced a hundred years later in the Federal Reserve system.

## Early Central Banking

A central bank is a banker's bank, one established by government to perform certain functions both for it (fiscal agent and the like) as well as for private banks (controlling reserve requirements, providing credit to the banks, affecting interest rates, and the like). Of course, accomplishing all these tasks is difficult enough in modern times. Imagine the information and control mechanisms necessary for the Federal Reserve system to do so in the late twentieth century. Imagine, also, how much more difficult this would have been in the late eighteenth and early nineteenth centuries. No typewriters, telephones, or printouts of data on economic activities. As J. R. Hicks might have observed, it would be easier for this kind of "central planning" to occur between the most remote village in even a poor nation and its capital city in 1980 than between Washington, D.C., and Boston in 1800.

Nonetheless, central banking (of a sort) was tried in the United States as early as 1791 with the chartering of the First Bank of the United States.* As we saw earlier, the First Bank earned the enmity of other banks and some politically powerful interests; their interests, together with those concerned about the constitutionality of a central bank, in 1811 defeated a proposal to renew the First Bank's charter.

For the five years from 1811 to 1816, there was no central bank or federal regulation. As we saw in Tables 9-4 and 9-5, the number of banks rose rapidly. Also, the specie reserves of the banks fell relative to their note issues. In response to a feeling that more central control of the system was needed, the Congress in 1816 created the Second Bank of the United States, with a much larger capitalization ($35 million) than its predecessor. Although recent research by Hugh Rockoff[17] and Peter Temin[21] has shown that the Second Bank was generally successful, there were problems in its administration of the money supply.

Much of the Second Bank's later political troubles can probably be traced to its reduction in loans in western states in 1818 and 1819. When it refused to accept the notes of western banks that did not pay in specie, the Panic of 1819 resulted. One of the western landowners who suffered sharp losses was Andrew Jackson. The so-called Jacksonian fear of central banks was either born or increased out of that experience.

During the 1820s, the Second Bank succeeded in expanding the money supply at a rate consistent with stable prices. The Second Bank's president, the usually able Nicholas Biddle, made a great mistake, however. Afraid that the bank's charter would not be renewed if Jackson was

---

*Neither the First Bank of the United States nor the Second Bank of the United States was a central bank in the sense of being a lender to other commercial banks.

elected president, Biddle openly campaigned for Henry Clay. Jackson campaigned on a promise to eliminate the Bank of the United States. He
started to make good on his promise, as early as 1832 when he withdrew
public deposits from the Second Bank. According to a widely accepted
view, the "bank war" between the Jacksonians and the Second Bank's supporters reduced its effectiveness, allowing a large increase in the money
supply, with inflationary results.

As Rockoff[17] and Temin[21] have shown, the money supply $(M)$ did
rise and the level of prices $(P)$ did rise. The reason, though, appears to have
been due to the very large inflow of specie from abroad. That inflow was
due to international trade conditions. As Peter Temin has observed, "It
would not be misleading to say that the Opium War was more closely connected to the American inflation than the Bank War between Jackson and
Biddle."

In fact, the United States did not have a true central bank before the
Civil War. Given the limitations of the country's metallic standard, it was
virtually impossible for one to function. The death of the Second Bank was
no great catastrophe; Temin has shown that its demise did not cause the
Panic of 1837 or the depression that lasted until 1843. It is generally
agreed that the major positive effect of the Second Bank was qualitative;
Arthur Fraas[9] has shown that its greatest contribution may well have
been to assure interregionally accepted monetary instruments. It probably
deserves to be well remembered for this, since it undoubtedly contributed
to the growth of interregional trade and the specialization of those regions
and the nation's resources we recounted in Chapter 8.

The federal government began withdrawing from bank regulation as
early as 1832. In that year, Jackson stopped the depositing of government
funds in the Bank of the United States and put those funds instead, in state
banks, which became known as "pet banks." The funds at least still served
the purpose of being the basis for loan creation and expanded economic
activity. In 1840, though, the Independent Treasury Bill was passed, which
attempted to eliminate any federal control over commercial credit. Under
this act, the U.S. Treasury would not accept bank notes in payment of
debts owed the government. Only specie became acceptable. The original
independent treasury was dropped in 1841, primarily because of opposition from Henry Clay. Reinstituted in 1846, however, all federal funds
were retained in the U.S. Treasury rather than in banks. The major effect
of this was to withdraw specie from circulation whenever the federal
government ran a budget surplus, thus further reducing the money supply.

The federal government withdrew entirely from bank regulation between 1832 and 1863. As a result, the number of banks more than doubled
and bank deposits more than tripled between 1843 and 1860. It is likely
that the ratio of specie to deposits and notes declined and that this created
some lack of confidence in the banking system as a result. There are two

sides to assess here, however. While it is true that banks with large reserves of high-powered money were viewed with great confidence, they also had a relatively low loan ratio. Yet banks with less high-powered money had less specie, because they had made more loans. In the great majority of cases, those loans were the basis for new and expanded economic enterprises in those areas where rapid economic development was occurring in the United States. In other words, a little less stability, even confidence, in the banking system may have been traded off for more development loans, which the United States and its business community needed. As Hugh Rockoff[19] has shown, even free banking (unregulated-banking) may have fostered this country's economic development in an era when a highly interest-elastic supply of money and credit was needed.

## Money and Economic Activity

Great problems exist in estimating the American money supply in the early antebellum period. The remarkable consistency of the various estimates, however, together with some calculations by Richard Vedder, has led to the relationships between the supply of money, its velocity, the level of prices, and the quantity of output, as we see in Table 9-6.

As Vedder points out, the seeming price stability between 1799 and 1819 is deceptive. In fact, there was a severe inflation during the War of 1812. Undoubtedly the money supply (M) grew more rapidly than output (Q). The reason why prices did not rise was because of a reduction in velocity (V). During the most effective period of the Second Bank of the United States, the 1820s, output rose rapidly while the money supply grew slowly. With a steady velocity, prices actually fell. Yet the very rapid growth of the money supply in the 1830s caused an inflation, while a decline in velocity in the 1840s caused a fall in prices. When the money stock increased more rapidly than real output in the 1850s, there was inflation. Also, in that period there was a slight increase in velocity (the gold discoveries in California had much to do with the specie increase and money supply increase in the 1850s).

## Summing Up

It was conventional for many years for historians to point with criticism to the banking system before the Civil War. Apart from the "bright periods" of the First and Second Banks of the United States, it was presumed that there was not enough control and regulation to make the system work toward the development ends of the nation. That view is now largely discredited. It appears that the system worked remarkably well. It even worked well without the regulatory functions of central banking, which should not be surprising, given the enormous problems of imposing correct central bank policy, especially in that very early era.

Table 9-6. Components of the Equation of Exchange, 1799–1859.

| Year | Money[a] | Velocity | Prices[b] | Quantity[c] |
|------|-------|----------|--------|----------|
| 1799 | 29 | 12.02 | 113 | 308 |
| 1809 | 66 | 7.16 | 116 | 408 |
| 1819 | 86 | 7.75 | 112 | 595 |
| 1829 | 120 | 7.03 | 86 | 981 |
| 1839 | 215 | 7.21 | 100 | 1,550 |
| 1849 | 330 | 5.12 | 73 | 2,316 |
| 1859 | 586 | 5.68 | 85 | 3,913 |

[a]In millions of dollars.
[b]1839 = 100.
[c]Transactions of final goods and services, in 1839 prices, in millions of dollars.
*Note:* The estimates of the money stock and prices are reasonably reliable; the estimate of quantity is very tenuous for the pre-1840 period and is based on Paul David's[5] work. The income velocity measure was calculated from the other components and must be viewed as subject to considerable error.
*Source:* Richard K. Vedder, *The Economy in Historical Perspective* (Belmont, Calif.: Wadsworth, 1976).

# Glossary

**American system**   The term given to the system of standardized products, continuous production, and interchangeable parts begun in the early nineteenth century.

**Clearinghouse**   A means by which the notes of different banks are cleared through some central bank or institution.

**Deposit multiplier**   The increase in money supply possible under a fractional reserve banking system given the size of the reserve requirement and the amount of excess reserves in the banking system.

**Gresham's law**   The rule that relatively overvalued money drives relatively undervalued money out of circulation.

**High-powered money**   The reserves of banks consisting of gold, silver, and coins and certificates to specie that could be readily loaned.

**Price elasticity of demand**   The rate at which the quantity demanded of a product changes as its price changes.

**Reserve ratio** The ratio of bank reserves to deposits and notes; this reserve indicates the amount of specie that banks chose to or were forced to maintain in relation to their loans and note issue.

# Questions

1. How did the classical economists view the effect of technological change on economic development? Does the experience of the United States in the period from 1815–1860 bear out that view? Why or why not?

2. What were the major differences between the factory system and the system of home manufactures? What impact did the factory system have on labor force participation?

3. Why were standardized products and interchangeable parts so critical to the rapid productivity growth of the "American system of manufactures?"

4. In view of the fact that early American manufacturers got their original ideas from Britain, what was unique about American manufacturing?

5. What happened to manufacturing's share of real commodity output, income, and workers between 1815 and 1860? What is the problem with inferring the relationship between these changes for 1840–1860 and the period from 1800 to 1840?

6. What was the reason for the lack of success of Slater's early textile factory? What changes had to be made to produce a viable American textile factory? When did the latter occur?

7. What was the reaction of American textile producers to imports of British textiles after 1815?

8. What were the five most important manufacturing industries in the United States in 1860? What influences tend ultimately to make an industry such as cotton goods a declining industry in terms of relative importance?

9. According to the study of Robert Zevin, what were the sources of the increased demand for cotton textiles?

10. How does one reconcile the impressionistic sense that the American iron industry was backward before the Civil War with the fact that it was a rapidly growing industry?

11. What were the major sources of demand for iron in the antebellum period? How important was railway demand (both rails and locomotives) to the growth of the iron industry?

12. What caused the development of a successful machine tool industry in the United States after 1800?

13. What happened to the relative position of agriculture in commodity output in the United States between 1839 and 1850? In what sense does this indicate that agriculture was a declining sector? Why should the decline not be surprising?

14. What happened to the role of agriculture and the mix of agricultural products in the Northeast between 1815 and 1860? What factors explain these changes?

15. What incentives existed to technological change in American agriculture between 1815 and 1860? What were some of the most notable changes in that technology?

16. Why is the money supply so important to a developing economy? What does the equation of exchange tell us about the relation between the money supply and overall economic activity?

17. What was the bimetallic standard? What problems are created when the mint ratio and the market ratio differ significantly?

18. What happened to the number of state chartered banks, to their authorized capital stock, and to their notes in circulation and individual deposits between 1803 and 1818? What happened to the amount of high-powered money held by such banks? At what rate did the banking system grow from 1834 to 1860?

19. What determined the supply of money and the deposit multiplier in the pre-Civil War period?

20. What seems to have determined the stringency with which states chartered and regulated banks in the antebellum period?

21. Why did the drive to regulate banking gain momentum in the United States? How did the Suffolk Plan illustrate private regulation?

22. Trace the history of the Second Bank of the United States. What ultimately caused its demise? Was it truly a central bank? Why or why not?

23. Why was it difficult to have successful central banking in the antebellum era? What was the major effect of the Second Bank of the United States? What happened to commercial banking after the federal government withdrew from its regulation?

24. What does the equation of exchange show about the relationship between the supply of money, its velocity, prices, and quantity of output between 1799 and 1859?

# Suggested Readings

1. Bagnall, William R. *Samuel Slater and the Early Development of Cotton Manufacture in the United States.* Middleton: Stewart, 1890.
2. Bogue, Allen G. *From Prairie to Corn Belt.* Chicago: University of Chicago Press, 1963.
3. Bidwell, P. W., and J. I. Falconer. *History of Agriculture in the Northern United States, 1620–1860.* New York: Smith, 1941.
4. Danhof, Clarence H. *Change in Agriculture: The Northern United States, 1820–1870.* Cambridge, Mass.: Harvard University Press, 1969.
5. David, Paul. "The Growth of Real Product in the United States Before 1840: New Evidence, Controlled Conjectures." *Journal of Economic History, 27* (June 1967).
6. Davis, Lowell, and others. *American Economic Growth.* New York: Harper & Row, 1972. Chaps. 10 and 11.
7. Engerman, Stanley E. "A Note on the Economic Consequences of the Second Bank of the United States." *Journal of Political Economy, 78* (July/August 1974).
8. Fogel, Robert W. *Railroads and American Economic Growth: Essays in Econometric History.* Baltimore: Johns Hopkins University Press, 1964. Pp. 111–146.
9. Fraas, Arthur. "The Second Bank of the United States: An Instrument for an Interregional Monetary Union." *Journal of Economic History, 34* (June 1974).
10. Gallman, Robert E. "Value Added by Agriculture, Mining and Manufacturing in the United States, 1840–1880." Unpublished doctoral dissertation, University of Pennsylvania, 1956.
11. Gates, Paul W. *The Farmer's Age: Agriculture, 1815–1860.* New York: Holt, Rinehart and Winston, 1960.
12. Gibb, George S. *The Saco-Lowell Shops: Textile Machinery Building in New England, 1813–1849.* Cambridge, Mass.: Harvard University Press, 1950.
13. Gunderson, Gerald. *A New Economic History of America.* New York: McGraw-Hill, 1976.
14. Habakkuh, H. J. *American and British Technology in the Nineteenth Century.* Cambridge, England: Cambridge University Press, 1962.
15. Hammond, Bray. *Banks and Politics in America.* Princeton, N.J.: Princeton University Press, 1957.
16. Redlich, Fritz. *The Molding of American Banking.* New York: Johnson Reprint, 1968.

17. Rockoff, Hugh T. "Money Prices and Banks in the Jacksonian Era." In *The Reinterpretation of American Economic History,* ed. Robert W. Fogel and Stanley L. Engerman. New York: Harper & Row, 1972.

18. Rockoff, Hugh T. "Varieties of Banking and Regional Development in the United States, 1840–1860." *Journal of Economic History, 35* (March 1975).

19. Rockoff, Hugh T. *The Free Banking Era: A Reexamination.* New York: Arno Press, 1975.

20. Shannon, Fred A. *The Farmer's Last Frontier.* New York: Farrar and Rinehart, 1945.

21. Temin, Peter. "The Economic Consequences of the Bank War." *Journal of Political Economy, 76* (March/April 1968).

22. Temin, Peter. *The Jacksonian Economy.* New York: Norton, 1969.

23. Timberlake, Richard. "The Specie Standard and Central Banking in the United States Before 1860." *Journal of Economic History, 21* (September 1961).

24. Van Fenstermaker, J. "The Statistics of American Commercial Banking, 1782–1818." *Journal of Economic History, 25* (September 1965).

25. Ware, Carolyn F. "The Early New England Cotton Manufacture." *American State Papers.* Washington, D.C.: U.S. Government Printing Office, 1931.

26. Woodbury, Robert S. "The Legend of Eli Whitney and Interchangeable Parts." *Technology and Culture, 2*(1), 1960.

27. Zevin, Robert Brooke. "The Growth of Cotton Textile Production After 1815." In *The Reinterpretation of American Economic History,* eds. Robert W. Fogel and Stanley L. Engerman. New York: Harper & Row, 1971.

# Chapter 10

---

# The Civil War:
# A Watershed?

We began in Chapter 1 by noting that the events recorded by historians can be viewed and interpreted in many ways. No major event better illustrates that than the Civil War. In terms of loss of lives, the war was clearly America's most important military conflict. It also was a series of political events that dramatically changed personal, regional, and national power relationships. The war, in other words, had multiple effects, and both its origins and effects can be viewed in many ways.

Until the 1920s, it was customary to view the causes of the Civil War largely in political terms. Southern historians often saw the conflict as having been fought over the issue of states' rights and having been initiated through the bungling and miscalculation of southern politicians urged on by abolitionists.* Northerners frequently saw the conflict in moral terms as a contest over the institution of slavery. Between 1927 and 1960, however, the focus of interpretation shifted strongly in favor of viewing the Civil War as a social and economic catalyst that had much to do with turning the United States into a predominantly industrial nation.

## A Model of Some Economic Effects of War

From a conceptual standpoint, the economic effects of war can be divided into the direct effects associated with military actions, especially the

---

*The pioneering article of Victor S. Clark[3] published in 1918 and cited in the Suggested Readings to this chapter is an important, although until recently largely neglected, exception.

destruction of human and nonhuman resources, and the indirect effects on growth, efficiency, and distribution. While it is impossible to hypothesize briefly about all those effects, we can center on some that are likely to be important.

The direct effects of battle are perhaps the clearest. Destruction of both human capital and physical capital reduces the productive capacity of a nation or region. This diminishes not only the total full employment output of the society, but also average productivity, to the extent that the resources destroyed are among its most productive. Although the physical capital that is destroyed can be replaced, the society still incurs the opportunity cost, the foregone output of goods and services that the capital could have been used to produce. This is a permanent loss.

A second set of microeconomic effects is on the efficiency of resource allocation. War may restrict the ability of a nation to maintain comparative advantage patterns of trade, those in which it exchanges goods that it produces with relatively few real resources for those produced with relatively few real resources elsewhere. When this happens, whether from a blockade or whatever reason(s), a society turns inward from necessity to produce the goods denied it by trade. Since productivity will fall, its full employment output declines. Of course, its output of civilian goods will be reduced in any case as it reallocates resources to the production of war goods.

The macroeconomic (income-employment-price level) effects of war are equally important. The effects of war on prices may be understood in terms of the society's **elasticity of output,** the rate at which output increases as effective demand increases. We can see the importance of this relationship in Figure 10-1.

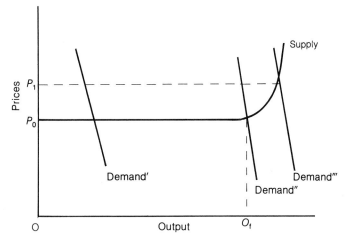

Figure 10-1. Elasticity of Output.

While the index of output represented on the horizontal axis is difficult to measure, statistically, it is conceptually a measure of the real goods and services of an economy. As effective demand increases from Demand' to Demand", there is no increase in the index of prices represented on the horizontal axis; in other words, output is perfectly elastic. The reason for this is that the society is producing more by bringing unemployed resources into use. Let us suppose that at output level $O_f$, full employment is reached or that bottlenecks exist in moving further toward fully employing the nation's resources. If demand increases further, say to Demand"', there are no further resources to employ (the elasticity of employment is zero) so all the increased demand must be translated into inflation, an increase in prices from $P_0$ to $P_1$.

What may this mean for wartime societies such as the North or South during the Civil War? If such a society begins the war at a condition of full employment ($O_f$ in Figure 10-1) and attempts to bid resources away from private production, does not finance its wartime expenditures by taxing or otherwise reducing private (civilian) expenditure, then the increasing effective demand (fueled by government deficits financed by newly created money) will result in inflation.

What happens to income distribution in these circumstances? If wage growth falls behind growth in price (a form of taxation of wage earners), it may well be that there will be an increase in profits (assuming that total real-factor incomes rise) that accompanies the decline in real or purchasing power wages (assuming no change in interest and rent shares). If profits rise, there may be an incentive to invest in capital creating activities on the part of entrepreneurs. In other words, there may be a heightened incentive to increase the rate of industrial growth.

# The Beard-Hacker Argument

Writing in 1927, Charles and Mary Beard referred to the Civil War as a Second American Revolution, which, although it wiped out some economic assets, especially those of the slaveowning aristocracy, "assured the triumph of business enterprise."[2] The Beards went on to say that the capitalists who financed the union efforts and those who supplied it with war material gained "profits greater than they had ever yet gathered in four years of peace." According to them, these huge profits or masses of capital were used to conquer the continent and exploit the natural resources of the nation. In addition to these direct effects on profits, capital accumulation and the distribution of wealth, the Beards alleged that the Civil War changed social and political relationships in a way that clearly favored the industrial development of the United States.

The Beards undertook no careful, systematic investigation of the data for the Civil War period. Nonetheless, their conclusions became widely accepted. Arthur Schlesinger, Jr., referred to the war as having a hothouse effect on the tender industrial growth of America. Harold Faulkner, in a well-known textbook, called the Civil War "terribly important" in our economic development. Writing in 1940, Louis Hacker[9] stated that the war resolved a critical situation, the conflict between the planter capitalist interests of the South and the industrial capitalist interests of the North. According to Hacker, the Union government was free after 1860 to pursue policies favorable to industrial expansion.

The approach of the Beards had been to cite specific acts after 1860 that seemed to them to favor industrialization. Among those cited were the subsidy and land grant programs to the railroads beginning in 1862 and the protective tariff legislation enacted by the Republican dominated Union Congress. Going beyond that type of casual empiricism, Hacker sought to produce the statistics to show that industry, especially heavy industry, made great strides between 1860 and 1865.

In the 1960s, economic historians began to systematically investigate the effects of the Civil War using recent research techniques and newly available data. One of the most important such efforts was by Thomas Cochran[4] in a 1961 article entitled, "Did the Civil War Retard Industrialization?" Taking various indices of economic activity and using data available since 1949, Cochran came to the conclusion that the war actually retarded the country's industrial growth. Cochran cites Robert Gallman's[7] constant dollar series for value added in manufacturing. That series rose 157% from 1839 to 1849, 76% from 1849 to 1859, and only 25% from 1859 to 1869. According to Cochran, this raises a presumption of slower rather than more rapid growth during the war. Looking behind these aggregate figures, Cochran cites pig iron production (up 17% from 1850 to 1855, and 17% from 1855 to 1860, but only 1% from 1860 to 1865), bituminous coal production (no change in its long-term rate of growth), and a low rate of growth in copper production. Also, railroad track mileage additions declined dramatically during the war, immigration declined, there was an actual decline in the value of machinery per farm, and the constant dollar value of loans fell. Cochran concludes that the "Civil War retarded American industrial growth."

In an article subsequent to that of Cochran, Stephen Salsbury[14] points out that the Cochran conclusions rest on a very unquantified if not unquantifiable assumption. That assumption is that by 1840 all of the conditions necessary to favor rapid industrial growth were set in the United States. If this assumption is granted, then Cochran's comparisons of the 1840s and 1850s with the Civil War period are fundamentally valid, because the trends of the war period either would continue the industrial growth patterns of the 1840–1860 period or would deviate from those patterns. On the other hand, it appears that what the Beards (and others) were earlier arguing in part was that the Civil War had a major impact on setting those conditions. Salsbury points out that if one looks at the production growth rates of pig iron, bituminous coal, and railway track construction after the war, there is evidence of a postwar boom with rates much above those of the prewar decades. One could then argue that the Civil War was, as Beard argued, the catalyst in which the conditions for rapid industrial growth were set.

If conclusions about the direct (production) effects of the Civil War seem to rest on less than universally agreed-on assumptions, what about the indirect effects? Cochran recognizes two kinds of such effects, those that reflected changes in the political and social system produced by the war and those stimulants such as inflation and large federal debt creation resulting directly from the war. Cochran confirms Wesley Mitchell's[13] 1903 conclusion that the rapid wartime inflation brought on by massive printing of greenbacks, redistributed incomes from wages (real wages fell) and salaries, and interest payments to profits. This action put "savings in the hands of entrepreneurs who would invest in new activities." Also, the inflation reduced the burdens of railroads with large mortgage debts, perhaps encouraging expansion of the railway system. Cochran concludes, however, that these effects have not been shown to be significant in terms of causing postwar growth. Salsbury agrees, but says that until their significance is systematically investigated we should be wary of concluding that the Civil War retarded industrialization.

Similarly, Salsbury finds room for disagreement with Cochran about the effect of the Civil War on the supply of money and credit and its industrial growth effects. Cochran states that the growth of the banking system between 1800 and 1860 had made credit readily available, and it continued to do so in the North during the war. Cochran says that the war destroyed southern banking and that, even in 1875, 40% of banks were outside the new national banking system. From this, Cochran seems to conclude that the war's effects did little or nothing to improve the availability of credit and, thereby, stimulate investment. Salsbury says that the evidence cited by Cochran neither proves nor disproves the thesis that the war retarded industrial growth. After all, he says, how easy was credit to obtain before 1860? Was it readily available to finance large scale ventures? Did this picture change after 1865? If it did, was the change the result of the war? All these questions remain unanswered.

Finally, did the Civil War, as the Beards assert, "enhance the capitalist spirit"? Cochran agrees that it may have, but that this is an argument that is very difficult to evaluate. What legislative and executive measures did the Republicans take? Was there an increase in federal aid to or subsidization of internal improvements (railroad land grants and the like)? Cochran feels that even if one shows such an increase in federal aid, some of it, such as the Union Pacific land grant, was wasteful, that it created uneconomic enterprises or at least enterprises before market demand would have warranted their private creation. Robert Fogel has shown that Cochran's assertion about the Union Pacific is probably unwarranted; the line earned an average of 11.6% annually on its cost outlays and 29.9% social return during the first decade of its operation.

Ultimately, Salsbury concludes, some of these issues press beyond the boundaries of subjects readily amenable to statistical analysis. For example, did the Civil War place businessmen in undisputed power and, thereby, enhance the industrialization of this nation? Salsbury says that comparative data on tariffs, land grants, and federal subsidies will help to answer that question. Beyond that, interpretation "based upon nonstatistical, social, political, and psychological analysis" is called for.

Salsbury's conclusion is generally reinforced in a study by Stanley L. Engerman,[5] who notes that much research remains to be done. Among other things, little is known about the effect of the conflict on invention, the size of the government budget or the location of financial markets. Engerman does note that a 1964 conference of economic historians concluded that, apart from commercial banking, the war had not "started or created any significant new patterns of economic institutional change," a conclusion directly contrary to the views of Beard and Hacker.* After looking at some specific commodity output figures, Engerman finds the relationships shown in Table 10-1 (based on Gallman's data).

As Engerman notes, per capita commodity output rose much more rapidly in both the non-South and the South in the decade of the 1870s than in the war decade. Indeed, per capita output fell significantly between 1860 and 1870 in the South, reflecting not only the direct destruction of labor and capital between 1861 and 1865 but also the productivity effects of freeing the slaves, fragmenting southern landholdings and the like.† The fact that per capita output grew much more rapidly in the decade after the Civil War than in the prewar decade is not enough to convince Engerman of the validity of the Beard-Hacker thesis. Indeed, it is not until almost 1885 that the trend value of per capita commodity output extrapolating from the 1840–1860 trend was reached.

## Industrial Growth, Summing Up

Following on the research of Cochran, Salsbury, Engerman, and others, few historians today appear ready to fully accept the Beard-Hacker thesis about the Civil War as a great industrial watershed. Yet, because of the

---

*This view appears to overlook the important institutional change of the abolition of slavery.

†Engerman notes that the construction of these indices precludes their use to accurately compare the absolute levels of per capita output in both regions. The rates of change in each region are accurate, however.

Table 10-1. Commodity Output per Capita, by Region, 1860–1880.

| | Non-South | Compound Rate of Growth per Year | South | Compound Rate of Growth per Year |
|---|---|---|---|---|
| 1860 | $ 74.8 | 0.9% | $77.7 | −4.8% |
| 1870 | 81.5 | 2.6% | 47.6 | 2.6% |
| 1880 | 105.8 | | 61.5 | |

*Source:* Adapted from Stanley L. Engerman, "The Economic Impact of the Civil War," *Explorations in Economic History*, 3(3), (Spring-Summer, 1966).

data and interpretation problems, few also are willing to dismiss the argument entirely in any form (especially in terms of power relationships). As we have noted, much research remains to be done within the limitations of available data (especially the lack of data for the war period itself) before a more definitive judgment is formed.

## The Scope of the War

There is at least one sense in which the Civil War was clearly a major watershed. In terms of the degree of involvement of the economies of the North and South, the War marked a dramatic change. Previous wars, even the American Revolutionary, had not involved all the American people and their land and capital. Although the leaders of both North and South entered the conflict expecting to put forth a relatively greater effort than in any previous war period, their expectations were, nonetheless, too low. In one battle in 1862, that of Antietam, over 23,000 soldiers were killed, more than the entire fatalities in all previous wars fought by the United States. It soon became clear (probably not long after the battle of Bull Run in 1861) that only the total involvement of both economies could raise the men and material necessary to successfully prosecute the war.

Some have asked why the Civil War was so much greater in scope than its predecessors. This was still basically a foot soldier's war. There were few dramatic changes in military technology; an exception was the rifling of gun barrels, which greatly increased the distance and accuracy of rifles and cannon. Ironically, the factor that appears to explain the broadening of the war is lowered transportation cost, the cost of delivering men and material over long distances. The railroads especially reduced the unit costs of such movements and, in a sense, became an external economy of scale to the fighting of wars. Gerald Gunderson[8] has pointed out that, following the battle of Chickamauga in Tennessee, a large part of the Union's western army was decimated. Within three weeks, however, several thousand troops had been moved over 3000 miles from the Army

Abraham Lincoln, President of an industrial North, and Jefferson Davis, President of an agricultural South. (Photo nos. 111-B-3656 and 111-B-5140 in the National Archives)

of the Potomac to Tennessee and the entire western army resupplied. In no previous war would this have been possible.

The South, of course, was sytematically denied some of these economies of scale. The Union blockade of southern ports forced a turn to contraband (high-priced goods brought into southern ports, especially to the well-protected port of Wilmington, North Carolina) and to producing goods previously purchased from the North or from Europe. The Union blockade of the Mississippi after 1863 prevented or made very expensive the movement of resources or goods from the Southwest to the "Old South." Many ordinary consumer goods became quite scarce. Consumer goods prices rose dramatically. The South had only one iron works, and its entire output was given over to armaments. Stoves and other consumer goods using iron became scarce. Ironically, textiles became relatively scarce in both North and South. The South had cotton; even the scorched earth policy of the Union in the latter years of the war did not prevent that. Most of the textile mills, though, were located in the North. The lack of that industry's main input resulted in the shutdown of many mills and a virtual depression in several northeastern states. As a result, a significant amount of illegal trade occurred, involving the sale of southern cotton in exchange for northern goods of various types. This illegal trade went on even in the face of opposition from Union generals who recognized not only that it prolonged the ability of the South to continue fighting but also that it was in contradiction to the generals' plan to destroy the economic base on which the South's government rested. Thus, at the same time that the Union's army and navy were attempting to strangle the transportation system of the South and destroy its ability to support a large-scale war, the

Union was actually importing substantial quantities of southern cotton and paying for those transactions with goods such as bacon, salt, shoes, and clothing that helped provide the goods to sustain Lee's troops. It is not surprising, then, that the end of the war was not caused by some ultimate military defeat, but by the success of the war of attrition; ultimately by the inability of the South to produce and distribute the food and clothing necessary to maintain the Army of Virginia around Richmond. Lee's retreat to Appomattox is directly attributable to the desertion of his soldiers in an effort to find such goods.

Northern troops, on the other hand, were among the best fed, clothed, and militarily outfitted in history. The northern transportation system worked so well at resupplying, as Gunderson points out, that the troops frequently discarded blankets, for example, at the end of a season, rather than carry them on marches.

# Financing the War

Both North and South were confronted early in the war with the necessity to finance an unprecedentedly large volume of military expenditures. In the South, this proved to be particularly difficult; according to Gunderson, the region's government was forced to find a means to finance purchases equal to more than half of the entire yearly income of the prewar South. Since output almost certainly fell in the South during the war, this was an enormous task. An early effort at property taxation proved very inadequate. Two other principal means of finance were available: sales of government bonds and the printing of money. Although early issues of southern bonds were even oversubscribed, the bonds sold later on only at tremendous discounts. This was especially true as the military fortunes of the South declined, particularly after 1863 and the battle of Gettysburg. In October 1864, only $362 million of the total Confederate government debt of $1,371 million was in the form of bonds, and, of that, only $125 million had taken the form of voluntary purchases.

As it became harder to finance its purchases of goods out of a declining real southern product with either tax or bond revenues, the South turned to the printing press. Eugene Lerner[12] reports that between 1861 and 1864 the stock of money in the (dwindling) Confederacy increased 11-fold. With an increasingly inelastic supply of goods and services as well as a reduced supply, prices rose dramatically—more than 2800% between 1861 and 1864. Data after 1864 do not exist for the disintegrating Confederacy. With the value of Confederate currency falling at a rate of 10% per month, the velocity of monetary circulation increased and further fueled the inflation.

The high rate of inflation ascribable in large measure to deficit government spending, was in effect a "tax." By 1864, even this tax was inadequate to finance military purchases. Southern commissary officers turned to simply taking the needed supplies (such as food, fence posts for firewood, horses, and mules). Since the owners were rarely repaid, much less at fair market prices and in currency of constant purchasing power, the practice was virtually one of resource conscription. Ultimately, even conscription, when combined with declining real product (especially once systematic destruction of southern property became Union policy) and a failing transportation and distribution system, became inadequate to provide the resources that would permit the continuation of large scale warfare.

Early in the war, little was done in the North to raise taxes or adopt other means to finance the war. Ultimately the North financed its wartime purchases in much the same way as the South, primarily with bond issues and the printing of money (the famous greenbacks).

In 1861, the Morrill Tariff Act was passed, raising tariffs. The tariff rates were so high, as the Beards note, that the apparent objective of the act was to provide protection for domestic industries rather than to raise revenue. Also, a direct tax of $20 million was levied, along with the nation's first federal income tax—on incomes in excess of $800 per year. These measures failed to raise substantial revenues, however, until late 1864 when rates were raised and internal taxes broadened to cover many commodities. For example, of the $350 million raised by the income tax, only $50 million was raised by the end of the war. Thus, most of the burden of financing the war fell on issuing bonds (whose value rose with the North's improving military fortunes after the battles of Vicksburg and Gettysburg) and on the printing of money.

The National Banking System was established in 1863 (and strengthened in 1864) to facilitate the sale of government bonds as well as the issue of currency (the greenbacks). By taxing state bank currency out of circulation, the Union government gave itself a monopoly of the currency supply in areas under its control. The extent of Union reliance on nontax sources of finances is reflected in the fact that of the $3,300 million spent by the federal government during the war period, only 20% came from tax sources.

The results of this financing, however, were quantitatively different from those in the South. Over the period of the war, from 1861 to 1865, prices of northern goods and services rose about 125%. This reflected a decreasing elasticity of output. According to Kessel and Alchian,[10] average incomes rose only about 90%, and private purchasing power fell correspondingly. The reason for the vastly different rates of inflationary tax is that real output probably rose in the North (other than for industries dependent on southern cotton). This is true for all output even though the supply of civilian goods doubtless declined. In addition, the

North continued to engage in comparative advantageous legal trade with foreign nations rather than to import high-priced contraband and both northern bonds and currency did not depreciate as much as those of the Confederacy. In general, then, the North did not suffer from an elasticity of output as low as that in the South. The amount of inflation and decline in northern real incomes (about 15 to 20% between 1862 and 1865) necessary to transfer resources from civilian goods to the war effort was, thereby, smaller. Indeed, the North *appeared* prosperous during the war, with the exception of the areas dependent on textile employment, which suffered from at least a partial withdrawal of cotton supplies.

## Summing Up

In spite of a spate of investigations of the Civil War period since 1960, much remains unknown about the period. Because of the absence of five-year data for the period for 1861–1865, there are severe limits to how far the quantitative investigations can be pushed. Within these limits, disagreements remain about the "watershed" arguments. Little doubt exists that the war left a legacy of destruction and institutional changes that greatly reduced the income position of the South relative to the rest of the nation. Was the destruction of a thriving southern slave agriculture more than offset by a Beard-Hacker effect on future industrial growth? As we have already indicated, there is serious doubt about the Beard-Hacker thesis. Nonetheless, once all the evidence is in, the tradeoffs between reduced output growth in one region and whatever enhancement of growth occurred elsewhere *may* give some validity to a very particular version of the argument.

## Glossary

**Elasticity of output**  The rate at which output increases as effective demand increases.

## Questions

1. What were the customary bases for interpreting the Civil War up to 1920? What different interpretation was given to the war by Charles and Mary Beard and restated by Louis Hacker?
2. According to the model set forth in this chapter, how may war directly and indirectly affect the loss of capital and other resources, the effi-

ciency of resource allocation and prices (in terms of the elasticity of output)? What may happen to profits and capital accumulation?

3. What was Thomas Cochran's basic conclusion about the effect of the Civil War on American industrial growth? How did Cochran reach that conclusion?

4. In what respects does Stephen Salsbury disagree with Cochran's conclusions about the effect of the Civil War on U.S. industrial growth? Is the disagreement complete?

5. What data and conceptual problems remain in assessing the industrial impact of the Civil War, especially the indirect effects of that war?

6. What conclusions does Stanley Engerman reach about the economic effects of the Civil War?

7. What happened to the growth of commodity output per capita in the decade of the 1860s and that of the 1870s? What are the interpretations of this in terms of the Beard-Hacker thesis?

8. In what important sense was the Civil War clearly a watershed? What appears to account for the enormous increase in the scope of the war as compared with previous wars?

9. What was the Union's economic strategy with respect to defeating the South? Why did the North continue to trade with the South in spite of that strategy?

10. How was the Civil War financed by the South? The North? Why was the North more successful in its efforts to finance the war?

## Suggested Readings

1. Andreano, Ralph, ed. *The Economic Impact of the American Civil War*. Cambridge, Mass.: Schenkman, 1967.

2. Beard, Charles A., and Beard, Mary R. *The Rise of American Civilization*. Vol. 2. New York: Macmillan, 1933. Chap. 18.

3. Clark, Victor S. "Manufacturing Development During the Civil War." *Military Historian and Economist*. Vol. 3 (1918). Reprinted in *The Economic Impact of the American Civil War*, ed. Ralph Andreano. Cambridge, Mass.: Schenkman, 1967.

4. Cochran, Thomas C. "Did the Civil War Retard Industrialization?" *Mississippi Valley Historical Review*, 48 (September 1961).

5. Engerman, Stanley L. "The Economic Impact of the Civil War." *Explorations in Economic History*, 2 (III), (Spring-Summer, 1966).

6. Friedman, Milton. "Price, Income and Monetary Changes in Three Wartime Periods." *American Economic Association, Papers and Proceedings*, 42 (May 1952).

7. Gallman, Robert E. "Commodity Output, 1839–1899." In *Conference on Research in Income and Wealth, Trends in the American Economy in the Nineteenth Century.* Princeton, N.J.: Princeton University Press, 1960.

8. Gunderson, Gerald. "The Origin of the American Civil War." *Journal of Economic History, 34* (December 1974).

9. Hacker, Louis M. *The Triumph of American Civilization.* New York: Columbia University Press, 1947. Chap. 24.

10. Kessel, Reuben A., and Alchian, Arman A. "Real Wages in the North During the Civil War: Mitchell's Data Reinterpreted." *Journal of Law and Economics, 2* (October, 1959).

11. Keynes, John M. *The General Theory of Employment Interest and Money.* New York: Harcourt Brace Jovanovich, 1935. Chap. 20.

12. Lerner, Eugene M. "Money, Wages and Prices in the Confederacy." *Journal of Political Economy, 62* (February 1955).

13. Mitchell, Wesley Clair. *A History of Greenbacks.* Chicago: University of Chicago Press, 1903.

14. Salsbury, Stephen. "The Effects of the Civil War on American Industrial Development." In *The Economic Impact of the Civil War,* ed. Ralph Andreano. Cambridge, Mass.: Schenkman, 1967.

15. Scheiber, Harry N. "Economic Change in the Civil War Era: An Analysis of Recent Studies." *Civil War History, 2* (December 1965).

# Chapter **11**

# Agriculture, 1865–1897

Through much of the last third of the nineteenth century, sizable sections of U.S. agriculture were in political ferment in efforts to solve the economic problems generated in part by falling prices. Now let's look at the economic history of U.S. agriculture from 1865 to 1897. The year 1865 is a good starting point because it marks the end of the Civil War and the beginning of a period of renewed agricultural expansion. The year 1897 is a good terminal point because it marks the end of the great depression of 1893 and the beginning of more than 20 years of prosperity for U.S. agriculture. Also, in some sense, it marks the end of a great era in U.S. history, the so-called end of the frontier.

This chapter explores the condition and development of U.S. agriculture from the end of the Civil War to the end of the nineteenth century. To begin with, we will review the various supply and demand factors as they affect agriculture in the period from 1865 to 1897. Then, we will examine the role of government and technology in agriculture. As a third element, this chapter analyzes agricultural development in the three major regions of the United States. Finally, we will review the various factors generating what has been called "the farmers' discontent" and show how farmers attempted to solve their problems. In exploring agricultural development in the last third of the nineteenth century, the concepts of demand and supply and elasticity are very useful. Included at the end of this chapter in our Review of Economic Concepts is a brief summary of the basic principles of these concepts for those students who feel the need for a review.

## Agriculture and Supply and Demand

Before going into the institutional and historical materials dealing with the economic development of U.S. agriculture from 1865 to 1897, it is useful to analyze how the various supply and demand factors may theoretically affect agriculture in that period. If the reader feels insecure about supply and demand theory, he or she should read the Review of Economic Concepts in this chapter. First, though, we shall look at the nature of the demand for agricultural products, then at their supply.

## Agriculture and Demand

Agricultural products adhere to the general law of demand: The quantities demanded increase as their prices decline. During the period from 1865 to 1897, the **price elasticity of demand** (a measure of responsiveness of quantity demanded to a change in price for a section of the demand curve) for agricultural products was low compared to that of other goods; that is, demand for agricultural products was price inelastic (the percentage change in quantity demanded was less than the percentage change in price). Agricultural products are "necessities," are perishable, and have few if any close substitutes; all these factors indicate a price inelastic demand. Although agricultural products take a significant part of total expenditures, which tends to increase elasticity (the percentage change in quantity greater than the percentage change in price), this factor was probably not strong enough to offset the other factors. Thus, while a particular kind of food may be price elastic, the demand for food in general is price inelastic.

The most important economic implication of price inelasticity is that a given change in supply has a much greater impact on prices than on quantity demanded. In Figure 11-1, the demand curve for agricultural products is presumed to be relatively price inelastic. When supply increases from $S_0$ to $S_1$ price declines from *A* to *B*, while quantity increases from *C* to *E. The rate of decline in price is greater than the rate of increase in quan-

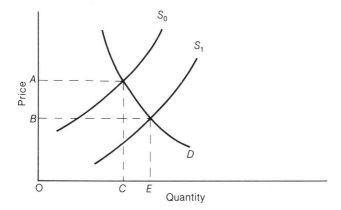

Figure 11-1. Inelastic Demand and an Increase in Supply.

*tity demanded.* To offset this disproportionate price effect of increases in supply, demand would have to increase (the demand curve shift up).

It is unlikely that tastes or preferences for food in general changed in the second half of the nineteenth century. It was not until the 1950s that medical knowledge of the effects of overeating could have had any effect on decreasing taste and preferences for food, thereby decreasing demand. During the nineteenth century, it may even have been fashionable to exhibit a bit of a "pot" to show one's affluence, thus increasing demand.

During the second half of the nineteenth century, considerable economic development occurred, and real income on the whole increased. When income increases, demand tends to increase; increased income then increased the demand for agricultural products. To measure how much, one needs to use the concept of **income elasticity of demand** (measures the responsiveness of quantity purchased to changes in income). Statistical studies of consumption patterns and income indicate that the demand for agricultural products is income inelastic. In the 1960s, income elasticity was about 0.2. To increase the demand for food by $1, income had to increase by $5. It is likely that in the period from 1865 to 1897, income elasticity was higher, although substantially less than 1. In effect then, increases in real income through economic development meant increases in the demand for food, but increases that were limited by low income elasticities of demand.

Increases in the number of buyers were the dominant factor in increases of demand for food. The population of the United States was increasing at a rapid rate from 1865 to 1897, both naturally and also from high levels of immigration into the United States. Both caused domestic demand to grow. World population also was exhibiting high rates of growth, which increased world demand for food.

In brief then, price inelasticity of demand for agricultural products caused increases in supply to affect price more than quantity. However, increases in demand occurred, in part due to economic development and thus increased incomes. Most of the demand growth, however, was due to rapid increases in both domestic and international population.

## Agriculture and Supply

Now let us look at the nature of the supply of agricultural products. The total supply of food adheres to the law of supply in that, as price rises, quantity supplied increases. **Price elasticity of supply** (measures the responsiveness of quantity supplied to changes in price for a segment of a supply curve)—at least in the short run—tends to be highly inelastic because of discontinuity in agricultural production. Once wheat, or any other field crop is planted, there is little that can be done to increase output until the next planting period. The same applies, although with variations in time involved, for animals and fruits. Therefore, between the beginnings of new production periods, quantities supplied of agricultural products have a limited ability to respond to price variations. (Elasticity is slight or even zero.) In the long run, farmers respond to profit or loss possibilities from the prior period. But these responses may not be appropriate for the present period. This lag increases the probability of error in management decisions and causes greater instability within agriculture.

Changes in supply (shifts of the curve) are influenced by the following: For one, improvements in technology increase supply. The technological revolution that has continued to increase productivity in agriculture started in the United States in the late 1830s and has continued to the present. A record of this increase in productivity is shown in Table 11-1.

Table 11-1. The Number of People One Farm Worker Could Feed.

| Year | Number of People |
|------|------------------|
| 1820 | 4 |
| 1930 | 10 |
| 1950 | 15 |
| 1970 | 46 |

*Source:* James F. Willis and Martin L. Primack, *Explorations in Economics* (Boston: Houghton Mifflin, 1977), p. 434.

Also in 1865 the frontier had passed the Mississippi River, and land was plentiful and cheap. The price of this resource remained low and thus did not restrict the increases in supply of agricultural products that occurred in the second half of the nineteenth century.

In addition, perhaps the single most important factor affecting supply was the tremendous increase in the number of farmers and the increase in farm acreage. Table 11-2 shows an increase in the number of farms in the United States from 1.5 million in 1850 to 5.7 million in 1900. Improved acres in farms also showed a remarkable increase from 114 million acres in 1850 to 416 million in 1900. World supply of agricultural products also was increased by similar increases in farmers and land, particularly in Argentina, Canada, Russia, and Australia, as well as in the United States.

As a fourth factor, with the large number of farms shown in Table 11-2, it is likely that very substantial conditions of competition existed and that excess demand and excess supply were eliminated as equilibrium theory suggests. Farmers could not act together and restrict supply (shift the curve up) to maintain higher prices. **Monopoly power** (the ability of a firm to influence price) *was not* present in agriculture.

Table 11-2. Farms, and Improved
Land (in millions).

| Year | Farms | Improved Acres |
|------|-------|----------------|
| 1850 | 1.5 | 114 |
| 1860 | 2.0 | 164 |
| 1870 | 2.7 | 196 |
| 1880 | 4.0 | 284 |
| 1890 | 4.6 | 358 |
| 1900 | 5.7 | 416 |

*Source:* U.S. Bureau of the Census, "Agriculture, General Report and Analytical Tables," *Fourteenth Census of the United States, Taken in the Year 1920,* Vol. 5 (Washington, D.C.: U.S. Government Printing Office, 1922), pp. 38–43.

Finally, the willingness of farmers to cut production when prices and profits are low depends on their opportunity costs. Opportunity costs represent what farmers could receive in income from alternative uses of their resources, their labor, land, and capital. It seems apparent that their opportunity costs (alternative uses) were indeed low. Alternative nonagricultural uses of land, especially in this period, were few (perhaps only hunting) and low in income. Although farm machinery was costly, alternative uses of machines were few, because these machines were specialized for agricultural production. Even though agricultural labor was highly skilled, it was also very specialized and not easily applicable to nonagricultural employment. These low opportunity costs were stronger in the short run than in the long run. Eventually farmers could leave agriculture. Since opportunity costs were low, prices had to be very *low* to cause economic forces to impel the movement of resources from agriculture. Of course, nonmonetary factors may have been very strong. How many farmers' sons and daughters went to the big city because of the bright lights and excitement?

## Some Conclusions

Despite the strong increases in demand caused by increases in real per capita income and increases in the population, the factors increasing supply—technological improvement, cheap land, and increases in the number of farmers—were much stronger. Because of the price inelasticity of demand for agricultural products, more of the effect of relative increases in supply resulted in decreasing prices than in increasing quantity demanded.

# The Role of Government and Technology

From its founding, the U.S. government has had significant effects on agricultural activity. Prior to 1860, the price and other terms of sale of federal and state land and land grants to the railroads had had a significant impact on the general availability and price of land. Also, in the early 1800s the patent office was instructed to collect and disseminate improved seeds.

The impact of government policy was even greater after 1860. In 1862, Congress created the Department of Agriculture, which was given cabinet status in 1889. Its function was primarily to study ways of increasing agricultural productivity and to disseminate this information to the farming community. Again in 1862, the Morrell Land Grant Act gave federal land to the individual states for the purpose of setting up agricultural colleges. The Hatch Act of 1887 provided funds for each state to establish experimental stations. By 1897, each of these colleges had a well-diversified set of offerings in agriculture, an experimental station, and an extension department, which became a vital force in adult education. This accumulation of knowledge and its dissemination were prime factors in increasing agricultural productivity and increasing supply.

## The Homestead Act

Southern opposition prevented the passage of the Homestead Act until 1862. Essentially, the act gave 160 acres of unappropriated public land to anyone who would live on the land and cultivate it for five years and pay minimal fees. Fred Shannon[15] described what he considered was "the hope and the myth" of the Homestead Act as the **safety valve theory.** Free western land given to the poor was the "safety valve" that would prevent eastern urban "exploitation" of the American working class. If eastern manufacturers pressed too hard, their workers could go to the frontier and get free land. The seemingly limitless frontier would prevent the United States from becoming like Europe with its "class distinctions and downtrodden working class," according to Shannon. Free land was the safety valve that would keep America free.

Both the hope and the myth of the Homestead Act were far from the reality. There were basic flaws in the Homestead Act. The act did not provide funds to transport workers from the eastern to the western frontier. Also, the act did not provide draft animals, necessary livestock, or machinery needed to commence farming. Perhaps most important, the act did not provide for subsistence of the new farm family for the first year until the first crop could come in. Most urban workers, many earning less than $250 per year, could not save enough to cover these costs of establishing a farm on the western frontier. Furthermore, in the drier parts of the frontier 160 acres was not enough land to provide a living for a farm family.

Shannon argues that the Homestead Act was not the major element in westward expansion after the Civil War as the myth implies.

> It is true that the number of farms in the United States grew from about 2,000,000 in 1860 to 5,737,000 in 1900, and that the total land in farms rose from 407,213,000 to 838,592,000 acres. It is equally true that not quite 600,000 patents for 80,000,000 acres of homesteads were issued in those same years. In other words, even if all the homesteaders had kept and lived on their holdings, less than a sixth of the new homes and little over a sixth of the acreage would have been on land that came as a gift from the government. Eighty-four out of each hundred new farms had to be achieved either by the subdivision of older holdings or by purchase. Furthermore . . . an astonishing number of homesteaders were merely the hired pawns of land monopolists who took over the land as soon as the final patents were received.

While the Homestead Act may not have provided a safety valve for the eastern industrial labor force, it may have provided the needed release for a portion of the farming community itself. Marginal farmers in the East and Midwest, instead of joining the rural to urban flow, could, because of the Homestead Act, more easily move to government lands on the frontier.

# Technology and Agricultural Productivity

The technological revolution in agriculture began before the Civil War, and many of the basic innovations in agricultural machinery were made by 1860. Improved iron and steel plows, mowing machinery, grain binders, threshers, and grain planters were invented in the 1840s and 1850s. In the North and the West, the Civil War drew off such a large proportion of farm labor for the Union armies that the resulting labor shortage increased the demand for this improved machinery. Mechanized agriculture was firmly established.

This use of machinery to replace labor was intensified in the period from 1865 to 1897. These machines became stronger, larger, and more efficient. Implements to prepare the soil included the John Deere steel plow (1837), the Oliver chilled-iron plow (1868 and 1877), the addition of a seat for the driver (1864), and the use of wheels (1884), plus multiple or gang plows. The spring tooth harrow (1869) was also an important contribution. These implements could be used to prepare the soil for most field crops.

Drill planters for grains such as wheat and oats were in general use by the 1870s. The corn planter and corn cultivator were perfected by the beginning of the 1880s. Hay mowers, loaders, and forks greatly decreased labor cost for haymaking. In 1866, Entel perfected the continuous hay baler. The binders and threshers increased productivity in the harvesting of grains.

Table 11-3 compares hand methods to machine methods in the 1890s. The greatest gains were achieved in wheat, oats, and hay. The smallest gains were in cotton, tobacco, and corn. The major problem was that harvesting machinery was very difficult to develop for these crops. The corn picker was a development of the 1920s, and a really effective cotton picker had to await the end of World War II.

Table 11-3. Hand Methods Versus the Machine Methods of the 1890s (per acre).

| Crop | Time Worked | | | |
|------|-------------|--|--|--|
| | Hand | | Machine | |
| | Hours | Minutes | Hours | Minutes |
| Wheat | 61 | 5.0 | 3 | 19.2 |
| Corn | 38 | 45.0 | 15 | 7.8 |
| Oats | 66 | 15.0 | 7 | 5.8 |
| Hay: loose | 21 | 5.0 | 3 | 56.5 |
| Potatoes | 108 | 55.0 | 38 | 00.0 |
| Cotton | 167 | 48.0 | 78 | 42.0 |
| Rice: rough | 62 | 5.0 | 17 | 2.5 |
| Sugar cane | 351 | 21.0 | 191 | 33.0 |
| Tobacco | 311 | 23.0 | 252 | 54.6 |

*Source:* U.S. Commissioner of Labor, *Thirteenth Annual Report: Hand and Machine Labor,* Vol. 1 (Washington, D.C.: U.S. Government Printing Office, 1899), p. 6.

Until an efficient mechanical cotton picker could be invented, the size of tenant holdings in the South was limited by the amount the tenant family could pick. On these small farms, the use of other improved implements was not great enough to justify their costs. As a result, technical improvement, its adoption, and the resulting increase in productivity were slowest in the South.

In the Northeast, the usefulness of improved implements was reduced not only by small farms, but also by the small fields that resulted from irregular, hilly terrain.

The north central and western prairie states were the ideal setting for improved machinery. On this relatively flat terrain, with larger fields, these machines created economies of scale, and the size of farm that could achieve lowest per unit cost increased substantially. In the 1880s and early 1890s, what were called "bonanza wheat farms" appeared in the wheat belt that extended from North Dakota south to Oklahoma and northern Texas. Tens of thousands of acres of wheat land owned by one person were prepared, seeded, and harvested by gangs of hired labor operating the most modern machinery.

# Southern Agriculture

### The Southern Economy, 1865

By the end of the Civil War, the southern economy was in general collapse. Direct damage was great, especially in the war zones of Virginia, Georgia, and along the Mississippi. An important target of the Union army had been the railroad system. Much of the rolling stock and a substantial amount of track had been destroyed. Southern financial capital was completely destroyed through the issue of large amounts of eventually worthless Confederate currency. The South was now primarily dependent on the North for financial capital. The small amount of industrial capital was either destroyed by military conflict or worn out because the South could not replace industrial equipment.

Productive potential in agriculture had been seriously reduced. There were substantial decreases in horses, mules, and other farm animals and in acreage and the value of farm buildings. Along the river systems flood control levees were seriously damaged, and the freeing of the slaves presented southern agriculture with the need to create a new labor system. Table 11-4 gives some measures of the depressing effects of the war on southern agriculture. According to Kirkland,[10] it took southern agriculture at least 10 years after the war to recover to 1860 output levels.

Table 11-4. Southern Agriculture, 1860–1870 (in millions).

|  | 1860 | 1870 |
|---|---|---|
| Number of Improved Acres |  |  |
| South East | 36.6 | 24.5 |
| South Central | 30.5 | 28.1 |
| Value of Farm Land |  |  |
| South East | 795.5 | 443.0 |
| South Central | 1,022.8 | 487.5 |
| Value of Farm Buildings |  |  |
| South East | 178.6 | 127.0 |
| South Central | 203.1 | 142.6 |

*Source:* U.S. Bureau of the Census, "Agriculture, General Report and Analytical Tables," *Fourteenth Census of the United States, Taken in the Year 1920,* vol. 5 (Washington, D.C.: U.S. Government Printing Office, 1922), pp. 38–43, 50–55; and Martin L. Primack, *Farm Formed Capital in American Agriculture 1850 to 1910* (New York: Arno Press, 1977), p. 177.

# Reconstruction

Kenneth M. Stampp[16] has characterized the traditional view of the southern Reconstruction era, 1865 to 1877, with the following description: "Various historians have called this phase of American history, 'The Tragic Era,' 'The Dreadful Decade,' 'The Age of Hate,' and 'The Blackout of Honest Government.' Reconstruction represented the ultimate shame of the American people, as one historian phrased it, 'the nadir of national disgrace.' It was the epoch that most Americans wanted to forget." It was not until the 1930s that this point of view was challenged and a group of revisionist historians appeared. Stampp, a revisionist, commented, "The history of an age is seldom simple and clear-cut, seldom without its tragic aspects, seldom without its redeeming virtues."

The radical Republican reconstruction of the South had three basic aims: first, to guarantee political equality to the blacks of the South; second, to prevent the southern planter aristocracy from regaining political control and thus opposing the Republican Party; and third, to initiate economic development in the South so as to achieve black economic independence.

Southern whites would not allow blacks political or economic equality. The Black Codes of 1866 relegated the black to "a twilight zone between servitude and freedom." Radical reconstruction from 1867 based its bid for black equality on the Thirteenth, Fourteenth, and Fifteenth Amendments to the Constitution and congressional and military support to state governments dominated by white Republicans and the now enfranchised exslaves.

Republican state governments concentrated on the formation of social overhead capital, economic structures that would create a more favorable overall or general climate for development. The areas emphasized were primarily railroad construction and the development of educational facilities primarily for the blacks. A primary emphasis for developing economies today is the self-same concentration on transportation facilities and education.

Historians have tended to emphasize the political corruption rampant in the southern state Republican administrations during Reconstruction. Corruption no doubt existed, but corruption was also rampant in other areas of the country. One should not forget the scandals of the Tweed political ring, in New York City, nor the Credit Mobilier scandal, in Washington itself.

Radical reconstruction, on the whole, was a failure. Although the blacks had gained paper equality with the Thirteenth, Fourteenth, and Fifteenth Amendments, the Compromise of 1877 returned the southern state governments to white rule in exchange for southern white support in the electoral college for the election of the Republican Rutherford B. Hayes. The use of white terrorist organizations, such as the night riders and the

Ku Klux Klan, and political subterfuge effectively disenfranchised the blacks.

Radical reconstruction also failed to provide the blacks with an economic alternative to the white cotton economy. Radical Republicans could not bring themselves to implement the "40 acres and a mule" plan that would have given each black family a small farm and the needed livestock and equipment. The Freedman Bureau set up by the federal government to help the exslaves was only of temporary help and provided only limited welfare support. The blacks were forced to accommodate themselves to a market system of labor. Of necessity, they returned to the white cotton economy.

## A New Labor System

After the freeing of the slaves, the southern agricultural economy had to devise a new system of labor. Southern landowners first tried to use hired gangs of wage laborers, but, according to Shannon,[15] this system was considered unsuccessful because the landowners lacked enough control over this form of labor. Absenteeism was high, and competition between landowners for labor during the busy seasons could be considerable.

The final solution adopted by southern landowners was **sharecropping**. The landowner rented land, frequently for a black family to use, and in return received one-half to two-thirds of the crop. The family had direct responsibility, but the landowner had control of what was to be planted. In this way, the landowners were no longer responsible for the condition of the exslaves. These owners were concerned with the growing of a cash crop, and they generally forced all effort into the growing of cotton. Very little homegrown food was produced, because it was a drain on land and labor that could be used for cotton (opportunity costs were too high for the landowners).

Since very little homegrown food was produced, the sharecroppers purchased their provisions from the local store, generally on credit. Fred Shannon[15] maintains that abuses of this credit system were substantial and produced a system of what might be called "debt slavery." To enforce this system of sharecropping and debt, most of the southern states passed vagrancy and credit lien laws. People without means of support (without a job or not in sharecropping) could be arrested for vagrancy. Because of racial discrimination, the laws were implemented more vigorously for blacks. Credit extended by the local stores was secured by a lien on the crop produced by the sharecropper. The sharecropper in effect became tied to the land and this reduced their mobility. This system was used not only for the blacks but also for poor whites. And whites who owned small farms often went into debt to the local store and became entrapped into the system.

Sharecroppers. (Photo no. 48-RST-3A-9 in the National Archives)

With southern financial capital impaired by the Civil War, the South became more dependent on northern financial capital. Substantial amounts of credit were extended from New York to southern local merchants, who in turn extended credit to both plantation owners and their tenants. Cotton, the means of paying the debt, moved back up the chain of debt to New York, as it had before the Civil War. This debt structure forced most of agricultural effort into cotton.

It is an open question whether or not at the high levels of output achieved, producing cotton was based on minimizing opportunity cost. For the sharecropper, probably some resources devoted to foods grown and consumed on the farm would have yielded a higher return than cotton. Both the debt and tenant relationships prevented producing home-grown food. The landowners, also entrapped in this system of debt, had fewer options as to the use of the land. Perhaps through experimentation and diversification the landowner could have emerged with a more productive mix of output. The need to service a large debt may well have pressured southern agriculture into an ever-increasing output of cotton. It was not at all obvious, then, that cotton production minimized opportunity cost.

Figure 11-2 describes cotton production from 1866 to 1898. Acres grown increased from 6 million in 1866 to 25 million in 1898. It is interesting that this increase in output was accompanied by a fall in prices from about 16 cents a pound in 1869 to a little less than 6 cents a pound in 1898. The system of debt and tenancy was substantially responsible for forcing greater effort into cotton as prices fell.

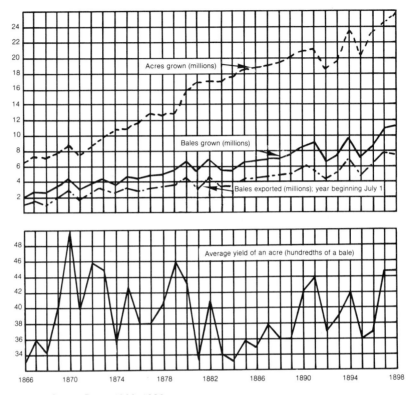

Figure 11-2. Cotton Data, 1866–1898.

*Source:* Fred Shannon, *The Farmer's Last Frontier: Agriculture 1860–1897* (New York: Harper & Row, 1945), p. 113.

Table 11-5 shows the increase in the number of farms in the South as the process of sharecropping developed. According to Fred Shannon[15], by 1900 five-sixths of black farmers were croppers or tenants and five-eights of the whites farming cotton were croppers. White croppers outnumbered the blacks by five to four.

The price decline in cotton (see Figure 11-2) was not only due to the increase in output of southern cotton stimulated in large degree by the share-cropper-credit lien system, but also to increased world supply, especially from such places as Egypt and India. England, starved for cotton for its textile mills during the Civil War, had stimulated cotton production in Egypt and India, which became serious competitiors. In addition, the rate of growth in textile production in the Northeast and Europe was relatively low after this industry had reached maturity around 1870. Prices fell because supply had increased very substantially, while demand experienced only a moderate rate of growth.

A further problem facing southern cotton production was the slow

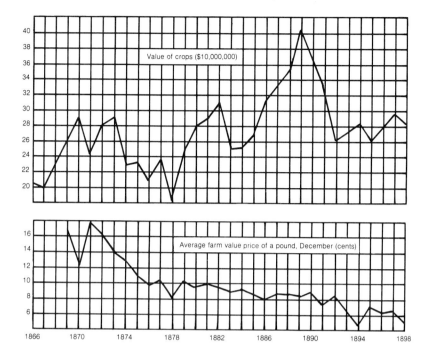

Figure 11-2. continued.

development of technology. Abundant and cheap supplies of labor, plus the difficulty of adapting machinery to cotton harvesting, contributed to this near absence of technological improvement in cotton production.

Improvement in technology would increase supply and thereby decrease prices, but it would also increase productivity and thus lower costs and perhaps increase profits. While the lack of technological advancement reduced one pressure toward increased supply and lower prices, it also meant the continuation of low levels of productivity and low incomes for cotton growers.

Despite the problems of increased output and falling prices, cotton was still the dominant cash crop in the South. In 1900, the cotton crop was

Table 11-5. Number of Farms in the South (in 1000s).

|  | 1850 | 1860 | 1870 | 1880 | 1890 | 1900 |
|---|---|---|---|---|---|---|
| South East | 242 | 304 | 367 | 637 | 740 | 953 |
| South Central | 255 | 327 | 448 | 772 | 849 | 1199 |

*Source:* U.S. Bureau of the Census, "Agriculture, General Report and Analytical Tables," *Fourteenth Census of the United States, Taken in the Year 1920,* vol. 5 (Washington, D.C.: U.S. Government Printing Office, 1922), pp. 38-43.

valued at approximately $280 million. The value of the second most important cash crop in the South, tobacco, was only about $40 million. Although his crown was tarnished, his robes ragged, and his house in great disrepair, cotton was still king in the South.

# Agriculture in the Northeast

The major problem of northeastern agriculture was increased competition from the developing West. The West's higher fertility and greater adaptability of improved machinery, plus declining fertility in the Northeast, increasingly pressured agriculture there. The completion of the railroad network west of the Mississippi provided an efficient transportation system to move western production to the East. The discriminatory system of railroad rates* that at times made long-haul rates less than short-haul rates often put eastern agriculture under a cost disadvantage.

Urbanization in the Northeast increased the demand for fresh milk and vegetables, and in areas near cities farmers specialized in these products. Railroads, especially after the development of refrigerated cars, greatly extended the agricultural area that could produce milk and vegetables. In regions farther removed from urban areas, the product of the dairy herds went into butter and cheese; factories to process the milk increased substantially in number.

But as western competition took its toll, marginal land and farms were abandoned. Table 11-6 shows that the decade with the highest number of improved acres in the Northeast was the 1880s (47 million acres). This total declined to 37 million by 1910. The high point in the number of farms also was reached in 1880 (705,000), which declined to 668,000 by 1910.

# Western and Midwestern Agriculture

On the basis of agricultural products, the West and Midwest can be divided into three areas: the corn belt, the wheat belt, and the livestock frontier. As Figure 11-3 shows, the corn belt spreads from Ohio through Iowa, the wheat belt lies in the prairie states, and the livestock frontier lies to the west.

## The Corn Belt

By 1860, the forested areas of the corn belt in Ohio, Indiana, and Illinois had been settled. After the Civil War, the areas of Iowa, eastern Nebraska,

---

*To economists, price discrimination exists for a good when prices of that good vary and the differences are not proportional to cost differences.

Table 11-6. Number of Improved Acres and Farms in the Northeast.

|  | 1850 | 1860 | 1870 | 1880 | 1890 | 1900 | 1910 |
|---|---|---|---|---|---|---|---|
| **Number of farms (in thousands)** | | | | | | | |
| New England | 168 | 184 | 181 | 207 | 190 | 192 | 189 |
| Mid-Atlantic | 328 | 388 | 429 | 498 | 478 | 495 | 479 |
| Total | 496 | 572 | 610 | 705 | 668 | 687 | 668 |
| **Number of improved acres (in millions)** | | | | | | | |
| New England | 11 | 12 | 12 | 13 | 11 | 8 | 7 |
| Mid-Atlantic | 23 | 27 | 30 | 34 | 32 | 32 | 30 |
| Total | 34 | 39 | 42 | 47 | 43 | 40 | 37 |

*Source:* U.S. Bureau of the Census, "Agriculture, General Report and Analytical Tables," *Fourteenth Census of the United States Taken in the Year 1920,* vol. 5 (Washington, D.C.: U.S. Government Printing Office, 1922), pp. 38–43.

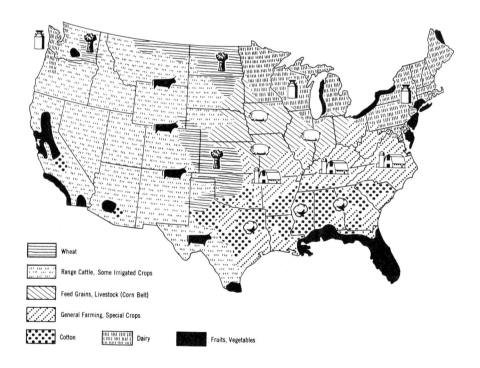

Wheat

Range Cattle, Some Irrigated Crops

Feed Grains, Livestock (Corn Belt)

General Farming, Special Crops

Cotton        Dairy        Fruits, Vegetables

Figure 11-3. Agricultural Regions, 1860 to 1897.

*Source:* Ross Robertson, *History of the American Economy,* 3d ed. (New York: Harcourt Brace Jovanovich, 1973), p. 300. Copyright 1955. Copyright 1964, 1973 by Harcourt Brace Jovanovich, Inc.

Missouri, southern Michigan, and Minnesota became the frontier and were quickly settled. But the problems found in the prairies were different from those of the forested areas.

By 1870, it took only 1.5 man-days to break an acre of sod in the prairie, while it took 15 to clear an acre of forest land for the plow. This decrease in clearing costs provides an important explanation for the rapid rate of settlement of the prairie. There were, however, severe disadvantages to the prairies. Wood was scarce for housing, farm buildings, and fencing, and the lack of fuel to heat the homes of the farmers was critical. Buffalo chips (dry dung) and later cow chips were a standard source of fuel, and the sod itself was used to build sod huts. The scarcity of streams and limited rainfall increased the problem of finding an adequate water supply. Locust plagues (the worst in 1874), blizzards, prairie fires, floods, and high temperatures during the summer were serious threats to people, animals, and crops. The vagaries of weather, especially the apparent recurrence of cycles of wet and dry seasons, was a serious problem. The wet part of the cycle enticed settlement much farther than was justified, and farms were brutally wiped out during the dry part of the cycle. These problems appeared to be greater the farther west toward the Rockies settlement went.

## The Wheat Belt

Wheat continued to be the major cash crop on the frontier until it reached the area of minimum rainfall, beyond which the growing of crops was too risky. By 1900, there was a well-defined wheat belt confined by rainfall sufficient for wheat but not great enough for more diversified agriculture. This area started with North Dakota and parts of Montana and then went south through South Dakota, western Kansas, Nebraska, Missouri, Oklahoma and parts of northern Texas.

California was a leading wheat-producing state until the development of refrigerated cars and irrigation shifted production to fruits and vegetables. Technological change contributes to changing opportunity costs. Refrigeration and irrigation increased the profits that could be obtained from fruits and vegetables, and thus wheat was abandoned for the now relatively more profitable alternatives. The opportunity costs of wheat (what wheat growers gave up by not producing fruits and vegetables) had increased.

These wheat areas in the western prairies had fertile soil and flat topography and were most suited for the use of the improved machinery of the second half of the nineteenth century. In the 1870s, cheap land, high levels of rainfall, completion of railroad transportation, high prices for wheat, and the development of flour-milling machinery for northern-grown spring wheat contributed to the rapid settlement of the northern wheat belt.

## The Cattle Frontier

When American agriculture first reached the prairie around 1860, the ranchers and herders outnumbered farmers along the frontier. As farms increased in number, cutting down the amount of free grazing land for the rancher, population pressure increased the price of land, and the livestock rancher moved farther west, leaving the land to be used more intensively for crop farming. Eventually livestock ranching reached areas where rainfall was too low and unpredictable for crop production. By 1900, the cattle belt was established west of the wheat belt and east of the Pacific coastal farming areas.

# Agricultural Discontent

The post-Civil War period, especially after the beginning of the depression of 1873, was known as the "age of agrarian discontent." Along with the creation of millions of new farms, and the bringing into production of hundreds of millions of acres, came a series of problems that vexed great sectors of U.S. agriculture. Many farmers saw these problems under three main categories: the steady fall in farm prices; discriminating practices by the railroads; and unfair practices by agricultural middlemen and food processors.

## Agricultural Prices

Figure 11-4 shows that the index of farm prices fell from a high of 161 in 1864 to 72 in 1878 and 1879, then to a low of 56 in 1896. General prices declined from 192 in 1864 to 90 in 1879 and 69 in 1896. The problem was not a deterioration in the terms of trade between farm prices and general prices, for although the relation between the two varied (as shown in Figure 11-4), prices in general fell somewhat more than agricultural prices. But general prices are a poor indicator in this case: Profit margins narrowed, because many items of cost more important to farmers than the general price index did not decline as fast as the prices of agricultural products.

Compounding the problem of narrowing and disappearing profit margins was the effect of falling prices on the burden of paying debts. As the West was filled by expanding agricultural settlement, agricultural debt mounted to pay for land, equipment, and livestock as well as for the cost

Figure 11-4. Index of Wholesale Prices of Farm Products and All Commodities, 1860–1900.

*Source:* George F. Warren and Frank A. Pearson, *Gold and Prices* (New York: Wiley, 1935), pp. 30–31; and Fred Shannon, *The Farmer's Last Frontier: Agriculture 1860–1897* (New York: Harper & Row, 1945), p. 294.

of maintaining the farmer until his land could provide enough cash income. As the prices of agricultural products fell and the dollar volume of debt did not decline, more products would have to be produced to pay off a given amount of debt. Primack and Willis have shown that this debt burden was indeed significant. If we assume that only the interest on mortgage debt was paid, it would have amounted to 17% of the net cash income of mortgaged farms in the United States as a whole, 16% in Iowa, and 32% in Pennsylvania. These figures become even more significant when nonmortgage debt is included.

## Railroads

The farmers' complaints about the railroads centered in two broad areas: the setting of rates and railroad monopolization of certain middleman functions.

Although farmers complained that general rates were too high, the statistical evidence seems to indicate that railroad rates in general fell at about the same rates as agricultural prices. Rather, the major problem with railroad rates involved rate discrimination. The specific rate for a particular farmer depended on a whole set of competitive forces that varied greatly in kind and intensity from place to place. Competition from other railroads and forms of transportation, such as river, lake, coastal, and canal transportation, created a complex system of shipping costs.

Short-haul versus long-haul charges was the subject of a very intense controversy. Often shippers found that charges on goods shipped a longer distance were less than charges for shorter distances. This inequity gave the long-haul shipper a per mile cost advantage over the short-haul shipper. Eastern farmers suffered substantially from this form of discrimination.

Rebates were another form of discrimination that created discontent. If the farming enterprise was large enough, it could pressure the railroads to rebate a portion of the shipping fees. This practice was a serious disadvantage to the smaller farmers.

Farmers in areas of considerable competition in transportation had advantages, while those in areas without competition, with perhaps a single railroad, were exposed to the use of monopoly power, the ability of the railroad to dictate price. Even in areas of competition and lower rates, the smaller farmers were at a disadvantage in comparison to the larger ones because they did not have the ability to negotiate rebates.

In the north central and midwestern prairie states, where wheat was the major crop shipped, railroads tended to branch into grain storage. Farmers often complained that the railroads were forcing them to use these storage facilities at high fees by refusing to ship wheat except from these storage facilities.

## Agricultural Middlemen

Farmers complained bitterly about the increased monopolization of middleman functions between the farmer and the ultimate consumer. Complaints also were expressed because combination movement in industries producing what the farmers needed to buy tended to generate higher prices. The former lowered the prices farmers received for their output. The latter increased the prices of the things farmers bought.

An example of a middleman organization that lowered the farmers' profits was the milk-marketing trust. The New York Milk Exchange, Ltd., formed around 1882, fixed the prices paid to farmers for milk around the Metropolitan New York City area. This kept milk prices to the farmers low in sections of the five states marketing milk in New York. In 1895, it dissolved and was reorganized as the Consolidated Milk Exchange after the courts had concurred that it was fixing prices in violation of the 1890 Sherman Antitrust Act.

Another example, the Illinois Grain Dealers' Association, formed in 1890. The aim was to kill the emerging farmer cooperative grain storage movement. The association pressured railroads and commission merchants in the central city markets to ship or sell wheat only from the association.

Many farmers reacted to these problems by direct political action and the development of the agricultural cooperative movement.

## Agriculture in the Political Arena, 1865-1897

The effort of many farmers to affect their economic situation by direct political action can be divided by decades into three distinct phases: the 1870s, the 1880s, and the 1890s. In the 1870s, a number of different farm organizations became directly involved in politics and captured a number of state legislatures and governorships with these third-party organizations. The group most numerous was the Grange, and the Grange name was given to a series of legislation passed by these farmer parties. These Granger laws, which imposed state regulation of railroads, were passed in 1871 in Illinois and Minnesota and in 1874 in Iowa and Wisconsin.

The railroads fought state regulatory laws, but in 1876 in *Munn v. Illinois* the Supreme Court upheld the right of states to regulate railroads. In 1886 and 1890, the Supreme Court reversed itself. State laws that regulated railroads were held to be invalid under first, the clause in the Constitution forbidding states to interfere with interstate commerce, and second, the Fourteenth Amendment due process clause.

In the 1880s, farmers' groups joined others to launch the national party that came to be called the Greenback Party. It advocated the issuance of unbacked paper currency (greenbacks) to increase the supply of money and to increase prices. (Remember the equation of exchange in Chapters 4 and 9.) Increases in prices would increase profit margins and reduce the burden of debt (how much the farmer would have to produce to pay off a dollar of debt). During the 1880s, farmers' clubs began to coalesce into alliances. By 1890, there were three grand alliances, one in the North, the second in the South, and the third a black farmers' alliance.

In the election of 1890, the farmers' alliances with labor allies gained control of seven state legislatures and elected three federal senators and 52 congressmen, mostly from the South. In 1892, in St. Louis, the People's or Populist Party was born out of a coalition of farmers, labor unions, and reform organizations. The party's presidential candidate polled 9% of the popular vote and received 22 electoral votes.

The Populist Party platform called for regulation of railroads and other monopolies, low tariffs to reduce monopoly power, free coinage of silver and issuance of greenbacks to increase the money supply and prices, a subtreasury plan that would scatter the national treasury across the country and enable it to issue very low-interest loans to farmers, and a plan to have the government buy up farm surpluses to keep farm prices higher.

By 1900, it seemed obvious that the farmers' efforts at third-party politics had failed. The Interstate Commerce Commission (1887) and the Sherman Antitrust Act of 1890 were rendered impotent by the Supreme Court, which undercut federal efforts to regulate railroads and monopolies. But by 1900 general prosperity returned, and farm prices and incomes began to climb. Farmers' discontent evaporated under the pleasant wave of prosperity.

## Farmers' Cooperative Movement

A U.S. Department of Agriculture bulletin reported that in 1907 there were about 85,000 farmer cooperatives (business enterprises, other than farms, owned by groups of farmers and operated for mutual benefit) affecting over 3 million farmers, half the farmers in the United States. Despite these seemingly impressive figures, by 1907 the farmer cooperative movement had achieved only limited success.

About 72,000 of these cooperatives involved irrigation, telephone, or insurance services. These forms of cooperation were necessary if the farmer was to get such services at all or at rates the average farmer could afford. These forms of cooperation were in areas in which private enterprise did not provide the needed services. Most of the 3 million co-op farmer members went no further in their cooperation than this.

Fred Shannon[15] summarizes the position of the rest of the farmers' co-op movement with the following:

> The stores, marketing associations, and elevators comprised about all the rest of the businesses of any economic significance and these totaled less than seven thousand by 1907, or possibly half as many a decade earlier. It was along these lines that the greatest growth occurred after 1907. If there were a thousand cooperative elevators by the end of the century, they may have benefited a hundred thousand grain growers. But as long as the farmers had no control over the exchanges, and did little if anything to limit their crops to the visible market—as long as the industrial worker was so poorly paid that he could not eat his fill—the saving on marketing costs often was not enough to do more for the farmer than allow him to break even. Much the same might be said for the marketing associations and stores. They were all very nice in their way, but they did not go far enough.

The farmers' co-ops had to overcome many problems, including the lack of skilled management. Knowledge about running cooperatives took time to acquire. Because financial capital was always in short supply, most co-ops operated without reserves against hard times. By charging as little as possible and thus encouraging privately owned competitors to enter price wars, the co-ops prevented the accumulation of desperately needed reserves. Toward the end of the century, the co-ops adopted the Rochdale principles, which included the idea of providing services or goods at the prevailing market price and giving dividends based on patronage at the end of the year. Another problem that plagued many co-ops was the lack of membership loyalty. When a private competitor offered a temporary advantage, many members would forsake their co-ops. Overall, the most important question was how the co-ops could compete against privately-owned and often large economic units in the marketplace.

Eventually, in the twentieth century, farmers' cooperatives carved out a place for themselves in the market economy of the United States. They performed important functions for the farming community, but they did not provide the panacea that many of their founders had envisioned. It was not until the depression of the 1930s and the New Deal that the federal government interfered heavily in the agricultural marketplace in order to raise farm incomes. But that is a story for a later chapter.

We are reserving for the next time period the theoretical analysis of monopoly and bilateral monopoly.

# Conclusions

The supply of agricultural products of all types increased at an astonishing rate in the United States from 1865 to 1897. This increase in supply was caused by increases in farm land and farmers, and increases in productivity resulting from acceleration of the technological revolution in farm machinery. Although demand also increased, the increase in supply caused prices to decline.

The farming sector was thus plagued by problems, and efforts to solve them resulted in institutional changes. One of these changes was the southern labor system in which tenant-debt bondage replaced slavery. But the farmers' efforts also produced changes in politics and political parties and attempts to establish a farm cooperative movement.

In studying agriculture, or any other sector of the economy, one must be aware of the forces affecting the market. But these forces are not simply technical or theoretical factors that give rise to quantifiable costs. They are also social, political, ideological, philosophical, and historical. One must understand both economic and social causes and also the economic and social consequences of particular choices made in response to economic situations.

# Review of Economic Concepts: Demand, Supply, Equilibrium Price, and Elasticity

## Demand

The main points about the theory of demand are as follows:
1. Demand is not a specific price-quantity relationship, but rather a schedule of the various quantities that buyers are *willing* and *able* to buy at various prices during a particular time period.
2. The demand schedule is constructed under the assumption that, except for price and quantity, all factors affecting demand are constant.
3. When the market demand schedule is diagrammed, the resulting demand curve slopes down, to the right. In other words, the law of demand states that price and quantity are inversely related. Check $D_0$ in Figure 11-5.
4. When factors other than price and quantity change, the demand curve shifts, changing all prices and quantities. The factors that shift the demand curve are (a) changes in tastes and preferences; (b) changes in money incomes; (c) changes in the prices of other goods; (d) changes in price expectations of buyers; and (e) changes in the number of buyers.
5. Again referring to Figure 11-5, observe that when demand increases, the demand curve shifts up from $D_0$ to $D_1$. When demand decreases, the demand curve shifts down from $D_0$ to $D_2$.

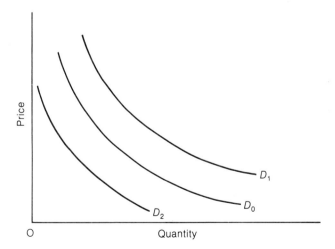

Figure 11-5. Demand.

## Supply

The main points about the theory of supply are as follows:
1. Supply is not a specific price-quantity relationship, but rather a schedule of the various quantities that sellers are *willing* and *able* to sell at various prices during a particular time period.
2. The supply schedule is constructed under the assumption that except for price and quantity, all factors affecting supply are constant.
3. When the market supply schedule is diagrammed, the resulting supply curve slopes up, to the right. In other words, the law of supply states that price and quantity are directly related. Check $S_0$ in Figure 11-6.
4. When factors other than price and quantity change, the supply curve shifts. The factors that can shift the supply curve are: (a) changes in technology; (b) changes in the prices of the factors of production used; (c) changes in the prices of other commodities using the same factors of production; (d) changes in price expectations of sellers; and (e) changes in the number of sellers.
5. Referring to Figure 11-6, observe that when supply increases, the supply curve shifts down from $S_0$ to $S_1$. When supply decreases, the supply curve shifts up from $S_0$ to $S_2$.

## Equilibrium Price

The main points of the theory of equilibrium pricing are
1. The equilibrium, or market clearing price and quantity, is that point at which supply and demand are equal. In Figure 11-7, equilibrium occurs at Price A and Quantitity B.

Figure 11-6. Supply.

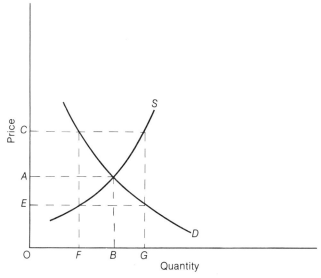

Figure 11-7. Equilibrium.

2. If price is above the equilibrium price (A), say at price C, the quantity supplied is G, but the quantity demanded is F. There is an excess supply (surplus) of FG, and sellers compete with each other, driving price C down toward price A.
3. If price is below the equilibrium price (A), say, at price E, the quantity supplied is F but the quantity demanded is G. An excess demand (shortage) of FG causes buyers to compete with each other, driving price up toward A.
4. The model assumes that there is competition, that no buyer or seller can influence price.

## Elasticity

The concept of price elasticity of demand analyzes the demand curve from a new direction. The law of demand simply noted the general slope of the demand curve, that as price declined, quantity demanded increased. Elasticity deals with the question of the rate at which quantity changes as price varies. **Price elasticity of demand** is a measure of the responsiveness of quantity demanded to changes in price along a given portion of a demand curve. In very simple terms, if quantity responds little to a given change in price, demand is **inelastic**; if it responds by a lot, demand is **elastic**. If the response of quantity is proportionate to the change in price, demand is **unit elastic**.

More precisely: If the percentage change in quantity demanded is greater than the percentage change in price, demand is elastic. If the percentage change in quantity demanded is less than the percentage change in price, demand is inelastic. If the percentage change in quantity demanded is equal to the percentage change in price, demand is unit elastic. Specific values for elasticity can be obtained by using the following formula:

$$E = \frac{(Q_1 - Q_2)/(Q_1 + Q_2)}{(P_1 - P_2)/(P_1 + P_2)}$$

Remember that $E$ is the *elasticity coefficient*, $Q_1$ is beginning quantity, $Q_2$ is ending quantity, $P_1$ is beginning price, and $P_2$ is ending price. If $E$ is greater than 1, demand is elastic. If $E$ is less than 1, demand is inelastic. If $E$ is equal to 1, demand is unit elastic. (Ignore the negative sign in the result for it has no economic significance.)

Figure 11-8 is a simple illustration of the concept of elasticity. Beginning price for both $D_1$ and $D_2$ is $B$ and ending price is $A$. For demand curve $D_1$ beginning quantity is $C$ and ending quantity is $E$. For demand curve $D_2$ beginning quantity is $C$ and ending quantity is $F$. For the same change in price, from $B$ to $A$, $D_2$ experiences a much greater increase in quantity demanded ($C$ to $F$) than $D_1$ (only $C$ to $E$). Demand curve $D_2$ is more elastic than $D_1$ between the price range $B$ to $A$. We do not know by how much or whether either curve is elastic, inelastic, or unitary because we do not have numerical values.

What are the factors that make the demand for a good more elastic or less elastic?

1. *Perishability (inelastic) or durability (elastic).* New purchases can more easily be postponed for durable goods than for perishable goods; hence, a consumer can respond more readily to changes in the prices of durable goods.
2. *Necessity (inelastic) or luxury (elastic).* Luxury goods may be regarded as those whose consumption can be postponed, while purchase of a necessity cannot. Thus quantity demanded of luxury goods varies more with price than quantity demanded of necessities.

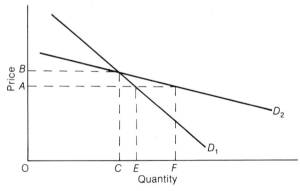

Figure 11-8. Elasticity.

3. *Number of close substitutes.* The larger the number of close substitutes for a good, the more easily one can respond to changes in its price, and the more elastic is its demand.
4. *Percentage of total expenditures.* The larger the percentage of a consumer's total expenditures is spent on a particular commodity, the more the consumer is aware of and affected by a change in price, and thus the more elastic is the consumer's demand for that commodity.

In brief, then, factors that contribute to an inelastic demand are perishability, necessity, small number of substitutes, and a small percentage of total expenditures. The factors that contribute to an elastic demand are durability, luxury, large number of close substitutes, and a large percentage of total expenditures.

The concept of elasticity can be applied to situations other than price and demand. Two further examples are of interest. **Price elasticity of supply** measures the responsiveness of quantity supplied to changes in price. **Income elasticity of demand** measures the responsiveness of quantity purchased to changes in money income.

---

# Glossary

**Elastic demand**   The result when quantity responds greatly to a given change in price; or the percentage change in quantity is greater than the percentage change in price; or the elasticity coefficient is greater than 1.

**Elasticity coefficient**   A number indicating the degree of responsiveness of quantity to something else as for example the price elasticity of demand represented by the following formula:

$$\frac{Q_1 - Q_2}{Q_1 + Q_2} \div \frac{P_1 - P_2}{P_1 + P_2}$$

$Q_1$ is beginning quantity, $Q_2$ is ending quantity, $P_1$ is beginning price, and $P_2$ is ending price. (Ignore the minus sign in the results.)

**Income elasticity of demand**   A measure of the responsiveness of quantity demanded to changes in money income.

**Inelastic demand**   The result when quantity responds little to a given change in price; or the percentage change in quantity is less than the percentage change in price; or the elasticity coefficient is less than 1.

**Monopoly power**   The ability of an economic entity to influence the price of a product, service, or resource.

**Price elasticity of demand**   A measure of the responsiveness of quantity demanded to changes in price along a given demand curve.

242 An Economic History of the United States

**Price elasticity of supply** A measure of the responsiveness of quantity supplied to changes in price along a given supply curve.

**Safety valve theory** The assumption that in the nineteenth century the free or nearly free land on the frontier would provide an alternative to eastern industrial employment and would limit the ability of industrial employers to "exploit or oppress" the American working class.

**Sharecropping** A system of tenancy in which the renter pays the landlord a certain percentage of his crop for the use of the land.

**Unit elastic demand** The relationship in which quantity responds proportionately to a given change in price; or the percentage change in quantity is equal to the percentage change in price; or the elasticity coefficient is equal to 1.

# Questions

1. Give examples drawn from agriculture of factors that can affect demand. Do the same for supply.
2. How does each of your example factors affect equilibrium price?
3. How does elasticity affect the agricultural market?
4. Was radical reconstruction in the South after the Civil War a failure? Why or why not?
5. What was the new labor system created to replace slavery? Did it increase or decrease economic flexibility? Why?
6. Describe various government policies that affected agriculture after 1860. How did they affect agriculture? Were they good policies? Why or why not?
7. What were the problems of applying the new agricultural technology to the post-Civil War South? The Northeast? The prairies? Was the new technology beneficial to the farmers? Why or why not?
8. What were some major economic problems facing the post-Civil War farmers in the Northeast?
9. What were major advantages and disadvantages of farming in the corn belt? The wheat belt? The livestock frontier?
10. What were the major problems causing the farmers' discontent after 1870? How did farmers attempt to deal with them? Were they successful? Why or why not?

# Suggested Readings

1. Bogue, Allan G. *From Prairie to Corn Belt.* Chicago: University of Chicago Press, 1963.

2. Bogue, Allan G. *Money at Interest: The Farm Mortgage on the Middle Border.* Ithaca, N.Y.: Cornell University Press, 1955.

3. Brown, Wiliam W., and Reynolds, Morgan O. "Debt Peonage Re-examined." *Journal of Economic History, 33* (December 1973).

4. DeConio, Stephan. "Cotton 'Overproduction' in Late Nineteenth-Century Southern Agriculture." *Journal of Economic History, 33* (September 1973).

5. Farmer, Hallie. "The Economic Background of Frontier Populism." *The Mississippi Valley Historical Review, 10* (March 1924).

6. Fite, Gilbert. *The Farmers' Frontier, 1865–1900.* New York: Holt, Rinehart and Winston, 1966.

7. Hayter, Earl. *The Troubled Farmer, 1850–1900.* DeKalb: Northern Illinois University Press, 1970.

8. Hicks, John D. *The Populist Revolt.* Minneapolis: University of Minnesota Press, 1931.

9. Higgs, Robert. "Race, Tenure and Resource Allocation in Southern Agriculture, 1910." *Journal of Economic History, 33* (March 1973).

10. Kirkland, Edward C. *Industry Comes of Age: Business, Labor, and Public Policy 1860–1897.* New York: Holt, Rinehart and Winston, 1961.

11. Mayhew, Anne. "A Reappraisal of the Causes of Farm Protest in the United States, 1870–1900." *Journal of Economic History, 32* (June 1972).

12. Miller, George H. *Railroads and the Granger Laws.* Madison: University of Wisconsin Press, 1971.

13. Primack, Martin L., and Willis, James. "Debt and Tenancy in American Agriculture." Unpublished paper.

14. Reid, Joseph D., Jr. "Sharecropping as an Understandable Market Response—The Post-Bellum South." *Journal of Economic History, 33* (March 1973).

15. Shannon, Fred A. *The Farmer's Last Frontier: Agriculture 1860–1897.* New York: Harper & Row, 1945.

16. Stampp, Kenneth M. *The Era of Reconstruction 1865–1877.* New York: Vintage Books, 1967.

17. Sutch, Richard, and Ransom, Roger. "Debt Peonage in the Cotton South after the Civil War." *Journal of Economic History, 32* (September 1972).

18. Willis, James, and Primack, Martin L. *Explorations in Economics.* Boston: Houghton Mifflin, 1977. Chaps. 3, 15, 16, and 17.

19. Wright, Gavin. "Cotton Competition and the Post-Bellum Recovery of the American South." *Journal of Economic History, 34* (September 1974).

# Chapter 12

---

# Transportation, Industry, and Labor

The Civil War took place following a half-century of industrial expansion. The last third of the nineteenth century saw a continuation of this expansion, stimulated by the completion of a national transportation network, especially the railroads. Accompanying and perhaps created by, this industrial expansion was the establishment and growth of national labor unions. But this expansion of the economy was not uniform or proportional in all sectors: Some sectors led and pulled along others. The leaders were the railroads, iron and steel manufacturing, and related activities. This chapter, then, starts out with an analysis of the history of the progress of railroads, of industry generally, and of labor unions in the 1865–1897 period.

## The Railroads

A sector that led the economy and was a primary factor in stimulating the economic development of the United States in the second half of the nineteenth century was the railway industry. In 1865, there were 35,000 miles of railway track; by 1900, there were over 242,000 miles of track. In 1860, railway construction had just begun to cross the Mississippi River. By 1897, there were five transcontinental railroads.

Table 12-1 shows another measure of the expansion of railroads after the Civil War. Per capita freight on railroads increased from 78 ton-miles in 1859 to 1,861 ton-miles in 1900, a 2500 percent increase.

Economic stimulus can be divided into three kinds: primary or direct,

Table 12-1. Railroad Freight Volume, 1859–1900.

| Year | Total Freight Volume (1,000,000 ton-miles) | Freight Volume Per Capita (ton-miles) |
|---|---|---|
| 1859 | 2,400 | 78 |
| 1882 | 39,302 | 744 |
| 1890 | 79,193 | 1,256 |
| 1900 | 141,597 | 1,861 |

*Source:* Richard K. Vedder, *The American Economy in Historical Perspective* (Belmont, Calif.: Wadsworth, 1976), p. 152.

secondary, and tertiary. The effects of railroad development on the economy were enormous. The primary or direct effects were in actual construction of the roads, which involved wages paid to the labor employed in construction and the facilities and services needed to maintain that labor.

The secondary effects included the stimulus to those industries that provided the materials used in construction. Two industries were of special importance in this context. Perhaps the most important was the iron and steel industry. It provided the iron and steel for the hundreds of thousands of miles of track and for the many bridges needed to cross rivers and mountains. The second major industry was the railway equipment industry, suppliers of the needed locomotives and railroad cars.

These two industries provide an excellent example of what Albert Hirschman meant by backward linkages. Hirschman[13], in *The Strategy of Economic Development*, maintained not only that historic growth was unbalanced but also that the best approach for rapid development was to unbalance investment in some deliberate, predesigned way. He pointed out that economic activities have both **forward** and **backward linkages.** These linkages and linkage effects are not just input-output relations (forming a demand-supply stimulus); they also establish the probability of the linkage activity or industry. The construction of the railroads clearly pointed to increased demand for the output of railroad equipment and steel ties. At first the demand was substantially filled by imports, but in time domestic development met the linkage needs. These linkage relationships increased the probability of profits large enough to justify the creation of such new domestic facilities.

Railways provided the stimulus for the expansion of plant and equipment to produce steel and rolling stock. The increased level of demand for output also permitted the use of the most up-to-date technology.

Tertiary effects included the general stimulus to the economy as a more efficient transportation system was created. Transportation costs fell. Isolated localized markets were integrated into larger market areas.

Competition between regions increased. Demand for individual firms' output increased, permitting efficiencies of larger scale and more up-to-date technology.

These tertiary effects can be interpreted as forward linkages: Transportation facilities created the opportunities for firms to find sources of supplies from outside their immediate geographic areas and new firms found wider markets for their products.

Railroad development was a classic example of Schumpeter's **innovation** theory. Joseph Schumpeter[23] also developed a theory of unbalanced growth—first in his 1911 book, *Theory of Economic Development*, and later, more fully, in *Business Cycles*. To Schumpeter, the process of development was discontinuous. Economies were disturbed from stable, no-development conditions by the introduction of one or more innovations (a new product, process, machine, or market).

When such innovations occur, the expectation of profit induces banks to lend funds to entrepreneur-innovators in the field. With these funds, resources are bid into these new activities and away from other possible uses. Schumpeter maintains that the required investment in new plant and equipment is made mainly by new firms under the leadership of "new men." The creation of new leadership becomes the basis of capitalist dynamics.

The first innovators obtain monopoly profit. But imitators quickly appear eager to share in the profitability of the new innovation. Clusters of development occur, expanding the economy. The innovation forces old industry to adapt to the changing pattern of economic conditions.

Eventually the innovation is fully developed, and the required new facilities are completed. Output pours forth from the completed facilities. Investment drops down to replacement level. Or overinvestment may occur, and capacity may exceed demand for the output. New investment falls, and the economy contracts until the excess capacity is worked off. The economy arrives at a new stable position but at a higher level of development.

Schumpeter feels that the "first innovators" pushed railroads to new areas and were followed by imitators who created clusters of investment. New railroads and new leaders emerged in the process. The total effects of these actions go far beyond the direct effects of railroad construction and operation. Existing industries had to adapt to the new situation as a comprehensive railroad system created opportunities for the development of new firms.

Was railroad expansion after the Civil War as significant in nineteenth-century development, as many economic historians believe? Robert Fogel,[5] among others, does not think so. In *Railroads and American Economic Growth*, Fogel claims that the fact that prior to the Civil War about 50% of the U.S. output of pig iron supposedly went into rails diminishes substantially on closer scrutiny, as imports and reuse of old rails are considered. The impact on coal mining was minimal, because wood was the widely used fuel. Further, the widespread use of wood for bridges and railway cars reduced demand for iron. Fogel's claim about the reduced significance of railroads on U.S. economic development was more relevant before the Civil War than after. After 1865, domestic steel production expanded rapidly, and imports of all kinds of steel or iron products decreased steadily, including rail and locomotive imports. As the forests were cleared and wood became less easily available, coal use increased, especially in the east. As the new steel technology (Bessemer's process for example) became more widespread, steel decreased in cost and was used more widely in construction.

There is no doubt that Fogel's analysis has substantially reduced the formerly presumed significance of railroad expansion. Even so, railroad growth from 1865 to 1897 was perhaps the most important single factor in the general expansion over those years.

## Railroad Construction and Finance

Railroad construction was not only an important factor in total effective demand and general economic activity, but it also played an important role in the financial world. In 1860, the value of stocks and bonds of U.S. railroads was $1.8 billion; by 1897, their value had risen to over $10 billion. However, after the Civil War only token issues of railroad stock were publicly offered, and the main instrument used to raise capital was debt (bonds). To give some idea of the importance of railroad financing, the federal debt in 1897 was only $1.2 billion.

The problems of estimating the financial needs and the business expected were considerable. There was little knowledge about the ultimate costs of construction, as there were large lapses of time from the beginning of construction to completion, and the conditions under which plans were made could change totally by completion time. Because the railroads were often developmental (they often were built in undeveloped areas, creating stimulus for development), there could be very little foreknowledge of how much traffic could be expected on a railroad line once it was operational.

The railroad **construction companies** were incorporated separately from the railroads they were to build. Their primary function was to raise capital and then to construct the railroad. Most often, however, the construction company received the railroad company's stocks for nothing and received the bonds at a discount. To many promoters, the impetus for the construction of railroads was not the potential profits of the completed railroads themselves, but rather the profits on the construction company.

There were two main disadvantages in using the construction company form of financing the building of the railroads. It substantially increased the possibility for speculation and manipulation of railroad securities, which could seriously weaken the future financial stability of the railroad. Also, the use of bonds as the main means of obtaining capital divorced those who provided the capital (the bondholders) from those who owned the railroad (the stockholders), thus increasing the possibility of management irresponsibility.

The most famous of the construction companies was the Credit Mobilier, the company that constructed the Union Pacific. The Credit Mobilier was the center of a huge scandal during the Grant administration. Senators, congressmen, cabinet members, and even President Grant's brother were accused of selling political influence to the Credit Mobilier. Some have estimated that a profit on the cost of construction of the Union Pacific Railroad as high as 80 to 100% was obtained by those who controlled the Credit Mobilier.

There were three sources of capital for financing of the railroads: federal, state, or local government; foreign investment; and domestic, private capital. Prior to 1860, funds from the federal government were less important than those that railroads received from state and local governments but included tariff remission, government surveys, and materials (wood) from public lands. The latter two levels of government contributed to the financing of the railroads in a number of ways. They gave the railroads almost 50 million acres of land—local rights of way, plus land within cities and towns for stations and railyards. They gave tax concessions to railroads, guaranteed railroad bond issues, and purchased railway bonds themselves. The future growth and at times the very existence of a town depended on whether a railroad came through the town. Towns, public bodies, and private individuals, therefore, vied with each other by offering incentives to attract railroads.

After 1860, the federal government became more important in financially aiding the railroads. Over 130 million acres of land, valued at over $500 million, were granted to various railroads after 1860. The federal government lent the railroads about $64 million, and by 1900 the unpaid interest on these loans amounted to $114 million. Aid by local governments in the form of donations, loans, guarantees, or subscriptions to securities issues after 1860 was estimated to be about $87 million.

Aid from the various levels of government probably approached $1 billion by 1900, about one-tenth of the total capital investment in U.S. railroads. However, despite the substantial financial contribution of the various levels of government, the dominant opinion in the United States was that the railroads should be under the sole control of private interests.

Foreign investment in U.S. railroads was very substantial. In 1869, $243 million railroad bonds were held by foreigners, and by 1900 this had risen to $3.1 billion, mostly held by British citizens. About 25% of railroad stock was also held by foreigners. This interest by foreign investors was, on the whole, a progressive element. They led the outcry against mismanagement and were a significant force in demanding more responsible management of the railroads.

Stock and therefore management control were highly concentrated. Even western and southern railroads were controlled either as stockholders or as financial underwriters by the "eastern money interests." Private domestic capital accounted for about 60% of the financial requirements of U.S. railroads.

The average return on railway bonds in 1869 was 6%; on stocks, 7%. This rate steadily declined, so that by 1900 average bond and stock returns were only 3.5%. The point is not that railroad bond and stock yields were so much less than from other economic activities but rather that railroad fortunes, on the whole, were not earned through railroad operations—they were earned through railroad construction, promotion, and manipulation.

## Rate or Pricing Policy

Rate making, or price setting for railroad service, involved a complex system of price discrimination. The practice was not simply one of discrimination in prices between different types of goods shipped, but also between shippers, distances, and roads. One factor increasing the intensity of this discrimination was the very strong system of rate warfare. The early monopoly of certain routes disappeared quickly when parallel railway lines were constructed. Also, in relevant geographic areas alternative forms of transportation on oceans, lakes, and rivers were still strong enough to affect rates. Alternative systems of transportation and parallel railway lines were especially strong in the Northeast and North Central states.

After the Civil War, rate wars became frequent, climaxing in 1877. Opposition to this rate cutting came from both stockholders and shippers. Shippers preferred predictable rates rather than uncertain, even if lower, rates. As a result, the railroads intensified efforts to reduce competition.

Various methods were used to reduce competition between the railroads. Railroads sometimes both entered into production of goods to be shipped and also became the shippers, as in the anthracite coal region of eastern Pennsylvania, where the Reading Railroad owned a large number of coal mines and dominated the transportation of coal out of the region. A second method involved special contracts with individual shippers to use only one road; rebates were given as inducements. Such contracts were made only with larger shippers, which placed smaller shippers at a cost disadvantage through higher transportation rates. Shippers might form shipping associations; but the railroads, in turn, could also organize. The two associations then would bargain over rebates to be made and would apportion the freight among the various railroads.

Often these arrangements were used as devices to discriminate against nonmembers of the shippers' organization. A famous example was the effort of John D. Rockefeller to set up the Southern Improvement Association in 1871–1872, which practiced severe discrimination against nonmembers. The association was dispersed under the pressure of an oil shipment strike by nonmenbers out of Titusville, Pennsylvania, in 1872. Another example was a livestock shippers' association west of Buffalo in 1875.

A more direct way to reduce competition was for the railroads to engage in **pooling**. Railroads maintained themselves as separate companies, but all cooperated together in pools and jointly decided important market questions. The first railroad pool was established in 1870 by railroads carrying traffic west from Chicago. The two primary issues these pools decided were the freight rate structure and the territory or share of total business to go to each railroad.

The pooling arrangement was a difficult anticompetitive structure to maintain. Pools had to set up a complex system of regulations to fix rates and shares of the market, regulations that required a bureaucracy, with all its attendant difficulties. Each road constantly jockeyed within the pooling arrangement to improve its position with respect to the rest of the industry. Individual roads also were not above cheating on the pooling arrangements when it was to their advantage, especially under the pressure of declining demand during depression or business contraction periods. Perhaps most importantly, pooling, according to English common law, was a conspiracy in restraint of trade and therefore illegal. Since the pooling "contracts" were contracts to commit illegal acts, these arrangements could not be enforced in the courts.

One way of avoiding the problems of pooling and of still reducing competition was through **consolidation**; that is, combining a number of smaller railroads into one large railroad company. Some consolidation occurred prior to 1897. Jay Gould had built a railroad empire in the Southwest and the western Great Lakes region. Commodore Vanderbilt had combined the New York Central, the Erie, and the Michigan Central into the most important railway line in the Northeast. However, by 1897 the United States had only experienced the beginnings of railroad consolidation; its heights were reached in the period from 1897 to 1910.

## Railroad Legislation

The basic but by no means the only complaint against railroad policies was the discrimination in rates between shippers. This discrimination took two forms. First, there were the **short-haul versus long-haul rates.** Often rates for a short haul, or short distances, were higher than for a long haul; or, when short haul rates were lower, they would not be reduced by an amount proportionate to the relative distances traveled. This form of discrimination could prove disastrous to farm enterprises in unfavorable locations. A second problem was the favorable rates granted certain shippers through drawbacks (refunds), special contracts granting favorable rates, and rebates. Small shippers were often put at a serious disadvantage through these practices.

Remember that in the 1870s and 1880s a number of states passed what were generally called **Granger laws** to regulate railroads either through legislative committees or through separate commissions. The railroads fought back, and part of this fight was carried on in the courts. In 1876, the U.S. Supreme Court upheld state regulation of railroads in the case of *Munn v. Illinois.*

In 1886, in the case of *Wabash, St. Louis and Pacific Railway v. Illinois,* the U.S. Supreme Court reversed itself by declaring that the states could not regulate interstate (between states) trade. The climax came in 1890 when the Court held that under the Fourteenth Amendment the states could not regulate the railroads, because this would deprive railroad owners of their property without due process of law. In effect, state regulation of railroads was now dead. The battle shifted to the federal level.

In 1887, Congress passed the Interstate Commerce Act, which established the Interstate Commerce Commission (ICC). The function of the ICC was primarily to regulate the railroads. Support for the act came from three main sources: eastern shippers who wanted an end to the various forms of discrimination, some parts of the railway industry itself who hoped national regulation would substitute for competitive anarchy, and investors, especially from England, who wanted an end to mismanagement in operation and fraud in the sale of securities. In addition, a role was played by farmer organizations seeking increased regulation.

The ICC, however, chose to rely on competition and prohibited the pooling wanted by some in the railroad industry. The ICC did attack the discriminatory practices, prohibiting rebates, and insisting that long-haul rates must be higher than short-haul rates. For a time, the railroads cooperated, hoping that the ICC could solve their competitive problems. Eventually, however, the industry opposed the ICC and went to the courts in an effort to diminish its authority.

In 1897, the Supreme Court held that the Interstate Commerce Act did not give the ICC the right to set rates, and thus destroyed its power to control discriminatory rate setting. By 1897, the ICC had moved from its position in opposition to pooling and had begun to experiment with pools. The Supreme Court reacted by judging these pools illegal under the Sherman Antitrust Act of 1890. Now, in effect, the ICC was powerless. But more legislation was soon to come.

# Industry

In 1860, the United States was the world's second most important manufacturing economy, led only by England. By 1900, however, the United States was the leader, contributing over 30% of the world's manufacturing output. An indicator of this phenomenal growth is the manufacturing output index, which was 7.5 in 1863 and 53.0 in 1897, a sevenfold increase. Also, the real output per worker in U.S. manufacturing increased from $223 in the period 1860–1873 to $632 in the period 1912–1916. Real wages increased about 50% from 1860 to 1890. Agriculture was the dominant U.S. industry in 1850, with 60% of the labor force employed in agriculture. By 1910, however, employment in agriculture had fallen to 30%, and employment in manufacturing was also 30%.

This growth in manufacturing was achieved through the establishment of the factory system of production. Edward Kirkland[16] defines the factory system as one where the "raw materials were converted into finished goods by consecutive harmonious processes carried along by a central power." Decisive in the spread of the factory into differing industries was the invention of critical machines or methods. For example, the perfection of the refrigerator car for the transportation of fresh meat was necessary to expand the market, increasing the optimum scale of operation in the meat-packing industry to create the factory system of organization there.

But the factory was as much a managerial as a technological problem. Scientific management in the 1880s, pioneered by Frederick Taylor, was developed to rationalize the internal flow of processes to increase productivity. Management had to learn to organize the procurement of sufficient supplies of raw materials, organize and discipline the larger amounts of labor necessary, rationalize the flow of productive processes, and find markets for the increased output. An excellent example of an early pioneer was Francis Cabot Lowell in the textile industry near Boston around 1815.

## Iron and Steel

A series of innovations revolutionized the steel industry and made it one of the most important industries in the development of the manufacturing sector in the United States. In 1867, only 1.6 *thousand* tons of steel were produced; by 1897, output had grown to the phenomenal figure of 7.2 *million* tons annually.

In 1856, Bessemer in England developed the forced air process which bears his name, and greatly reduced the costs of producing steel. At around the same time, Kelly in the United States developed similar processes. Martin and Siemens perfected the open hearth method, which gave the steel maker more control over the quality of the finished product. Now, much like the baker making a cake, the steel producer could add different ingredients and make steel to specifications. In the 1870s, steel makers began to use a limestone lining in their furnaces, a practice that allowed them to use iron ore containing phosphorus. Previously these ores had made very poor-quality steel.

These innovations made raw materials more useful, increased productivity, and, of course, greatly reduced the costs of producing steel. The innovations also increased the optimum size of the steel mill. By 1897, the steel industry had become "big business," and the output of workers employed in operating blast furnaces increased 30 times between 1850 and 1914.

This revolution in steel production had substantial backward and forward linkages. The expansion caused by the technological changes forced a conversion from charcoal to coke and caused the development of the soft coal industry in western Pennsylvania, West Virginia, Ohio, Kentucky, Tennessee, and other places. Other backward linkages led to the development of the Mesabi iron ore field in the peninsula of Michigan. As the cost of steel fell under the technological explosion, forward linkages appeared. Steel and iron could now be used not only in the railroad industry but also in other forms of construction and for consumer use. In total output, stoves became as important as rails. Obviously, the iron and steel industries were stimulated by developments in other fields, railroads for instance, but in turn they provided the stimulus for other forms of development.

## Electricity

While Europeans were most important in developing the scientific principles of electricity, it was primarily Americans who innovated its practical application. The first applications revolutionized communications, with the subsequent economic impact of quickened business communication and reduced information cost. In 1837, Morse invented the telegraph, and in 1876 Bell invented the telephone.

Electricity was applied to lighting homes and businesses by Edison, and the first commercial operation of electric lights was made in New York by 1881. Another application of the use of electricity as a source of power was the electrification of street railways by Sprague in 1887. Before electricity could be used widely as a source of power, however, the cost of transporting it over long distances had to be reduced. Westinghouse in the early 1890s solved that problem with the perfection of alternating current.

The use of electricity as a source of power to compete with steam and water power was just beginning by 1897. The basic innovations had been made, however, but it was not until after 1900 that electricity became dominant as the primary source of power in the United States.

## Water and Steam

As late as the 1870s, water power was still as cheap as steam power, and in 1870 about half of the power generated to run the machines of the United States came from water power. The main advantage of steam power was its mobility (it was not stopped by lack of water or by winter ice). Parsons in 1884 invented the steam turbine, greatly increasing the amount and efficiency of steam power generation, and by 1899 water power provided only one-seventh of the total power needs of the United States. In 1900, Westinghouse coupled the steam turbine to the electric generator to produce electricity.

## Government Aid to Manufacturing

Direct government financial aid to manufacturing was small, especially when compared to aid provided for the railroad system. The federal government gave very little venture capital; aid from local and state governments was somewhat more plentiful. A number of local governments gave manufacturers land for factory sites and control over water power. Sometimes state and local governments gave exemptions from taxes. Overall, however, direct government aid was unimportant to manufacturing, although it may have been significant for a specific enterprise.

Of more importance than direct (transfer) payments was government protection of U.S. manufacturing through the use of tariffs. These import taxes raised the prices of imports and thus increased potential profits in the United States industries so protected. Prior to the Civil War, tariffs levied by the United States were moderate, in large measure due to the opposition of southern legislators whose region depended on exports of cotton and imports of manufactured and semimanufactured goods. During the Civil War, high tariffs were imposed partly to help finance the northern war effort. With the South now absent from Congress, this was relatively easy to do. Some higher tariffs were also due to political pressure from particular industries. There was no general reduction of these higher tariffs immediately after the war, and the Tariff Acts of 1883, 1890, and 1894 saw no general reduction either. The Dingley Tariff of 1897, in fact, raised tariffs to all-time highs for a broad range of goods.

The major rationale used for these high tariffs was the infant-industry argument—that these industries needed tariff protection until they were developed enough to withstand world competition. But the industries benefiting from the Dingley Tariff of 1897 were not, on the whole, infant industries. The rates from that tariff act seemed less to reflect economic need than the political influence of representatives of particular industries.

The federal government's patent system also gave substantial assistance to many firms. A patent granted by the federal government conveyed exlusive monopoly rights to the inventor of a product or process for 16 years, with the possibility of renewal for another 16 years. In 1860, 4363 patents were granted; in 1879, 22,098 were granted. This growth in patents granted not only reflects the tremendous increase in the pace of technological development but also provides a crude measure of the importance of the patent system as an aid to industry. These exclusive rights to produce certain products or to use certain processes gave the patent holders **monopoly power,** the ability to influence price, and allowed the favored firms to increase prices and obtain **economic profits** (a profit larger than necessary to keep the firm producing).

## The Monopolization Movement

The post-Civil War period saw the beginnings of the combination movement in U.S. industry. The aim of the movement was to reduce competition and increase control of prices through the use of various organizational devices. The first organizational device used to reduce competition was the pool.

## Pools

A pool is created when a number of firms in the same industry get together and jointly decide on prices, shares of the market, and other conditions of the industry. Each firm maintains its own separate legal independence. As described earlier, pools were pioneered in the United States by sections of the railroad industry and by John D. Rockefeller in the oil industry. Thus, the producers of railroad ties formed a pool in 1887 and established production quotas for each firm and, in consultation with officials of the chief railroads, stabilized prices. The limitations of pooling discussed earlier in this chapter with respect to railroads also apply generally here to manufacturing.

## Trusts

The next form of monopoly organization used was the **trust.** Firms in an industry would turn over their common stock to a board of trustees and would receive trust certificates in return. Only the trust had voting stock in the individual companies and thus it could control them, even though each firm remained a legally separate entity. The trustees did not control the formerly competing firms in any managerial or detailed way. The idea was to get each firm's independent management to do what the pool could not legally get them to do—adopt noncompetitive strategies.

In 1882, John D. Rockefeller established the Standard Oil of Ohio trust. In 1892, the General Electric Company trust was formed for firms in the electric light industry. The core organization of the American Telephone and Telegraph Company (AT&T) had formed a trust comprised of firms in the telephone industry by 1899. Of course, many other trusts were formed in other industries.

The primary defect of the trust form, from industry's point of view, was that it was specifically declared illegal by the Sherman Antitrust Act of 1890.

## Holding Company

A **holding company** is a company formed for the purpose of buying stock in other companies, a device used for controlling major segments of particular industries through controlling their voting common stock. The holding companies did not violate the Sherman Antitrust Act, perhaps because they were not named in the act. While the trust involved only loose coordination of the firms, the holding company would impose a centralized, integrated management of the subsidiary companies. Centralized, supermanagement became the order of the day.

In the 1890s, John D. Rockefeller converted the Standard Oil trust into a holding company form, with Standard Oil of New Jersey as the basic holding company. At the beginning of the 1900s, AT&T was also converted into a holding company.

Around 1897, another device of the movement toward monopolization involved using the consolidation form. Consolidation involved combining a number of independent firms into one large corporation, unlike the pool, the trust, and the holding company wherein the individual companies maintained their separate legal existence. The high point of consolidation came at the turn of the twentieth century—but that story will be told in the next section.

# The Labor Movement

The concept of workers in the same craft or industry organizing into an association or union seems to stem from three sources. The first is probably as old as manufacturing itself and was embodied in the guild organizations of the Middle Ages, whereby workers in the same craft or trade bonded together for mutual comfort, both economic and social. These guilds were carried over into the craft unions of the nineteenth century. A second source, at least as argued by many, was the emerging large-scale firm of the post-Civil War period in the United States. Many have concluded that workers felt these large firms could only be challenged by a consolidated labor movement. A third source stemmed from rapid technological change. With the development of new processes and machinery and the adoption of the factory system, many skills and trades were eliminated and those who had been employed in them experienced decreases in income and standards of living. Such workers were affected not only economically but also socially and psychologically.

Although the movement toward the organization of labor unions began before 1860, it was during the period 1865–1897 that labor unions became firmly established on the American scene. In this period, two basic policy approaches concerning the direction of the labor movement were often in conflict. The first approach was reformism, aimed at either eliminating or controlling the wage system and corporate capitalism. This approach relied on the use of direct political action to achieve reform. The second approach was simple, straightforward trade unionism, an approach that recognized and accepted the wage system and corporate capitalism; what was demanded was an increased share of income and greater job security for the workers. Although conflicting theories about what approaches to take continued into the twentieth century, it seemed apparent by 1897 that straightforward trade unionism was the path the labor movement had decided on.

## The Early Years

The lack of a unified transportation system prior to the Civil War kept markets scattered and contributed to the local or regional nature of the labor movement prior to 1860. The need for national organizations became pressing only with the establishment of national markets. A taste of what was to come after the Civil War was the founding in 1859 of the first successful national union, the typography union in the printing industry.

The first effort at an organization of national unions, the National Labor Union, was founded in 1866 and centered its brief life on a campaign for an eight-hour day. Its organizational nature contributed to its demise in 1872—its trade union members were in constant conflict with its independent reformist members over the issues of women, blacks, and direct political action.

## The Knights of Labor

The Knights of Labor was an organization founded in Philadelphia in 1869 by Uriah S. Stephens. Stephens kept the order secret and control highly centralized. In 1879, when Terrence W. Powderly became Grand Master, Powderly abandoned secrecy, and as a result the organization began to grow. The local unit was the assembly of which there were two kinds, **a trade assembly** with all members belonging to the same craft or occupation, and a **mixed assembly** with members from a variety of different occupations. The self-interest of the two forms separated as the trade assemblies became more concerned with obtaining direct benefits for their members through trade union activities.

In 1884, a group of trade assemblies in the railroad industry conducted successful strikes on the Kansas Pacific and other railroads. Thereafter, membership in the Knights of Labor rapidly expanded from 52,000 in 1884 to a peak of 700,000 in 1886. Attempting to repeat the successes of 1884, the trade assemblies in railroading struck the Southwestern Railroad in 1886. The strike failed, and as it crumbled violence occurred. Partly as a result, membership in the Knights of Labor fell to 100,000 by 1890, and the organization had all but disappeared by 1900.

There were many other factors contributing to the rapid decline of the Knights, including the general incompetence of Terrence Powderly and the continuing internal conflict between Powderly and others who aspired to take over the Knights. Powderly had based the thrust of the order in two directions—the establishment of producer cooperatives to avoid the wage system and the use of political pressure on Congress to obtain more favorable laws for workers. Because of inadequate management and insufficient capital, the cooperatives failed. The Knights' political agitation also failed to generate any noteworthy political gains.

Powderly was opposed to the use of the strike as a labor weapon, on the grounds that it was an acceptance of the wage system, and he withheld the support of the national organization for the strike activities of the trade assemblies. The numerical strength of the Knights was in the mixed assemblies, to which trade union activities were not of much interest. After the formation of the American Federation of Labor in 1886, the trade assemblies left the Knights.

The strikes of trade assemblies in the railroads of the Midwest in 1886 and 1887 degenerated into violence as the strikes were lost. Large segments of the press blamed the Knights for this violence, causing bad public relations. Ironically, the Knights were blamed for the strikes despite the national organization's opposition to strikes.

Defections from the Knights were massive by the end of the 1880s, and, as stated earlier, by 1900 the Knights of Labor were no longer an important force in the American labor movement; dominance had shifted to the American Federation of Labor.

## The American Federation of Labor

The American Federation of Labor (AFL), a federation of national trade unions, was founded in 1886 under the leadership of Samuel Gompers of the Cigar Makers Unions.

The basic philosophy of Gompers was stamped on the AFL. In brief, this philosophy was called **trade unionism.** The only concern of the union was to be the welfare of its members; that is, concern centered on wages, hours of labor, and the various conditions of work. No political or reformist agitation was to be engaged in by the union; the union would not affiliate in any way with any particular political party. The aim was to help labor's friends and punish its enemies through the ballot box, not through direct involvement.

Another basic principle of Gompers' labor philosophy was a reliance on **craft unionism.** Union membership was to be in a union representing the worker's trade or craft—not representing an entire industry. This concentration on craft rather than industry gave advantages to small groups of highly skilled workers in organizing the unions and bargaining with employers. However, such craft concentration led to the neglect of masses of unskilled and semiskilled workers and contributed to the inability to effectively organize important major industries, such as steel, until the late 1930s.

This "craft versus industry" approach introduced a major conflict within the labor movement. Eugene V. Debs, later to run several times for U.S. president under the Socialist banner, organized the National Railway Union in the early 1890s as an industrial union. Soon after its formation the NRU tried to assist the workers of the Pullman strike by boycotting trains with Pullman cars. But after interference by the courts and federal troops the strike and boycott failed, and the NRU collapsed.

By 1897, the only existing **industrial union** (a union drawing its members from an entire industry) was the newly reconstructed United Mine Worker's Union. Further efforts at industrial unionism were made, but widespread success did not come until the late 1930s.

The final principle of Gompers' trade unionism was complete opposition to **dual unionism.** There was to be only one union in each craft or industry. As rivals to the AFL appeared in the twentieth century, however, dual unionism and its attendant conflicts became a reality.

Data in the nineteenth century on the numbers of members in the various labor organizations is scanty and open to question. These numbers were probably inflated. Table 12-2 contains estimates of membership in labor unions and of this membership as a percentage of total employment. The data show growth in membership in the 1880s and 1890s as the American Federation of Labor and the Railroad Brotherhoods became firmly established. But the percentage of the total labor force who were union members remained under the 5% that had existed in 1870.

## Consequences of Trade Unionism

The trade unionism of the AFL meant a retreat from the opposition to the factory-corporate market system so resented by the Knights of Labor. The

AFL accepted the legitimacy of the wage system, technological change, factories, and corporate capitalism. The AFL seemed to be saying that it wanted a full piece of the pie for workers; workers wanted their share of "the action."

Table 12-2. Membership in Labor Unions and Percentage of the Total Labor Force.

| Year | Union Membership (thousands) | Percent of Total Labor Force |
|------|------------------------------|------------------------------|
| 1870 | 300 | 5.0 |
| 1880 | 200 | 2.3 |
| 1890 | 400 | 3.2 |
| 1900 | 868 | 4.8 |

*Source: Historical Statistics of the United States* (1960), pp. 72–73, 98; J. G. Royback, *A History of American Labor* (New York, 1959), pp. 104, 118, 156, 163; L. Wolman, *The Growth of American Trade Unions* (New York, 1924), p. 21.

Philip S. Bogwell and G. E. Mingoy, *Britain and America, A Study of Economic Change 1850–1939* (New York, 1970), p. 207.

To get that share, the AFL concentrated on a select group of highly skilled workers organized in crafts where the union could more easily control the supply of labor. As a result, mass production industries were neglected because of the economic strength of the individual firms and the semiskilled nature of the employees. The AFL also neglected the immigrant workers, on the grounds that they could not be organized; in fact, the AFL was strongly opposed to the U.S. policy of unrestricted immigration. Members of the AFL saw the immigrant as a competitor, not as a fellow worker. The AFL also neglected the organization of black workers and women workers.

The AFL was an unimportant force in politics and had minimal effect on legislation. The union developed a deeply pessimistic view of government relationships with unions; often governments became more the enemy than were employers. Gompers, in the nineteenth century, wanted government to leave unions alone.

Socialists and other left-wing groups within the AFL provided the only challenge to Gompers and his program. In 1894, the Socialists confronted Gompers on the issue of the AFL presidency and challenged his program. Although the threat to the program was defeated, Gompers lost the presidency for two years. The next challenges came from rival organizations— the program was not challenged again from within the AFL until the 1930s.

## Tactics of the AFL

The basic goal of the AFL was to obtain union recognition and a contract with the employer that set wages, hours of work, and other conditions of employment. If it was impossible to achieve recognition and a contract through negotiations, then the union would use its ultimate weapon—the strike. Outside of the highly skilled crafts, where the union had control over the supply of labor, it was very difficult to win a strike. In the second half of the nineteenth century, use of the strike was reserved mostly for resisting a cut in wages and to sue for union recognition.

A technique used with the strike was picketing, aimed at "persuading" workers or customers not to enter the premises of the struck firm. In many instances, persuasion became intimidation.

The boycott was another important union weapon. In a **primary boycott,** the striking union urged people not to buy from the struck firm. In a **secondary boycott,** the union urged people not to buy from another firm that did business with the struck firm.

At times, in desperation because a strike was failing, a union resorted to violence. This violence was directed at physical intimidation of non-striking workers and at the productive facilities of the firm.

## Weapons of the Employer

The **lockout** was the employer's equivalent to the union's strike. Often the lockout was used to crush developing union organizations. The great Homestead Steel strike of 1892 was, in effect, a lockout, as the owners closed the mills in an effort to destroy the union.

Another important weapon of employers was the **yellow-dog contract.** Workers, on being hired, would be required to sign a contract stating that they were not members of a union and would quit if they did join one. These were called yellow-dog contracts because supposedly only a "yellow dog" would sign one. The contracts were used as the basis for court injunctions against union-organizing activity on the grounds that the union's organizer was encouraging workers to violate their contracts.

An especially effective weapon against unions was the use of the **blacklist.** Union leaders, organizers, members, and any other category of worker that it would be "undesirable" to employ were put on a so-called blacklist distributed to all employers. A blacklisted worker found great difficulty in obtaining employment.

When a strike occurred, the employer could and did hire thugs and often had them deputized by the local police to break up the strike. Strike-breakers, often using violence, broke up picket lines and physically intimidated union members. In the case of the Homestead Steel strike, a pitched battle took place between the strikers and strikebreakers brought in by the

Pinkerton Detective Agency. The union beat off the strikebreakers after 12 people had died.

The Pinkerton Detective Agency enjoyed a brisk business in providing what were called "company spies" to infiltrate the ranks of the union and report to the employer on union plans and the names of prominent union members. Perhaps the most famous use of a company spy was the agent who infiltrated the Molly McGuires, a labor terrorist group in the Pennsylvania coal fields in the 1880s, and gained evidence needed to convict the leaders of murder. In 1935, firms paid $80 million a year to 230 detective agencies to provide 40,000 company spies; or so it is estimated.

The employer firms very often owned the houses that the workers lived in, and if an individual irritated the employer or if workers struck, they could be evicted from these homes. When the unions struck at the Pullman plant in 1894, one of the first acts of Pullman's managers was to evict the striking workers from the company homes.

In this period, the unions maintained that government at whatever level often interfered on the side of the employers. The courts rarely decided in favor of the unions. The courts prohibited a wide variety of activities by unions and were a very strong deterrent to the unions' ability to effectively organize. The use of the yellow dog contract to enjoin unions against organizing activity was an especially serious problem.

The use of local and state police, the national guard, and even federal troops in labor-management disputes was condemned by the unions. Unions charged that they were primarily used to end strikes by breaking up picket lines, intimidating strikers, and jailing strike leaders. The trade unions called state police the American Cossacks. Often local police forces deputized people who worked for and were paid by the employers. During the great Pullman boycott of 1894, called by the United Railway Union led by Eugene V. Debs in support of the striking Pullman workers, federal troops were called out to protect the U.S. mail being transported by railroads, but the unions charged that they went far beyond protecting the mails and were considered by many unionists to be a prime factor in defeating the boycott causing the collapse of the United Railway Union.

## A Conclusion

In the period 1865 to 1897, except in skilled crafts, union strength was small, especially when compared to the economic and political strength of employers. It is quite surprising, then, that union membership grew to the point where the American Federation of Labor and the various railroad brotherhoods were firmly established. The struggle was a bitter one; violence was practiced on both sides. This early labor movement history in the United States involved more violence than any other labor movement history in the world.

# One More Comment

Beyond doubt, an important factor in the economic development of the United States from 1865 to 1897 was the rapid growth and final completion of the railroad network. This network finally helped to create one large free-trade economy from coast to coast, breaking down the transportation barriers restricting economic expansion. It also provided direct economic stimulus through its demand for labor and materials in its construction and operation.

But institutional changes occurred. The factory system became the dominant form of organizing the processes of production under the impact of expanding demand and developing technology. By 1897, the United States had become an industrial society. In the process, various forms of business organization developed in a rush to reduce competition and raise profits. The pool, trust, holding company, and combining of several firms into one firm (consolidation), strongly contributed to the rise of "bigness" in industry. Largely because of this trend, the government began to experiment with intervention; for example, in the form of the Interstate Commerce Act of 1887 and the Sherman Antitrust Act of 1890. A further response to the economic forces of the time was the establishment of a national labor union movement as workers attempted to gain a larger share of the benefits of the economic changes. These unions aimed to monopolize the supply of labor and raise wages.

# Glossary

**Backward linkages**  Effects of input-output relationships or demand-supply stimuli from one economic activity to probable economic activities that existed in prior stages of production. For example, expansion of steel production through technological change increases the probability of developing coal and iron deposits.

**Blacklist**  A list, distributed to employers, of workers considered "undesirable" for employment; used against union members.

**Consolidation**  Forming one larger company out of a number of smaller companies.

**Construction companies**  Separately incorporated firms whose primary function was to raise financial capital and construct the railroads.

**Craft unionism**  Union representation of workers by trade or craft rather than by industry.

**Dual unionism**  More than one union existing for a single craft or industry.

**Economic profit**   Any profit above a return "necessary" to keep a firm producing.

**Forward linkages**   Effects of input-output relationships or demand-supply stimuli from one economic activity to probable economic activities closer to the ultimate user of the activity. For example, wheat production provides raw materials that could be used in flour milling.

**Granger laws**   State laws passed in the 1870s and 1880s to regulate railroads.

**Holding company**   A company formed for the purpose of buying stock in other companies and thereby controlling these other companies.

**Industrial union**   A union that draws its members from a specific industry rather than from a specific trade or craft.

**Innovation**   According to Schumpeter, innovation means new products, new processes, new machines, or even new markets that open up new opportunities for profits.

**Lockout**   The employer's equivalent of the strike; occurs when the employer locks the door of the plant and does not allow workers to work.

**Mixed assembly**   A local unit of organization in the Knights of Labor, consisting of union members from a variety of occupations.

**Monopoly power**   The ability of a seller to directly influence price by varying supply in the market.

**Pooling**   Firms jointly deciding prices, shares of market, and other conditions of the market, as a method of reducing competition between firms.

**Primary boycott**   When a striking union urges people not to buy from the firm that the union is striking against.

**Secondary boycott**   When a striking union urges people not to buy from another firm that does business with the firm that the union is striking against.

**Short-haul versus long-haul rates**   Often discrimination in railroad rates occurred when rates for short hauls (distances) were either higher than for longer hauls or were higher per mile, giving a price advantage to those shipping over longer distances.

**Trade assembly**   A local unit of organization in the Knights of Labor consisting only of union members from the same craft or occupation.

**Trade unionism**   A philosophy of union organization in which the concentration is primarily on gaining benefits for union members in terms of increased wages, reduced hours of work, and other conditions of employment; avoids direct political involvement.

**Trust**   A form of business organization in which firms in an industry turn over their common stock to a trust company and receive in return trust certificates. As a result, the trust company controls each individual firm.

**Yellow-dog contract**   A contract with an employer wherein a worker agrees not to join a union; often used as the basis for a court injunction against a union's organizing activities.

# Questions

1. In what ways did the growth of railroads in the second half of the nineteenth century affect the economic growth of the United States?
2. What were the advantages, disadvantages, and functions of the railroad construction company? Do you think they were a useful institution in the construction of the railroad system?
3. What were the ways in which railroads attempted to reduce competition in the last third of the nineteenth century? Why was the pool so unsatisfactory as a way to reduce competition?
4. What were the two forms of rate discrimination that were strongly opposed by many railroad shippers? Why were they opposed?
5. How did the courts frustrate the workings of the Interstate Commerce Commission? The workings of the state laws regulating railroads?
6. What economic conditions had to exist in order for the factory system to be established?
7. What was the series of innovations that transformed the iron and steel industry in the second half of the nineteenth century?
8. What were the major innovations in the field of electricity and power in the second half of the nineteenth century?
9. Do you think government aid to manufacturing was important to the growth of manufacturing in the second half of the nineteenth century?
10. Describe the various forms of organization that were used to reduce competition, pointing out their advantages and disadvantages.
11. What new conditions did workers have to face in the nineteenth century that may have contributed to the drive toward unionization?
12. What were the principal factors causing the rapid decline of the Knights of Labor after 1886?
13. Outline the major elements of Samuel Gompers' trade union philosophy.
14. What were the consequences of Gompers' trade union philosophy?
15. What were the primary weapons of the labor unions?
16. What were the weapons used by employers in labor disputes?

# Suggested Readings

1. Cantor, Milton, ed. *Black Labor in America*. Westport, Conn.: Negro Universities Press, 1970.

2. Clark, Victor S. *History of Manufacturers in the United States*. Vol. 2: 1860–1893. Washington, D.C.: Carnegie Institution, 1929.

3. Cochran, Thomas C. *Railroad Leaders, 1845–1890*. Cambridge, Mass.: Harvard University Press, 1953.

4. Dubofsky, Melvyn. *Industrialism and the American Worker 1865–1920*, New York: Crowell, 1975.

5. Fogel, Robert W. *Railroads and American Economic Growth*. Baltimore: Johns Hopkins University Press, 1964.

6. Gates, Paul W. "The Railroad Land Grant Legend." *Journal of Economic History*, 14 (Spring 1954).

7. Habakkuk, H. J. *American and British Technology in the Nineteenth Century*. Cambridge, England: Cambridge University Press, 1967.

8. Hacker, Louis M. *The World of Andrew Carnegie, 1865–1901*. Philadelphia: Lippincott, 1968.

9. Harbeson, Robert. "Railroads and Regulations, 1877–1916: Conspiracy or Public Interest." *Journal of Economic History*, 27 (June 1967).

10. Henry, Robert S. "The Railroad Land Grant Legend in American History Texts." *The Mississippi Valley Historical Review*, 32 (September 1945).

11. Higgs, Robert. *Transformation of the American Economy 1865–1914*. New York: Wiley, 1971.

12. Hidy, Ralph, and Hidy, Muriel. *Pioneering in Big Business: A History of the Standard Oil Company of New Jersey 1882–1911*. New York: Harper & Row, 1955.

13. Hirschman, Albert. *The Strategy of Economic Development*. New Haven, Conn.: Yale University Press, 1960.

14. Jenks, Leland. "Railroads as an Economic Force in American Development." *Journal of Economic History*, 4 (May 1944).

15. Josephson, Matthew. *The Robber Barons*. New York: Harcourt Brace Jovanovich, 1962.

16. Kirkland, Edward Chase. *Industry Comes of Age: Business, Labor, and Public Policy*. New York: Holt, Rinehart and Winston, 1961.

17. Kolko, Gabriel. *Railroads and Regulation, 1877–1916*. Princeton, N.J.: Princeton University Press, 1965.

18. Lindsy, Almont. *The Pullman Strike*. Chicago: University of Chicago Press, 1942.

19. Nerlove, Marc. "Railroads and American Economic Growth." *Journal of Economic History, 26* (March 1966).

20. Passer, Harold C. *The Electrical Manufacturers, 1875–1900.* Cambridge, Mass.: Harvard University Press, 1953.

21. Porter, Glenn. *The Rise of Big Business, 1860–1910.* New York: Crowell, 1973.

22. Reed, L. S. *The Labor Philosophy of Samuel Gompers.* New York: Columbia University Press, 1930.

23. Schumpeter, Joseph A. *Business Cycles.* New York: McGraw-Hill, 1964.

24. Stover, John F. *American Railroads.* Chicago: University of Chicago Press, 1961.

25. Stover, John F. *The Railroads of the South 1865–1900: A Study in Finance and Control.* Chapel Hill, N.C.: University of North Carolina Press, 1955.

26. Temin, Peter. *Iron and Steel in Nineteenth-Century America.* Cambridge, Mass.: MIT Press, 1964.

27. Vatter, Harold G. *The Drive to Industrial Maturity: The U.S. Economy 1860–1914.* Westport, Conn.: Greenwood, 1975.

28. Ware, Norman. *The Labor Movement in the United States, 1860–1895.* New York: Vintage Books, 1964.

29. Williamson, Jeffrey. "The Railroads and Midwestern Development, 1870–1940: A General Equilibrium History." In *Essays in Nineteenth Century Economic History,* ed. David C. Klingamen and Richard K. Vedder. Athens: Ohio University Press, 1975.

30. Williamson, Jeffrey G. *Late Nineteenth-Century American Development: A General Equilibrium History.* Cambridge, England: Cambridge University Press, 1974.

# Chapter 13

---

# Economic Instability, 1815-1920

To this point, we have examined American economic growth and development to the year 1897. Economic growth—simple increases in output—did increase steadily as population, and hence the labor force, increased by natural growth and immigration; as land was cleared for agricultural production; and as capital was formed to aid in the process of production and distribution. Intensive growth—increases in per capita output—also occurred. Technological improvement in broad sections of the economy increased productivity. The size of markets increased through population growth, urbanization, reduction in the noncash economy, and transportation developments. Larger market sizes increased the opportunities for specialization within firms and industries, thus increasing productivity. Education progressed both formally, in educational institutions, and informally, in on-the-job training. Increased skills meant increasing productivity. Lastly, institutional changes of a political, social, and economic nature may have created a more favorable environment for production. (Keep in mind that for some of these institutional changes it is not at all clear that net gains to output occurred as a result of the institutional changes.)

Long-term intensive growth measured in the increase in real output per capita, had increased from about 0.5% per year around 1820 to about 1.7% per year by 1920. Nonetheless, there were considerable variations in the output of the American economy from one year to the next; those one hundred years were characterized by considerable economic instability as may be seen in Figure 13-1. This instability has been called business cycles, or business fluctuations. However, cycles implies a regularity in these fluctuations that did not exist, and these variations were more than simply fluctuations in business activity. So we will use the term **economic instability** to mean variations in the level of economic activity around the long-term trend.

To begin, we will examine the record of economic instability for the period 1815–1897. Then, as our introduction to the next period, we will examine the record of instability for the period 1897–1920. Finally, for those in need, a macro and a monetary model of the factors determining output are presented in a Review of Economic Concepts at the end of this chapter.

# Economic Instability to 1865

In this chapter, we are going to divide economic instability into several time periods—the period up to 1815, from 1815 to 1865, from 1865 to 1897, and finally, from 1897 to 1920. The analysis to 1897 will provide a summary review of these time periods, while the analysis of the period from 1897 to 1920 can serve as an introduction to the next period.

## Instability to 1815

Let's summarize the record of economic instability for the period 1783–1815 that we examined in Chapters 4 and 6. The economy experienced a recession, or contraction in economic activity, in 1784–1786, primarily stemming from the inability of the American economy to export enough goods to earn sufficient foreign exchange to pay for the high levels of imports in 1783 and 1784. Only one-third of imports were paid for by earnings on exports. Part of the imports were paid for by a flow of gold and silver to the English exporters, which substantially decreased the supply of money. This decrease in $M$ contributed to a decrease in prices and, to some extent, output. There were increased difficulties in the payment of debts, including the debts owed to English exporters, and there were some commercial bankruptcies.

This recession was primarily a commercial one, especially involving commerce connected with international trade. The large share of noncash production (for home use) cushioned the economy from the recession. However, the problems associated with this recession help to point up problems in the workings of the Articles of Confederation and encouraged the formulation and adoption of the Constitution.

From 1792 through 1815, the dominant factor in U.S. economic activity was the long European conflict known as the Napoleonic Wars. These wars created the opportunity for rapid growth in American shipping, both exports and reexports. These sectors expanded until a lull in the

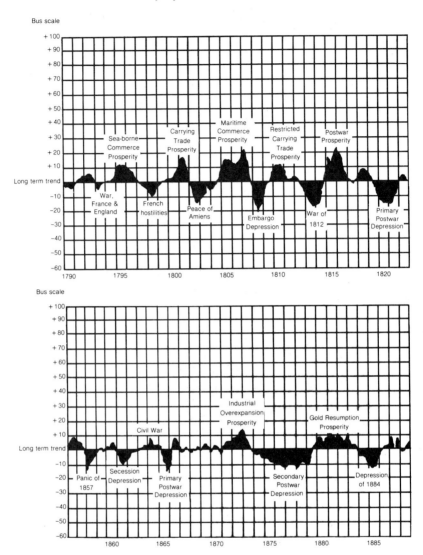

Figure 13-1. American Business Activity, 1790–1920.

fighting in 1798, when trade collapsed. They expanded again from 1799 to 1802. Peace in 1802 and 1803 caused a drastic reduction in U.S. shipping and international commercial activity. With the resumption of war in 1804, our trade expanded again until the Embargo Act of 1807, when trade collapsed as the federal government forbade all trade with Europe in retaliation for British and French seizure of U.S. ships. With the Non-Inter-

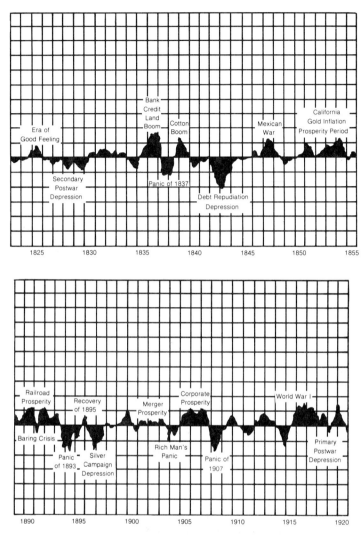

Figure 13-1. continued.

course Act of 1809 and the removal of the prohibition of trade with France, trade revived to some extent. From 1809 to 1812, there was moderate recovery, but not to the levels that existed prior to 1807. Our War of 1812 against Britain caused a further collapse of our international trade until the end of the war in 1815.

It seems apparent that the U.S. record of economic instability for the period from 1782 to 1815 was primarily confined to the international trade sector, involving shipping and commerce. The effects of such instability were minimal on a generally agricultural economy, affecting only those sectors of the economy tied to the international trade sector.

## Economic Instability, 1815-1865

There was a mild depression in 1815 as trade resumed with the end of the War of 1812, and many of the new, small manufacturing enterprises found they could not compete with British imports. These enterprises had appeared under the protection of trade restrictions against British goods from the time of the Embargo of 1807 through the war.

Then there was strong prosperity through to the end of 1818. Aggregate demand was high. Exports increased as the restrictions on trade existing before the war disappeared. There was a spurt in agricultural exports as the industrial revolution in Britain increased the demand for southern cotton to provide raw materials for the expanding textile industry of Britain. Also, there was a growing demand for general foodstuffs from the North and West to feed the expanding industrial labor force of Britain. Investment increased as high levels of construction were achieved, with increases occurring in ship building, turnpike construction, and construction of the Erie Canal, begun in 1817.

Substantial growth in state banks occurred, which increased the availability of credit to finance the expansion of investment. This increase in banking and credit increased the supply of money with its stimulus to output and prices. Even in manufacturing, many of the firms established before 1815 survived the renewal of trade. These grew in size and were joined by new firms as a textile industry became firmly established in the Northeast.

## The Panic of 1819

In 1819, there was a banking panic and a downturn in economic activity. There were two events originating from Britain and Europe that precipitated this contraction. First, Europe had an excellent agricultural harvest in 1818 that reduced demand for United States exports of food crops from the North and West. At the same time, Britain was going through a financial and industrial crisis that sharply reduced the demand for cotton by the British textile industry. These causes indicated a continuing dependence of United States prosperity on international trade.

Besides the decrease in U.S. exports of agricultural products, the financial crisis in Britain led to a banking panic in the United States. In response to their own financial difficulties, the British called in large amounts of their loans in the United States. This caused an outflow of gold and sharp reductions in reserves of urban banks. Some that had insufficient reserves to survive the outflow of gold collapsed. This banking crisis spread to the rural banks outside of the large coastal cities. Prices of agricultural exports dropped sharply as the supply of money was curtailed. The urban economy, so dependent on foreign trade activity and commercial stability, suffered.

## The Expansion of 1820 to 1837

Next, a long period of substantial growth occurred between 1820 and 1837. An important factor in this expansion was the prolonged increase in investment. First, there was a rapid expansion in the small manufacturing sector. There was substantial growth in iron, machinery, shoes, leather, and in textiles, both cotton and woolens. Second, construction activity was high. Between 1816 and 1840, over $125 million was expended on canal construction alone. In 1821, 1400 tons of steamboats were constructed; in 1837 this had risen to 33,500 tons. There were substantial increases in the construction of sailing vessels, turnpikes, and bridges, including over 3000 miles of railroads, by 1840. As population grew in cities, increased construction of housing and other forms of urban building occurred.

Consumption within the money economy also increased. Home products produced and consumed in the home began to decrease in the 1830s as factory-produced products became more readily available and as the opportunity cost of home manufacture increased. Growing population, both through immigration and natural increase, further raised consumption.

In the 1820s, there was a slow rate of growth in the banking system—from 307 banks in 1820 to 330 by 1830. Also, the growth of the supply of money did not keep pace with output, and prices moved gradually downward. In the 1830s, the number of banks grew more rapidly, especially after the Second Bank of the United States was refused a renewal of its charter. The supply of money increased sharply, and prices rose in the 1830s.

## The Banking Crisis of 1837

The growth of the 1820s began to deteriorate in the 1830s, as an increased emphasis on speculative ventures spread throughout the economy. In the westward movement, land speculation became almost universal, as both small farmers and large landowners speculated on increases in land values, most often on credit. Manufacturing expanded rapidly, and many new firms were started with insufficient prospects for success. Many canals proved disappointing—profits earned proved inadequate because traffic did not live up to expectations. Overall, this speculation was financed by expansion of the banking system and, through it, of the supply of money.

In 1836, the balance of trade turned sharply against the United States as exports fell. In the following year, gold flowed to Britain as British merchants tightened their credit to southern cotton growers. Reserves in the urban coastal banks fell, and a banking crisis developed; but this contraction was restricted to commercial interests in international trade and the banking system.

The economy revived quickly in 1838 and 1839. The manufacturing sector was still strong, and exports revived. Internal improvements, especially those in railroad construction, were strong. Reserves in the banking system increased, as British investors increased their purchases of bonds from various state governments.

## The Crisis of 1839 and Depression

The revival of 1838 and 1839 was not maintained, and a crisis developed by the end of 1839. Credit was again tightened in England, and gold flowed out of the United States, reducing bank reserves and the supply of money. The former Second Bank of the United States, now a Pennsylvania state bank, closed its doors as its speculation in cotton proved disastrous. These factors precipitated a general panic and more bank failures. The overexpansion in manufacturing caused many low-productivity firms to fold. Speculation in land values in the West collapsed, and many rural banks were unable to survive the default on land loans. The result was depression and unemployment that lasted until 1843.

The expansion of the 1820s and 1830s was based on sustained expansion of investment with its multiplier effects on income. This expansion in income increased the quantity consumed, with its increases in induced investment and the positive accelerator, reinforcing the multiplier effect on income. As the expansion began to slow up, induced investment declined and a negative accelerator began to contract the economy; there were falls in aggregate demand and a reverse in the multiplier effect. (If this is confusing, read the Review of Economic Concepts at the end of this chapter.)

## The Expansion of 1843-1857

By 1843, the economy had recovered and had entered another long period of expansion, which lasted until 1857. The primary stimuli to that expansion were sustained increases in investment, increases that substantially raised aggregate demand and caused a multiplier effect, expanding income.

Railroad construction played a major role in this increase in investment, a role it was to maintain until the 1890s. In 1840, there were 3000 miles of track. This had increased to 24,000 miles of track by 1857. The direct effects on aggregate demand were substantial: Employment was provided in the building of the roads, and manufacturing was stimulated to provide materials needed for construction. The indirect effects were perhaps even greater, because transportation costs fell, increasing the opportunities for broadened economic activity. Other forms of investment were also high: Factories were built, ships constructed, telegraph lines completed, and urban areas created and expanded, and as the westward movement in agriculture continued.

This expansion required credit and substantial financial facilities. These facilities were provided primarily by expansion in the banking system. Historians have pointed out that part of the banking expansion was provided by what have been called "wildcat banks" with insufficient reserves and, at times, fraudulent issuance of currency. Despite the confusion of a great variety of currencies of varying reliability, this surge in banking capacity provided, along with foreign investment, the financial capital for expansion.

This expansion in the supply of money can also explain the stimulative effects on the growing economy. Increasing supplies of money increased Q (transactions; that is, real output) by increasing demand for investment and consumption. Prices also increased moderately. (See Chapter 4 for a discussion of the equation of exchange. Also, check this chapter's Review of Economic Concepts.)

## The Crisis of 1857 and Depression

As we approached 1857, a series of factors weakened the economy and precipitated another panic and depression. New investment was discouraged, because it became increasingly clear that wide areas of investment had been overextended, including railroads, and profit expectations on many projects were not fulfilled. The end of the Crimean War in 1856 decreased demand for U.S. wheat, lowering its price, and also reducing demand for American shipping. The effects were not felt until 1857.

Adverse events also occurred in the area of finance. In 1858, there was a sharp increase in the demand for credit. This increased interest rates in France and drew financial capital of Britain from the United States to France. It reduced British investment in the United States and drew gold from the New York banks.

By this time, the securities market in New York was significant, and the New York banks had taken to lending their reserves on the call market. Those buying securities in the New York stock market would borrow to pay for these securities from the banks; these loans could be called in at any time, forcing the borrowers to sell the securities in the stock market. With the flow of gold to Britain, the reserves of the New York banks were low, and they called in many loans. To pay for these loans, investors sold the securities on the exchange, and the stock market collapsed. Some banks could not recapture their loans, and a banking panic developed.

This stock market and banking panic was severe, but short. The resulting disruption in the supply of money and confidence in the banking system contracted demand and output. The depression that ensued lasted until the end of 1859.

The confusion that occurred at the outset of the Civil War caused a contraction in economic activity in the North. This contraction was short, because the economy in the North expanded under the impact of increased government expenditures for the military.

## A Brief Recap

On analyzing economic instability from 1815 to 1865, two observations can be made. On the one hand, the American economy was very much influenced by economic conditions in Europe, especially in Britain. Variations in the demand for American exports, as well as financial decisions originating in the British economy, had substantial impact on the United States economy. On the other hand, as the American economy developed and became larger during these 50 years, internal factors affecting aggregate demand and the supply of money played an increasingly important role. As late as 1860, the stability of the U.S. economy was still dependent on European economic conditions, but that dependence was weakening.

# Economic Instability, 1865-1897

## The Expansion to 1873

Many warned that the economy would severely contract after the Civil War. However, the economy expanded until 1873, with only two mild recessions. The long war, with its concentration on the armed conflict, caused postponement of considerable amounts of demand in the civilian economy. Thus, after the war, construction both of housing and of the railroads was high, and capital goods production for industry was also high. In addition, high levels of investments were obtained in the newly developing petroleum industry. The new steel technology of Bessemer, Siemens, Martin, and others had revolutionized steel production, increasing investment in that new technology. Finally, the economy continued to be stimulated by large government expenditures as bounties, pensions, and back pay were paid to the returning soldiers. Settlement of over $700 million in war-related contracts took four years to pay.

Once again, expansion occurred as aggregate demand, consumption, investment, and government expenditures increased, causing a multiple increase in income. (In turn, a positive accelerator reinforced the expansion.)

## The Depression of 1873

By 1872, it was becoming apparent that the expansion was weakening, especially as railroad construction had pushed lines into areas that could not at the time provide sufficient earnings. A general contraction of the economy was held off by a wave of speculation and overoptimism in the now fully developed New York stock market.

In September 1873, a stock market crash and a banking panic were triggered by the failure of Jay Cooke and Company (the great marketeers of Union bonds during the Civil War). There had been overspeculation in railroad securities, which were the backbone of the issues sold in the stock market. First the market collapsed. Then the collapse spread to the urban banks, and a general banking panic ensued. The overexpansion, especially in railroad construction, produced a decrease in investment and a depression in the economy. The slow-up in investment caused a decline in aggregate demand and a multiple decrease in income. In turn, induced investment declined, and a negative accelerator further reduced income and output. The economy's recovery was weak until 1878.

## The Expansion of 1878–1883 and Depression Again

Under the stimulus of increased railroad construction as well as immigration and urban construction, the economy expanded after 1878. This expansion remained vigorous until the end of 1882, when a slow contraction set in. Again railroad construction overexpanded, with the resulting low earnings on a number of lines, caused a slow-up in railroad construction.

In May of 1884, a stock market and banking panic again signaled a collapse in the economy and a depression. Once again the depression was protracted, and a new expansion did not become vigorous until 1886. Once again first the workings of the multiplier and positive accelerator expanded the economy then, and, as this growth slowed and declines occurred, a negative accelerator and multiplier caused contractions in the economy.

## The Expansion of 1886–1892 and the Depression of 1893

The expansion of 1886–1892 was not as vigorous as that in the 1878–1882 period. Railroads still paced the expansion, but their rate of growth had declined. By 1892, railroad expansion had begun to fall off again. In 1892, the import surplus (imports exceeding exports) substantially widened, and there was an outflow of gold, weakening the reserves of the New York banks. In February 1893, there was, once again, a stock market and banking panic and collapse. The ensuing depression lasted until 1897. As before, the multiplier-accelerator sequences expanded and then contracted the economy.

## General Observations

In regard to economic instability, the period from 1865 to 1897 had a number of important characteristics. The most frightening and dramatic aspects of the depressions of 1873, 1883, and 1893 were the coupling of stock market collapses with banking and monetary crises. These depressions began with the collapse of security prices on the stock exchange and with a number of bank closings.

Stock market health and the banking system were linked through the call market for securities. Banks would make call loans on securities; that is, payment could be demanded at any time, and the securities could be sold to pay off the loan. New York bank reserves were heavily committed to the call market; also, deposits of banks outside of New York in the New York banks were heavily involved in the call market. It was the only way that interest could be earned on these funds and that they could also be made immediately available.

Any weakness in either the stock market or the banks could be transmitted to the other. If the banks had a drain on their reserves through either a flow of gold to Europe to cover an import surplus or through withdrawal of deposits by rural banks to meet adverse agricultural situations, then the banks might well call in their loans. This meant selling large amounts of securities in the stock market, causing securities prices to fall. In turn, the banks would call in more loans to protect themselves against falling securities prices, causing more securities to be sold, further decreasing prices in the stock market. The cycle would escalate until a stock market panic resulted. Securities prices could fall so rapidly that banks might not recover the full value of their loans, in turn suffering losses and resulting in bank closings. However, the original stimulus might come from a decline in prices on the stock market, causing banks to call in loans to protect themselves, and so on down the slide.

What was equally frightening about economic instability in this last third of the nineteenth century were the long periods of depression that followed these panics. These periods of business stagnation lasted four to five years (1873–1878, 1882–1885, and 1893–1897). Periods of prosperity were shorter than before the Civil War; the recovery of 1878 lasted until 1882, the less-certain expansion of 1886 lasted until 1892.

Also, the record of instability was closely correlated to the pace of railroad building. The nature of the railroad industry and its effects on the economy were especially destabilizing. First, the cost of constructing a railroad was very high, and the length of time from the start of construction to completion was considerable. By the time a line was completed, the favorable expectations for certain areas, on which the decision to build had been based, might have dissipated; economic conditions might have changed considerably. Or, since the rail lines were developmental in nature, in that many areas along the lines were not yet settled and developed, expectations about their earnings potential may have been too high. Earnings might prove less than anticipated, and further expansion, for a time, was discouraged.

Railroad construction also had impacts on industries such as steel and railroad equipment industries. Changes in the rate of construction functioned with an accelerator impact on the need for increased capacity for those industries supplying materials for construction. Decreases in the rate of growth in railroad construction not only decreased railroad construction, but also introduced a strong negative accelerator effect on broad sectors of the economy.

A fourth characteristic of this last third of the nineteenth century was the long-term decline in prices. Using 1873 for a base price index of 100, the price index in 1890 was 78, a 22% decline, and in 1896 it was 71, a further decrease of 7%. Looking at the equation of exchange $(MV = PQ)$, we see some of the reason for the decline in prices. Output $(Q)$ was increasing, due to increases in productivity and resources (population, investment, and so forth). The supply of money $(M)$ was not increasing fast enough to prevent a fall in prices $(P)$. The fall in prices was not proportional throughout the economy—for some industries and firms, cost fell more slowly than the prices of what was sold, and as a result profits were squeezed. Some income-receivers found that the prices of their resources (labor, land, and so forth) fell more rapidly than the prices of what they bought. As a result, their real demand was reduced. In this way, the fall in prices may have created potentially unstable economic conditions.

Government policy seemed to work in a perverse manner; that is, it tended to reinforce contractive forces in the economy. Federal fiscal policy (government expenditures and taxes) tended to be contractive. The aim of the federal government was to reduce the national debt incurred during the Civil War. To achieve this, the federal government generated a budget surplus. Taxes tended to be high, thus reducing consumption. Expenditures tended to be low, thus reducing aggregate demand and the level of income.

More importantly, the federal government engaged in a deliberate policy of restricting the growth of the money supply. In order to alleviate the confusion of a multiplicity of different currencies and to have a more uniform form of currency stemming from the newly created national banks, the federal government in 1866 taxed out of circulation currency issued by state banks.

In addition, the federal government committed itself firmly to a return to the gold standard. Beginning in 1866, it began to contract the supply of Civil War-issued greenbacks (they were not backed by gold). By 1879, the remaining greenbacks in circulation were being exchanged at par for gold.

Finally, the federal government severely restricted the coinage of silver. From 1873 to 1878, no silver was coined. The government then limited the coinage of silver. This effectively eliminated the use of silver as a method of increasing the supply of money.

There was substantial political opposition to these restrictive money supply policies. The Greenback Party, one that called for increased issues of unbacked currency in the 1870s, was replaced by the demand for the free coinage of silver in the 1880s and 1890s, especially in the short-lived Populist Party and in the Democratic Party under the leadership of William Jennings Bryan.

Another problem relating to the supply of money was the inability to expand national bank currency during financial crises. In fact, the opposite tended to occur, a restriction of the currency supply, itself tending to decrease prices further. According to the National Bank Act of 1864, the supply of national bank currency had to be backed 100% by federal government bonds. When a contraction occurred, interest rates fell, and as interest rates fell the sale price of bonds increased. Banks, now holding government bonds priced higher in the market, tended to sell them to realize the profit. As they sold the bonds, they had to decrease their currency issues. The result was a decrease in the supply of money, decreased prices, and contracting pressures on the economy.

Some historians have argued that an additional factor explaining the recurrent security market crisis was the action of the so-called robber barons in the railroad securities market. Rampant exploitation of railroads for short-run immediate gains of promoters left railroads financially weak; ruthless speculation and manipulation of railroad securities by such "barons" as Vanderbilt, Gould, Fisk, Huntington, and Stanford eroded the confidence and security of railroad securities and left the whole stock market itself unsettled.

The term "robber baron" has been severely criticized in more recent research. While it is not our intent to review that debate, it is true that the most extreme elements of Mathew Josephson's *The Robber Barons*[6] have been discredited. These barons look less and less like heroic commanders of the strategic heights of the American economy and more and more like businessmen trying to make profits both from productive enterprise and also from the exercise of monopoly power, whichever was available.

But the point is that significant manipulation of railroad securities and property had occurred that substantially weakened the financial soundness of many railroads and at times undermined the workings of the stock exchange. Some examples are the Credit Mobilier scandal of the Grant administration concerning the construction of the Union Pacific; the stock market fight between Vanderbilt (controlling the Long Island Central) and Gould (controlling the New York Central) for control over railroad transportation out of New York City in the early 1870s; and, lastly, at the beginning of the twentieth century the fight between Harriman and Morgan for control of the Northern Pacific.

# Economic Instability, 1897–1920

## Expansion, 1897–1907

The recovery from the 1893–1897 depression was caused by a combination of very favorable demand and monetary factors. Furthermore, international factors were also favorable. Europe recovered faster than the United States from the depression of 1893, which generally increased U.S. exports. In 1897, there was a drought in France and floods in Austria, the Balkans, and Russia, which more than doubled U.S. wheat exports.

Railroads, many of them in bankruptcy during the depression, recovered sufficiently by 1897 to engage in much-needed repairs, plus a resurgence of new construction. New construction averaged 3400 miles of track a year from 1897 to 1902. This expansion increased the demand for iron and steel, railroad cars and locomotives, and new bridges and terminal facilities. Obviously the multiplier and accelerator effects were substantial.

With the resumption of prosperity and increases in employment opportunities, large-scale immigration resumed, producing labor for the urban manufacturing centers. As a result, urbanization, with its construction activity, expanded. Finally, the Spanish American War began in 1898, increasing government expenditures, especially for the U.S. Navy. As a result, steel, munitions, and shipbuilding expanded.

Besides these expansions in aggregate demand, there were very favorable monetary developments. The very favorable balance of trade in 1896 brought in $122 million in gold, which went into the reserves of the banks. Gold strikes in the Yukon in Alaska and in South Africa doubled world gold production after 1896. An increased world supply of gold increased the supply of money, increased prices, and expanded demand.

With this renewal of prosperity, profits rose. Financial speculation followed this glut of investment funds in the market. In the spring of 1901, speculation in the stock market went rampant. A climax was reached on May 9, 1901, with the fight for control of the Northern Pacific Railroad between Morgan and Harriman. Both bought at high prices as much Northern Pacific stock as they could. Some brokers sold stock they didn't have, hoping to buy the stock at lower prices for later delivery. On May 9, it seemed that more stock was sold than existed. In six hours, the stock price went from 160 to over 1000. However, a truce was called, and a panic was avoided.

Again in 1903, speculation and stock prices rose and the stock market panicked; but this rich man's panic had little effect on the rest of the economy.

## Panic and Depression of 1907

Speculation and stock manipulation contributed to the stock market panic of 1907. This panic spread from the stock market to the banks, with a number of bank failures. The depression that followed was acute and lasted into 1911.

The economy recovered in 1912 but lapsed again in 1913. Recovery had started by the beginning of 1914, but the economy contracted again as war began in September 1914. But by the middle of 1915 the U.S. economy boomed, because the United States was the primary country capable of filling the production needs of the belligerents. The demand for U.S. exports by the warring nations of Europe, especially the Allies, tremendously stimulated the U.S. economy. These large export surpluses of the United States were paid for at first by the liquidation of large amounts of European-held investments in the United States. Later in the war, especially after the entry of the United States on the side of the Allies, large loans were extended by the United States to the Allies. By the end of the war, the United States had shifted from a **net debtor nation** (Americans owed foreigners more than they owed us) to a **net creditor nation** (foreigners owed Americans more than we owed them).

A number of reasons have been offered to explain the fits and starts of the U.S. economy from 1907 to 1914. One important explanation was the inefficient and inelastic credit system existing under the national bank system. A serious deficiency lay in the lack of a central bank that could lend to the banking system during crises so as to shore up reserves and expand the ability to lend. Also, the existing tie between currency and government debt restricted the ability to expand the currency supply during crises. Both were serious inadequacies of the national bank system. The efforts to deal with these problems resulted in the overhaul of the banking system with the Federal Reserve Act of 1913.

Some charged that promoters and financiers had so overloaded railroads and the recently created large corporations with such a high ratio of debt to total assets that they impaired the efficient working of these firms. Also some charged that, of the firms created through the combination

Northern factories. (Photo nos. 165-WW-203A-8 and 165-WW-203C-1 in the National Archives)

movement, those large enough to greatly influence prices were reluctant to lower prices after 1907 in the face of weakened demand. This use of monopoly power (control over price) restricted the stimulating effects of price declines after or during recessions.

Because wages barely kept up with rising prices, some concluded that increases in productivity (technological change and so forth) increased profit margins, not consumption. As a result, consumption was restricted more than investment expanded, and aggregate demand was less than it would have been.

Some also have argued that during the first decade of the twentieth century, the antibusiness articles written by muckrakers, government committees investigating business practices, and higher levels of antitrust action aimed against monopolizing practices of business caused a loss of confidence in investors and thus a decrease in the willingness to invest.

What this indicates most of all is that business cycle theory was far from adequate then or even now. Each issue is strongly debated as to its quantitative importance. The presentation here is not made for the purpose of entering into debate about the significance of the "robber baron" thesis of Josephson[6] or the decline of competition thesis of Faulkner.[3] That these factors were present is debatable and whether they were sufficiently strong to cause the instability between 1907 and 1914 is very much in doubt. A more probable explanation lies in the slowing up of a long-term expansion (1897–1907) and the resulting negative accelerator effects.

## A Small Conclusion

The record to 1920 shows that the impressive long-term development of the U.S. economy was accompanied by periodic variations in the level of output, prices, and employment. Economic development was a fact of the nineteenth century, but so was economic instability. The nature of that instability changed as the century progressed. In the beginning, instability was transmitted by the actions of the European economies, especially that of the British. In time, though, through the dynamics of internal development in the United States (the westward movement, transportation, manufacturing development, immigration, and urbanization), instability became more and more a function of the country's internal dynamics and less determined by trade relationships with Britain and Europe. At the end of 1919, the tables had turned. Not only was the country "independent" of the European economies—but those economies had become dependent on the new industrial and financial giant, the United States.

---

# Review of Economic Concepts: Macro and Monetary Models

## A Macro Model of Output

To explore the question of economic instability, one must examine what basic factors determine, at a point in time, the level of output and income in an economy. The model to be constructed is a **macro** one, a model concerned with activity on the level of the whole economy—as distinct from a **micro** model, the analysis of the activities of the smaller units in our economy, such as the individual market, consumer, or firm. This macro model can be approached from two directions: (a) analyses of total or aggregate demand and (b) analyses of the effects of variations in the supply of money. By necessity, our treatment will be brief. (For a more complete presentation, the student should consult a text on the principles of economics.)

**An Aggregate Demand Model**     John Maynard Keynes[10] maintained that the equilibrium level of income and thus output in our economy is determined by its level of effective or aggregate demand.* Five principal factors influence the level of aggregate demand: First, the **consumption function** represents the various quantities that the society is willing and able to consume at differing levels of income. Increases in consumption (a

---

*Note that this model takes aggregate supply as given.

shift upward of the curve) increase aggregate demand, while decreases in consumption (a shift downward of the curve) decrease aggregate demand. The position and shape of the curve are determined by (a) habits, customs, and institutions; (b) the stock of consumer durables; (c) the amount of liquid assets (those easily converted into money) held by the society; and (d) the level of taxes.

Second, the **savings function** represents the various quantities that the society is willing and able to save at differing levels of income. What a society does not consume out of income is either saved or paid in taxes. Therefore, the same factors that determine consumption also determine savings, but in the reverse direction. Increases in savings (shifts upward of the savings function) decrease consumption and thus decrease aggregate demand, while decreases in savings (shifts downward of the savings function) increase consumption and thus increase aggregate demand.

Third, the **investment function** represents the various quantities that the society is willing and able to invest at different levels of income. There are two kinds of investment: autonomous and induced.

**Autonomous investment** is determined by factors outside the model; that is, it is not affected by income or consumption. The quantity of autonomous investment depends on the interest rate (the cost of investing) and the marginal efficiency of capital (the expected rate of return). Investments will be made as long as the marginal efficiency of capital is equal to or greater than the interest rate. The primary factors determining the marginal efficiency of capital are expectations of investors about future returns and productivity of the investment (technology). The quantity of autonomous investment will increase if (a) the interest rate falls, (b) expectations become more optimistic, or (c) technological change occurs, increasing the productivity of investment. A decrease in the quantity of autonomous investment will occur if the opposite happens.

**Induced investment** is investment induced by or caused by changes in the model, changes in income, and changes in consumption. For now, let us leave induced investment out of the model; we will consider it later.

Fourth, the government expenditure function represents the various quantities of government expenditure that will be made at different levels of income. Such expenditures are obviously determined by governmental decision-making. Aggregate demand increases as these expenditures increase and decreases as they decrease.

Fifth, the tax function represents the various quantities that society pays in taxes at different levels of income. Taxes are also determined through governmental decision-making. An increase in taxes is paid for in part out of income that would have been spent on consumption; thus consumption and aggregate demand are decreased by taxation. If taxes decrease, the additional private income is spent in part on consumption; thus consumption and aggregate demand are increased.

In summary, aggregate demand determines the level of income and thus output in the economy. Aggregate demand is made up of consumption, investment, and government expenditures. Increases in savings and taxes decrease aggregate demand, while decreases in savings and taxes increase aggregate demand. Aggregate supply equals consumption, plus savings, plus taxes.

## The Model

Figure 13-2 shows the elements of aggregate demand in a diagram relating income on the horizontal axis and consumption, investment, and government expenditure on the vertical axis. The top line, marked $C + II + G$, represents aggregate demand. The line emanating from the origin divides that quadrant in half (two 45-degree angles) and is called the 45-degree line. The distance from the vertical axis to the 45-degree line is equal to the distance from the horizontal axis to the 45-degree line. The vertical distance to the 45-degree line is equal to income or value of output. The 45-degree line, then, is aggregate supply.

Now for the analysis. The equilibrium income level of the economy (the central tendency of the model) is the level of income that equates aggregate demand and aggregate supply at Point B, or Income Level 0A. Any other level of income would not be stable and would cause a movement

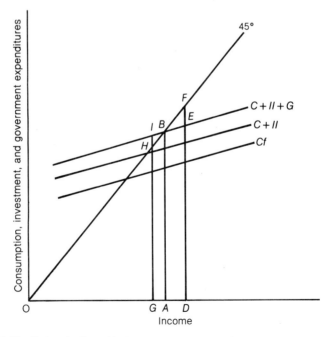

Figure 13-2. The Determination of Income.

toward the Equilibrium Level 0A. At any level of income above the equilibrium (for example, 0D), aggregate supply (DF) exceeds aggregate demand (DE)—more is produced than is demanded. Inventories of business firms therefore become greater by EF than the firms wish, causing them to reduce orders to manufacturers. In turn, these actions reduce output, employment, and income. The level of income shifts to 0A. At any level of income below the equilibrium (for example, 0G), aggregate demand exceeds aggregate supply—more is demanded than is produced. Inventories of business firms decrease below what they have planned as people consume more than was produced for them by IH. To replenish these depleted inventories, firms increase orders to the manufacturers, who in turn increase output, employment, and income. The level of income moves to 0A.

Since the level of income and output is determined by the level of aggregate demand, any change in the latter's components (consumption, investment, government expenditure) will change the level of income. In Figure 13-3, we see, though, that this relationship is not a simple one. The increase in aggregate demand (AB) is much smaller than the increase in income (DE). This is known as the **multiplier effect,** or a multiple change in income from any given change in aggregate demand. The size of the multiplier depends on the marginal propensity to consume or save. The **marginal propensity to consume** is the percentage of any change in income that is spent on consumption. The marginal propensity to consume meas-

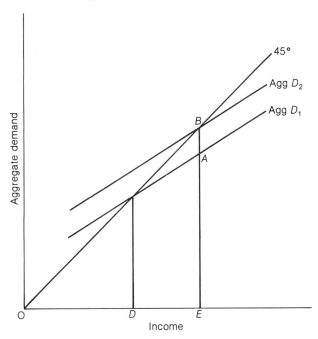

Figure 13-3. The Multiplier.

ures the portion of the income generated by a change in aggregate demand that is returned to demand once again as additional demand. But the main point is that income changes by an amount larger than the original changes in aggregate demand.

Let us assume that the marginal propensity to consume (*MPC*) is one-half, and the government decides to build a post office for $100,000. That $100,000 is an increase in aggregate demand through an increase in intended investment. Income will increase by $100,000 as this office is built and the people who build it are paid. Now the people who have this additional income will (remember that *MPC* is one-half) save only one-half and will demand more goods and services with the other one-half. Output then will increase by $50,000 as goods and services are produced to satisfy that increased demand. Income increases by another $50,000. People who receive that income also spend one-half of it (*MPC* equals one-half), and output and income increase by $25,000. The process continues until there is virtually no additional demand for output. The point to remember is that income increases by more than the original increase in aggregate demand, the $100,000 for the post office. In this example, the multiplier is two, and income would increase by $200,000. The multiplier formula is $1/1 - MPC$. Substituting an *MPC* of one-half in the formula gives us $1/1 - \frac{1}{2} = 1/\frac{1}{2} = 1 \times 2/1$ or 2.

The last factor to keep in mind about the aggregate demand model is the **accelerator principle**. When induced investment increases, the accelerator is positive, thereby expanding the economy. When induced investment is negative, the accelerator is negative and the economy contracts. Remember that induced investment is induced or caused by changes in the level of income and thus changes in the quantity of consumption. These increases in the quantity consumed increase the need for additional capacity to produce the additional output. These increases in capacity result from induced investment.

But induced investment is not increased simply by increases in total consumption demand, but rather by increases in the *rate* of growth in consumer demand. When the *rate* of growth in consumer demand is increasing, then induced investment is increasing, and the accelerator is positive, thereby expanding the economy. When the rate of growth is constant, induced investment is zero. When the rate of growth in consumer demand is decreasing, induced investment decreases, and the accelerator is negative, resulting in a contraction of the economy. Forces can thus be contracting the economy even when total consumer demand is still expanding.

## Summary

In summary, according to the aggregate demand model, the following factors expand the economy:

1. Increases in the consumption function caused by (a) changes in habits and institutions that decrease savings, (b) increases in liquidity (proportion of assets that could quickly be converted into money), (c) decreases in inventories of consumer-held durables, and (d) decreases in taxes.
2. Increases in investment, both autonomous and induced. Increases in autonomous investment occur when (a) interest rates decrease, (b) expectations become more optimistic, and (c) technological development occurs. Increases in induced investment occur when the rate of growth in demand increases, creating demand for increases in productive capacity.
3. Increases in government expenditures. Here we are faced with the fact that government expenditures result from political processes. Variations in such expenditures are not closely related to variations in income. Thus we still take government expenditures as given.

Decreases in the level of income result from the opposite occurring.

Keep in mind that small variations in aggregate demand will cause larger variations in income and output through the functioning and interaction of the multiplier and the accelerator.

## A Monetary View

In recent years, a number of economists, including Milton Friedman, have emphasized the role of the supply of money in determining the level of economic activity. These monetarists maintain that money is the primary thing that matters, not that it is the only thing that matters. "Keynesians," however, maintain that money is important but that aggregate demand is also important. Now let's examine how variations in the supply of money affect the level of economic activity.

The model we shall use is the equation of exchange or quantity theory of money already presented in Chapter 4. Let's review it briefly. The equation of exchange is $MV = PQ$. $M$ is the supply of money; $V$ is the velocity of exchange or the number of times $M$ changes hands in a given period of time; $P$ is the price level; and $Q$ is the number of economic transactions in real rather than money terms.

We can distinguish two types of money, $M_1$ and $M_2$. $M_1$ consists of all demand deposits (checking accounts) and all currency and coins in circulation. $M_2$ adds savings accounts and highly liquid (easily converted into money) assets. The velocity of exchange ($V$) depends on the customs, habits, and so on of the population (how strongly they want to hold on to money), on the degree of efficiency of the financial institutions (how quickly money can be transferred), and on people's expectations about economic activity, including the security of financial institutions.

If there are unemployed resources and the supply of money increases with a velocity that is constant, output or Q tends to increase as more resources are employed. As the economy approaches full employment and the supply of money continues to increase, P or prices also begin to rise. When full employment is reached, only prices will increase (not output) with increase in the supply of money. The reverse of these effects occurs when the supply of money decreases.

# Glossary

**Accelerator principle**  The principle that as the rate of growth of consumer demand increases, the need for additional facilities increases and induced investment increases. These increases create a positive accelerator and the economy expands. The reverse occurs where the rate of growth of consumer demand declines.

**Autonomous investment**  Determined by factors other than changes in income or consumption.

**Consumption function**  A function representing the various quantities that the society is willing and able to consume at different levels of income.

**Economic instability**  Variations in the level of economic activity, primarily variations in output, employment, and prices. It is considered a more appropriate term than *business cycles* or *business fluctuations*.

**Induced investment**  Investment induced, or caused by, changes in income and consumption. When the rate of increase in consumer demand is increasing, induced investment increases.

**Investment function**  A function representing the various quantities that society is willing and able to invest at different levels of income.

**Macro model**  One concerned with economic activity on the level of the whole economy.

**Marginal propensity to consume**  The percent or portion of any change in income that becomes personal consumption expenditure rather than savings or tax payments.

**Micro model**  The analysis of the activities of the smaller units in the economy such as the individual market, or consumer, or firm.

**Multiplier effect**  A multiple change in income from any given change in aggregate demand. The size of the multiplier depends on the marginal propensity to consume or save.

**Net creditor nation**   A nation to which foreigners owe more than it owes to foreigners.

**Net debtor nation**   A nation that owes more to foreigners than they owe to it.

**Savings function**   A function representing the various quantities that the society is willing and able to save at different levels of income.

# Questions

1. What was the basic source of instability in the period 1792 to 1815?
2. What internal factors expanded the economy from 1820 to 1837 and from 1843 to 1857?
3. On comparing the contractions in 1819, 1837, 1839, and 1857, which seemed to be more important, internal factors or factors external to the American economy? Does there seem to have been any change in relative importance between the two over time?
4. List the periods of expansion and the periods of contraction from 1865 through 1897.
5. What four major characteristics of economic instability in the last third of the nineteenth century are listed in the text?
6. How were banking and stock market panics linked in the period 1873 to 1897?
7. In what ways did railroad construction from 1865 to 1897 increase economic instability?
8. What factors contributed to the long-term decline in prices from 1865 to 1897?
9. What various factors caused a recovery and then expansion in the economy from 1897 to 1907?
10. What are the various explanations for the fits and starts of the U.S. economy from 1907 to 1914?
11. Which factors—external ones generated by international economic relations, or internal ones generated by domestic economic development—are more descriptive of the causes of U.S. economic instability in the nineteenth century? Why?

# Suggested Readings

1. Barnett, Paul. *Business Cycle Theory in the United States, 1860–1900.* Chicago: University of Chicago Press, 1941.

2. Dillard, Dudley. *The Economics of John Maynard Keynes.* Englewood Cliffs, N.J.: Prentice-Hall, 1948.

3. Faulkner, Harold U. *The Decline of Laissez Faire, 1897–1917.* New York: Holt, Rinehart and Winston, 1961. Chap. 2.

4. Fels, Rendig. *American Business Cycles, 1865–1897.* Chapel Hill: University of North Carolina Press, 1959.

5. Kirkland, Edward C. *Industry Comes of Age.* New York: Holt, Rinehart and Winston, 1961. Chap. 1.

6. Josephson, Mathew. *The Robber Barons: The Great American Capitalists, 1861–1901.* New York: Harcourt Brace Jovanovich, 1934.

7. Friedman, Milton, and Schwartz, Anna J. *A Monetary History of the United States, 1867–1960.* Princeton, N.J.: Princeton University Press, 1963.

8. Hoffman, Charles. "The Depression of the Nineties." *Journal of Economic History, 16* (June 1956).

9. Hughes, J. R. T., and Rosenberg, Nathan. "The United States Business Cycle Before 1860: Some Problems of Interpretation." *Economic History Review, 15* (April 1963).

10. Keynes, John Maynard. *The General Theory of Employment, Interest and Money.* New York: Harcourt Brace Jovanovich, 1936.

11. North, Douglass C. *The Economic Growth of the United States, 1790–1860.* Englewood Cliffs, N.J.: Prentice-Hall, 1961.

12. Smith, Walter B., and Cole, Arthur H. *Fluctuations in American Business, 1790–1860.* Cambridge, Mass.: Harvard University Press, 1935.

13. Taylor, George R. *The Transportation Revolution, 1815–1860.* New York: Holt, Rinehart and Winston, 1951.

14. Temin, Peter. *The Jacksonian Economy.* New York: Norton, 1969.

15. Willis, James F., and Primack, Martin L. *Explorations in Economics.* Boston: Houghton Mifflin, 1977. Chaps. 7–9.

# Chapter 14

---

# Agriculture, Industry, and Transportation, 1897-1920

The depression of 1893 was over by 1897, and America's economy entered into a new era. Prosperity was the order of the day as the economy continued its growth. Agriculture, troubled and dissenting for the last 30 years, now enjoyed unprecedented prosperity. The seemingly limitless frontier had been occupied and technology continued to advance as the internal combustion engine and the tractor began to replace the horse. Manufacturing development continued as the United States became the world's leading industrial society. But this growth was increasingly accompanied by the formation of larger and larger enterprises. Partially in response to this quickening of the combination movement in industry, the labor movement increased union organization, and the federal government strengthened and expanded the regulation of business.

First, we will look at the progress of agriculture and industry from 1897 to 1920. Then we will briefly discuss transportation changes in the same period. Finally, for those who wish to review the model of economies of scale or what economic and technical factors affect the size of firms, a simple model is included in the Review of Economic Concepts in this chapter. In the following two chapters, we will examine first the combination movement in business enterprises, the strengthening and expansion of government regulation, and the expansion of organized labor. The last chapter in this section on the period from 1897 to 1919 will be concerned with the United States in the international economy.

# Agricultural Prosperity

### 1897-1914

The end of the depression in 1897 began a period of agricultural prosperity that lasted more than 20 years. Agricultural prices and farm incomes were not only high but they were also high relative to prices and incomes in the other sectors of the economy. The prices of what farmers sold rose much more rapidly than the prices of what farmers bought both for production and for their own consumption. The terms of trade turned sharply in favor of the agricultural sector. In fact, farmers have tried ever since to use that period as the ideal for relative incomes and prices between agriculture and the remainder of the economy.

The reasons for this prosperity can be found in the farmers' supply and demand conditions. The rate of increase in the supply of agricultural products dropped drastically as the frontier finally became settled. The rate of growth of new lands and new farms being created and brought into production dropped sharply after 1900. The rate of growth in major crops also fell; in wheat production, there was even a decrease in acreage from 1900 to 1910. The productivity of the fairly constant supply of farm laborers (11 million in 1900, 1910, and also 1920) increased.

While supply experienced a decrease in its rate of growth, demand continued its rapid increase. World population, as well as that of the United States, continued to increase. Importantly, domestic demand increased as immigration swelled and as people moved primarily into industrial, urban areas. Total U.S. population grew from 76 million in 1900 to over 106 million by 1920. From 1901 to 1910, almost 9 million immigrants arrived in the United States. Due primarily to the war, this dropped to about 6 million for the period from 1911 to 1920. Also, both domestic and foreign demand grew as economic development increased real incomes in Europe and the United States.

This relatively more rapid increase in demand than supply caused agricultural prices to increase. The index of farm wholesale prices (1926 = 100) was 50 in 1900 and had risen to 74 in 1910, an increase of almost 50 %. The general wholesale price index increased by only 25 % or half of the percentage increase in agriculture during the same period. In addition to higher incomes and more favorable terms of trade (agricultural purchasing power), agricultural prosperity was expanded by a decrease in the real debt burden due to the increases in agricultural prices.

### 1914-1920

The surge of prosperity in agriculture continued unchecked until the recessions of 1913 and September 1914. In 1915, foreign demand for agricul-

Table 14-1. Selected Agricultural Statistics, 1890–1920.

|  | 1890 | 1900 | 1910 | 1920 |
|---|---|---|---|---|
| Number of farms (thousands) | 4,565 | 5,737 | 6,406 | 6,518 |
| Acres in farms (millions) | 623 | 838 | 879 | 956 |
| Acres in corn (millions) | 75 | 95 | 102 | 101 |
| Acres in wheat (millions) | 37 | 49 | 46 | 62 |
| Farm laborers (millions) | 9.9 | 10.9 | 11.6 | 11.4 |
| Number of tractors (thousands) | — | — | 1 | 256 |
| Number of horses (thousands) | 153 | 170 | 192 | 198 |
| Value of land (millions of dollars) | — | 13,048 | 28,469 | 54,825 |
| Value of mortgages (millions of dollars) | — | — | 3,207 | 8,449 |

Source: U.S. Department of Commerce, Historical Statistics of the United States Colonial Times to 1970, Part 1 (Washington, D.C.: U.S. Government Printing Office, 1975), pp. 449–525.

tural products as well as for all forms of U.S. output surged ahead as the belligerents of World War I, especially the Allies, increased their demand for American products. Prosperity returned to agriculture as farm prices again began to increase.

Farmers strove for greater output, to keep up with the wartime demand. Mechanization increased in order to replace the labor that was moving to the urban industrial areas and going into the armed forces.

During this time, tractors became firmly established, and the horse began to be replaced. The use of tractors had two expansionary effects on output for the market. The tractor was faster and more powerful than the horse, and thus increased labor productivity; also, each horse displaced released two acres of land for human food rather than for horse food.

The drive to increase output increased the demand for land; thus land values rose. With the exhaustion of the frontier by 1900, this increased demand for land could not be satisfied through additional land being brought into production except through the use of less productive land. Consequently, the increased demand for land resulted in competitive bidding for a scarce supply of land and hence in higher land values. As farmers strove to buy more land, total mortgage values rose. The value of land in agriculture increased dramatically, from $28.4 billion in 1910 to over $57 billion in 1920. At the time, higher mortgages seemed justified to farmers because of the existing higher prices for agricultural products. However, the higher mortgages and expanded agricultural supply later created problems in the 1920s.

These conditions of high agricultural output, prices, and incomes were maintained as the United States entered the war in 1917. After the war and through 1920, these conditions were maintained by high levels of foreign demand for U.S. agricultural products, because of the wartime devastation in wide areas of Europe.

Along with the prosperity of agriculture from 1897 through 1920, other trends established in the second half of the nineteenth century continued. Governments provided agricultural education and research through the state land grant colleges and universities, experimental stations, and county agents. Continued and expanded, the activities of the Department of Agriculture contributed significantly to increased productivity.

Increased mechanization, especially the tractor, improvements in livestock and crop varieties, development of superior fertilizers, and chemical sprays continued to increase agricultural productivity. In 1900, 108 man-hours were required to produce 100 bushels of wheat. This dropped to 87 hours by 1920. For corn, the drop was from 147 man-hours per 100 bushels to 113 man-hours. These improvements stemmed from activities of government, from private enterprise providing resources to agriculture, and from the agricultural sector itself.

Regional specialization continued, as the South concentrated on cotton. Production of wheat, cattle, animal products, and mixed farming each continued in the regions established by 1900. Moreover, local areas increased specialization in vegetable fruit raising and in dairying. Technological change, especially in refrigerated forms of transportation, continued to facilitate this form of specialization as it became possible to transport perishable products over longer distances.

These 20 years of prosperity left a legacy of problems for farmers in the 1920s. High mortgages and higher output deviled the farmers as demand moved to more normal levels and prices fell.

# Industry

Manufacturing continued its impressive expansion in the two decades from 1897 to 1920. As shown by Table 14-2 real output more than doubled, while the number of workers in manufacturing slightly less than doubled. The money value of products increased almost 600%, while money wages increased almost 500%. Thus with price increases the increase in productivity was not entirely passed on to workers; as a result, profit margins increased. These impressive gains were matched and at times exceeded in earlier time periods, but in this period there was also strong inflation, especially in the price increases from 1914 to 1919. What must be kept in mind is the contribution to economic development: Industrial output increased twice as fast as the total population.

Although the process is more complex and controversial, a moderate inflation could encourage economic development, as rising prices encourage business expectations of future higher profit. This in turn encourages higher investments to create the facilities that would produce the output

Table 14-2. Index of Manufacturing Production.

| Census Year | Production Index (1899 = 100) |
|---|---|
| 1899 | 100 |
| 1904 | 122 |
| 1909 | 159 |
| 1914 | 169 |
| 1919 | 214 |

Source: Edmund E. Day, and Thomas Woodlief, *The Growth of Manufactures, 1899–1923,* U.S. Bureau of the Census, Census Monograph VIII (Washington, D.C.: U.S. Government Printing Office), 1928, pp. 32–33.

that would earn the expected higher profits. This process would occur if prices of products were expected to increase more rapidly than costs increase.

Industry increased its importance relative to agriculture. In 1900, agriculture and industry employed equal percentages of the total labor force—30%. By 1920, however, agriculture employed only 25% of the labor force, while industry's share had grown to 42%.

## Causes of the Expansion

On the whole, the same factors fueled the 1897–1920 expansion as had caused expansion in earlier periods. Some of these factors were technological change and accompanying increases in productivity, a labor force expanding through high immigration and natural increase, and rapidly increasing demand, due in part to expanding population and real income. In addition, the stimulus of the Spanish American War of 1898 started the period, which closed with the end of World War I. A number of new industries also appeared. The most important was probably the automobile industry, while the most glamorous was the motion picture industry.

The factory system continued to spread, encroaching on both home and small handicraft production. The factory system penetrated the garment industry, utilizing the sewing machine, reduced the number of tailors and dressmakers making clothes to order, and also reduced the making of clothes in the home by the family. The labor force increased in numbers as immigrants, especially from eastern and southern Europe, flocked to U.S. cities. This was especially true in the 1904–1909 period. Perhaps equally important was the increase in labor skills and improved management. Frederick W. Taylor's ideas on scientific management, that is, the application of scientific analyses of management and labor to production processes, developed in the 1880s, gained further adherents. Increased attention was paid to the flow of work. These studies and attitudes were especially important in the development of assembly lines and other mass production techniques.

The continuing advances in technology increased productivity in a wide range of industries. Two developments of special relevance, which will be treated in greater detail a little further on, were expansion in the use of electricity and mass production and assembly-line techniques.

Changes in international trade also provided stimulus to manufacturing expansion. The proportion of U.S. exports that were agricultural products decreased, and the proportion that were semifinished and finished manufactured products increased substantially. In the period from 1896 to 1900, 21% of U.S. exports were finished nonagricultural goods. By 1917, this had increased to 44%.

## Characteristics of the Expansion

Of prime importance was the continuation of the high levels of production of investment goods (capital equipment needed for further production). It averaged about 20% of the value of output during the 1897–1920 period. Frederick Mills[9] estimates that from 1901 to 1913 capital equipment increased at a rate of 5% per year, while consumption goods increased at an average of only 2.6% per year.

Processing of agricultural and forest products became relatively less important as the growth of manufacturing that used minerals as raw materials increased. Textiles, furniture, and grain processing grew more slowly than iron and steel, chemicals, and petroleum processing and the manufacture of automobiles.

A very important characteristic of manufacturing expansion from 1897 to 1919 was the continuation of the tendency toward larger firms. Faulkner[5] shows that the average manufacturing establishment increased from an average product output of $13,429 in 1859 to $215,157 in 1919, in dollar terms, and, in average number of wage earners, from 9.34 in 1859 to 20.49 in 1899 to 31.36 in 1919.

In addition to the increased average size of firms, the largest size firms dominated wide sections of manufacturing. In 1919, those firms producing over $1.2 million in output, while comprising only 3.6% of all firms, produced more than 67% of the total value of output and employed 56% of the workers.

There were two basic reasons for this increase in size of firm. First, by combining into larger firms competition might have been reduced, prices increased, and profits raised. (The combination movement is reviewed in the next chapter.) Second, the available economies of scale encouraged increased size of establishments to obtain resulting cost savings.

Increased economies of scale came about for a number of reasons. There were increases in the size of markets that created opportunities to utilize improved production techniques and specialization. There were technological improvements in communication and transportation. World and domestic population increased. There were increases in real income as the United States and western Europe continued to develop economically. Finally, there was expansion in foreign trade. The technology of the time, such as assembly-line mass production techniques, required larger machines and facilities, and higher levels of output were needed to fully utilize these new techniques. Also, the growing use of Taylor's scientific management techniques introduced methods that postponed rising average costs or diseconomies of scale, increases in per unit costs due to management inefficiencies appearing as the increased size of firms created communication problems. Finally, the relatively faster rate of growth in industries requiring larger scale to reach minimum average cost (iron and steel, automobiles, and petroleum, for example) increased the average size of enterprises. Note that some of these economies of scale increased the average size of each plant. Technological change required larger facilities. Others increased the size of the firms by increasing the number of plants, such as increases in the size of markets, improvements in communication, and improvements in management.

Although there were some geographic shifts of manufacturing, the Northeast maintained its dominance in that sector. According to Keebe and Danhof,[7] the share of manufacturing wage earners in New England and the Middle Atlantic states dropped from 52.2 to 46.5% from 1899 to 1910. The East North Central states gained, as their percentage went from 22.8 to 26.3. The rest of the gains were in the West. The West South Central, Mountain, and Pacific states increased from 5.9 to 9.1%. These increases, although small in total, were a clear indication of future trends in the United States.

Technology also continued to improve: there were larger and more productive facilities, new management techniques, and increased use of electricity. In 1900, each worker in the steel industry produced an average of 85 tons of steel; by 1920, this average had risen to 114 tons. From 1900 to 1914, a 76% increase in the volume (not dollar value) of manufactured goods was achieved, with an increase of only 36% in the number of workers.

## Electric Power

By 1897, the pioneering giants in the generation and utilization of electric power (Edison, Westinghouse, Parsons, Thomas, and Tesla) had brought the industry to the point that electricity could be carried cheaply over long distances and also be easily applied as a source of power. Faulkner[5] comments that "The fundamental inventions were made before 1897, and the great fruition of a century of research came after the first World War. The two decades under study [1897–1919] appear to be chiefly a period of extension, application, and improvement."

The total available horsepower per worker for each year noted in industry increased, according to Harry Jerome,[8] from 2.11 in 1899 to 3.24 in 1919, and from 1909 to 1919 the increases were even higher in agriculture and mining. In 1899, only 5% of all power used in manufacturing came through electric motors; by 1919, this had risen to 55% and by 1925 to 73%.

The advantages of electricity were numerous. Once electricity could be cheaply transported over long distances, the plant was freed from the necessity to locate near sources of other kinds of power. For instance, water power required location near streams, and steam power needed a cheap nearby source of coal. Industry could now locate anywhere.

Especially for light industries, it was cheaper to use electricity than steam or water, because the latter forms of power required that each firm build its own power plant. And electricity was much more convenient, because the portable electric motor could be used for portable machine tools. Electricity provided more uniform speeds and could be controlled in ways that permitted fine variations of speed.

## Assembly-Line Production

**Assembly-line production,** or what many call **mass production,** is one of the best known technological innovations of the first two decades in the twentieth century. Henry Ford, of the Ford Motor Company, became famous as one of its early exponents. The process depending on standardization, interchangeability of parts, and systems of material flows logically arranged to facilitate product assembly continued the **American System.**

These production concepts were not new. A prominent example of their earlier use was Eli Whitney's assembly of guns for the military in the very early nineteenth century. Standardization of parts required sufficient improvements in the machine tool industry so that identical parts could be produced. The development of high-speed carbon tool steel at the turn of the twentieth century was one of the more important of the very many advances in machine tools that made the making of standard parts practical. Taylor's scientific management method advocated systematic management analyses of the work flow, which strongly encouraged assembly-line techniques. The adaptability of electricity to portable tools used along the assembly line was an important contribution. Finally, in order to justify mass production techniques, there had to be sufficient demand to buy the output. By 1900, domestic plus foreign demand had reached that level in many industries.

An early light bulb, and early telephone service. (Photo nos. 119-M-2B-4 and 16-G-95-6 in the National Archives)

By 1913, Ford had shifted from stationary assembly to moving assembly in the production of Ford automobiles. Now instead of hand carrying the parts to the waiting workers, a system of motor-powered conveyors delivered the work at a preset speed. Assembly-line production reduced costs. Ford's Model T fell in price from $950 in 1909 to $490 in 1914, mostly because of the assembly line and interchangeable parts.

## Conditions of Wage Earners

Several factors changed the conditions of wage earners in the period 1897–1919. For example, unionization of labor was expanding, both in numbers and in industries organized—but more on this in the next chapter.

Large-scale immigration continued until 1914. The total immigration to the United States from 1897 to 1914 was over 14 million people. These immigrants were primarily from southern and eastern Europe, were mostly unskilled, and concentrated in urban areas of the United States after immigration. They experienced considerable difficulties adjusting to the culture and language of the United States, and they were for varying periods of time isolated from the general society.

Also, there was an accelerated movement of women into the labor force. In 1890, women were only 14% of the total labor force. This increased to over 20% by 1920 under the impact of labor shortages during World War I. Increased urbanization reduced female work requirements in the home (smaller apartments, no farm chores, or such things as canning and food preserving), and mores were changing toward a more favorable view of women in the labor force. No doubt an important factor was the economic pressure forcing women to supplement family incomes, especially immigrant and black women. But many working women were young and single, with their wages as their sole financial support.

Finally, blacks began to move out of agriculture into industry and to move out of the South into northern urban areas. This movement into northern industry was accelerated as labor shortages after 1914 partially overcame racial prejudice in employment.

The unions were especially hostile to the influx of immigrants, women, and blacks and provided considerable pressure for antiimmigration regulations. In addition to the possible racial, ethnic, and sexist prejudice existing among many union members and leaders, unions considered it hard to organize these groups. Thus, besides their other cultural and language problems, these groups of workers had the least experience with unionization and were the most exposed to economic reprisal.

It should also be noted that there was a sharp reduction in this period in the use of child labor. In 1910, 18% of the labor force were under 16 years of age; this had fallen to 9% by 1920.

The statistics indicate that real income rose little from 1897 to 1914 for hired labor. Wage rates rose about 16% to 1914, while prices rose 39%. The wages of unionized workers and the skilled tended to increase more rapidly. The real wage index for manufacturing—that is, how much can be bought by the total wages earned—increased from 98 in 1897 to only 103 in 1914. That increase came about because of decreases in unemployment, both full and part-time, as well as because of the increase in wage rates. In manufacturing, the wage earner's share of the net product dropped from 45% in 1889 to 40% in 1909.

Although there was some improvement in real income to wage earners, Hunter,[6] for one, considered that income inadequate for the support of many employee families. He estimated that in 1910 the minimum poverty-level income (income necessary to maintain health) for a family of four in an urban area was $640 to $800. In 1909, the average family income for those engaged in manufacturing was $721.

Hours worked per week improved somewhat from 1897 to 1914. In 1897, the 10-hour day and the six-day week were prevalent in most industries. The average work week was 59 hours. This had declined to 55 hours by 1914.

## 1914-1920

Wage earners made economic gains under the impact of full employment, as war orders started to flow in from the Allies after 1914, as the U.S. econ-

Eugene V. Debs, union leader, socialist and presidential candidate. (Photo no. 165-WW-418-P97 in the National Archives)

omy converted to military production after 1917, and as the leaders of the labor movement gained important positions in the planning structure of the wartime federal government.

Hours of labor per week fell for both union and nonunion labor. Average weekly hours for all manufacturing labor fell from 55.2 in 1914 to 51 in 1920, and union manufacturing labor fell from 48.8 hours per week in 1914 to 48.7 in 1920. Average annual earnings for all labor increased from $627 in 1914 to $1407 in 1920, a 224% increase. Hourly wages for all labor in manufacturing rose by 231%; union labor's increase was a little over 200%. These impressive gains shrink when compared to a 200% increase in the consumer price index from 1914 to 1920.

# Transportation

## Railroads

The heyday of the railroads was over. This form of transportation reached its maximum growth and began to decline in the period 1897–1920. The year of highest railroad construction in U.S. history was 1906, when 6262 miles of new track were laid. After 1906, additional miles built declined, and after 1917 more track was abandoned than built. In addition, the rate of growth in tonnage shipped decreased by 60% from 1906 to 1916, and the rate of growth in passenger mileage dropped by at least two-thirds.

Railroading was now a mature industry. It had expanded into many of the profitable market areas. In fact, it overexpanded, establishing some marginal lines that were eventually abandoned as unprofitable. The slowdown in expansion and eventual contraction of total track mileage was encouraged by competition from the developing auto industry. Private automobiles competed for passenger traffic, and trucks competed for cargo shipment. The competition intensified after 1920. The test of the ability of private enterprise-controlled railroads to service the needs of the economy came during World War I. The federal government concluded that they had failed, and took over the running of the railroads in December 1917, claiming that private operation was not capable of meeting the transportation needs of the war economy. There is still considerable controversy about whether government takeover was necessary and whether in 1919, when the railroads were restored to private ownership, they were in as good a condition as when received.

By 1917, government regulation of the railroads had gone quite far, with a series of new laws that greatly strengthened the original 1887 Interstate Commerce Act. A detailed discussion of regulation is reserved for the next chapter.

## Urban Transportation

By the 1880s, street rail cars had appeared in urban areas, providing a method of transportation within cities. At first these cars were drawn by horses over rails laid down on city streets. In the early 1890s, however, electricity was applied, greatly increasing the speed of travel. Eventually, streetcar lines were established throughout major cities. These street railroads also established suburban routes, greatly widening the commuting range for cities and for the first time making suburban structures possible, with all their advantages and problems.

## Automobiles

There was rapid development of the automobile following its invention in 1895; in that year, there were only 4 autos in the entire United States. But by 1916 there were over 5 million. Capital invested in production facilities for autos reached $1 billion by 1919. The rate of growth would be even greater in the 1920s. The early period, prior to 1910, was one during which the development of necessary inventions was made to produce a practical and relatively cheap means of private transportation. Such inventions included the brake, air cushion tires, windshield wipers, safety glass, and many others.

The combination movement appeared here too. Between 1903 and 1926, as many as 181 firms had produced cars. Of these, 44 were still in production in 1926, and significant price competition still existed. But the Ford Motor Company held 45% of automobile production in 1914; General Motors was formed in 1908, and the future pattern of long-term consolidation into only a small number of firms was becoming apparent.

The automobile had a tremendous impact on the U.S. economy. Ford's pioneering application of interchangeable parts and assembly-line production was not only used eventually in the entire auto industry but also served as an example for the rest of manufacturing. The auto expanded commuting distance for the cities and intensified the suburban shift in population. It helped break down rural isolation, providing a more efficient transport for farmers to get to each other and to town. It stimulated, more after 1920 than before, other industries, especially the petroleum industry, to greater growth. And, of course, it established the automobile culture, with all its costs and benefits.

## Water Transportation

The water transportation industry suffered mixed conditions. Coastal and Great Lakes transportation was expanding, while ocean, canal, and river transportation was contracting. The basic underlying factors causing these relative movements depended on competitive and opportunity cost relationships.

America's comparative advantage in the coastal trade had continued since colonial days, and coastal shipping in the hands of Americans continued to grow vigorously. This trade had reached almost 4 million tons by 1897 and climbed to over 6 million tons by 1917.

Great Lakes transportation was equally prosperous. Long distances covered by large ships gave this form of transportation cost advantages over the railroads. In 1900, lake shipping of one bushel of wheat from Chicago to New York cost only half of railroad shipping. The advantage was intensified by a system of canals that linked the Great Lakes; for example, the Sault Ste. Marie Canal, between Lake Huron and Lake Superior, and the Welland Canal, between Lake Ontario and Lake Erie.

Active competition served to maintain high levels of efficiency and keep rates low. Railroads, while owning some lines—the New York Central owned Western Transit Company, for example—could not control enough of the fleet to affect market conditions. Faulkner[5] points out that "By 1910 the Great Lakes fleet was larger than that of any foreign nation except Great Britain and Germany."

The major product moving east was wheat, in part from Canada, and iron ore from the Mesabi range in Michigan. Important return cargoes were soft and hard coal.

Transoceanic foreign trade, however, had reached its low point, with American registry falling to under three-quarters of a million tons by 1898. In 1901, only 8% of U.S. trade was carried in U.S. ships. U.S. ownership of transoceanic vessels fell after the Civil War because (a) profits in shipping were not high enough to justify the opportunity costs of drawing resources from internal development, and (b) foreign governments gave much higher subsidies to shipping than did the United States.

This created a special problem for the United States: When World War I began, there were insufficient U.S. ships to carry the cargo no longer carried by British and German ships. The U.S. government established the Emergency Fleet Corporation in 1917 to build merchant vessels, but it was not until after the armistice and the end of the war that the first ship was actually completed. However, the government decided to complete construction of the vessels, and this sharply expanded the U.S. merchant fleet by 1920.

Canal and river transport not connected to the Great Lakes route steadily declined under the impact of railroad competition. The most successful of the canals, the Erie, saw tonnage fall from 4.6 million tons in 1880 to 2.4 million tons by 1906. One factor causing contraction in the use of the canals was widespread purchase of canals by railroads—by 1909 railroads owned almost one-third of total mileage—and their subsequent almost universal—some charged, deliberate—neglect of the canals.

## Summary

The period 1897–1919 was one of general prosperity spurred by high levels of domestic and international demand. This was especially so between 1897 to 1907 and during World War I. Not only did agriculture and industry continue to expand, but technological improvement also continued uninterrupted. By 1897, agricultural machinery had been generally adapted to horsepower, and by 1919 the horse was being replaced by the internal combustion engine. Industry was now widely using electricity for power and was experimenting with the economies of interchangeable parts and mass production. Technological transformations (including those in communications) increased the available economies of scale. Supported by increasing levels of demand, the most efficient sizes of enterprises increased.

In transportation, the railroad reached maturity and began to lose, first, relative importance, and subsequently, absolute size. The new transportation miracle, the internal combustion engine, utilized in autos, trucks, and buses, was by 1919 beginning to capture significantly the former railroad transportation market.

By 1919, an industrial, urban component was firmly entrenched as the most dynamic and dominant feature of American society.

---

# Review of Economic Concepts: Economies of Scale

Two important time periods that economists use are the short-run and the long-run. In the **short-run time period,** production of goods and services takes place as factors of production are used in varying amounts. However, in the short run not all factors of production can vary in their use. At least one factor input is fixed in outlay to the individual firm and provides a limiting factor in the firm's ability to respond to changing conditions. Often the limiting resource is fixed plant size.

In the **long run,** all factors of production for the individual firm can vary, including plant size. In the long-run, or planning period, the firm can choose from an array of different possible plant sizes (size of the individual plant can vary as well as the number of plants). Each plant size represents a different **scale of operation.**

Figure 14-1 is a long-run average cost curve for an individual firm. Since the scale of the firm can vary in the long run, Figure 14-1 depicts the long-run average cost (*LRAC*) curve as an **envelope curve,** one that encloses or envelops a series of possible scales or short-run average cost (*SRAC*) curves. From Output 0 to Output *A*, average costs are declining as scale in-

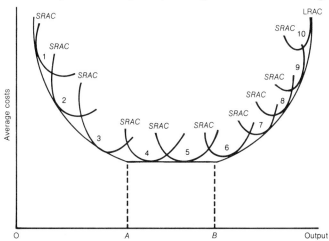

Figure 14-1. Long-run average cost curve of a firm.

creases (SRAC$_1$ through SRAC$_3$). This condition is called **economies of scale** or **increasing returns to scale.** From Output *A* to Output *B*, average costs are constant as scale increases (SRAC$_4$ and SRAC$_5$). This is called **constant returns to scale.** After Output *B*, average costs increase as scale increases (SRAC$_6$ through SRAC$_{10}$). This is called **diseconomies of scale** or **decreasing returns to scale.**

In drawing the long-run average cost curve, we are assuming a few things. For example, that technology is fixed or a menu of choices. If technology improved, the entire *LRAC* curve would shift down. Also, we assume that the firm is small and thus cannot affect the economic environment outside the firm. Lastly, because of the preceding assumption, prices of factor inputs are constant as the output of the firm varies.

There are a number of factors that will cause economies or increasing returns to scale. First, a certain minimum output may be necessary before the most improved technology can be used. The first scale in Figure 14-1, SRAC$_1$, may represent a scale so small that it doesn't pay to buy sewing machines, so clothes are sewn by hand. In Scale SRAC$_2$, output is large enough to justify the use of machines for sewing. Second, as output increases people and machines can be used more fully; that is, they are indivisible or cannot be subdivided below a certain minimum size. In Scale SRAC$_2$, output is large enough to justify the use of the sewing machine but not large enough to use it full time. In Scale SRAC$_3$, output is large enough to utilize the machines full time, increasing output without a comparable increase in costs (no need for additional machines). Finally, as output increases people and machines can become more specialized. At Scale SRAC$_3$, output is only large enough to employ small numbers of workers, each having to do the whole garment. At Scale SRAC$_4$, more workers are hired, each doing a different part of the garment. Productivity (output per worker) increases as less time is lost going from one job to another, as the worker learns a smaller number of operations better, and as the actual aptitude of the worker can be better fitted to the job. Also, at Scale SRAC$_4$, output is large enough to justify the use of special attachments or special machines such as a button sewer.

In brief, economies of scale occur because (a) better technological choices can be used with a larger scale; (b) capital and labor can be used more fully as output increases (they are indivisible or cannot be subdivided below a certain minimum size); and (c) advantages of labor and machine specialization can be realized as output increases. At some point, those advantages are used up and constant returns to scale occur.

Diseconomies, or decreasing returns to scale, occur because of management problems causing inefficiencies as scale goes beyond some point; in Figure 14-1, beyond SRAC$_6$. As scale becomes larger, problems of communication between the various segments of the enterprise become more complicated and difficult. Inefficiencies appear as miscommunication becomes more frequent and as information and communication costs rise.

Remember that changes in technology shift the long-run average cost curve. This occurs in the historic time period, one longer than the long run. These changes may intensify the economies to scale and may increase the economic advantage of larger firms. The development of assembly-line techniques, especially in the automobile industry, is of this kind. These changes may, however, reduce the economies obtained from increased scale. The development of small portable electric motors increased the flexibility of applying or using energy, reduced the need for large furnaces and fixtures for steam energy, and consequently reduced the optimum scale or size of firms. Improvements in communications such as the telephone increased the speed and efficiency of communication and thereby slowed down the development of diseconomies of scale due to management inefficiency or discommunication with large scale.

It is important to understand that the level of demand—or, in other words, the size of the market—must be large enough to enable the firms to move down the long-run average cost curve. Large scale, in turn, enables the firms to take advantage of economies of scale. In Figure 14-1, demand must enable the firm to move to the scale represented by $SRAC_4$ to take advantage of all economies of scale. There are many activities that may increase demand. Improvements in transportation and the elimination of barriers to larger geographic markets, improvements in communications and lowering of consumer information costs, increases in population and increases in money income from resources growth—all facilitate increases in demand and permit exhausting economies of scale and, thereby, larger enterprises.

---

# Glossary

**Assembly-line production** or **mass production**  A process depending on standardization and thus interchangeability of parts and the development of a system or systems of flow of materials logically arranged so as to facilitate assembly of the product.

**Constant returns to scale**  The return when long-run average costs are constant as scale (size of plant or number of plants) increases.

**Decreasing returns to scale**  See **Diseconomies of scale.**

**Diseconomies of scale** or **decreasing returns to scale**  The return when long-run average costs are increasing as scale (size of plant or number of plants) increases.

**Economies of scale** or **increasing returns to scale**  The return accruing as the long-run average cost curve slopes down as successive short-run average total cost curves, each showing a larger scale or size of operation, result in lower average costs.

**Envelope curve**   The long-run average cost curve as it encloses or envelops an array of short-run average total cost curves, each representing a particular scale of operation.

**Increasing returns to scale**   See **Economies of scale.**

**Long-run time period**   A period of time long enough such that all factors of production used by the individual firm can vary, including plant size.

**Mass production**   See **Assembly-line production.**

**Scale of operation**   A firm's operations when utilizing a particular size of plant or number of plants.

**Short-run time period**   A period of time short enough such that at least one kind of factor is fixed in amount for the individual firm. Often the limiting factor is fixed plant size; that is, fixed floor space.

# Questions

1. List the various factors that lead to larger-size economic enterprises.
2. What were the primary factors increasing agricultural demand from 1897 to 1920? What were the factors increasing agricultural supply? Why did agricultural prices increase?
3. What conditions were being created in 1914 to 1920 in agriculture that would become problems after 1920?
4. What factors cited in the text contributed to the expansion of industry from 1897 to 1920?
5. List and comment briefly on the characteristics of the expansion of industry noted in the text.
6. What were the advantages to industry in the use of electricity? What problems in the use of electricity had to be overcome before it could be widely used as a source of power?
7. What were the various factors that encouraged the development of assembly-line techniques?
8. What were the major factors affecting the conditions of wage labor from 1897 to 1920? Were there significant differences between 1897–1914 and 1914–1920? Why?
9. What were the major characteristics of the railroad industry from 1897 to 1920?
10. What were the economic effects of street railway development in the period?
11. Which forms of water transportation were expanding and which forms were contracting from 1897 to 1920? Why?

# Suggested Readings

1. Barger, Harold. *The Transportation Industries, 1889–1946.* New York: National Bureau of Economic Research, 1957.

2. Barger, Harold, and Landsberg, H. H. *American Agriculture, 1899–1939: A Study of Output, Employment and Productivity.* New York: National Bureau of Economic Research, 1942.

3. Day, Edmund E., and Woodlief, Thomas. *The Growth of Manufacturers, 1899–1923.* U.S. Bureau of the Census, *Census Monograph VIII.* Washington, D.C.: U.S. Government Printing Office, 1928.

4. DuBoff, Richard B. "The Introduction of Electric Power in American Manufacturing." *Economic History Review, 20* (December 1967).

5. Faulkner, H. U. *The Decline of Laissez-Faire.* New York: Holt, Rinehart and Winston, 1961.

6. Hunter, Robert. *Poverty,* ed. Peter d'A. Jones. New York: Harper & Row, 1965.

7. Keebe, Harold D., and Danhof, Ralph H. *Changes in Distribution of Manufacturing Wage Earners, 1899–1939.* U.S. Bureau of the Census. Washington, D.C.: Government Printing Office, 1942.

8. Jerome, Harry. *Mechanization in Industry.* New York: National Bureau of Economic Research, 1942.

9. Mills, Frederick C. *Economic Tendencies in the United States.* New York: National Bureau of Economic Research, 1932.

10. Nevins, Allan. *Ford: The Times, The Man, The Company.* Vol. 1. New York: Scribner's, 1954.

11. Rees, Albert. *Real Wages in Manufacturing, 1890–1914.* Princeton, N.J.: Princeton University Press, 1961.

12. Soule, George. *Prosperity Decade: From War to Depression, 1917–1929.* New York: Holt, Rinehart and Winston, 1947.

13. U.S. Department of Commerce. *Historical Statistics of the United States Colonial Times to 1970.* Washington, D.C.: U.S. Government Printing Office, 1975.

14. Williamson, Jeffrey G. "Migration to the New World: Long-Term Influences and Impact." *Explorations in Economic History, 11* (Summer 1974).

# Chapter 15

---

# The Decline of Competition

The prominent economic historian Harold Faulkner[3] characterized the period 1897–1919 in U.S. history as one in which significant decreases in competition occurred in the American economy. Indeed, Faulkner called his history of this period *The Decline of Laissez-Faire* to point up his conviction that, especially from 1897 through World War I, the classic competitive economy, composed of small-scale firms functioning within highly competitive markets in which no individual buyer or seller could significantly influence price and in which government did little to influence the market, had been very seriously eroded. Faulkner maintained that this competitive economy was replaced by one in which monopoly power (the ability to influence market price) was widely used in the market and in which government regulations became a significant factor. This movement toward the creation of monopoly power and government regulations precedes 1897, and the movement continued after 1919, but during those years, according to Faulkner, the decline of a competitive economy was most pronounced.

A major weakness of Faulkner's position is that the classical competitive economy that he assumed existed may not have existed, especially prior to the completion of the transportation network. With an inadequate transportation system, isolated markets existed, and within these small markets barriers to competition from outside the local area due to inadequate and high-cost transportation existed. Even though the firms within these markets were small, market size was also small, and these small firms held considerable market power. It can be argued that the completion of the railway system by 1897 broke down these barriers and increased the size of these markets and, by creating a national market, increased competition.

A second weakness of the Faulkner argument lies in the failure to precisely define the scope of the market within which competition and its decline is measured. Faulkner seems to utilize an *intra*-industry measure based upon the (declining) number of firms in certain industries (such as the number of firms in the steel industry). Some recent studies in industrial organization suggest that *inter*-industry measures relating competitiveness among products of different industries may be more appropriate (such as the competitiveness of steel, concrete, aluminum and similar products in the building materials industry.)

According to Faulkner, however, a decline in competition occurred from three sources: The combination movement contributing to the creation of larger-size firms, the increases in unions and union membership, and the continued extension of government regulations. We will look at the combination movement in manufacturing and transportation, the further development of unions, the Federal Reserve Bank, antitrust legislation, and at government regulation through the Interstate Commerce Commission. The Review of Economic Concepts in this chapter outlines a theory comparing monopolistic firms to competitive firms.

# The Combination Movement

## Industry and Transportation

Although an increase in the size and power of business enterprises began before 1897, it was during the years of 1897 through 1920 that the increase in large business organizations was most marked. Specifically, the combination movement started in the late 1870s, increased in the 1880s and early 1890s, and reached a climax from 1897 to 1904. This process of creating large business entities then slowed, but it revived again in the 1920s.

Up to 1904, the combination movement was concentrated in railroads, heavy industry, and raw materials extraction. From 1904 to 1920, combinations were concentrated more in public utilities and the new industries (autos, motion pictures, and certain chemicals), and in the 1920s the major industries concerned were retailing and banking. For example, in 1901 U.S. Steel was formed, in 1908 General Motors was formed (and then reorganized in 1916), Paramount Studios in 1916, Alcoa and Union Carbide both in 1917. By 1903, there were total assets of $6 billion in industrial combinations and $20 billion in combinations of public service industries (including railroads). In the railroad industry by 1910, 80% of total railroad track was organized into only six financial groups.

As described earlier, the first measures used to create larger business enterprises were the pools in the 1870s and 1880s. Later trusts were formed in the 1880s. The Interstate Commerce Act of 1887 and the Sherman Antitrust Act of 1890 made pools and trusts specifically illegal. After 1897, the methods used to effect combinations became the holding company and the consolidation. (See Chapter 12 for a more detailed discussion of these methods.)

Consolidations were carried out partly through promoters, who organized the formation of the new corporation. It was essential that some of the promoters be connected to investment banks. Also, it was useful if some of the promoters came from the industry to be combined. Promoters had to get options to buy the assets of all the individual companies to be consolidated into the larger corporation. Another requisite was that the promoters form an underwriting syndicate to market the new corporate securities in order to obtain funds to purchase these assets. Profits from this underwriting function were often high. Finally, the promoters would form the new corporation. The owners of the assets in the former independent companies would often receive preferred stock, while often the promoters would receive common stock.

For example, U.S. Steel Corporation was formed as a consolidation in 1901. J. P. Morgan was the financial promoter, and Judge Gary managed the huge consolidation. Total capitalization was about $1.4 billion, with about $400 million in bonds, $500 million in preferred stock, and about $500 million in common stock. The actual market value of the assets that went into the new corporation was $700 million at the time of the consolidation. Profits were high enough to meet the interest charges on the bonds, dividends on the preferred stock, and dividends on common stock for every year between 1901 and 1929 except two. The underwriting syndicate formed by the promoters received $62.5 million in fees.

Combinations in the railway industry were equally spectacular. These consolidations were accompanied by bankers' control. The movement started with the depression of 1893, when one-fourth of the total track mileage belonged to roads that went into receivership. Railroad lines were bought up, and the two leading investment banking houses, J. P. Morgan & Company and Kuhn and Loeb, invested heavily.

## Reasons for Combinations

In examining the characteristics that tended to encourage combinations and the creation of larger business firms, it is important to distinguish between two types of factors. First, there are the factors that increased the economies of scale, both in terms of increased size of individual plants and size of enterprise. Here costs are reduced with increased output and the economy as a whole can benefit. The second factor was that of encouraging larger size in order to decrease competition. The motivation for increased size, of course, was increased opportunities for profits. These could be obtained either by economies of scale and lower costs or by reduced competition and higher prices.

Changes in technology in this period tended to encourage the increase in size of firms. First, mechanical innovation led to higher fixed costs in plant and equipment, such as in steel and oil refining. In the second half of the nineteenth century, the shift from water to steam power required an enlargement in power-generating facilities.

By 1900, a technological revolution in transportation and in communications, connected with the completion of railroad and telephone networks, broke down locally isolated markets and created a national market for many products. This expanded market increased demand, so that economies of scale were available and increases in scale toward the optimum size took place. An expanded market also required an enlarged structure of distribution, increasing the size of firms.

Taylor's development of the concepts and techniques of scientific management introduced management methods to deal more efficiently with the problems of managing larger-scale enterprises. Scientific management techniques contributed to increased economies of scale. Furthermore, the techniques of financing large enterprises developed with the increased sophistication of securities markets and the rise of investment banking. The use of these techniques was predicated on the application to manufacturing of the corporate structure pioneered in large measure in the railway industry.

Government itself contributed to the rise of large firms. Since the Civil War, tariffs had remained high, reaching their highest level with the Dingley Tariff of 1897. Taxes on imports raised the prices of foreign goods and reduced the effectiveness of foreign competition.

The patent system also encouraged the formation of monopolies by giving one producer exclusive control over a new invention for 16 years, with the possibility of renewal of the patent for another 16 years. The United Shoe Machinery Company, for instance, maintained a monopoly in 1900 through the control of over 6000 patents. The agreement of Westinghouse and General Electric in the 1890s to share patents gave these two companies substantial monopoly power in the electric industry.

The social benefit claimed for patents is that exclusive use of inventions and thus monopoly profits encourages research and causes the rate of technological improvement to remain high. Society thereby experiences a more rapid rate of productivity increase and the introduction of new and improved products. The loss of competition is the negative factor that reduces these benefits. The controversy over whether patents provide a net benefit to society is still going on, with little prospect of any immediate resolution.

In brief, at the turn of the century the combination movement, the creation of large firms, was at its height. The profit motive for the creation of these large firms had three basic components: (a) to take advantage of potential economies of scale in order to reduce costs; (b) to reduce competition, raise prices, and thus increase profits; and finally, (c) to obtain profits for the promoters and underwriters out of the very act of creating the new corporation.

## The Opposition

Opposition to the combination movement was considerable, although singularly unsuccessful in stemming its progress. There were many criticisms of these new giant firms. The first, but not the least, was that they reduced competition and increased prices to the consumer.

Increased size by itself may not create monopoly power (the ability to influence price), as the various restraints on the use of monopoly power must be considered. These restraints include lack of complete control over the quantities demanded by consumers, competition within the same industry and from other industries producing substitutes, threat of entry of new firms to take advantage of higher profits, and possible adverse public and government reaction. Furthermore, increased monopoly power must be actually exercised to be effective.

Second, not only was competition reduced, but unfair and perhaps illegal methods of competition were also applied to smaller business people. For example, it was widely held (and some still hold the view) that Rockefeller's Standard Oil Company eliminated competition by lowering prices below costs in local markets to drive out the small local firms, while keeping prices higher in the rest of the country. McGee[9] (among others), however, maintains that there is no historical evidence nor theoretical analysis to support this belief in predatory pricing.

Charges were made that the new firms reduced economic opportunities and that the number of small firms was reduced in many industries. With the reduction of small businesspersons and the concentration of wealth, a less flexible social structure may have been created in the United States. Insofar as these larger-scale firms stemmed from increases in optimum size of the enterprise, however, they became more efficient than smaller firms. Insistence on smaller firms for greater social flexibility incurs the cost of reduced efficiency, because optimum scale is not achieved.

Also, some people were concerned about the inability to organize the workers in these large firms, to afford them some protection from the "exploitation" of the employers. These large firms were too strong for labor unions and in fact were not unionized until the middle to late 1930s.

Concern was also expressed about the increase in absentee ownership and the separation of ownership and management that took place with the creation of larger corporations. One fear was that the workplace would become more impersonal as larger size and greater "distance" appeared between the worker and the owner. Another fear was that the separation of management from ownership would make management more irresponsible.

Finally, in the American political system concern over economic power and political decision-making was always present. Would these large economic entities exert disproportionately large influence in the political process for their own self-interest? Could democracy withstand the onslaught of the economically powerful?

# Labor Unions

## Railroad Brotherhoods

By 1900, the railroad unions were organized into four independent brotherhoods—engineers, firemen, brakemen, and conductors. After the violent strikes in the 1870s and 1880s, strikes became rare, as the brotherhoods tended to avoid strikes to safeguard their insurance resources. Railroading was a dangerous occupation, and the brotherhoods became more and more mutual insurance and benefit societies. Strikes might expose the unions, and thus their insurance funds, to court damage claims. The unions concentrated on the skilled trades and gradually won company recognition. In turn, they were able to increase wages and to establish a seniority system.

The federal government became involved in labor management relations with the Hepburn Act of 1906, which required mediation and arbitration of labor difficulties. In the Adamson Act of 1916, the railroad workers were granted an eight-hour day.

## Union History, 1897 to 1909

The "great advance" of 1897 to 1904 saw total union membership increase from 447,000 to two million, more than a 400% increase in seven years. The American Federation of Labor (AFL) was the major beneficiary of this expansion, increasing from 265,000 members to 1,676,000, more than a 600% increase. Much of this expansion was concentrated in the skilled occupations of the building trades, a stronghold of AFL craft unions from the beginning. The coal-mining industry finally experienced a revival of union organizing with the successful founding of the United Mine Workers (UMW) toward the end of the nineteenth century. Against Gompers' craft union principle, the UMW became the first industry-wide union to join the AFL. There was no practical way to organize it along craft lines.

The prime factors in this union growth were the prosperity and low unemployment of the time. In the face of this advance, employers staged a counteroffensive. A number of employers' organizations were active in this period. The most famous was the National Association of Manufacturers. Others were the Citizens Alliance, the Citizens Industrial Association, and the American Anti-Boycott Association. Their main objectives were opposition to the closed shop (a firm where only union members could be hired) and to the boycott. Not only did they try to influence public opinion through various forms of propaganda, but they also provided, at times, financial help to those in conflict with unions.

There were other factors beside this counteroffensive by employers that slowed the advance of unions. The depression of 1907 reduced the demand for labor, increasing unemployment and making it more difficult for labor to pressure management for recognition. This unemployment made union membership less attractive to workers as well. Internal friction, as well as outside rivalry, distracted union attention from making further advances. Adverse public opinion plagued the unions.

In 1905, the governor of Idaho was assassinated and Big Bill Haywood and other leaders of the Western Federation of Miners were charged with the murder; however, Clarence Darrow obtained an acquittal. In 1910, the *Los Angeles Times* building was bombed, and the McNamara brothers, leaders of the International Association of Bridge and Structural Iron Workers (which was striking against the *Los Angeles Times*), were charged with the act. Darrow again came to defend these labor leaders, but the brothers confessed to the deed. These and other acts of violence charged against the unions generated unfavorable public reaction.

A series of court decisions unfavorable to organized labor caused the unions to view the courts as a major enemy. The following are two examples. In 1902, the United Hatters staged a strike and boycott against a Connecticut firm. They were charged with violating the Sherman Antitrust Act and were sued for damages. The union lost the case, and in addition the homes of some union members were attached. In 1907, a federal lower court issued a sweeping injunction against an AFL boycott of a St. Louis stove company. The union tried to test the injunction's validity before the U.S. Supreme Court, but the Court refused to review. The use of the injunction became an even more crippling antiunion weapon in the 1920s.

Within the AFL, the socialists actively opposed the conservative attitude of the federation toward the unskilled, immigrants, women, and blacks. This internal dissension, while persistent, failed to change the policies of the AFL during that time.

## The Industrial Workers of the World

Competition to the AFL appeared with the formation of the Industrial Workers of the World (IWW) in 1905. The IWW was formed primarily of four groups: the Western Federation of Miners, the Socialist Party of Eugene V. Debs, the Socialist Labor Party of Daniel De Leon, and a large group of radical unionists. This peculiar combination of socialists, syndicalists, and anarchists perceived a revolutionary class struggle as being achieved through industrial unionism.

The IWW was mainly an outgrowth of union conditions in the West. It was produced by the oppressively violent conditions of the frontier mining and lumber camps. Western strikes involved the most bitter and violent labor warfare in American, if not world, labor history. Primarily, the IWW attracted unskilled and migratory workers, although the IWW was never more than 60 to 70 thousand strong.

They led a series of strikes started by unorganized, unskilled workers neglected by the AFL. In 1912 at Lawrence, Massachusetts, and again in 1913 at Paterson, New Jersey, textile workers struck for higher pay and better working conditions. In both cases, the workers were inexperienced in running a strike, and after the AFL refused to help they asked the IWW to provide leadership. At Wheatland, California, in 1913, the migrant workers in the hop fields struck and asked for IWW help. After a bitter strike, this first effort at a union of migrant fieldworkers failed.

The IWW was widely condemned. It was anticapitalistic and thus engendered general public hostility. It was a rival to the AFL, and that organization did whatever it could to counter the IWW. In 1907, the Western Federation of Miners left the IWW, and at about the same time the IWW ousted De Leon and his Socialist Labor Party. But what eventually destroyed the IWW was its opposition to U.S. involvement in World War I. Partially as a result of this opposition and their radical anticapitalist philosophy the IWW became a prime target of Attorney General A. Mitchell Palmer, who in response to the mass hysteria stemming from U.S. public reaction to the Russian Revolution, arrested and imprisoned thousands of IWW members.

## 1910–1917

By 1917, union membership had increased to over three million. The increase came about primarily in four industries: transportation (mainly railroads), the building trades (the traditional stronghold of the AFL), mining (primarily in coal), and the clothing industry (newly organized).

The United Mine Workers extended their base from western Pennsylvania and Ohio into West Virginia; in the strike of 1912, they expanded their membership into the anthracite coal fields of eastern Pennsylvania. Their strike in the Colorado coal fields in 1913–1914, which failed, was one of the most bitter in U.S. labor history. The striking miners were evicted from the company houses, and they set up a tent city at Ludlow, Colorado. National guard units, plus guards from the mines, surrounded the tent city one morning and fired into it, killing several men, two women, and eleven children. John D. Rockefeller, who owned the mines, afterward refused to deal with the union.

In 1909 the International Ladies' Garment Workers Union (ILGWU) declared a general strike in the women's garment industry in New York. Two immigrant groups, the Eastern European Jews and the Italians, provided the bulk of the workers in the industry. Together, they forged an effective coalition that won the strike and firmly established the ILGWU. In 1910, Sidney Hillman successfully led another union, the United Garment Workers (UGW), in the Chicago strike against Hart, Shaffner, and Marx, the largest men's clothing firm in the country. This established the UGW in the men's clothing industry. With these two sections of the garment industry successfully organized, immigrants became an active force in the U.S. labor movement. These two unions strengthened the industrial unionist approach within the AFL.

After World War I broke out, the Allies relied heavily on the U.S. economy for supplies of all sorts. Between January 1915 and the entry of the United States into the war in 1917, the Allies spent over $5 billion in the United States. This stimulus, plus increased spending on the army and navy as the United States prepared for entry into the war, expanded the economy to full employment, shortages, and rising prices.

## World War I, 1917-1920

Samuel Gompers, the president of the AFL, fully supported the war effort and cooperated wherever possible with that effort. President Wilson, to assure labor union support, placed union representatives on the various planning committees set up to plan for a more efficient allocation of the nation's scarce resources for war production.

Labor benefited from these arrangements, and favorable conditions were written into many government contracts, as no strike pledges were given by labor. Cost-of-living clauses and favorable conditions of work were easily obtained as business profits soared during the war. Under these favorable conditions, union membership rose from 3 million in 1917 to over 5 million by 1920.

With the end of the war, both unions and employers were in strong positions, as full employment and increased membership filled union treasuries and high wartime profits made businesses financially prosperous. Unions, however, were dissatisfied with the progress made during the war. From 1914 to 1919, average annual earnings of the employed increased 87%, but their purchasing power had only increased 5% during the same period. Business was not happy with this imposed wartime labor-management cooperation. The years 1919–1920 saw management-labor confrontation.

Strikes increased rapidly in 1919. The most spectacular was the 1919 Steel Strike, the first effort made since the Homestead Strike of 1892 to organize the steel industry. Despite a massive effort, the strike failed, but as a result of the strike public pressure brought an end (several years later) to the 12-hour day, seven-day week that had prevailed in much of the industry. Other notable strikes took place in the men's clothing industry, in railroads by the newly organized shop crafts, and in soft coal mining.

But the unions still had basic weaknesses. First, they had not penetrated the primary manufacturing industries, especially steel and auto. The obstacles of the unions' craft orientation and large, powerful corporations were difficult to overcome. Second, the Bolshevik revolution and the reaction from the U.S. Justice Department, the press and major sections of the American public created a very negative attitude toward anything that appeared in opposition to American capitalism. This led to vigorous anti-union activity. The unions started the decade of the 1920s with adverse public sentiment.

# Government Regulation

When Harold Faulkner[3] referred to "the decline of laissez-faire" as the main characteristic of the 1897 to 1917 period, he was not simply describing the rise of the large corporation or the establishment of national unionism. He was referring also to the developing commitment of the federal government to interference in certain kinds of business activity and industries. By 1920, government regulation of various areas of economic activity had become an established fixture of the economic scene.

In this section on government regulation, we will first examine railway legislation, especially the continued development of the Interstate Commerce Commission. Then we will look at the continued use and development of antitrust legislation. Finally, we shall consider the Federal Reserve System.

## Railroad Regulation

The foundation of federal regulation of railroads was laid with the Interstate Commerce Commission Act of 1887, creating the Interstate Commerce Commission (ICC). For the first few years, the ICC had the cooperation of the railroad companies. They hoped the ICC would solve the problem of what they considered too much competition in railroad industry. However, the ICC tried to maintain, if not encourage, competition, and after 1890 the railroad companies opposed the actions of the ICC, looking to combinations as the device through which to control competition. The conflict between the ICC and the railroads was fought out in the courts, and the commission lost.

The U.S. Supreme Court in effect nullified the Interstate Commerce Commission Act by 1900. From 1887 to 1905, there were 16 decisions handed down by the U.S. Supreme Court on the act, 15 of them in favor of the railroads. The courts refused to accept the findings of the ICC as valid. In 1897, the Supreme Court ruled that the ICC could not set rates, concluding that the 1887 act did not give the ICC that power. This undercut the ICC's power to eliminate discrimination.

In response to the crippling rulings of the Court, the ICC attempted at first, and with limited success, to use the Sherman Antitrust Act as a legal basis to control discriminatory railroad practices. Then an effort was made to strengthen the ICC. The Expediting Act of 1903 established that ICC and antitrust suits in the courts would be given preference over other cases. This substantially increased the speed with which ICC cases were decided. The Elkins Act of 1903 forbade the giving of rebates, eliminating that form of discrimination. The Hepburn Act of 1906, which increased the size of the ICC and its budget, greatly strengthened the commission by explicitly requiring it to establish rates on railroads, pipelines, and terminal facilities. The Mann-Elkins Act of 1910 introduced two important provisions. New rates issued by the ICC were to remain in force for at least 10 months if the railroads chose to challenge them in the courts. Prior to this act, the rates were not in force until the question was decided in the courts. The act also stated that charges for shipment must be higher for longer distances. This definitely resolved the short-haul versus long-haul problem that had been an important motive for the original act establishing the Interstate Commerce Commission.

By 1920, railroad regulations had been firmly established. The courts had recognized the authority of the ICC to set rates, and the obvious forms of discrimination, rebates, and short-haul versus long-haul discrimination, had been declared illegal. However, the ICC still lacked the power to regulate the financial structure of the railroads and could not (according to Kolko[7] and Faulkner[3]) control the mismanagement and corruption that had generated substantial financial strain on many of the roads. But much of the damage had already been done, and the age of the railroad magnates and control by financiers of railroads was mostly over. Practical railroaders were mainly in control.

Kolko and Faulkner argue that by 1920 regulation was still trying to foster competition in an industry that should have been considered a monopoly. They argue that, instead of relying on competitive forces to establish prices, the ICC should have been more vigorous in deciding price policy.

Some opponents of that view maintain that there are very substantial competitive forces in transportation, if not specifically in railroading, and that railroading is not an example of a natural monopoly. They maintain

Theodore Roosevelt, the "trustbuster." (Photo No. 200S-M-5 in the National Archives)

that government regulation inhibited the functioning of a competitive market and created inefficient allocation of resources, higher costs, and higher prices. They further maintain that, especially after 1920, the auto, truck, bus, and later the airplane, coupled with water transportation, would assure a sufficiently competitive market to prevent any abuses of the past.

Robert Harbeson's[5] opinion was that the ICC eventually carried out the plans of the railroad industry by helping to lessen competition through eliminating much of the price cutting. He finds it interesting that the official rates of the ICC were very similar to those of an informal railroad cartel.

## Antitrust Legislation

By 1900, the U.S. Supreme Court had also weakened and confused the interpretation of the Sherman Antitrust Act. The 1897 Supreme Court "rule of reason" decision meant one had to be "reasonable" about what constituted monopoly. Also, the Court maintained that having the power to utilize monopoly techniques was not important if the power was not used. In effect, then, there were to be no objective standards that could be applied to test violations of the act. The Court became the arbiter of the act. What especially irked the labor movement was the use of the act against labor unions.

Antitrust legal actions increased during Theodore Roosevelt's administration, with 25 indictments under the Sherman Act from 1901 to 1908. The most famous of these was the Northern Securities Case of 1904. This company had succeeded in controlling all of railroad transportation in the entire Northwest. Although the government won the case, this had little practical result. The government could think of no effective way to break up the Northern Securities Company, and the Hill-Morgan group maintained ownership of the company and control of the railway system in the Northwest.

During William Howard Taft's administration (1908–1912), there were 43 indictments under the Sherman Act. In the American Tobacco case, an important example, the results were encouraging in that new companies entered the industry and competition in cigarettes did increase.

As with regulation of the railroads, legislation was passed to strengthen antitrust activity. The Expediting Act of 1903 also applied to antitrust cases and substantially speeded up the handling of these cases in the courts. In the same year the U.S. Department of Justice received a $500,000 appropriation to set up a special branch and to create a special staff to handle antitrust cases.

The Clayton Act of 1914 was an important addition to antitrust legislation. It tried to deal with some of the problems created by earlier court rulings. The act specifically forbade discrimination in pricing and exclusive selling or leasing contracts; both had often been used as weapons to lessen competition. Also forbidden was the use of interlocking directorates and holding companies for the purpose of reducing competition. (When the same people appeared on the boards of directors of a number of different corporations in the same industry, these governing bodies were called **interlocking directorates**; policies could then be more easily formulated in these several corporations that would eliminate competition and substitute cooperation.) Finally, the Clayton Act exempted labor unions and farmer cooperatives from government antitrust actions.

In 1914, Congress also passed the Federal Trade Commission Act. The commission set up under this act was responsible for defining and preventing "unfair" competition in commerce. It was given the power to investigate, issue cease-and-desist orders, go to court, and enforce court decrees.

## Antitrust Success or Failure?

Harold U. Faulkner[3] concluded that antitrust legislation and activity was a failure by 1917. He maintained that the legislation was meant to restore competition in a "changing economic order" now not meant for competition. If the monopoly power of large firms was to be controlled, a different approach would have to be used. Even after 1903, when the U.S. Justice Department's small staff and budget were earmarked for antitrust activities, antitrust prosecutors did not have resources at their disposal equal to those of the large corporations. Even when cases were won by the Justice Department, the government had difficulties obtaining and evaluating data, and it was ignorant of how to break up such trusts; it often recommended fines that were too small to be a deterrent. The vigor of enforcement varied with the interest and initiative of the incumbent U.S. president. It was fairly vigorous in the period 1901 to 1917 and very weak in the 1920s. Furthermore, the effectiveness of enforcement was sharply affected by the shifting point of view of the U.S. Supreme Court. Faulkner concludes that by 1914 it was already too late: In many industries, the large corporations were already formed, and little competition remained.

Other economists, such as Yale Brozen,[1] concur on the failure of antitrust legislation but approach the problem from a very different direction. Their argument is that government regulation replaced the workings of the marketplace with bureaucratic decision-making. Under these conditions, the allocative function of the market is disrupted, inefficiencies in the allocation of resources occur, and the combination of goods produced is not the one that consumers prefer.

Which is worse?—bureaucratically induced economic inefficiency and threats to liberty, or economic inefficiency and threats to liberty through manipulation of the market through the use of monopoly power and influencing of the political process by large firms. Or indeed, was either of the two really the only alternative? Was the U.S. economy still vibrantly competitive, making constant adjustment to changing technology and economic conditions? Extensive historical research and endless theoretical debate have led to very few areas of broad agreement. The debate continues to rage.

What is apparent is that by the end of this period there were large economically powerful firms, large union organizations, and strong steps by the government into regulation. Whatever the consequences, large economic interests and government economic involvement were to be part of the U.S. economic scene.

## The Federal Reserve Act of 1913

The inadequacies of the U.S. banking system under the National Bank Act of 1864 have already been noted. These inadequacies culminated in widespread bank failures in the crises of 1893 and 1907. Both congressional and banking leaders recognized that reform was needed. As a result, the National Monetary Commission was established in 1908 to investigate the structure of the American banking system.

In its report in 1912, the commission condemned the following conditions. First, there was no adequate national clearing system for checks. Second, the supply of currency was not elastic; that is, it could not readily vary in response to the needs of the banking system. Finally, and perhaps most importantly, the individual commercial banks had no lender of last resort available in case of financial crisis.

The Federal Reserve Act of 1913 established the Federal Reserve System and, in varying degrees, met these inadequacies in the banking sector. But a deep-seated reluctance to establish one central bank, a philosophy dominant in American banking since Jackson vetoed the rechartering of the Second Bank of the United States in 1832, was mirrored in the act. Instead of establishing 1 bank, the act established 12 banks, one in each of 12 districts. Instead of making it mandatory that all commercial banks belong to the system, the act required only the national banks to join and made membership optional for state banks. By 1917, only 37 state banks had joined.

Despite this reluctance, the Federal Reserve System had sufficient power to eventually become an instrument of control over the commercial banking process of the United States. The control increased with experience and with further legislation that enhanced the powers of the "Fed."

Although there is much controversy about *how* the Federal Reserve System should behave, there seems to be little dissent that some kind of "Fed" was needed to regulate the supply of money and to serve as a lender of last resort to protect the banking system. However, the Fed had little impact in its early years on the supply of money.

---

# Review of Economic Concepts: Monopoly Power Versus Competition

The following is a brief review of the theory about the advantages and disadvantages of monopoly as compared with competition. First we must assume that costs are the same between the two types of markets. Afterward, we will drop that assumption and consider other relationships.

Under the assumption that costs are the same, the competitive firm in the long run under the pressure of other firms entering the industry will produce at the lowest level of average costs at a price just high enough to cover normal or minimally necessary profits. A firm with monopoly power, however, will be able to restrict entry and thereby increase prices, by reducing quantity supplied to a level that probably results in higher profits (including an economic profit) and, because of reduced output, in higher average costs.

From the point of view of society, the competitive industry, then, has the advantage over the monopoly power firm by producing a larger output, at a lower cost and price, and with only normal profits. Figure 15-1 shows diagrammatically the relationships just described. The demand, average revenue, and marginal revenue curves for the competitive firm are horizontal or perfectly elastic because the competitive firm cannot influence the market price, and thus as output increases the same market price is charged. The demand, average revenue curves for the monopoly power firm slope down to the right, showing that this firm does influence the price in the market, and thus if the firm wants a larger quantity demanded they must lower price in order to get consumers to buy more. Once price falls as output increases, marginal revenue (the additions to total revenue as output increases) falls more rapidly and lies below demand and average revenue. Remember, we assume that the cost curves are the same for both types of firms. Remember also that the most profitable rate of output is that at which marginal cost is equal to marginal revenue, but the price for that output is determined on the demand curve.

Output under competition will be at $Q_c$ and price at $P_c$. Price is equal to average cost and revenues just cover costs, including a normal profit. The monopoly power firm would produce at $Q_m$, where marginal cost equals marginal revenue and price (determined on the demand curve) is $P_m$. Average costs are $C_m$, and price is higher than costs; thus an economic profit is obtained equal to $P_m$ minus $C_m$ times $Q_m$. So, now using diagrams, we see that price and costs are lower for the competitive industry and output is higher. Only a normal profit can exist for the competitive firm in the

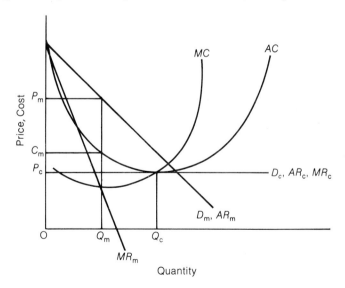

Figure 15-1. Monopolistic Firm and Competitive Industry.

long run, while an economic profit is likely for the monopoly power firm.

Note that the competitive firm has price equal to marginal cost. This is an important relationship. Price indicates the value that consumers place on the last unit purchased. Marginal cost measures the opportunity cost (what society gives up in other goods not produced) of that last unit purchased. When the two are equal, the value of the unit to the consumer is equal to its cost to society. With prices providing the needed signals for activities, this situation means the resources are distributed most efficiently to produce that combination of goods consumers prefer.

For the monopoly power firm, price is above marginal cost. Thus consumers place a higher value on the last unit produced by the monopolist than the cost to society through the loss of alternative goods not produced. In effect, the consumer, in terms of other goods, prefers the good produced by the monopolist more than the goods that could have been produced by the resources used by the monopoly firm. As less of the good is produced than society prefers, there is a misallocation of resources because firms are not producing that combination of goods consumers prefer. Inefficient allocation of resources, then, is an additional disadvantage of monopoly power firms.

Now it is time to look at the assumption that costs are the same in the two market situations. A larger-size monopoly power firm may use a technology requiring larger scale than that existing in a competitive industry, and costs are not the same. The situation may be the one depicted in Figure 15-2. If the monopoly power situation existed, the short-run average cost curve would be $SRAC_m$ at quantity $Q_m$ and cost $C_m$. If the market were subdivided among enough firms to create a competitive situation the size of the firm might be too small to take advantage of economies of scale. The short-run average cost curve might be at $SRAC_c$, and average costs would be much higher at $C_c$. The disadvantages previously listed to society for a monopoly power firm may be compensated for by the economies of scale and lower cost obtained with the larger-size firm. But if the size of the monopoly power firm exceeds the optimum, $SRAC_m$ in Figure 15-2, added size results without economies of scale. Finally, these cost advantages through economies of scale are not necessarily passed on to consumers through lower prices. Because of barriers to entry from monopoly power, these gains can remain with the monopolist through increased profits.

Another problem that makes comparing competitive and monopoly power firms complex is the question of technology. First, which firm will more rapidly adopt already perfected technology? Second, which firm will more rapidly develop new technology? The answers to both questions are not simple.

It is generally accepted that the competitive firm, in order to survive the pressures of the other firms in the industry, will rapidly adopt already developed improved technology. In this way, costs are kept as low as possible. For the monopoly firm, pressures to increase efficiency from other

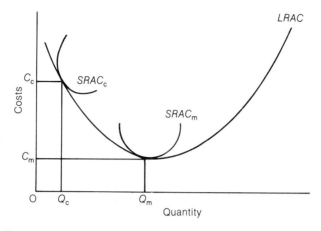

Figure 15-2. Economies of Scale and Monopoly and Competitive Firms.

firms are substantially less, and thus pressures to adopt new technology are less. There is a "but" to be added. "But" if the improved technology leads to increased size (increased size of plants and/or number of plants) and if, to achieve optimum size, the competitive firm had to move from $SRAC_c$ in Figure 15-2 to $SRAC_m$, it would become a monopoly power firm.

The question of which firm would more rapidly increase the development of improved technology is also not simple. Some innovations require extensive research facilities, large staffs, and considerable financing. Competitive firms may not be able to afford such research. For example, in the second half of the nineteenth century research in steel or petroleum or electrical power generation would have been beyond the means of competitive firms. However, this does not mean, especially one hundred years ago, that with larger size, more research and more technological development would have taken place.

At the time, much of the development of technology *was* taking place in small firms, and individual inventors were making the inventions. Bell and the development of the telephone he invented is one example; barbed wire, invented by a farmer in the Midwest, is another. Furthermore, a great many productivity innovations came from small changes most often made by people close to the production line. The larger the firm, the more communication obstacles exist to prevent this kind of innovation. Furthermore, in the twentieth century research increasingly became publicly financed by the government and nonprofit organizations.

In Josephson's *The Robber Barons*, one gets the impression that the "captains of industry" who controlled those large monopoly power firms operated without restraint. As with a number of other concepts associated with the "robber barons," this one too has been largely discredited. Restraints on monopoly power firms stem from a number of sources.

First, while the monopoly power firm has significant control over price, the nature of demand (the shape and position of the curve) determines the quantity bought at each price. The firm may set price but not quantity. It does not have control over both.

Second, the monopoly power firm is restrained by competition—if not from within the industry, then at least from industries producing substitutes.

Third, as profits become higher through the use of monopoly power, the gains to be made by new firms penetrating the industry increase. Firms have an incentive to work vigorously to overcome barriers to entry.

Finally, monopoly power firms are very visible and must be aware of the potential reaction of the public and the government. This was especially relevant after passage of the Interstate Commerce Act in 1887 and the Sherman Antitrust Act in 1890.

In brief, in looking at the problems caused by the exercise of monopoly power one must distinguish between increases in size in response to increased economies of scale and increases generated for the purposes of exercising monopoly power. The first benefit the entire economy, through lowered costs and increases in efficiency. The other benefit the monopolistic firm at the expense of the economy, through higher profits through increased prices and possibly decreases in efficiency and high costs. In addition, one must add the net effects of the development and utilization of technology.

The problems generated by the existence of monopoly power go beyond the simple economic ones of distribution of resources and income and questions of efficiency. They also become social, political, and philosophical problems.

## Glossary

**Interlocking directorates**   Situations in which the same people appeared on the boards of directors of a number of different corporations in the same industry; policies could then be more easily formulated in these several corporations that would eliminate competition and substitute cooperation.

## Questions

1. How was the typical consolidation formed in the 1897–1904 period?
2. List the various reasons for the formation of large firms in the period 1897–1920. Which of them were beneficial to society in general?

3. What were the arguments in opposition to the creation of large-scale monopoly power firms?
4. What was the structure of unions in the railroad industry from 1897 to 1920?
5. Why was union expansion rapid from 1897 to 1904 and slower from 1905 to 1909?
6. Describe the basic characteristics of the Industrial Workers of the World.
7. In what major industries did unions expand their membership between 1910 and 1917?
8. Describe the strengths and weaknesses of organized labor in 1920.
9. By 1920, was regulation concerning transportation successful? Why or why not? What do you mean by "successful"?
10. Describe the various acts that strengthened antitrust legislation from 1900 to 1920.
11. Evaluate antitrust legislation by the end of this period. Was it successful? Why? Why not?
12. What problems in the banking system was the Federal Reserve, in 1913, designed to overcome?

# Suggested Readings

1. Brozen, Yale. "Antitrust Witch Hunt." *National Review,* November 24, 1978.
2. Chandler, Alfred D., and Galambos, Louis. "The Development of Large-Scale Economic Organizations in Modern America." *Journal of Economic History,* 30 (March 1970).
3. Faulkner, Harold U. *The Decline of Laissez-Faire, 1897–1917.* New York: Holt, Rinehart and Winston, 1961.
4. Friedman, Milton, and Schwartz, Anna J. *A Monetary History of the United States 1867–1960.* Princeton, N.J.: Princeton University Press, 1963.
5. Harbeson, Robert. "Railroads and Regulations, 1877–1916: Conspiracy or Public Interest?" *Journal of Economic History, 27* (June 1967).
6. Klehamer, Benjamin. "Potential Competition and the American Antitrust Legislation of 1914." *Business History Review, 38* (1964).
7. Kolko, Gabriel. *Railroads and Regulation, 1877–1916.* Princeton, N.J.: Princeton University Press, 1965.
8. MacAvoy, Paul. *The Economic Effects of Regulation.* Cambridge, Mass.: Massachusetts Institute of Technology Press, 1965.

9. McGee, John S. "Predatory Price Cutting: The Standard Oil (N.J.) Case." *Journal of Law and Economics, 137* (1958).

10. McGraw, Thomas R. "Regulation in America: A Review Article." *Business History Review, 49* (1975).

11. Nelson, R. *Merger Movements in American Industry, 1895–1956.* Princeton, N.J.: Princeton University Press, 1959.

12. Rayback, Joseph G. *History of American Labor.* New York: Macmillan, 1959.

13. Soule, George. *Prosperity Decade, From War to Depression, 1917–1929.* New York: Harper & Row, 1947.

14. Thorelli, Hans B. *The Federal Anti-Trust Policy: Organization of an American Tradition.* Baltimore: Johns Hopkins University Press, 1955.

15. Ulman, L. "American Trade Unionism, Past and Present." In *American Economic History,* ed. Seymour E. Harris. Berkeley, Calif.: University of California Press, 1961.

16. Willis, James F., and Primack, Martin L. *Explorations in Economics.* Boston: Houghton Mifflin, 1977. Chap. 16.

# Chapter **16**

---

# The United States in the International Arena

In 1790, the United States was economically dependent on Europe, especially England. But by 1920 the United States had the most powerful economy, in terms both of production and finance, in the world. In 1790, the United States was dependent on foreign investment, again especially from England, to pay for a large share of its imports and encourage economic growth. It was a net debtor nation, owing more to other countries than was owed to it. But by 1920 the United States was a net creditor nation, with investments in other countries far greater than these other countries had in the United States.

In 1790, the United States was bordered by the Mississippi River on the West. By 1920, the United States stretched westward from the Atlantic to the Pacific, south to Mexico, and north to Canada. In addition, the United States had gained direct control of territories outside the continental United States, such as Alaska, Hawaii, the Philippines, territory in the Caribbean, and islands in the Pacific. However, in the 1920s the United States, despite its territorial expansion, was still inexperienced in the ways of world economic leadership.

This chapter will review the role of the United States in world economic affairs to 1920. It will be helpful if the reader has some knowledge of the balance of payments. We have included at the end of this chapter, a Review of Economic Concepts concerning balance of payments.

## The Balance of Payments to 1920

The period of 1850–1920 saw dramatic changes in the balance of payments as the United States continued its development toward becoming a mature industrial society. There were changes in the growth and composition (both as to products and countries) of the various balance of payments accounts. The balances of the individual accounts changed as the United States shifted from being a net importer of products and capital to being a net exporter of both. Table 16-1 will be used as a basis for much of our discussion of the period through 1913. (Because of the special effects of World War I, the period from 1914 to 1920 will be discussed later separately.)

Table 16-1.  U.S. Balance of Payments 1850–1913 (millions of dollars).

|  | 1850 | 1870 | 1876 | 1900 | 1913 |
|---|---|---|---|---|---|
| 1. Imports | 195 | 449 | 470 | 854 | 1829 |
| 2. Exports | 153 | 413 | 562 | 1395 | 2600 |
| 3. Balance of merchandise account | − 42 | − 36 | + 92 | + 537 | + 771 |
| 4. Balance of invisible items | + 4 | − 97 | − 134 | − 265 | − 604 |
| 5. Balance of long-term capital account | + 29 | + 97 | + 42 | − 271 | + 87 |
| 6. Balance of current account and gold (+ credits, − debits) | + 9 | + 36 | 0 | + 1 | − 70 |

*Source: Historical Statistics of the United States; Trends in the American Economy in the Nineteenth Century* (Princeton, N.J.: National Bureau of Economic Research, 1960), pp. 699–705.

## Imports and Exports

Not only was the international trade of the United States increasing dramatically in this period but also it was increasing more rapidly than the total of world trade. In 1850, the United States' share of world trade was about 10%; by 1913, that share had risen to about 15%. The change is even more dramatic when one looks at the U.S. share of the world's exports of manufactured goods, which increased from 2.8% in 1880 to 12.6% in 1913.

Not only did the volume of U.S. trade increase, both absolutely and relatively in terms of world trade, but the composition of that trade as to both products (see Table 16-2) and countries involved also changed. These changes reflected the long-term continuation of industrialization.

As shown in Table 16-2, the dominant place held in U.S. exports by raw materials, primarily cotton (Column I) gave way first to foodstuffs, including manufactured foodstuffs (wheat, flour, processed meats—Columns II and III) in the 1870s and 1880s. They, in turn, surrendered first place to manufactured goods, both semifinished and finished (Columns IV and V) by 1910. Imports also showed the effects of U.S. industrialization, as imports of raw materials and semimanufactured goods increased to provide needed materials for the finished goods manufactures that were

Table 16-2. Percent Composition of U.S. Exports and Imports, 1851–1910.

|  | I | II | III | IV | V |
|---|---|---|---|---|---|
|  | Raw Materials | Nonmanufactured Foodstuffs | Manufactured Foodstuffs | Semimanufac- tured Goods | Finished Goods Manufactures |
| Exports |  |  |  |  |  |
| 1851–1860 | 61.7 | 6.6 | 15.4 | 4.0 | 12.3 |
| 1876–1880 | 32.2 | 23.9 | 24.4 | 4.6 | 14.9 |
| 1896–1900 | 26.1 | 18.9 | 24.0 | 9.6 | 21.4 |
| 1906–1910 | 31.7 | 8.9 | 18.1 | 14.2 | 27.1 |
| Imports |  |  |  |  |  |
| 1851–1860 | 9.6 | 11.7 | 15.4 | 12.5 | 50.8 |
| 1876–1880 | 18.6 | 18.2 | 21.5 | 12.4 | 29.3 |
| 1896–1900 | 29.5 | 15.1 | 15.9 | 13.3 | 26.2 |
| 1906–1910 | 34.6 | 11.0 | 11.8 | 17.8 | 24.8 |

Source: U.S. Department of Commerce, Bureau of the Census, Historical Statistics of the United States, Colonial times to 1970, Part 2 (Washington, D.C.: U.S. Government Printing Office, 1975), pp. 889–890.

later exported, and imports of finished goods manufactures declined by 1910 to less than half the 1851–1860 percentage level.

Of all U.S. exports, 75% went to Europe in 1860; this had fallen to 68% by 1906–1910. The share of exports going to Canada rose from 7% to 10% in the same period, and those going to Asia rose from 2.4% to 5.5%. In 1860, 60% of U.S. imports came from Europe; this had fallen to 51% by 1906–1910. The share of U.S. imports coming from Asia and South America increased in the same period.

Starting in 1876 (and except for 1887–1889 and 1893), significant credit balances in the **merchandise account** became the rule. These **credit** balances meant that exports from the United States exceeded imports into the United States. This was a favorable balance of trade; U.S. residents were obtaining claims to foreign currencies in greater amounts than foreigners were obtaining claims to dollars from exports to the United States. This reversed the long-term condition of imports exceeding exports, which had generated a **debit** balance as the rule prior to 1876.

## Invisible Items

Table 16-1 shows an increasing debit balance in the **invisible items accounts** between 1870 and 1913. Invisible items represent a number of different accounts that, together with the merchandise account (imports and exports of goods), make up what is called the current account. They include tourist expenditures; transportation and insurance fees; the flow of dividends, profits, and interest on foreign investments; and transfer payments. The single most important reason for this outflow of funds from the

American economy (debit entries, or balances, result from transactions where residents are obligated to pay nonresidents) was to pay the profits, dividends, and interest on foreign investment in the United States. This outflow of funds increased as foreign investments made in the United States rose from approximately $1.5 billion in 1870 to about $6.3 billion in 1913.

A second reason for the growing debit balance (whereby residents must pay nonresidents) in invisible items stemmed from a substantial shift after the Civil War from the carrying of U.S. exports and imports by U.S.-owned ocean vessels, to carrying by foreign, especially British, vessels. As more U.S. goods were shipped on foreign vessels, transportation fees paid to nonresidents—a debit—increased.

Another reason for these debit balances was increased tourism by Americans in Europe. After the Civil War, the U.S. upper- and upper-middle-income classes expanded substantially. These groups began to seek the "higher culture" of Europe, and the flow of U.S. tourists increased. Expenditures they made in Europe put U.S. purchasing power in the hands of nonresidents, resulting in debits in the U.S. invisible items account.

Finally, European immigration into the United States increased markedly between 1880 and 1914. Many immigrants sent funds back to their original countries to bring their relatives to the United States, or sent funds back to help support their families still in Europe, or returned to Europe themselves, taking their American savings with them. These are called **unilateral transfers,** in that the nonresident recipients of these funds are not obligated to pay back funds, goods, or services, either immediately or in the future. Since these funds transfers went to nonresidents (the immigrant who returned to the old country now became a nonresident), they were debits, or outflows, of claims to U.S. money.

## The Current Account

By 1876, the U.S. economy had achieved an export surplus in the merchandise account (imports and exports). These credit balances in the balance of trade became large enough by 1881 to offset the growing debit balances in invisible items. The **current account** is the sum of the merchandise and invisible items accounts, Lines 3 and 4 in Table 16-1. Credit balances in the current account were modest until 1896 and then became much more marked, a factor that reduced the U.S. dependence on foreign inflows of capital to balance the overall payments accounts.

## Capital Movements

Except for the period from 1897 to 1905, annual foreign investment in the United States exceeded U.S. investment in foreign countries from 1850 up to 1914. The **long-term capital account** held a credit balance, except for the years 1897 to 1905, when debit balances were achieved ranging from $23 million in 1897 to $245 million in 1901. A credit balance in the long-term capital account meant that nonresidents, mostly English, had invested more in the United States than U.S. residents had invested in other countries. This caused an inflow of foreign exchange into the United States. By the end of the nineteenth century, credit balances in the current account reflected the fact that the United States had become a source of international capital.

Until 1914 and the start of World War I in Europe, the United States remained a **net debtor nation** (more total foreign investment in the United States than U.S. residents had invested in other countries). The U.S. net debt position was $75 million in 1803, $1.5 billion in 1869, $2.7 billion in 1897, and $3.7 billion by 1914. Of this net debt, almost all of it was with Europe. One-half of the net debt was held by English residents, and one-half was in railroad stocks and bonds.

Despite its net debtor position, the United States had made substantial amounts of foreign investment of its own by 1914. These foreign investments totaled $2.6 billion in 1914, up from $634 million in 1897. Over half of the investments were in the two closest neighbors of the United States: over $860 million in Canada and $850 million in Mexico.

In Canada, a great deal of the U.S. investment was attracted to the manufacture of products for sale in the Canadian market. High Canadian tariffs encouraged the effort to "jump the tariff walls" by direct investment. But a substantial amount of investment also went into raw materials, especially lumber and minerals, items needed for the growing manufacturing sector of the United States. In 1914, U.S. investment in Canada was only one-half the amount of investment there by the English. But by the 1920s U.S. investment in Canada had become greater than English investment in Canada.

In Mexico, the so-called Peace of Dictator Diaz created a favorable environment for foreign investment until the Madera revolution of 1911. Afterward, nationalistic sentiment seriously threatened foreign investment. From 1897 to 1914, an average of $40 million a year from the United States flowed into investments in Mexican railroads, mining, oil, agricultural properties, and public utilities.

In Cuba, U.S. investment rose rapidly after Cuban independence, from $50 million in 1897 to $200 million in 1914. After 1914, foreign investment in Cuba was largely monopolized by Americans. In Central America, about one-third of the $93 million invested by U.S. residents by 1914 was in the fruit industry. Investments in South America by U.S. citizens rose from $38 million in 1897 to about $366 million in 1914. Of this, about two-thirds were in mining. Investment in oil in South America developed later, after 1916.

The Asian market proved small for the United States. Exports to Asia in 1897 accounted for 4% of the United States' total exports, and this had grown only to 6% by 1914. The United States was a latecomer on the China scene, arriving after the European powers and Japan had carved up China into their own spheres of influence. The international **open door policy** (that everyone should be equally able to trade and invest throughout China) advocated by the United States was largely ignored. The deep poverty of the masses in Asia contributed to a relatively low level of demand for U.S. products and investment. U.S. investments in all of Asia grew from $23 million in 1897 to $235 million by 1914; most of this was invested in Japan.

## After 1914

In 1914, the United States was a net debtor nation by $3.7 billion. With the advent of World War I, however, U.S. exports expanded rapidly. By April of 1917, over $3 billion of U.S. securities held by Europeans had been sold to U.S. residents in partial payment for these purchases. In addition, $2263 million in loans to the allied countries were made, plus $45 million in loans to Germany and $365 million in loans to neutrals. By the end of 1918, the United States had become a **net creditor nation** of about $7 billion. Nonresidents owed American residents $7 billion more than Americans owed them.

A fundamental shift had occurred in the structure of international finance. The United States had now become the strongest financial power in the world. Eventually, the United States would have achieved such status anyway, as shown by the historical trends with the relative increases in exports and foreign investment by U.S. residents. But the war catapulted the United States into that position in just a few years. The big issues to be answered in the next chapter are, then, could the world adjust to this fundamental shift, and, indeed, could the United States adjust to its responsibilities?

## Summary

From 1790 to 1876, the United States was a **young debtor nation.** Its import surplus (a debit balance in the merchandise account) was paid for by substantial inflows of long-term capital (a credit balance in the long-term capital account). This inflow not only paid for the excess of imports over exports but also led to increased productivity from the capital goods (machines, factories, and so forth) created by investments. This resulted in greater output that could increase exports so as to pay for the interest, dividends, and profits earned by the foreign investment.

From 1876 to 1914, the United States was becoming a **mature debtor nation,** as its export surplus became large enough to pay for the outflows (debits) of dividends, profits, and interest in the invisible items account created by the prior foreign investment in the United States. The United States became increasingly less dependent on foreign investment to balance its payments.

After 1914, under the impact of the outbreak of World War I in Europe, the United States became a **young creditor nation.** The export surplus was large enough to provide funds for significant amounts of foreign investments made by Americans in other countries. In terms of the balance of payments, a young creditor nation is one that generates a credit balance in the merchandise account that provides the foreign exchange for debit balances in the long-term capital account.

# Tariffs

The tariff policy of the United States is an important factor to review in this consideration of the United States and the international economy. Tariffs are taxes on imports that raise the price of these imports. As the prices of the imports increase, competing domestic goods acquire a greater competitive advantage. But this is not a net gain, because governmental interference in international relative prices raises domestic prices and causes a less efficient allocation of resources. Exports may be adversely affected also, as when other countries retaliate and raise their tariffs against U.S. goods, causing a decreased demand for U.S. exports.

Prior to the Civil War, tariffs in the American economy were moderate and were essentially for revenue. Opposition, in large measure from the agricultural South, which was a primary importer of manufactured goods, kept tariff rates from becoming significantly protectionist in nature. In fact, tariff rates were on the decline after 1832.

But now, with the South out of the Congress and with the Civil War creating needs for large amounts of revenue, this low-tariffs trend was reversed after 1860. From 20% in 1860, average tariff rates had risen to 47% by 1864. After the war, these "temporary" rates became permanent, and high protectionist rates became the policy of the federal government.

The Dingley Tariff of 1897 pushed tariffs to the highest rates in U.S. history, an act that triggered retaliatory rate increases against U.S. products, especially by England and Canada. The next tariff passed was the Payne-Aldrich Tariff of 1909. Faulkner[3] concludes that there was no essential difference between the two tariffs—that perhaps the Payne-Aldrich Tariff was a little less aggressively protectionist but was more obviously logrolling, with those groups with more political influence obtaining the greatest benefits (higher rates for those commodities the politically powerful wish to protect).

The Democratic party made these high tariffs a campaign issue in the congressional elections of 1910. The party made enough congressional gains to pass a lower tariff bill, but President Taft (a Republican) vetoed the bill. In 1913, the Underwood Tariff was passed, in an effort to reduce tariff rates. However, the tariff structure of the United States was still basically protectionist.

What arguments can be made in favor of these relatively high tariff rates? Some have argued that tariff protection is needed to protect American labor against cheap foreign labor. This hardly seems a valid argument in the face of unrestricted immigration and the very high level of immigration into the United States from 1880 to 1914 by this selfsame "cheap foreign labor." Besides, U.S. labor achieved higher productivity and wages because of higher skills and larger amounts of capital invested per worker.

The tariffs certainly reduced imports. However, the United States was not suffering from any chronic balance of payments problems that would have required higher tariffs to counter deficits in the balance of payments. Furthermore, the United States was moving steadily toward a mature debtor position (export surplus covering U.S. foreign investment abroad). Thus, there seems to have been little reason to decrease imports, as regards the balance of payments.

Some also argued that high tariffs would foster United States manufacturing. No doubt some industries were begun under tariff protection and needed that protection to develop. But that cannot be said about industry in general. By 1900, manufacturing in the United States was firmly established in conditions very favorable to the American producer. The sector had a large domestic market, with ready access to supplies of materials, large amounts of capital, and a rapidly developing system of technological innovation.

Finally, some argued that the tariff was needed to obtain revenue for the federal government. Tariff revenues did provide a significant portion (at least 50%) of total federal government receipts after the Civil War. But, these receipts produced a federal government budgetary surplus through most of the period from 1870 to 1914. In addition, tariffs frequently are a regressive form of taxes, falling more heavily on the lower-income groups, which raises a serious question about equitable taxation.

Against whatever gains one could rationalize from high protective tariffs, they also had distinct disadvantages. The interference in comparative advantage trade reduced efficiency in the allocation of resources and increased prices. High tariffs also fostered retaliation by other governments, which increased their tariffs against U.S. exports, thereby reducing U.S. output and employment in export industries. Lastly, perhaps Faulkner was right that tariffs were made high to reduce foreign competition and thus encourage combinations in the United States by monopoly power producers who set higher prices.

# Territorial Expansion

Prior to 1897, the territorial expansion of the United States was primarily internal. The basic aim was to reach from the Atlantic to the Pacific. As may be seen in Figure 16-1, land was obtained either by purchase, such as the Louisiana Purchase in 1803 and the purchase of Florida in 1821, or by other means—Texas was admitted into the union in 1845, the Gadsden purchase took place in 1853, and California was admitted in 1846—or by negotiation, such as for the Oregon Territory in 1846. In addition to the territories included in the continental United States, Alaska was purchased in 1867.

These territories were acquired for settlement and for the utilization of the areas' resources. The native populations (Mexicans and Native Americans) were essentially shunted out of the way in this process of economic development.

The territories obtained after 1897 were not for direct colonization nor for the purpose of exploiting the native populations. They were primarily acquired for strategic purposes. One objective was to obtain

Construction of the Panama Canal. (Photo no. 185-G-71 in the National Archives)

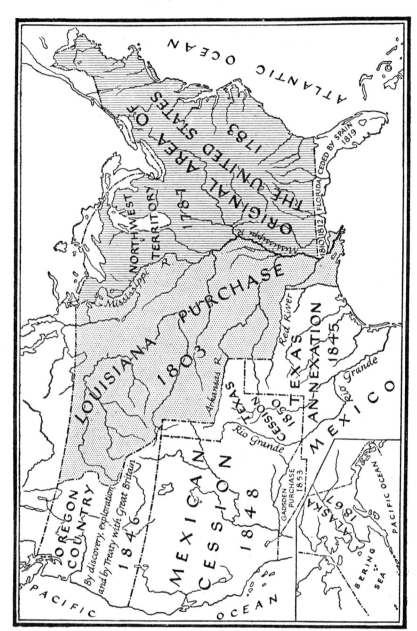

Figure 16-1. Territorial Growth of the United States, 1783–1867.

*Source:* Excerpted from *The Beard's New Basic History of the United States* by Charles A. Beard and Mary R. Beard. Copyright © 1944, 1960, 1968 by Doubleday & Company, Inc. Reprinted by permission of the publisher.

naval coaling stations, to maintain a two-ocean navy. Thus, the United States managed to "acquire" the Philippines and Samoa as part of the Pacific fueling system. In addition, these countries gave overseas access to the Asian markets.

Another economic (and political) objective was to obtain a protected canal route across the Isthmus of Panama. The U.S. acquisition of Puerto Rico, a naval base in Cuba, the Virgin Islands, and the Canal Zone itself all contributed to satisfying this objective.

The case of the Hawaiian Islands was substantially different. The United States took over the islands mostly by accident. According to Faulkner,[3] the McKinley Tariff of 1890 increased the tariff duties on imported sugar to help the Louisiana sugar producers. The American sugar producers in Hawaii wanted to take advantage of the new tariff by making Hawaii a part of the United States, so they organized a revolt against the native Hawaiian government. They lost; however, to stop the Hawaiian queen from executing the American rebels, the commander of the U.S. Naval Squadron at Hawaii "reluctantly" placed the islands under the "protection" of the United States. In the end, the U.S. sugar growers achieved their objective. Few people in the United States were unhappy with the annexation of Hawaii in 1898. The islands were dominated by American economic interests, and the Hawaiian harbors were important during the 1898 war with Spain. Furthermore, there was growing fear of Japan's intentions toward the islands.

## Summary

A number of observations can be made about the U.S. economy and the international economic setting before 1920. Perhaps the most important is that, as the U.S. economy developed and matured into the largest industrial complex in the world, the center of economic power shifted. No longer did the U.S. economy depend on the tempo of economic activities and financial decisions in Europe, especially Britain. Even more, the dependence was being reversed. Europe was now to react to the actions of the new economic giant, the United States.

A second point deserves notice. Until 1897, U.S. investors and entrepreneurs were primarily occupied with utilizing the economic opportunities of the continental United States. In addition to U.S. investment and enterprise, significant infusions of European capital and enterprise were productively utilized. By 1897, however, U.S. enterprise began to vigorously seek opportunities for profit beyond U.S. borders. Foreign investments by U.S. citizens rose rapidly to exploit foreign profit-making opportunities. The U.S. government, too, went beyond the boundaries of the United States, as more territory was acquired to satisfy the strategic needs of two-ocean trade.

The last point to consider deals with the fundamental shift in international economic power that resulted from World War I. Not only did the United States shift from a net debtor to a net creditor position, but this shift resulted in a $7 billion net credit position. The large size of these credits would put a severe strain on the ability of the European debtors to meet their debt obligations. In addition, this large net creditor position put the United States under an obligation to create conditions to enable those countries to pay or meet these debts, an obligation the United States met poorly in the 1920s.

World War I also caused significant shifts in international markets. Europe lost markets heavily in North and South America and in Asia to the United States and the emerging economy of Japan. The loss of these markets compounded the European postwar economic adjustments. The drama begun in 1914 continued long after the war was over. However, the international economic strategy of the United States that would be used after the war was already clearly defined by the beginning of the war. High protective tariffs with a tendency toward increases (except for the Underwood Tariff of 1913) were the policy of the U.S. government after 1860. To allow for repayment of loans and to increase export markets in the 1920s, the U.S. would have had to increase its own imports, largely by lowering tariffs. Instead, however, the high tariff policy was continued.

---

# Review of Economic Concepts: The Balance of Payments

The **balance of payments** is a summary of all economic transactions between the residents of one country and the residents of all other countries during a given time period. It is important to point out, first, that the balance of payments accounts are summaries of transactions and do not contain a record of each individual transaction. In that sense, they are like balance sheet items in accounting, not like journal entries. Second, the accounts reflect transactions between residents, not citizens of countries. The important thing is where people are living or residing. Lastly, the balance of payments is for a specific time period—usually, one year—and only includes transactions of that time period; it is not cumulative.

The balance of payments is set up in a T-account, or double-entry system: For every transaction, two equal and offsetting entries are made, a credit and a debit. Therefore, if all the debits are added up and all the credits are added up they will be equal; thus the balance of payments always balances.

Credits are all economic transactions that create an immediate obligation for a nonresident to pay a resident. Debits are all economic transactions that create an immediate obligation for a resident to pay a nonresident. Credits thus create inflows of payments (foreign exchange), and debits create outflows of payments (foreign exchange).

We can also define debits and credits in the balance of payments accounts from another point of view. Credits are all economic transactions that increase the demand for dollars in a foreign exchange market as nonresidents seek dollars to pay residents or increase the supply of foreign exchange, as nonresidents offer their own monies to obtain dollars to pay residents. Debits increase the demand for foreign monies, as residents seek foreign exchange to pay nonresidents or increase the supply of dollars to obtain foreign monies to pay nonresidents.

## The Major Accounts of the Balance of Payments

Figure 16-2 is a schematic presentation of the balance of payments accounts that are most relevant to the period through 1920. The first major account is the current account, which is divided into two major subaccounts, the merchandise account and services or invisible items. The merchandise account consists of exports (credits) and imports (debits). Invisible items consist of a number of different accounts: First, services, including fees for transportation and insurance; second, expenditures of tourists in other countries; third, payments of profits, dividends, and interest on prior foreign investment; fourth, funds spent in other countries to maintain military forces and diplomatic missions; and finally, transfers not requiring repayment, such as immigrants sending money back to the family in the old country.

The second major account is the short-term capital account. It consists of changes in demand deposits (checking accounts) and short-term debt (debt that matures in less than one year).

The third major account is the long-term capital account. This account records foreign investment, nonresidents investing in the United States or U.S. residents investing in other countries, in the form of purchase of corporate stock or equity instruments, or purchase of corporate debt or bonds, or direct investment in noncorporate forms.

The last major account is the gold account. Exports or outflows of gold

I. Current Account
   A. Merchandise Account
   B. Invisible Items
II. Short-Term Capital Account
III. Long-Term Capital Account
IV. Gold Account

Figure 16-2. Major Accounts in the Balance of Payments.

are credits, and imports or inflows of gold are debits. The gold account was only relevant up to 1971.

## Balance of Payments Deficit

Since debits always equal credits, by the nature of the way the accounts are set up, the balance of payments always balances. But the various accounts *individually* need not balance. There are stable sets of balances between the accounts, and there are unstable ones. The stable balances can be maintained for extended periods or can contain self-correcting mechanisms. A debit balance in the merchandise account (imports exceeding exports) can remain stable as foreign investment flows into the economy. Credit balances in the long-term capital account, as capital is formed, increase the productive capacity of the economy. Eventually output increases, and this import balance can be reversed.

Deficits in the balance of payments occur when these balances in the individual accounts are potentially not stable. Credit balances in the short-term capital account (bank balances), as well as credit balances in the gold account, are considered potentially unstable. Increases of bank balances by nonresidents cannot be maintained indefinitely, because if those nonresidents cannot use their balance to buy the output of the U.S. economy or use them to obtain investments, they would wish to use these funds in their own economies. Prior to the 1930s, this would result in a withdrawal of gold. Since gold was the main reserve of the banking system in the nineteenth and early twentieth centuries, the loss of gold would have reduced both credit activities of the banking system and the supply of money. The level of general economic activity could then be affected. However, according to gold standard theorists, these changes in the supply of money would change prices, so as to introduce self-correcting activities.

---

# Glossary

**Balance of payments**   A summary of all economic transactions between the residents of one country and the residents of all other countries in a given time period.

**Credit**   All transactions that generate an immediate obligation for a nonresident to pay a resident in the balance of payments accounts. Or, all transactions that increase foreign demand for dollars or increase the supply of foreign monies in the foreign exchange market; for example, an export.

**Current account**   The sum of the balance of payments merchandise and invisible items accounts.

**Debit**  All transactions that generate an immediate obligation for a resident to pay a nonresident in the balance of payments accounts. Or, all transactions that increase foreign supply of dollars or increase the demand for foreign monies in the foreign exchange market; for example, an import.

**Favorable balance of trade**  When exports exceed imports or there is a credit balance in the merchandise account.

**Invisible items account**  A major subaccount within the current account of the balance of payments. It contains primarily services such as expenditures by tourists; transportation; insurance fees; dividends, profits, and interest on foreign investments; and transfer payments.

**Long-term capital account**  A balance of payments account containing all entries in the balance of payments concerning investments (the purchase of stock or bonds or direct investments) by residents in other countries or nonresidents in this country.

**Mature debtor nation**  A nation that has a credit balance in the balance of payments merchandise account that provides the foreign exchange to pay for the debit balance in dividends, interest, and profits resulting from outflows of income earned by prior foreign investment in the nation's economy.

**Merchandise account**  A major subaccount within the current account of the balance of payments. It reflects the exports and imports of goods.

**Net creditor nation**  A nation that has more investment in other countries than foreigners have in that country.

**Net debtor nation**  A nation that has more investment by foreigners in its economy than its residents have in other countries.

**Open door policy**  A policy advocated by the United States in the late nineteenth century to allow all countries to trade and invest throughout China.

**Unilateral transfers**  Funds transfers arising when nonresidents receive funds, in money, goods, and services, that they are not obligated, now or in the future, to pay back. An example is an immigrant's savings of American dollars that he takes with him when he moves back to his original homeland.

**Young creditor nation**  A nation that has a credit balance in the balance of payments merchandise account that provides the foreign exchange to permit long-term capital investment in other countries; it has a debit balance in the long-term capital account.

**Young debtor nation**  A nation that has a debit balance in the balance of payments merchandise account, paid for by credit balances in the long-term capital account.

## Questions

1. List the changes in the current account of the United States from 1850 to 1913. Which of these changes attest to the growing industrial nature of the American economy? Why do they do so?
2. Trace the changes in the long-term capital account of the United States from 1850 to 1920. Did these changes indicate an increasing or a decreasing dependency of the U.S. economy on Europe? Why?
3. U.S. investment in other countries to 1914 was concentrated primarily in which countries and what industries? Why do you think this was so?
4. What fundamental change occurred during World War I in regard to the U.S. balance of payments? Why was this change important?
5. Evaluate the arguments made in favor of high tariffs.
6. What are the disadvantages of tariffs?
7. What were the basic economic motives for territorial expansion of the United States? First, within the continental United States? Second, outside the continental United States?
8. What were the four points made about the United States and the international economy in the summary to the chapter?

## Suggested Readings

1. Ashworth, William A. *A Short History of the International Economy, 1850–1950.* New York: Longmans Green, 1952.
2. Bagwell, Philip S., and Mingay, G. E. *Britain and America 1850–1939: A Study of Economic Change.* New York: Praeger, 1970. Esp. Chaps. 4 and 9.
3. Faulkner, Harold U. *The Decline of Laissez-Faire, 1897–1917.* New York: Holt, Rinehart and Winston, 1951. Esp. Chaps. 3 and 4.
4. La Feber, Walter. *The New Empire: An Interpretation of American Expansion, 1860–1898.* Ithaca, N.Y.: Cornell University Press, 1963.
5. National Bureau of Economic Research. *Historical Statistics of the United States: Trends in the American Economy in the Nineteenth Century.* Princeton, N.J.: Princeton University Press, 1960. Pp. 699–705.
6. Novak, David, and Simon, Mathew. "Commercial Responses to the American Export Invasion, 1871–1914." *Explorations in Economic History,* 3 (1966).

7. Scheiber, Harry N. "America and the World Economy." In *America: Purpose and Power*, ed. Gene Lyons. New York: Quadrangle, 1965.

8. Scheiber, Harry N. "World War I as Entrepreneurial Opportunity." *Political Science Quarterly, 84* (1969).

9. Taussig, F. W. *The Tariff History of the United States.* New York: Capricorn Books, 1964.

10. U.S. Department of Commerce, Bureau of the Census. *Historical Statistics, Colonial Times to 1970.* Washington, D.C.: U.S. Government Printing Office, 1975.

11. Wilkins, Mira. *The Emergence of Multinational Enterprise: American Business Abroad from the Colonial Era to 1914.* Cambridge, Mass.: Harvard University Press, 1970.

12. Williamson, Jeffrey G. *American Growth and the Balance of Payments, 1820–1913.* Chapel Hill: University of North Carolina Press, 1964.

13. Willis, James F., and Primack, Martin L. *Explorations in Economics.* Boston: Houghton Mifflin, 1977. Esp. Chap. 25.

14. Woodruff, William. *America's Impact on the World.* London: Macmillan, 1975.

15. Zevin, Robert. "An Interpretation of American Imperialism." *Journal of Economic History, 32* (March 1972).

# Chapter 17

---

# The Prosperity of the 1920s

The decade of the 1920s was a dramatic time in the economic history of the United States. The economy boomed, and the 1920s became synonymous with the idea of prosperity. Indeed, George Soule[23] titled his excellent economic history of the 1920s *The Prosperity Decade*. The automobile led this expansion; the American people began their rush to a life on four wheels. At the same time, the United States had become the most powerful financial power in the world, and Americans had their first taste of being world economic leaders. But, ironically, this was the same decade that started with the depression of 1921 and ended with the stock market crash of 1929. Although that crash was not the beginning, it was the first dramatic sign of the international economic disaster known as the Great Depression of the 1930s.

## The Beginning

Remember that, after a brief pause during the conversion to civilian production, the U.S. economy after World War I continued to expand. Government expenditures were still relatively high in 1919, due especially to bonus and discharge pay to the armed forces and the decision to complete the construction of merchant vessels under the Emergency Fleet Corporation. Exports were high, because agricultural and industrial products were needed by Europeans to tide them over until their countries' war damages could be repaired. Consumer demand was also high, because purchases had been postponed in 1917 and 1918 when resources were mobilized for the war effort. Purchasing power to pay for the increased demand came from high levels of savings, both in saving banks and through government bonds (Liberty Bonds) accumulated during the war. Investment, both in residential construction and in industrial plants and equipment, was high because such investment had been postponed during the war. Also, the supply of money continued to increase.

Under the impact of this expanding demand, inflation continued to increase. The inflation created the usual wave of speculation in inventories. Business people bought goods not only to make a "regular" profit on their economic functions (retailing, for instance) but also to profit from an increase in prices from the time they bought the goods until the time they sold them. In 1920, inventories increased beyond the normal needs of business. Apparently price increases exceeded the interest cost of holding inventories. This not only further increased demand but also made the economy more unstable.

The speculative expansion of inventories increased the rate of growth in demand to manufacturers for consumer goods. This resulted in increased investment, because new plants and equipment were needed to produce the additional goods, producing a positive accelerator effect and thus expanding the economy. Later, as the speculative buying of inventories slowed up, the demand for investment in additional production capacity also decreased, and this negative accelerator effect contracted the economy.

Government expenditures decreased toward the end of 1920 because salaries for the discharged military were not paid any longer, construction under the Emergency Fleet Corporation was completed, and war contracts were no longer paid. Exports declined as Europe completed war reconstruction. Also of considerable importance, the inventory bubble had burst by the end of 1920. In late 1920, the U.S. economy contracted, and a severe, although short, depression took place during 1921.

Some charged that the Federal Reserve System was responsible for the collapse of the inventory speculation, because it ordered the banks under its regulation to cease making loans to allow speculative buying of inventories. But probably this actually had little effect on the outcome. Any wave of speculation must end, because (among other things) any hesitation in price increases brings a crash as people rush to get out from under the fall. In any case, excess inventories accumulation contributed to the severity of the depression. Remember the income determination model: As the level of income falls due to declines in total demand, business people have larger inventories than they wish, and they cut orders to their suppliers. This, in turn, decreases output, employment, and income. In 1920, inventories were much higher than normal, due to the swollen inventories resulting from speculation. This decreased income even more than would have occurred without the speculation.

The depression in 1921 was severe. Constant GNP fell by about 6%, and unemployment rose to about 12% with almost half a million workers unemployed. By the end of 1921, the index of industrial production had dropped from its September 1919 high by almost 18%. A major characteristic of the depression was the sharp drop in prices. The wholesale price index dropped from 227 in 1920 to 150 in 1921 (1913 = 100). Industrial prices decreased somewhat less than the average, while raw material prices decreased more than the average.

Agricultural prices declined almost to their prewar levels. This relatively greater decline in agricultural prices stemmed from four factors. Agriculture was highly competitive, and farmers, individually or collectively, could not reduce supply to stem the fall in prices. Also, war and immediate postwar demand encouraged farmers to expand output, which, by 1921, created excess supply. Furthermore, with the end of the war and renewed freedom of shipping, foreign supplies (for example, from Argentina and Australia) could reach the European markets. Finally, war reconstruction had advanced to the point that European demand for imported food fell. Europeans did not wish to continue to buy the same quantities of imported goods at the same prices.

# The Prosperous Twenties—1922-1929

However, the depression of 1921 was short. The basic demand for consumer goods and investment remained sound, and the U.S. economy renewed its expansion by the beginning of 1922. This expansion continued throughout the 1920s into 1929, with only a mild interruption in 1924 and an even milder one in 1927. Current GNP increased from $69.5 billion in 1921 to $103.1 billion in 1929. Unemployment dropped from 11.7% in 1921 to 3.2% in 1929. The price level itself fell very moderately, from 53.6 (1967 = 100) in 1921 to 51.3 in 1929.

## The Automobile

The rapid growth of automobile production was probably the single most important factor in the 1920s expansion. The direct and indirect effects of the widespread use of the auto had an enormous impact on the U.S. economy in the 1920s. Auto production performed the same kind of leading sector role that railroad construction had played in the period from 1865 to 1893. As in the 1865–1893 period, one could see the 1920s period in terms of Hirschman's unbalanced growth concept with forward linkages (the creation of the service station industry and increased road building) and with backward linkages (stimulus to the industries that provide the materials used to construct cars, such as steel and rubber). Also, the Schumpeter innovation-imitation model is useful to explore the role of the auto industry in the expansion of the 1920s.

Although the auto was first used around 1895 (there were four autos in the United States in 1895), its period of greatest growth was the 1920s. In 1921, 1.5 million passenger cars were produced and about 10.5 million motor vehicles were registered in the United States. By 1929, these figures had increased 300%, to 4.5 million passenger cars produced and 26.7 million registered motor vehicles, 23 million of which were passenger cars. In 1929, almost 13% of the value of all manufactures was automobiles, and over 7% of all manufacturing sector wage earners were employed in making cars.

The growth in the number of cars produced obviously had a major direct impact on the U.S. economy, reflected in total demand and thus in aggregate income. It also had substantial impact on the output of industries that provided materials to build the cars. It was the largest single source of demand for many industries—for example, plate glass and rubber—and used 15% of the nation's total steel production. In petroleum refining, it caused the substantial shift to gasoline production that revolutionized the industry.

This rapid increase in consumer demand and thus in induced investment caused high levels of demand for plant and equipment, not only in the auto industry but also in those industries that provided the materials to construct the cars. Remember that as the rate of growth in consumer demand increases there is additional need for plant and equipment (induced investment) to meet the increased demand. This positive accelerator (increases in induced investment) had substantial impact on raising the level of personal, real income in the economy.

While it is certain that increased real income during the 1920s brought about increased demand, and improvements in the auto made the car even more attractive, the following two factors seemed most responsible for the expansion in demand. The first was an innovative method of financing auto purchases. The introduction and subsequent widespread use of time payment plans or installment credit made the sale of cars to those of only moderate income possible, since it was difficult for such consumers to save the full purchase price. By 1925, over 68% of the dollar purchase amount of new cars was "on time," although this dropped to about 58% by 1928. The second factor was helped by the first and also by decreases in price as productivity increased and competition remained strong; that factor was the large **primary demand** that existed in the early 1920s because many people had not yet bought their first car. Although automobile output increased by a total of 19% in 1929, most of the increase was at the beginning of the year; output began to fall by the middle of the year, several months before the stock market crash.

It is hard to estimate the total impact of the auto industry. Its growth

Table 17-1. Important Statistics of the 1920s.

| | 1920 | 1921 | 1922 | 1923 | 1924 | 1925 | 1926 | 1927 | 1928 | 1929 |
|---|---|---|---|---|---|---|---|---|---|---|
| 1. Current GNP (in billions of $) | 91.5 | 69.5 | 74.1 | 85.1 | 84.7 | 93.1 | 97.0 | 94.9 | 97.0 | 103.1 |
| 2. Percent unemployment of civilian labor force | 5.2 | 11.7 | 6.7 | 2.4 | 5.0 | 3.2 | 1.8 | 3.3 | 4.2 | 3.2 |
| 3. Consumer price index (1967 = 100) | 60.0 | 53.6 | 50.2 | 51.1 | 51.2 | 52.5 | 53.0 | 52.0 | 51.3 | 51.3 |
| 4. Production of passenger cars (in millions) | 1.9 | 1.5 | 2.3 | 3.6 | 3.2 | 3.7 | 3.7 | 2.9 | 3.8 | 4.5 |
| 5. Registered motor vehicles (in millions) | 9.2 | 10.5 | 12.3 | 15.1 | 17.6 | 20.1 | 22.2 | 23.3 | 24.7 | 26.7 |
| 6. Percent of the value of manufacturing in the auto industry | | | | | | | | | | 13 |
| 7. Percent of manufacturing wage earners in the auto industry | | | | | | | | | | 7 |
| 8. Consumer debt (in billions of $) | 3.0 | 3.0 | 3.2 | 3.7 | 4.0 | 4.7 | 5.2 | 5.3 | 6.3 | 7.1 |
| 9. Value of new construction (in billions of $) | 6.7 | 6.4 | 8.0 | 9.7 | 10.8 | 12.0 | 12.6 | 12.4 | 12.0 | 11.2 |
| 10. Index of manufacturing production (1921 = 100) | 124 | 100 | 124 | 148 | 140 | 156 | 164 | 164 | 172 | 188 |
| 11. Agricultural parity (1910–1914 = 100) | 99 | 80 | 87 | 89 | 89 | 95 | 91 | 88 | 91 | 92 |
| 12. Index of farm prices (1967 = 100) | 83 | 49 | 52 | 56 | 56 | 61 | 51 | 55 | 58 | 58 |
| 13. Index of prices of what farmers consume (1967 = 100) | 71 | 51 | 48 | 48 | 48 | 50 | 49 | 48 | 48 | 48 |
| 14. Index of prices of what farmers buy for production (1967 = 100) | 68 | 45 | 44 | 48 | 49 | 51 | 49 | 49 | 52 | 51 |

| | | | | | | | | | | |
|---|---|---|---|---|---|---|---|---|---|---|
| 15. Value of agricultural exports (in billions of $) | 3.9 | 2.6 | 1.9 | 1.8 | 1.9 | 2.3 | 1.9 | 1.9 | 1.8 | 1.8 |
| 16. Value of farm property (in billions of $) | 78.4 | 71.4 | 62.0 | 60.1 | 58.5 | 57.4 | 57.4 | 56.4 | 56.7 | 57.7 |
| 17. Gross farm income (1910–1914 = 100) | 209 | 139 | 146 | 160 | 169 | 180 | 174 | 174 | 189 | 182 |
| 18. Agricultural bankruptcy rate as percent of all farms | 8.7 | | | | 18 | 18 | 18 | | | 9 |
| 19. Farm tenancy as percent of all farms | 38 | | | | | | | | | 42 |
| 20. Sales of bituminous coal (in millions of short tons) | 569 | 416 | 422 | 565 | 484 | 520 | 573 | 518 | 501 | 535 |
| 21. Employment in bituminous coal mining (in thousands) | 639 | 664 | 688 | 705 | 620 | 588 | 594 | 594 | 522 | 503 |
| 22. Capital investment in railroads (in billions of $) | 19.8 | 20.3 | 20.6 | 21.4 | 22.2 | 23.2 | 23.8 | 24.5 | 24.9 | 25.5 |
| 23. Railroad passenger revenue (in billions of $) | 1.3 | 1.2 | 1.1 | 1.2 | 1.1 | 1.1 | 1.0 | 1.0 | .9 | .9 |
| 24. Railroad freight revenue (in billions of $) | 4.4 | 4.0 | 4.1 | 4.7 | 4.4 | 4.6 | 4.9 | 4.7 | 4.8 | 4.9 |
| 25. Railroad employment (in millions) | 2.0 | 1.7 | 1.7 | 1.9 | 1.8 | 1.8 | 1.8 | 1.8 | 1.7 | 1.7 |
| 26. Value of textile production (in billions of $) | | | | 3.9 | | | | | | 3.6 |
| 27. Index of physical output of textiles (1929 = 100) | | 64 | | 83 | | 86 | | 92 | | 100 |
| 28. Members of organized labor (in millions) | 5.0 | 4.8 | 4.0 | 3.6 | 3.5 | 3.5 | 3.5 | 3.5 | 3.5 | 3.5 |

*Source:* U.S. Department of Commerce, Bureau of the Census, *Historical Statistics of the United States, Colonial Times to 1970* (Washington, D.C.: U.S. Government Printing Office, 1975).

encouraged state and local governments to expand road construction, and even the federal government began to lay plans for a national network of interstate highways. It created a new service industry, the retailing of gasoline. As more families took to four wheels, the automobile encouraged movement away from urban areas to the suburbs and the establishment of the commuting life.

The auto and the truck competed seriously for passenger and freight demand with the railroads, a factor that contributed to the problems of the already troubled railway industry. The auto also restricted the use of trolley systems to city cores.

## Other Durable Goods Industries

A number of other durable goods industries also had surges of growth in the 1920s. These industries, including radios, refrigerators, and other electrical appliances, experienced increased demand for the finished products plus increases in induced investment and a positive accelerator effect as plant and equipment had to expand to provide additional needed production capacity. Furthermore, as these products increased in quantity, the rising demand for the electricity needed for their use caused demand for

A "modern" kitchen of the 1920s. (Photo no. 16-G-227-8 in the National Archives)

construction of new and expanded electrical power facilities. Similarly, more use of radios increased the demand for radio stations.

These increased demands stemmed from rising real income or purchasing power; lowered price of electricity, resulting from its more efficient production; and decreases in the share of total expenditures for food, because food prices were low after the 1921 depression. Of equal importance was the application of consumer installment credit, developed for autos but also used for other consumer durables. There are no estimates of the distribution between autos and other consumer durables of total consumer credit. Total installment credit for 1925 was $4.7 billion; for 1929, it was estimated at $7.1 billion. By 1929, it is estimated that 15% of all consumer purchases of nonfood items was on credit.

The rapid rise in consumer credit obviously stimulated demand by making possible a higher level of consumption. But mortgaging future income introduced a greater instability into business activity. As long as incomes were climbing and people were optimistic, the process of expansion could continue. But if incomes leveled off or declined or if people became insecure about their economic future, retrenchment in consumer purchases would more readily take place, because people also had to pay off debts already accumulated, and debt repayment reduced funds available for new consumption.

## The Construction Industry

During World War I, resources were channelled away from civilian to military production, at the same time that incomes and profits remained high. Personal and business savings substantially increased in the process. After the war, families and businesses rushed to make up the postponed demand for residential housing and business construction. The growing use of cars increased the demand for roads, and construction of roads at all three government levels increased. Thus, demand for construction survived the depression of 1921 and accelerated during the 1920s.

Building construction in 120 cities increased by almost 300% between 1919 and 1925. In 1926, total construction peaked at $12.6 billion, of which $5.4 billion was residential construction. Government construction of roads increased steadily throughout the 1920s, and by 1929 road construction comprised 8% of total construction. Residential construction peaked in dollar value in 1926, and then began to fall. Business construction took up the slack for awhile, but by the end of 1927 it too began to fall.

## Productivity Gains

So far we have seen that the U.S. economic expansion from 1922 to 1929 was supported by high levels of demand for consumer goods, especially consumer durables; by high levels of demand for investment; and by construction in all three categories: residential, business, and government (primarily road building). Perhaps equally important was the sustained growth in productivity, both labor productivity (output per unit of labor) and capital productivity (output per unit of capital).

Some rough indicators of this rise in productivity are represented in the following data. The index of manufacturing production rose from 100 in 1921 to 188 in 1929; it was 124 in 1920. Real gross national product per capita rose from $375 (in 1913 dollars) in 1921 to $500 in 1929. Real gross product per man-hour rose 28% from 1920 to 1929. Productivity of labor increased about 2.2% per year from 1919 to 1929. In manufacturing, it rose at the astonishing rate of 5.6% per year during that period.

Four main developments brought about these productivity gains, especially as they related to manufacturing. The first was the final general adoption of electricity to production processes. The use of electric power spread widely as refinements were made in electricity-generating steam turbine engines and electric motors. A second factor was the widespread application of the concepts of assembly-line and mass production techniques. Automatic feeding devices, conveying systems, and more widespread mechanization, especially that powered by electricity, increased productivity, not only in the automobile industry but also in such industries as glass, rubber tires and tubes, and cigarette making. A third factor was the accelerating use of science as applied to production processes. This was especially true in the chemical industry; for example, in rayon production and in the production of gasoline. Many larger-scale firms established special research divisions where the application of scientific knowledge to production was systematically explored. Finally, the 1920s witnessed the continued growing application of Frederick Taylor's theories of scientific management; through new management techniques, many producers obtained increases in output without expanding plant size.

Lessons learned during wartime mobilization about expanding production without expanding plant size were applied. The drastic reduction of immigration due to the war and the restrictive immigration laws passed during the early 1920s gave added incentive to increase labor productivity, especially that of unskilled labor.

These factors were all interrelated; changes in one area created opportunities for improvements in productivity in others. For example, refinements in the generation and use of electricity in electric motors greatly facilitated the spread of assembly-line techniques. This, in turn, encouraged the development of new management techniques, while expanding consumer demand made it possible to sell the increased output that resulted. As output and market sizes grew, specialization could be extended by the establishment of special divisions for production, accounting, and sales.

Who benefited from this increased productivity? The answer to this question could help explain the expansion of the 1920s and perhaps the subsequent depression of the 1930s. The benefits may go to consumers, to wage earners, or to business firms. They may go to consumers, for example, via a decrease in prices; to wage earners via increases in real wages, and to business firms via an increase in their rate of profit.

The consumer price index fell only slightly between 1921 and 1929; thus, the gains from increased productivity did not go primarily to consumers. We know that average real income of employees increased by about 30% in the 1920s, but not all of this can be attributed to passing on productivity gains to employees through higher wages. High average levels of employment after 1921, the availability of overtime, and the slight fall in prices, as well as higher productivity, contributed to higher real income. When George Soule[23] compared this 30% increase in real income to the 40% increase in productivity from 1919 to 1928, he concluded, "Business did not fully share its productivity gains with wage earners and consumers by a combination of wage increases and price reduction."

These apparently increasing profit margins during the expansion of the 1920s tended to keep investment levels high. Business people experiencing high and expanding total profits and profit margins were highly optimistic about the prospects of continued profits and were inclined to continue their high levels of investment.

# Weaknesses in the Economy

But not all sectors of the economy experienced the benefits of the prosperity decade. A number of significant sectors experienced economic difficulties. These included agriculture; coal mining; textiles, especially in New England; and the railway industry. In addition, situations were developing in the area of international economic relationships that were to intensify the 1930s contraction.

## A Faltering Agriculture

From 1897 to 1920, American agriculture experienced prosperity. The depression of 1921 caused this prosperity to collapse, and agriculture was unable to recover to predepression conditions. The Great Depression of the 1930s gave U.S. agriculture a further staggering blow. While much of the rest of the economy was celebrating the Roaring Twenties, agriculture was going through a dress rehearsal for the Great Depression of the 1930s.

One measure of this distress is found in the concept of **parity.** Parity is a measure developed by the U.S. Department of Agriculture to express the purchasing power of farm products. It compares an index of farm prices to an index of the prices of what farmers buy. In 1921, with the period 1910–

1914 equal to 100, the parity index fell to 80; in other words, each dollar of agricultural output in 1921 only brought 80% of what it did in 1910–1914. At no time in the 1920s did parity reach 100; it touched a high point of 95 in 1925. Parity is criticized as a measure of relative purchasing power between the agricultural and nonagricultural sectors. Relative purchasing power not only depends on the parity ratio but also relative changes in technology and thus changes in productivity.

The problem was in part due to a greater fall in farm prices in 1921 than in nonfarm prices. Farm prices fell from an index of 83 in 1920 to 49 in 1921. Prices of what farmers consumed fell from 71 to 51, and prices of items they used for production fell from 68 to 45.

Agriculture had expanded output during the war, in part due to high levels of exports. After the war, the value of these exports sharply declined. From July 1919 to July 1920, agricultural exports were $3.8 billion. Exports fell to $1.9 billion during the period from July 1921 to July 1922. The annual value of exports remained below the 1920 figure. A number of factors contributed to this collapse, including a shortage of foreign exchange in Europe, European protection of its own agricultural sectors, the renewal of worldwide exports in competition with the United States, and expanded U.S. capacity left from the high levels of war demand. Although U.S. domestic demand did increase in the 1920s, because of higher incomes, that increase was not enough to offset declining exports.

Agricultural losses were further emphasized by the decline in the value of farm property. Farmers tended to put their savings into their land, and thus this decline was especially burdensome to farmers. The value of agricultural property fell from $78 billion in 1920 to $56 billion in 1927. In 1921, the value of agricultural property was 57% of its 1910–1914 value. The value had dropped to 35% by 1928, which, if computed on a constant purchasing power basis, was an additional 20% below the prewar figure. Moreover, the index of gross farm income (1910–1914 = 100) for 1920 was 209 and fell all the way to 39 in 1921. While it rose again, it was still only 82 by 1929.

But the major calamity resulted from the high level of farm mortgages accumulated during the war through efforts by farmers to obtain more land for expansion. With the fall in prices in 1921, farmers had to produce more in order to meet payments on the high mortgages. Many were unable to do so; as a result, the bankruptcy rate increased from 1.7% of all farms in 1920 to almost 18% in 1924–1926, declining afterward to almost 9% in 1929.

Farm tenancy increased as farmers forced from ownership took to renting land in order to continue farming. Tenancy, instead of being the traditional method for farmers to climb the ladder to farm ownership, became the ladder down which increasing numbers descended to become farm laborers and then moved out of agriculture. Farm tenancy increased from 38% of all farms in 1920 to 42% in 1930.

As in manufacturing, farmers strove to increase their productivity to counter the lower, post-1920 prices. During the 1920s, the move to internal combustion machines, especially tractors and more efficient combines, continued. Productivity increased by about 26% for the decade. The more efficient farmers gained, but the high level of competition and the release of even more acres to output as the shift from horses continued both tended to restrain a general recovery from low prices.

As in the Populist revolt of the 1890s, farmers turned to the government for help. The major piece of farm legislation in the 1920s came with the Agricultural Marketing Act of 1929. After vetoing, for the second time, the McNarey-Haugen bill (an effort to establish a two-price system—a higher domestic price and a lower foreign price for agricultural products), President Hoover agreed to the formation of the Federal Farm Board with an appropriation of half a billion dollars. The board would loan to cooperatives so that they could buy and store surplus agricultural products to restrict supply and raise prices. During periods of shortages, these supplies could be sold and prices could be stabilized.

The story of the Farm Board's failure is best told in the next chapter. Perhaps the board could have been successful in more normal times. But the advent of the depression of the 1930s, with its falling agricultural prices, plus the inability of the board to control agricultural production doomed this effort at controlling the agricultural market. By mid-1932, the Federal Farm Board had lost $354 million, without stemming the further collapse of the agricultural economy.

## Coal Mining

Another industry that failed to share the blessings of prosperity was coal mining, especially bituminous or soft coal. Bituminous coal sales in 1920 reached 569 million short tons. But except for 1926 sales were below the 1920 figure throughout the 1920s decade. Prices fell from $3.75 a short ton in 1920 to $1.78 in 1929. Employment dropped from 639,000 in 1920 to 502,800 in 1929. Net income decreased from 1.7% of national income in 1920 to 0.73% in 1929. Jobs shrank from 2.6% of the national total in 1920 to 1.2% in 1929. Wages fell from 1920 to 1929 by about half a billion dollars.

The reasons for this disastrous record were many. During the war, demand was high and supplies relatively short. Substantial expansion occurred. With the 1921 collapse, however, the industry, because of its highly competitive nature based on ease of entry (the low cost of opening a mine) and because there were many small-scale individual firms, could not easily reduce output. Thus the industry suffered from chronic oversupply. Although competition from electricity and oil was beginning to be felt, coal still provided the country's primary source of energy. But demand was inelastic; the already low prices and the relatively fixed relationship between output and the technical requirements for coal reduced any stimulating effects of falling prices.

A major problem was the slow and painful process of moving resources out of coal mining. The less efficient mines could be left idle, providing standby capacity for peak periods of demand, but the miners themselves were slow to move out of mining, because they lacked local employment alternatives and were tremendously reluctant to leave localities they had lived in for generations.

## The Railroads

The relative position of the railroads had already begun to decline with the decrease in total track mileage beginning in 1916. The statistical evidence of the 1920s clearly shows substantial weakening in the position of the railroads. While capital investments rose substantially, from $19.8 billion in 1920 to $25.5 billion in 1929, passenger revenue declined from $1.3 billion to $0.9 billion (passenger miles dropped from 47 million in 1920 to 34 million in 1927), and freight revenue rose barely enough to off-set the decline in passenger revenue. High investment, with its accompany-ing increases in productivity, caused a decline in employment from 2 million in 1920 to 1.7 million in 1929.

Two reasons are generally given for this stagnation and relative decline in the economic position of the railroads. First, competition from new modes of transportation began to make serious inroads into demand for railroad services. The explosion in the number of automobiles and trucks, coupled with a substantial increase in roads, reduced railway passenger demand and restricted the growth in freight revenues. Some people charge that this competition was unfair, in that the government subsidized autos and trucks through the construction of roads, which were not directly paid for by the road users. But the same government subsidy charge could have been made against railroads, in the 1800s, by canal owners. Highway user taxes, in the form of tolls and gasoline taxes, did not come into real use until after the 1920s.

A second major reason advanced by many was the failure of the In-terstate Commerce Commission to imaginatively and efficiently regulate railroads so as to maintain the railroads' competitive position. The Hoog-enbooms,[10] in their book *A History of the ICC,* maintain that the ICC was a very significant factor in the stagnation of railroads in the 1920s.

The Transportation Act of 1920, the Esch-Cummins Act, made major revisions in the power of the ICC as well as changing its basic objective. The act mandated that the commission set rates so as to give a "fair return upon the aggregate value of the railroad property"; thus the commission's responsibility was shifted from protecting the public from railroad discrimination to the duty to see that the railroads made a "fair return" on their investment.

Furthermore, it was recognized that increased efficiency was needed to assure such a fair return. The act not only authorized but required that the commission work out a national plan and implement it to combine the railroads into from 20 to 35 railway networks. Further, the act included a recapture clause. Half of any road's net income over 6% would be turned into a fund that could be used for loans to weaker roads. Some questioned the economic logic of the recapture clause in that it tended to penalize efficiency and reward inefficiency.

The commission failed to carry out, in many significant ways, the major provisions of the act. It was especially reluctant to carry out the recapture clause, and under pressure of the stronger railroads it asked Congress in 1930 to eliminate the recapture clause provision. And it was not until the end of 1929, almost ten years after the act was passed, that the commission formulated a tentative scheme for consolidating railroads into 21 networks. Even then very few consolidations, none of them significant, were put through. In 1940, Congress relieved the commission of this responsibility.

The Hoogenbooms conclude that the timidity of the commissioners, the lack of strong leadership, the growing bureaucratic power of the ICC staff, and the complex and conflicting pressures of railroads and shippers caused the failure of the commission to act effectively. It took the easy way out and opted for the maintenance of the status quo at a time when change was essential to improve or even to maintain the railroads' competitive position.

## New England Textiles

The textile industry also did not share in the prosperity of the 1920s. The value of output of both cotton and woolen textiles declined from its peak in 1923 of $3.9 billion to $3.6 billion in 1929. This decline was due solely to falling prices, because the index of physical output increased from 64 in 1921 to 100 in 1929. Thus, increases in productivity occurred as better machines and methods were introduced. Also, there was an increase in the work week, so that the increased output was achieved with a 2% reduction of the labor force.

As with agriculture and coal mining, the textile industry was an old, established industry and was characterized by intense competition. Its age of rapid growth had long passed. Demand for textiles was probably price and income inelastic (clothing was a necessity). The effects, then, of changes in supply would more strongly affect prices than quantity (see Figure 17-1). In addition, demand declined because of changes in fashions that substantially reduced the amount of cloth per dress.

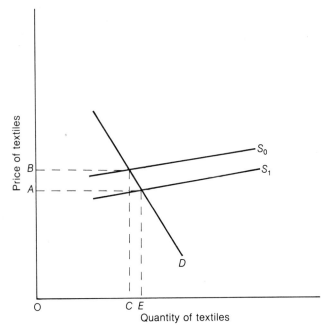

Figure 17-1. Elasticity and Quantity Demanded.

In Figure 17-1, demand is relatively inelastic. Where supply increases from $S_0$ to $S_1$, price falls from 0B to 0A. This fall in price is much larger than the increase in quantity that takes place from C to E.

Compounding the problem of general stagnation was the marked shift of textile production into the noncoal Appalachian South. Textile mills were created in North Carolina, Virginia, and Georgia in response to their cheaper labor costs, both as to wages and regulation of hours of work. Most of the 39% increase in wage earners in that region in the 1920s was due to textile employment. Only the northern mills with exceptionally good management, or those with special advantages, escaped the effects of the move south.

## The United States and the World Economy

Fundamental changes had occurred during the war and as a result of the Peace Treaty of 1919. The shift of the United States from a net debtor to a net creditor position, and the large amounts of the war debts owed the United States plus the impossibly high levels of reparations to several countries demanded from a defeated Germany, required fundamental changes in the international economy. The adjustments made in financing international economic transactions during the 1920s seemed, on the surface, to keep international activity stable, an agreement that scaled **down** the yearly reparations payments by Germany, especially after the Dawes Plan of 1924. But by the end of the decade it became apparent that this stability was easily shaken.

Table 17-2 shows that for 1919 private net assets (what U.S. residents were owed minus what U.S. residents owed others) were almost $3 billion in the United States' favor, plus $9.6 billion in net debt owed to the U.S. government. The net government debt was primarily war debts owed by the Allies. At the same time, the Allies (excluding the United States) demanded reparation payments from Germany. The Reparations Commission in 1921 set these payments at $375 million a year from 1921 to 1925 and afterward at $900 million a year. In order to pay these debts, a profound change would have to take place in international economic relations.

Table 17-2. America's International Balance Sheet (billions of dollars).

|  | 1914 | 1919 | 1929 |
|---|---|---|---|
| Assets (private account) | | | |
| Securities | .9 | 2.6 | 7.9 |
| Direct investments | 2.6 | 3.9 | 7.6 |
| Short-term credits | — | .5 | 1.6 |
| Total | 3.5 | 7.0 | 17.1 |
| Liabilities | | | |
| Securities | 5.4 | 1.6 | 4.3 |
| Direct investments | 1.3 | .9 | 1.4 |
| Sequestrated properties and securities | — | .7 | .2 |
| Short-term credits | .5 | .8 | 3.1 |
| Total | 7.2 | 4.0 | 9.0 |
| Net assets privately held | − 3.7 | 3.0 | 8.1 |
| Intergovernmental debts | | | |
| to the United States government | — | 10.0 | 11.7 |
| by the United States government | — | .4 | — |
| Net assets on government account | | 9.6 | 11.7 |
| Total net assets on private and government account | − 3.7 | 12.6 | 19.8 |

*Source:* Cleona Lewis, *America's Stake in International Investments* (Washington, D.C.: Brookings Institution), 1938, pp. 447–450.

One way in which these loans could be paid back was for the debtor countries to increase their exports of goods and services to the creditor country (here, the United States). In effect, then, the United States would need to increase imports of goods and services from its former allies in order for the latter to be able to pay off war debts. Instead, the United States increased its already high tariffs. The Emergency Tariff of 1921 and the Fordney-McCumber Tariff Act of 1922 pushed tariffs to all-time highs on a wide variety of imports. It was unlikely that the United States would voluntarily decrease its exports to reduce this drain on European foreign exchange, and also the U.S. invisible items account remained with a credit balance, further drawing foreign exchange from Europe as the flow of dividends, profits, and interest from U.S. foreign investment more than offset U.S. tourist expenditures in Europe. The Allies were following a similar policy with Germany, so that what little surplus Germany could generate was not enough to meet reparation payments in 1922.

Another way in which these war debts and reparations could be dealt with was to cancel them. England perceived the seriousness of the international money problems by 1921, and it was willing to cancel both reparations from Germany and the substantial debt owed to England by the other European Allies if, in turn, the United States would cancel the war debts owed by England to it. Instead, the U.S. government demanded payment. A more sensible arrangement was made under the Dawes Plan in 1924. But this happened only after Germany had defaulted on reparations, France had taken over the industrial Ruhr area in Germany, and Germany's hyperinflation in 1922–1923 had made its assets worthless in fixed money values. Economic chaos had preceded the Dawes Plan.

As a result, reparations payments were scaled down. Further negotiations between the former Allies and the United States reduced the interest rate on war debts from 5% to 3%. In effect, it reduced, for example, the debt by 30% for England and over 80% for Italy. But war debt and reparation payments still had to be made. In addition to government debt relations, the private net credit position of the United States required payments of interest, profit, and dividends that could not be made while the United States remained in a credit position in the balance of payments merchandise account.

The answer was largely found through foreign investment by the United States. The private net creditor position increased from the $3 billion position in 1919 to over $8 billion in 1929 (see Table 17-2). Although direct investment increased from $3.9 to $7.6 billion, securities bought by Americans increased even more—from $2.6 to $7.9 billion. Private investment, mostly in Germany and, because of the multilateral nature of international trade, in Latin America, provided the foreign exchange for Germany to pay reparations to the European Allies, which in turn provided them with the exchange to pay the U.S. government on their war debts. In effect, then, there was no net reduction of international debts with the United States but rather a shift from government debt relationships to private investments and to private means of international payments.

These relationships would not have threatened stability so much if they had been productively used so that increased productive facilities would provide the surplus to repay the investments. George Soule[23] concludes that securities investments were used so that "Many of the loans were not used for productive purposes or were made to countries that would have difficulty in making repayments if the flow of new capital would stop, since they could not be expected to develop an export surplus. Germany was in this category." Furthermore, Soule charged that American investment companies were more interested in the profits from floating these loans than in their repayment.

Direct investment had a better record in regard to the security of the investments. Most of the direct investments were controlled by the larger corporations with international business relations and were used to provide sources of raw materials and semifinished goods for U.S. production or to jump the tariff walls of many countries by producing finished goods within the tariff-protected economy. These investments had ample evidence of their potential profitability. Soule concludes, however, that even with direct investment a sizable minority were also of doubtful profitability.

In brief, the problem caused by the war debts and reparations repayments should have been resolved either by cancellation or by increases in exports from the debtor countries to the creditor countries. Neither alternative was allowed to operate to the point of resolving the questions with stability. Instead, the U.S. government encouraged increases in foreign investment of U.S. citizens to provide the foreign exchange needed. Some of this investment, especially in securities, was unstable; that is, with poor prospects of being repaid. A circular pattern was created as private investment from the United States provided the foreign exchange for the European Allies to pay war debts to the U.S. government. Rather than reducing the overall levels of debt, government debt relationships were converted into private debt. The process could only continue if private U.S. investors continued their foreign investment at ever-increasing rates to cover war debt and reparations repayments plus the servicing of a growing private investment. But if private U.S. foreign investment decreased, the process would not only collapse but would also seriously impair private international means of payments.

Investments in foreign securities began to fall by the middle of 1928, as the unprofitability of many of the investments became apparent and as U.S. corporate securities increased in price on Wall Street. The decrease was hidden by increases in foreign direct investment. With the onset of the depression in June 1929 and the stock market crash in the following October, U.S. foreign investments collapsed, as did imports from Europe. Not only did the circular system of capital movements evaporate, but also the international means of private payments were seriously impaired.

# The Decline of Organized Labor

The successes of labor unions since the founding of the American Federation of Labor (AFL) in 1886, at least in terms of the number of union members, had been impressive up to 1920. Although this increase in union members was not uniform but proceeded in fits and starts, union membership rose from 0.3 million in 1870–1872 to 0.9 million in 1900, to a high point of 5 million in 1920, as estimated by Leo Wolman.[25] Of these 5 million, about 4 million were members of the American Federation of Labor.

With the onset of the 1920s, the upward trend was sharply reversed. By 1929, total union membership had declined to 3.5 million, with only 3 million in the AFL. While most of this drop came early in the decade—by 1923, only 3.6 million members remained in unions—there was hardly a year in the 1920s that did not see a decline in union membership.

The largest gains in union membership had occurred during the war, as full employment and government production planning created a favorable environment for union expansion. Following the war, these industries saw the largest contraction in union membership as output and employment fell. But traditional strongholds of unionization also had trouble maintaining membership.

The United Mine Workers were especially hard hit as stagnant demand, overproduction, and strong antiunion activity by employers reduced UMW membership. The Textile Union was also hard hit, as productive capacity moved from the Northeast, a stronghold of unionism, to the Southeast, where antiunion public sentiment was very strong.

There were a number of reasons for this decline. One of the more important was the unsympathetic and basically antiunion position of the U.S. courts in general and the U.S. Supreme Court in particular. When the Republicans returned to power with the election of President Harding in 1920, the senate confirmed former president Taft as chief justice of the Supreme Court. Taft was a strong opponent of unions, and his leadership intensified the antiunion attitude of the court in the 1920s. But even prior to 1920 a number of decisions adverse to unions had already been made. Two examples of substantial importance were the Danbury Hat case of 1908 and *Hitchman Coal and Coke* v. *Mitchell* in 1917. In the first case, the Supreme Court ruled that the individual members of the union were liable without limit for monetary damages resulting from the actions of their union officials. In the Hitchman case, the Supreme Court enjoined the United Mine Workers from attempting to organize workers who had signed a "yellow-dog contract" (a pledge by the workers not to join a union).

In the 1920s, with Taft as chief justice, the Supreme Court ruled consistently against unions. Two areas of special difficulty were the use of the injunction to abridge union activities and the court's interpretations and use of antitrust legislation to condemn as illegal many actions of unions. Irving Bernstein[1] in *The Lean Years* points out that "At the end of the twenties the leading students of labor law were in accord that the marriage of the labor injunction with the yellow-dog contract was a peril to the survival of trade unionism in the United States." In the decade of the 1920s, 921 injunctions limiting union activities were issued by federal and state courts, half of the total injunctions of that kind issued from 1845 to 1930. By 1929, a union had to presume that an injunction would be issued if any strike was called.

Despite the seeming exemption of unions from antitrust legislation in the Clayton Act of 1914, the Taft Court in the 1920s used the Sherman Act of 1890 to judge such actions as strikes, picketing, and boycotts as illegal restraint of trade. Taft found that the Clayton Act only stated that unions in themselves were not a conspiracy, but what they did was. Besides interfering in union activities, these rulings laid unions open to monetary damages and the possibility of criminal prosecution. Bernstein's[1] conclusion about the courts in the 1920s was summarized thus: "The law recognized the equal freedom of the employers to destroy labor organizations and to deny the rights of employees to join trade unions."

Another important factor in the decline of labor unionism in the 1920s was the antiunion activities of employers beyond the courts and the yellow-dog contract. An important weapon was the use of the **company union,** where membership was only for employees of the particular firm and was dominated by company officials. The trade unions' attitude toward these organizations is mirrored in the words of an old union song: "The Hatmakers union is a no good union. It's a company union for the boss."

The spread of welfare capitalism and an increased effort to have employees buy stock in the firm undermined union loyalty and increased employee company loyalty. Major companies had programs to provide full medical care, educational projects, encourage workers to own their own homes, stock sharing, and especially forms of group insurance and pensions. Although humanitarian motives were involved, Scheiber and his associates[21] conclude that the main motivations were antiunion.

Equally important in reducing the strength of unions in the 1920s was the severe antiunion atmosphere among the general public. The Bolshevik revolution, which occurred in Russia in 1917, and other revolutions and revolts in Europe in 1919, especially in Germany and Hungary, created in the United States an atmosphere of fear of the "Red Menace" (communism). The wave of strikes in 1919 and 1920 convinced many that unions were somehow un-American. These strikes, generally made to resist declines in wages, often failed. For example, the Railroad Strike of 1919, the Great Steel Strike of 1919, and the coal miners' strike of 1920 all terminated unfavorably to the unions. In 1919, there were nine major industrial strikes, and more than 4 million workers were on strike.

Adding to these problems were some basic flaws in the union camp itself. The craft orientation of the AFL continued to limit the ability of organized labor to unionize the major mass production industries such as steel, autos, and petroleum refining. In addition, Samuel Gompers, who had dominated the AFL with his organizational genius since its founding in 1886, died in the early 1920s. The new leadership was far less competent and was much too cautious for the trying conditions facing labor unions in the 1920s.

# The Beginning of the End

A detailed analysis of the causes and the sequence of events of the Great Depression of the 1930s must await the next chapter. But that human and social catastrophe started in 1929. The two main supports of the 1920s expansion—construction and manufacturing, especially of that major consumer durable, automobiles—were contracting output by June 1929. Foreign investment also was contracting in 1929.

The value of construction reached its high point, over $17 billion, in 1928, and declined to a little over $16 billion in 1929. George Soule[23] comments about the auto industry: "The final burst of prosperity in 1929 brought a gain of 19 percent, but output began to fall off several months before the stock market crash. The index of industrial production reached a high of 188 (1913 = 100) in June of 1929 and began to fall."

The signs were there. The sustained investment that accumulated productive capital from 1923 to 1929 was now approaching a point of producing more than consumers would buy. The weakening of output in construction, autos, and manufacturing in general was added to the near-decade-long weaknesses in coal mining, agriculture, textiles, and railroads. Some significant contraction was imminent. But no one seemed to notice. A wave of speculative expansion on the stock exchanges maintained optimism and diverted attention from the growing signs of economic difficulty.

## Wall Street, 1929

The 1920s are an excellent example of speculative tendencies in the American people. The decade opened with speculation in normal business inventories. That bubble broke when prices fell with the depression of 1920–1921. In 1925, there was the Florida land speculation, as people bought land in Florida at rapidly increasing prices. In the end here, too, values collapsed, and many lost their investments. In late 1928 through

Wall Street of the 1920s. (Photo no. 306-NT-168310C in the National Archives)

October 1929, broad sections of stocks listed on the New York Stock Exchange increased rapidly in price. On October 24, 1929, these prices collapsed, and the great stock market crash of 1929 entered history.

Many trace the origins of the boom in stock prices to efforts of the Federal Reserve to support the faltering English pound in 1928 by reducing interest rates in the United States. These lower interest rates and the greater availability of credit increased the demand for stocks on the call market of the stock exchanges; that is, where stocks were purchased on margin, or through the borrowing of significant portions of their purchase price. This higher demand increased stock prices, and these rises in prices caused people to expand their demand in anticipation of even further price increases. Thus, the process snowballed.

By September 1929, the prices of stocks were too high to be justified by their earnings. A contraction in the economy had already started with the decrease in construction in 1928 and a decrease in manufacturing in June of 1929. By October 24, the high stock prices could no longer be maintained, and the market crumbled. The collapse was intensified because of the high proportion of securities purchased on margin, borrowing the bulk of the purchase price, and, when prices collapsed, the selling of these securities to protect lenders.

Briefly, the stock market collapse intensified the already developing contraction in a number of ways. First, the stock market had always been a very important measure of what the public thought was the state of the economy. When stock prices rose in the first three quarters of 1929, people felt very optimistic. But the gathering signs of a contraction were ignored, and consumption and investment demand were probably higher than would have existed without the stock market expansion. After the crash and the collapse of stock prices, the public became pessimistic, discouraged about prospects for high levels of economic activity. This pessimism probably caused lower levels of consumption and investment.

Second, the prime economic function of the stock exchanges was to facilitate the issuance of new stock to raise financial capital needed by corporations to expand productive capacity. With the collapse of stock prices, obtaining new financial capital became difficult and costly. No doubt this contributed to the decline in investment and added to the decrease in aggregate demand and total income in the economy.

Third, the crash dried up the flow of U.S. financial capital to Germany that funded the circular flow of reparations payments from Germany to the former Allies, that in turn flowed back to the United States as war debt repayments. If the circular flow had been confined to payments between governments, little economic damage would have resulted; but unfortunately the payments had been intertwined with private means of international payments, and these private payments were seriously impaired. The results weakened the international exchange system and decreased international trade. This decrease in international trade further decreased worldwide demand and, thus, output, income, and employment.

Finally, the decline in stock prices reduced the financial wealth of stockholders. Being now "poorer," these investors tended to decrease their consumption.

# Conclusion

Were the 1920s a period of prosperity built on a bed of quicksand, or were they a decade of new beginnings, a predecessor of the modern era that was to blossom after 1945 and the end of World War II? The question has not yet been resolved.

On the one hand, W. Elliot Brownlee,[2] in *Dynamics of Ascent*, titles his chapter on the 1920s, "The 1920s: A Glimpse of Modernity." He states,

> To understand the economy during the 1920s, we should view it, not as a sick decade, full of foreshadowings of the depression to follow, but as a period that bears a strong resemblance to the best years of the post-World War II era in its rising standards of living, sustained high employment, stable prices,

and strong market for articles of mass consumption. Despite our retrospective awareness that a major depression was to follow, the prosperity was unprecedented and was sustained from 1922 through much of 1929, with only modest pauses in 1924 and 1927.

On the other hand, Scheiber, Vatter, and Faulkner, in *American Economic History*,[21] in the chapter on the 1920s, "The Great Illusion," state,

Not all economists of the era were willing to grant unreservedly that this decade was a period of prosperity. Prosperity, if such it was, was exceedingly uneven, for it did not include all sections or all groups. Coal mining, cotton manufacturing, shipbuilding, the shoe and leather business, the railroads, and particularly agriculture were stagnant or declining. The Middle Atlantic, East-North-Central, and Pacific states seemed prosperous; but New England, which suffered from the textile depression, and the South, the agricultural areas of the Middle West, and the mountain sections, which suffered from the virtual failure of farm output to grow, did not participate greatly in the economic boom. Even in the most prosperous of these years, there was considerable unemployment, due in part to technological improvements. Indeed, it is a striking fact that manufacturing employment was constant from 1919 to 1929, despite a strong rise in the index of manufacturing production.

These were not the only sour notes in the paean of self-congratulatory praise. Some students were quick to point out that, notwithstanding the increase in profits, in wages, and in the consumption of consumers' goods, practically no progress was being made in solving the problems of unemployment or of economic and old-age security. Moreover, the move for gambling and speculation was a warning signal to the experienced economic navigator.

However, the debate cannot be oversimplified as optimism versus pessimism. One must integrate both positions, because both give insight into the economic nature of that decade and into the future—the Great Depression of the 1930s and also the expansion of the post-1945 period.

# Glossary

**Company union** A union whose membership consists only of the employees of a particular firm and that is dominated by that firm's officials.

**Parity** A measure to express the purchasing power of farm products. It compares an index of farm prices to an index of the prices of what farmers buy.

**Primary demand**  The initial demand for a product stemming from those who had never before bought the product.

# Questions

1. What factors expanded the economy from the end of World War I to the end of 1920?

2. What factors contributed to the depression of 1921? What was the role of inventory speculation?

3. Why did agricultural prices fall more than industrial prices during the depression of 1921?

4. What were the various ways in which expanded auto production and use affected the economy in the 1920s?

5. What were the major factors expanding the demand for consumer durables other than autos in the 1920s?

6. What factors contributed to the high levels of demand for construction during the 1920s?

7. How were the productivity gains of the 1920s distributed between business, labor, and consumers? Was this distribution favorable to the expansion of the 1920s? Why?

8. Why did agriculture fail to share in the general prosperity of the 1920s?

9. Was the legislative relief given to agriculture in 1929 a wise move? Why, or why not?

10. Why did coal mining fail to share in the general prosperity of the 1920s?

11. What were the factors that restricted the growth of output in the railroad industry in the 1920s? What was expected of the Transportation Act of 1920? Was it achieved? Why?

12. What were the various ways that reparation payments and war debts could be paid off? What was the way chosen in the 1920s? Was this a wise method of payment? Why?

13. A number of factors contributed to the contraction in union membership in the 1920s. What were they?

14. In what ways did the stock market crash in 1929 intensify the contraction of 1929?

15. Take either position, that of Brownlee or that of Scheiber, Vatter, and Faulkner, as to the essence of the 1920s, and defend it.

# Suggested Readings

1.  Bernstein, Irving. *The Lean Years: A History of the American Worker, 1920–1933.* Boston: Houghton Mifflin, 1960.

2.  Brownlee, W. Elliott. *Dynamics of Ascent.* New York: Knopf, 1974. Esp. Chap. 12.

3.  Chandler, Alfred D., Jr. *Strategy and Structure: Chapters in the History of American Industrial Enterprise.* Cambridge, Mass.: M.I.T. Press, 1962.

4.  Cochrane, Thomas C. *The American Business System, 1900–1955.* Cambridge, Mass.: Harvard University Press, 1965.

5.  Feis, Herbert. *The Diplomacy of the Dollar, 1919–1932.* Baltimore: Johns Hopkins University Press, 1965.

6.  Friedman, Milton, and Schwartz, Anna J. *A Monetary History of the United States 1867–1960.* Princeton, N.J.: Princeton University Press, 1963.

7.  Galbraith, John Kenneth. *The Great Crash.* Boston: Houghton Mifflin, 1955.

8.  George, P. J., and Oksanen, E. H. "Saturation in the Automobile Market in the Late Twenties: Some Further Results." *Explorations in Economic History, 11* (Fall 1973).

9.  Gordon, Robert A. *Economic Instability and Growth: The American Record.* New York: Harper & Row, 1974.

10. Hoogenboom, Ari, and Hoogenboom, Oliver. *A History of the ICC from Panacea to Palliative.* New York: Norton, 1976. Esp. Chap. 3.

11. Keller, Robert. "Factor Income Distribution in the United States During the 1920s: A Reexamination of Fact and Theory." *Journal of Economic History, 33* (March 1973).

12. Leuchtenbury, W. E. *The Perils of Prosperity, 1914–1932.* Chicago: University of Chicago Press, 1958.

13. Lewis, Cleona. *America's Stake in International Investments.* Washington, D.C.: Brookings Institution, 1938.

14. Lewis, W. Arthur. *Economic Survey, 1919–1939.* London: Allen & Unwin, 1949.

15. Lorant, John H. "Technological Change in American Manufacturing During the 1920s." *Journal of Economic History, 27* (June 1967).

16. Mercer, Lloyd J., and Morgan, W. Douglas. "Alternative Interpretations of Market Saturation: Evaluations for the Automobile Market in the Late Twenties." *Explorations in Economic History, 9* (Spring 1972).

17. Perlemen, Selig, and Taft, Philip. *History of Labor in the United States, 1896–1932.* New York: Macmillan, 1935. Esp. Chaps. 37–44.

18. Potter, James. *The American Economy Between the World Wars.* New York: Macmillan, 1974.

19. Rae, John B. *The American Automobile: A Brief History.* Chicago: University of Chicago Press, 1965. Esp. Chaps. 6 and 7.

20. Rothbard, Murray. *America's Great Depression.* Kansas City, Kansas: Sheed and Ward, 1972.

21. Scheiber, Harry N., Vatter, Harold G., and Faulkner, Harold A. *American Economic History.* New York: Harper & Row, 1976. Esp. Chap. 21.

22. Schumpeter, J. A. "The Decade of the Twenties." *American Economic Review,* Supplement (May 1946).

23. Soule, George. *Prosperity Decade: From War to Depression, 1917–1929.* New York: Holt, Rinehart and Winston, 1947.

24. U.S. Department of Commerce, Bureau of the Census. *Historical Statistics of the United States, Colonial Times to 1970.* Washington, D.C.: U.S. Government Printing Office, 1975.

25. Wolman, Leo. *The Growth of American Trade Unions, 1880–1923.* New York: National Bureau of Economic Research, 1924.

# Chapter **18**

# The Great Depression of the 1930s

The end of the 1920s "prosperity decade" was the beginning of the unparalleled economic disaster of the 1930s. Never before in the history of the United States had the economy suffered such a severe and prolonged depression. Never before had it taken so long to recover to former levels of output.

## Gross National Product

The value of all final goods and services produced annually fell from a high of $104.4 billion in 1929 to a low of $55.6 billion in 1933 (Table 18–1). Even when the data are adjusted for the fall in prices, real output declined by about 25% (Table 18–2). It was not until 1937 (Table 18–2) that the economy would recover to its 1929 level of output. Unemployment rose from 3.2% of the labor force in 1929 to a high of almost 25% in 1933 (Table 18–4). In addition, in 1933 almost another 25% of the labor force was only partially employed. Unemployment was still about 10% when the United States entered World War II on December 7, 1941.

Net private domestic investment, which is especially important in providing increases in capacity and therefore the ability to increase output, was particularly hard hit. In 1929, it stood at $8.3 billion (Table 18–1). By 1933, it had dropped to minus $5.6 billion. This meant that the economy had not even replaced worn-out capital equipment. The total stock of capital, the machines, and factory buildings needed to produce output, had decreased $5.6 billion. In 1937, net private domestic investment was still only $4.6 billion.

Table 18-1. Current GNP and Selected Components 1929 to 1939 (billions of dollars).

|  | Gross National Product | Consumption | Net Investment | Construction |
|---|---|---|---|---|
| 1929 | $104.4 | $79.0 | $8.3 | $8.7 |
| 1930 | 90.4 | 69.9 | 2.1 | 8.7 |
| 1931 | 75.8 | 60.5 | −2.2 | 6.4 |
| 1932 | 58.0 | 48.6 | −6.3 | 3.5 |
| 1933 | 55.6 | 45.8 | −5.6 | 2.9 |
| 1934 | 65.1 | 51.3 | −3.6 | 3.7 |
| 1935 | 72.2 | 55.7 | −0.4 | 4.2 |
| 1936 | 82.5 | 61.9 | 1.4 | 6.5 |
| 1937 | 90.4 | 66.5 | 4.6 | 7.0 |
| 1938 | 84.7 | 63.9 | −6.6 | 7.0 |
| 1939 | 90.5 | 66.8 | −4.0 | 8.2 |

*Source:* U.S. Department of Commerce, Bureau of the Census, *Historical Statistics of the United States, Colonial Times to 1970* (Washington, D.C.: U.S. Government Printing Office, 1975).

Table 18-2. Real GNP and Selected Components 1929 to 1939 (billions of 1929 dollars).

|  | Consumption | Gross Investment | Construction | Gross National Product |
|---|---|---|---|---|
| 1929 | 79.0 | 16.2 | 8.7 | 104.4 |
| 1930 | 74.7 | 10.5 | 6.4 | 95.1 |
| 1931 | 72.2 | 6.8 | 4.5 | 89.5 |
| 1932 | 66.0 | 0.8 | 2.4 | 76.4 |
| 1933 | 64.6 | 0.3 | 1.9 | 74.4 |
| 1934 | 68.0 | 1.8 | 2.0 | 80.8 |
| 1935 | 72.3 | 8.8 | 2.8 | 91.4 |
| 1936 | 79.7 | 9.3 | 3.9 | 100.9 |
| 1937 | 82.6 | 14.6 | 4.6 | 109.1 |
| 1938 | 81.3 | 6.8 | 4.1 | 103.2 |
| 1939 | 85.9 | 9.9 | 4.9 | 111.0 |

*Source:* U.S. Department of Commerce, Bureau of the Census, *Historical Statistics of the United States, Colonial Times to 1970* (Washington, D.C.: U.S. Government Printing Office, 1975).

Table 18-3. Government Fiscal Operations (billions of dollars), 1929–1939.

| | Total Government Debt | Federal Receipts | Federal Expenditures | Federal Deficits | State and Local Deficits and Surpluses |
|---|---|---|---|---|---|
| 1929 | 16.9 | 3.9 | 3.1 | +0.7 | — |
| 1930 | 16.2 | 4.1 | 3.3 | +0.7 | — |
| 1931 | 16.8 | 3.1 | 3.6 | −0.5 | — |
| 1932 | 20.8 | 1.9 | 4.7 | −2.7 | — |
| 1933 | 23.6 | 2.0 | 4.6 | −2.5 | −0.2 |
| 1934 | 28.5 | 3.0 | 6.6 | −3.6 | −2.3 |
| 1935 | 30.6 | 3.7 | 6.5 | −2.9 | +1.5 |
| 1936 | 34.4 | 4.0 | 8.4 | −4.4 | −1.0 |
| 1937 | 37.3 | 5.0 | 7.7 | −2.8 | +1.5 |
| 1938 | 39.4 | 5.6 | 6.7 | −1.2 | +0.7 |
| 1939 | 41.9 | 5.0 | 8.8 | −3.9 | −1.3 |

*Source:* U.S. Department of Commerce, Bureau of the Census, *Historical Statistics of the United States, Colonial Times to 1970* (Washington, D.C.: U.S. Government Printing Office, 1975).

Table 18-4. Unemployment and Consumer Prices, 1929 to 1939 (1929 = 100).

| | Unemployment Rate | GNP Price Deflator |
|---|---|---|
| 1929 | 3.2 | 100 |
| 1930 | 8.7 | 96 |
| 1931 | 15.9 | 85 |
| 1932 | 23.6 | 77 |
| 1933 | 24.9 | 75 |
| 1934 | 21.7 | 80 |
| 1935 | 20.1 | 79 |
| 1936 | 16.9 | 82 |
| 1937 | 14.3 | 83 |
| 1938 | 19.0 | 83 |
| 1939 | 17.2 | 82 |

*Source:* U.S. Department of Commerce, Bureau of the Census, *Historical Statistics of the United States, Colonial Times to 1970* (Washington, D.C.: U.S. Government Printing Office, 1975).

# The Causes

The economy was beginning to contract before the stock market crash in October 1929. By June 1929, demand for autos and general manufactured goods had begun to decline. The index of manufacturing production reached 188 in June and then began to fall. Primary demand on the part of those who had not purchased autos and other consumer durables had been temporarily satisfied. Replacement demand, or **secondary demand,** had not yet reached levels that could sustain demand.

These decreases in consumer demand created a negative accelerator (see Review of Economic Concepts Chapter 13) as induced investment (facilities needed to expand output to meet expanding demand) fell. Thus, contraction in investment involved not only the auto and other consumer durable industries but also the various industries that provided materials for their production such as steel and other metals, rubber, glass, and textiles.

Residential construction, the second major prop to the prosperity of the 1920s, had begun to crumble before 1929. The industry had been saturated by 1926, although business construction continued to expand the total of all construction until the middle of 1927. By June 1929, both of these segments of construction had substantial excess capacity.

Rising profits and profit margins, obtained in part by business firms retaining much of the advantages of rising productivity, were beneficial during the 1920s. They maintained optimism and encouraged continued investment. But as demand began to decrease after June 1929, these increased profit margins became a liability to the general economy. There was insufficient purchasing power to purchase the increased output. Put in Keynesian terms, the large savings caused by the widening of the profit margins reduced consumption demand. As investment fell, aggregate demand, income, and output also fell.

At the very least, the economy was in for a severe contraction. However, a number of aggravating factors turned this contraction into a major decline.

## Weak Spots in the Economy

Chapter 17 noted that several industries did not share in the prosperity of the 1920s. As the contraction developed, these industries could not provide any compensating offset in aggregate demand. These industries included the textile areas, especially in New England; agriculture, especially the agricultural South, corn belt, and mountain states; coal, especially the soft coal areas of western Pennsylvania, West Virginia, Kentucky, and Tennessee; and the railway industry in general.

## The Stock Market Crash of 1929

Beginning in 1928, there was an accelerated increase in prices of corporate securities on the New York Stock Exchange. The *New York Times* industrial averages increased from 245 at the beginning of 1928 to 452 on September 3, 1929. These price increases, although based primarily on an expectation of further price increases, became much too high to be justified by current earnings. A collapse of the price expectations and of stock prices was inevitable. On October 24, 1929, the stock market declined by over 30 points on the *New York Times* index, but this was only a preview of the future. The market continued to fall until it reached a *New York Times* industrial average of 58 on July 8, 1933.

It is important to keep in mind that the contraction in the economy had begun before the stock market decline. The decline of the market seriously aggravated the developing depression. Perhaps the most important effect of the market crash on the contracting economy was psychological. Many people used the relative state of the stock market as an indicator of the health or lack thereof of the general economy. The disastrous decline of corporate securities prices created more strongly pessimistic expectations about the future of the economy than conditions warranted. This further reduced investment and accelerated the contraction.

A second effect of the crash was to further decrease the availability of investment funds for capital formation. One function of the stock exchanges was to make it easier for corporations to raise financial capital by issuing stocks. With the progressive collapse of the stock market, this function evaporated. Since much of corporate investment apparently came from retained earnings, the significance of this effect is questionable.

A third effect involved the international means of payments and foreign trade. Remember, from Chapter 17, that the United States had become a net creditor nation, in part by making war loans to the Allies. To avoid canceling war debts or to avoid the need to increase imports to provide the foreign exchange to pay the debts, the U.S. government encouraged private U.S. citizens to invest in foreign countries. This was especially true of Germany, so that it might obtain the foreign exchange necessary to pay reparations to the Allies, who in turn might make payments to the United States on their own war debts.

This circular system was beginning to encounter difficulties prior to the crash. U.S. foreign investment had already begun to fall by the beginning of 1929. The collapse of the stock exchanges caused foreign investment to virtually disappear. The circular flow evaporated as Germany ceased reparation payments. The adverse effect of this on world and U.S. economic activity stemmed from the intertwining of the circular system with the international private means of payments. As these payments became significantly impaired, international trade and investments contracted, decreasing U.S. and world output.

A fourth way in which the collapse of stock prices affected the economy was through decreases in consumption by those who were affected by the decreases in the prices of their securities. A reduction of financial wealth in this manner on the one hand reduces purchasing power, forcing decreases in consumption, and on the other hand makes stockholders feel poorer and encourages them to cut back on consumption. Many writers minimize the indirect effect of the crash on consumption. Those who actually suffered losses were a minority of the population, even a minority of the middle class. But, whatever the total amount of the effect was, it was in the direction of contracting consumption demand.

Finally, the collapse of the stock market seriously undermined the financial security of broad sections of the banking system, especially the New York banks. Before the crash, call market loans amounted to over $8 billion; over half of this came from banks. The share of call loans held by banks increased during the crash—banks were forced to replace funds nonbanks withdrew as the panic developed, to try to prevent total collapse. At times, stock prices fell so fast that banks could not cover their loans by sales of securities. The margins on call loans were as low as 10% (that is, the purchaser of the security paid only 10%, and the bank lent 90%). Despite the high interest rate (10%) on the call market, the collapse caused significant losses to a number of banks.

## The Banking Crises of 1930-1933

Starting in 1929, the crisis-ridden U.S. banking system gave the deepening depression an additional series of blows. The first banking crisis occurred in November and December 1930, when bank failures increased in the agricultural states of Missouri, Indiana, Iowa, Arkansas, and North Carolina. These, plus the failure of the Bank of the United States of New York, caused people to increase their holdings of currency and to reduce deposits. Some banks were not able to withstand the withdrawals.

Peter Temin[21] describes the money hypothesis about the great contraction of 1929 to 1933 in these terms: "The assumption is that the banking panics turned a short depression into a sustained decline in national income." If variations in the supply of money are more important than variations in aggregate demand in causing the depression, then these banking panics must be independent of contractions in aggregate demand. The panics in 1930 were the first and thus the most crucial. According to Temin,[21] falling agricultural prices and deepening depression in farm areas were the primary causes for these failures. These bank failures, then, were caused by the developing depression and were not the cause of the depression, as suggested by Friedman and Schwartz.[8] Nonetheless, bank failures aggravated and worsened the depression.

The late 1930 panic resulted in the failure of banks that held $600 million, or 3% of the U.S. supply of money. In March 1931, the second banking panic took place. Bank failures continued, the worst wave occurring in 1933. When President Franklin Delano Roosevelt took office, he declared a three-day bank holiday, closing all banks.

Perhaps the most devastating effect of this almost three-year wave of bank failures was the decrease in the supply of money. It decreased by about one-third from 1929 to 1933 (Table 18-5). Part of this decrease came from the failure of banks. When they closed, their deposits were no longer available to serve as part of the supply of money. Also, as bankers became afraid that panic withdrawals of deposits in the form of currency would occur, they reduced their lending both for new loans and for loan renewal, in order to increase their reserves or liquidity. This contraction of loans not only reduced deposits created through lending and thus reduced the supply of money, but also equally important, it reduced the availability of credit for investment, as well as for consumption. The effect of both was to decrease the level of economic activity and to deepen the depression.

---

Table 18-5. $M_1$ Supply of Money (Currency in Circulation and Demand Deposits) 1929–1939 (billions of dollars).

| Year | $M_1$ Money | Year | $M_1$ Money |
|------|-------------|------|-------------|
| 1929 | 26.4 | 1935 | 25.5 |
| 1930 | 25.4 | 1936 | 29.2 |
| 1931 | 23.6 | 1937 | 30.3 |
| 1932 | 20.6 | 1938 | 30.0 |
| 1933 | 19.4 | 1939 | 33.6 |
| 1934 | 21.5 | | |

Source: M. Friedman and A. J. Schwartz, *A Monetary History of the United States, 1867–1960* (Princeton, N.J.: Princeton University Press, 1963), Table A-1, pp. 709–716.

---

We know, from the familiar equation of exchange ($MV = PQ$), that a decrease in the supply of money ($M$) and a decrease in velocity ($V$) will decrease prices ($P$) and also output ($Q$). And in fact prices declined by 24% from 1929 to 1933, and real output fell by about 25% in the same period.

But the widespread failure of banks also had other effects. First, large amounts of people's deposits became valueless as banks failed. This had a depressing effect on consumer demand. Second, these failures created a depressed psychological outlook, as the banking system and the whole economy seemed on the verge of total collapse. Postponable consumption and investment were deferred.

## International Trade

As devastating as the statistics were for declines in domestic output and employment, the collapse of international trade, which can be seen in Table 18–6, was even more dramatic. U.S. exports fell from $5.2 billion in 1929 to $1.6 billion in 1932. U.S. imports experienced a similar decline during the same period, from $4.4 billion to $1.3 billion. Growing depression in European countries decreased their demand for U.S. exports, depressing U.S. output and employment.

Table 18-6. U.S. Exports and Imports (millions of dollars).

| Year | Exports | Imports |
|------|---------|---------|
| 1929 | $5241 | $4399 |
| 1930 | 3843 | 3061 |
| 1931 | 2424 | 2091 |
| 1932 | 1611 | 1323 |

*Source:* U.S. Department of Commerce, Bureau of the Census, *Historical Statistics of the United States, Colonial Times to 1970* (Washington, D.C.: U.S. Government Printing Office, 1975).

The collapse of U.S. foreign investment after the stock market crash in 1929 partly explains the decrease in U.S. exports, since some of the dollars were used to finance the export surplus from the United States. Generally, however, falling demand due to the developing depression in both the United States and the rest of the world accounts for a great deal of the decline in international trade. Making matters even worse was the passage of the Smoot-Hawley Tariff of 1930, which raised U.S. tariffs and touched off a wave of retaliatory protectionism in Europe.

Aggravating the situation further were developing difficulties in the international financial markets. As we have already noted, the cessation of foreign investment with the collapse of the New York Stock Exchange dried up sources of foreign exchange for German payments of reparations. In 1931, Germany defaulted on reparation payments. Although President Hoover arranged for temporary suspension of reparation and war debt payments, tightening credit in England caused many Austrian and German banks to close, and caused those countries to abandon the gold standard. Britain abandoned the gold standard soon after, and the United States followed suit in 1933. The multinational payments system collapsed as na-

tions jockeyed for favored positions through **"beggar thy neighbor"
policies.** These were programs designed to increase exports while decreasing imports, for the purpose of increasing domestic employment.

## A Recap

The depression began in mid-1929 with declines in manufacturing output, construction, and investment in plant and equipment. A series of aggravating forces appeared that deepened the depression. These included the stock market crash of October 1929, widespread bank failures, a sharp decline in the supply of money, sharp reductions in international trade, and disruptions in the international payments system.

   The analysis in this book places primary responsibility for the severity of the depression on decreases in aggregate demand (see the Review of Economic Concepts in Chapter 13). Friedman and Schwartz,[8] in their classic *Monetary History of the United States,* present an alternative view. They argue that the depression stemmed from the drastic decline in the supply of money, starting with the first banking crisis described above in 1930. Peter Temin,[21] in his excellent study *Did Monetary Forces Cause the Great Depression?,* concludes, however, that the contraction in the supply of money and bank failures stemmed from the decline in demand (spending), not the other way around. These failures were concentrated in the agricultural Midwest and were caused by declining agricultural demand.

# The Hoover Years, 1929-1933

Contrary to the popular view of the politically ill-fated Hoover administration of 1928 to 1932, the president actively tried to improve the country's economic condition. As we shall see in the ensuing discussion, Hoover tried moral suasion or jawboning and the use of fiscal policy to achieve economic objectives. He also made substantial changes in U.S. economic structure, and tried to effect an improvement in international economic conditions. Could Hoover have done a better job of holding back the depression and inducing a recovery? Or was Hoover a victim of history, a man in the presidency at the wrong time?

## Moral Suasion, or, Can One Talk an Economy into Prosperity?

President Hoover called a number of conferences of manufacturing and financial leaders, especially in the early period of 1929 and 1930, to consider the problems of the evolving depression. He asked for and received pledges from these business leaders that they would hold the line on

Herbert Hoover worked to improve economic conditions. (Photo no. 208-PU-95P-18 in the National Archives)

wages, employment, and investment. He called for firms to resist the temptation, given the fall in demand, to cut wages or decrease employment. He called for increases in investment rather than cuts.

Murray Rothbard concludes[17] that these attempts by the president did indeed restrict the fall in wages and employment. Rothbard considers this a grievous error, however, because he believes it prevented the market from causing necessary liquidations of marginal enterprises. In his view, eliminating inefficient enterprises would have reallocated resources to more productive uses. Few share his view. Whether Hoover's jawboning was at all successful in holding back the fall in economic indicators is not as important as the fact that the jawboning did not cause a revival of favorable economic conditions. People became tired of continually hearing that recovery was around the corner. Many concluded that this jawboning was all that Hoover could do, and people became, in fact, more pessimistic as a result.

## Hoover's Fiscal Policy

President Hoover's first response to the contraction at the end of 1929 was to increase government spending and cut taxes. He also encouraged local and state governments to increase expenditures. In 1930 and 1931, he increased federal public works expenditures. The **full-employment budget** is a statement of federal government revenues and expenditures that contrasts actual revenues and expenditures with those that would exist at full employment. In 1929, there was a full employment surplus of $1 billion. This fell to a full employment deficit of $3 billion in 1931, a substantial deficit that was not duplicated until 1936.

In 1932, President Hoover reversed fiscal policy and asked Congress for a tax increase, which was granted and was embodied in the Revenue Act of 1932. This act increased taxes by one-third, the highest peacetime tax increase in U.S. history. The increase in taxes reduced demand and worked to contract the U.S. economy. Why did Hoover perform such a turnabout?

Reasons given vary. Some argue—Scheiber, Vatter, and Faulkner[18]—that the large (for that time) deficits in the federal budget in 1930 and 1931 were simply too much for a president raised in a world of "sound" fiscal policy and that Hoover's conservatism prevented him from using the more "radical" programs the occasion demanded. Others are more understanding of economic predicaments of the time. They argue—for example, W. Elliot Brownlee[4]—that Hoover was concerned that the federal government would have to finance its deficit by borrowing in capital markets in competition with private investors. A question still exists whether this concern was valid. Also, Hoover thought a move toward a balanced budget would discourage the export of gold and strengthen the international gold standard and thus encourage a recovery of international trade.

Overall, we must conclude that in the early period of the depression, from 1929 to 1931, federal fiscal policy was expansionary (but obviously not expansionary enough to stop the depression). In 1932 and 1933, however, federal fiscal policy sharply reduced aggregate demand, doing more harm than any possible good that may have resulted from the encouragement of domestic investment and international trade.

## Changes in Economic Structure

The Federal Farm Board was set up by the Agricultural Marketing Act of June 1929. The board was given $500 million to stabilize farm prices at some acceptable level. The law did not state what those acceptable levels were. The depression precipitated sharp declines in agricultural prices. The board tried to stem the decline by purchasing grains and cotton. But, except for some temporary successes in 1930, by the summer of 1932 the board had lost $354 million without achieving much of significance. The severe demand-decreasing effect of the depression and the inability of the board to control supply doomed the board's efforts at price stabilization. Much of the cotton and wheat bought with the fund was given away or sold at a loss, without accomplishing the board's objective.

The major structural change initiated by the Hoover administration was the creation of the Reconstruction Finance Corporation (RFC) in January of 1932. By July 1932, the RFC had capital and a borrowing ability of almost $4 billion. It was empowered to lend to various corporations, cooperatives, states, and public and private agencies. By the time Roosevelt took office in March 1933, the RFC had lent over $3 billion, about 80% of it to railroads and, especially, banks. It provided the needed liquidity to keep many banks solvent.

The Roosevelt administration continued the RFC and also used it as a major instrument to foster recovery. Its lending ability was increased, and its activities were shifted significantly from the support of banks to a wider range of lending. This was especially true after the bank holiday of March 1933.

## Hoover and the International Economy

Hoover maintained from the beginning that economic recovery in the United States required recovery in the rest of the world, and much of his policy was formulated around that concept. In 1931, he initiated the temporary halt to reparation and war debt payments. Some argue that his tax increase in 1932 was to reduce the federal budget deficit and discourage withdrawal of gold, which was undermining confidence in the international gold standard.

What confounds this interpretation of Hoover's policies, however, was his signing of the Smoot-Hawley Tariff of 1930. This tariff initiated a wave of retaliation by European countries and a marked shift away from trade based on comparative advantage. Thus, in the end, Hoover's policies regarding the international economy were contradictory and on balance probably contracted both the U.S. economy and that of the rest of the world.

## The Federal Reserve System

The Federal Reserve System (the "Fed") was established in the United States in 1913, a central bank given essentially two functions and the power to perform them. The functions were to provide stability to the country's banking system and to influence the supply of money and interest rates. Both functions were intended to provide greater stability within the economy. However, the Federal Reserve apparently did not perform its functions too well from 1929 through 1933.

From October 1929 to October 1931, the Federal Reserve—especially the New York bank—followed an easy money policy, purchasing $160 million of government securities in October 1929 and reducing the **rediscount rate** (the rate charged banks for borrowing from the Fed) in 1929 and 1930 and to May 1931 to a low of 1.5%. From October 1931 to February 1932, the Fed tightened credit, selling government securities and increasing the rediscount rate. These actions were in response to Britain's abandonment of the gold standard in September 1931 and to a flow of gold out of the United States. Between April and August 1932, the Fed purchased $1 billion of government securities. The New York bank eased credit in

Franklin D. Roosevelt, architect of the New Deal. (Photo no. 208-N-4704 in the National Archives)

February and June of 1932. Unfortunately, the rest of the Fed did not follow suit. When gold began to flow out of the banks after November 1932, as speculators presumed Roosevelt would abandon gold, the Federal Reserve banks again contracted the reserves of the banking system.

The record indicates then that the Fed seemed more concerned with the international gold problem than with internal U.S. economic stability. When the Fed did engage in easy money policies, they were not consistently followed but were pushed primarily by the New York bank. Also, the amount of action by the Fed was probably far less than the amount needed, especially in **open market operations** (the buying and selling of government securities). When the Fed contracted credit, it put heavy burdens on the banking system, burdens it was not prepared to carry. The action or inaction of the Federal Reserve must be given a substantial portion of the blame for the more than one-third reduction in the U.S. supply of money from October 1929 through March 1933 and for the negative economic consequences.

The Federal Reserve did not cause all the contraction of the money supply. Banks themselves substantially decreased the supply of credit, out of deep pessimism about repayment. At the same time, decreases in demand were heavy; business people looked pessimistically at the potential profitability of new investment. Both of these actions decreased the supply of money as both new and renewed loans fell. Doubt exists that further increases in reserves and decreases in interest rates by the Fed would have substantially changed the situation.

Temin[21] shows that the first bank panic, in 1930, centered in the agricultural Midwest and South, originated from the deepening depression and its effects on profits in agriculture. This started a wave and then, over time, recurring waves of distrust of banks and heavy withdrawals of deposits. In turn, this caused both a negative multiplier effect on reserves and waves of bank closings. Anticipating the waves of withdrawals, banks fought to become more liquid by reducing lending and converting existing loans into reserves. But many banks had become financially unsound, not necessarily because they had made unsound loans in the 1920s but rather because many loans that were sound under conditions of prosperity in the 1920s became unsound under the press of the deepening depression. The waves of withdrawals became too much for the weakened conditions of the banks.

Perhaps the Fed could have saved more banks by increasing overall liquidity more than it did. Lending to banks by the RFC did contribute to easing the liquidity problem. We must not forget, though, that falling incomes and rising bankruptcies, coupled with bank losses due to the banks' involvement in the call market of the collapsed stock exchange and to banks' large holdings of real estate mortgages in a drastically declining real estate market, would have left the banking system shaky no matter what the Fed might have done.

We draw the conclusion that the banking panics and the drastic decline in the supply of money with its accompanying fall in prices were not simply the result of an inadequate monetary policy by the Federal Reserve. The long-term contraction of aggregate demand stemming from declines in consumption and investment played a key role in the banking and monetary problems of 1929–1933.

# The Recovery: Roosevelt and the New Deal

In March 1933, President Roosevelt took office and initiated what became known as the New Deal. The intent of the new administration was to initiate a recovery from the disastrous decline of 1929 to 1933, to rectify what were perceived as structural weaknesses in economic institutions that aggravated the contraction, and to create what the administration perceived to be a more ethical, if not economic, balance between the various sectors in the economy. Most often these three elements were intertwined and difficult to separate.

Roosevelt's New Deal was primarily concerned with saving the private enterprise society of the United States. The new administration was not out to make a revolution. It had no coherent plan, however, and this was indeed a serious lack. The New Deal tended to "assault" each sector separately, often with little concern for how actions in one sector affected the other sectors.

## The Economic Record

After Roosevelt's inauguration in March 1933, the economy began to recover. From $55.6 billion in 1933, current GNP rose to $90.4 billion in 1937. From May 1937 to June 1938, the economy contracted once again, with current GNP falling to $84.7 billion in 1938, but recovered in 1939 to $90.5 billion (Table 18–1). **Current GNP** includes the effects of changing prices and thus is not the best measure of economic performance. **Real GNP** takes out the effects of price changes. Since prices fell after 1929, real output computed in 1929 prices would be higher than the current GNP figures. The record of recovery seems better when viewed in real GNP computed with 1929 prices (Table 18–2). Real GNP fell from the high of $104 billion in 1929 to $74.2 billion in 1933, and then rose to $109.1 billion in 1937, somewhat higher than in 1929. The recession of 1937–1938 brought real GNP down to $103.2 billion in 1938, but the economy recovered to $111 billion in 1939.

While the record of real GNP shows that under the Roosevelt administration the economy had recovered to predepression real output by 1939, the record for unemployment is decidedly not as good (Table 18–4). Unemployment had climbed to 25% by 1933, declining to 14.3% by 1937.

During the recession of 1937–1938, unemployment rose again, to 19%; it then fell in 1939 to 17.2%.

If one wished to look at the record optimistically (that is, "the glass is half full"), one could say that, 10 years after the beginning of the depression in 1929, real output had recovered to predepression levels and unemployment had fallen by one-fourth. If one wished to be pessimistic (that is, "the glass is half empty"), one would say that after 10 years of depression the economy had only just managed to recover to 1929 real output. Unemployment, however, remained at the very high level of over 17%, and the economy had to wait for World War II and the huge increases in war-related expenditures to achieve full employment.

## Fiscal Policy

The "new economics" of John Maynard Keynes[13] revolutionized traditional viewpoints about government expenditures and taxes. In his book *The General Theory of Employment, Interest, and Money*, published in 1936, Keynes advocated the use of government expenditure and budget deficits to increase aggregate demand, which would also create jobs and thus decrease unemployment.

Both the Hoover and Roosevelt administrations adhered to the conservative concern for the balanced budget. During the presidential campaign of 1932, Roosevelt continually attacked the deficits of the Hoover administration that were created by falling tax receipts under the impact of the depression's falling incomes. Again during the 1936 campaign, Roosevelt promised a return to a balanced budget. This concern with budgetary deficits prevented the generation of enough demand by the government to more vigorously counteract unemployment.

Table 18–3 shows that the federal deficit increased from $2.7 billion in 1932 to $4.4 billion in 1936. At this point, Roosevelt attempted to reverse the trend, and deficits fell in 1937 and 1938 to a low of $1.2 billion in 1938. This failure to pursue deficit financing is generally considered to be the cause of the sharp contraction that occurred in 1937–1938. The administration then reversed itself, and the federal deficit rose in 1939 to $3.9 billion, but still less than the deficit of 1936. Friedman[8] dissents from this position and argues instead that incorrect decisions and timing on the part of the Fed in regard to the supply of money were the major causes of the contraction.

The fiscal policies of the states were generally contractive, with substantial surpluses generated in 1935, 1937, and 1938. When the fiscal policies of all levels of government are considered together, in 1931 and 1936 combined fiscal efforts were clearly more expansionary than in 1929. The expansionary efforts of combined fiscal policy in 1930, 1932, and 1939 were mild. In 1933, 1937, and 1938, combined fiscal policy was

John Maynard Keynes, founder of the "New Economics." (Photo no. 306-NT-169294C in the National Archives)

substantially less expansionary than in 1929. To quote E. Cary Brown,[3] "In brief, then, it took the massive expenditures forced on the nation by the Second World War to realize the full potentialities of fiscal policy. Until then, the record fails to show its effective use as a recovery measure."

## Monetary Policy

The story of monetary policy is more complicated than simply the policy of the Federal Reserve about the supply of money. It also involves policy concerning the value of the dollar in terms of gold, and institutional changes in the Federal Reserve System and the banking system as a whole. The institutional changes will be discussed further on.

Monetary policy on the part of the Federal Reserve was expansionary from 1933 to 1937. In addition to the normal expansionary actions of purchases of government securities by the Fed and lower discount rates, the federal government greatly increased its holdings of gold and silver. This resulted from executive orders of March and April 1933 forbidding the exportation of gold, the executive order of October 1933 resuming the gold standard, and the Gold Reserve and Silver Purchasing Acts, both of 1934.

The resumption of the gold standard was accompanied by substantial changes. The price of gold increased from $20.67 per ounce in October 1933 to $35 per ounce in January 1934. Also, gold itself could only be purchased for international transactions. The first factor, a price increase for gold, devalued the dollar, but retaliatory devaluation by the major international trading countries kept exchange rates relatively constant. The second factor reduced the ability to speculate on possible future changes in the gold content of the dollar. This protected the domestic and foreign money markets from the effects of such speculation.

The increase in U.S. government holdings of gold and silver coming from these actions increased the supply of money. The decrease in the gold content of the dollar and the increase in the supply of money were aimed at increasing prices. This inflationary policy was successful to some extent, as the index of prices (1929 = 100) rose from a low of 75 in 1933 to 83 in 1937 (Table 18–4).

Although the inflationary policy of the government was not as successful as desired, the increase in the supply of money from 1933 to 1937 did expand the economy. People ended up with more of their assets than they wished in the form of money. In response, they increased their consumption and investment, which increased total demand and the output of the economy (read the Review of Economic Concepts in Chapter 4).

## Recap

Federal fiscal policy was mildly expansive from 1933 to 1937. Deficits in the federal budget occurred as expenditures rose faster than depression-restrained taxes. The administration reversed itself in 1937 and sought to reduce the deficits, perhaps precipitating the recession of 1937–1938. In any event, fiscal policy, if it did not precipitate, it did increase the severity of the contraction.

Monetary policy, including policy concerning gold and silver, was more expansive than fiscal policy in the period of 1933 to 1937. The supply of money rose from $19.4 billion in 1933 to $30.3 billion in 1937 (Table 18–5). The reversal of monetary policy in 1937 and the cutting of the supply contributed to the contraction of 1937–1938.

# Institutional Changes

Perhaps of greater importance than the monetary and fiscal policies of the Roosevelt administration were the widespread changes in the institutional structure of most sectors of the economy. These changes were not a part of an overall plan on the part of the administration, but rather were a piecemeal attack on the problems of the economy. These changes stemmed from the desire to revive the economy, to rectify what the administration perceived to be problems in various sectors of the economy, and to "balance" the structures and benefits of the economy.

## Industry and the NRA

The administration's direct efforts to revive industry were embodied in the National Industrial Recovery Act of 1933 (NIRA), which set up the National Recovery Administration (NRA). The traditional government policy in regard to industry had been to encourage competition. Traditionally, our legal system, derived from English common law, and special antitrust legislation, such as the Sherman Act of 1890, the Clayton Act of 1914, and the Federal Trade Commission Act of 1914, had made it illegal for companies to collude with a view to setting the various conditions of the market such as prices and market shares. The NIRA was a complete aboutface.

The act sought to enforce cooperation in industry by establishing associations of producers in each industry who, together with representatives from the government (from the NRA) and, where present, from labor, were to set up a code of fair practices for each industry. These industrial codes were issued over the president's signature and had the force of law. Roosevelt's aim was "the elimination of practical methods and practices which have not only harassed honest business but also contributed to the ills of labor."

Competition had failed, and now industrial self-regulation would reduce overproduction, raise prices, and increase wages and profits. The act gave labor the right to organize and to be represented in drawing up an industry's codes. The public was to be protected by open hearings and the government's representatives.

Bernard Bellush[1] charges that in practice many industries were dominated by the larger companies, and if organized labor already existed, their representatives may have been effective in protecting their interests. Most industries were not organized and were not represented by labor unions, and Bellush[1] says that the charge was persistently made that labor was not adequately protected in most codes; and even those codes with labor protection were being consistently violated.

Charges were continually being made that the larger firms were dominating the industries and that the codes favored them over the smaller firms. The consumer was in effect ignored. The intent of the act was to reduce output and increase prices. The interest of consumers, whether with government representation or not, was not of prime concern.

A flood of complaints moved the administration to appoint the National Recovery Review Board, but the U.S. Supreme Court, in the 1935 Schechter case, declared the NIRA unconstitutional as being an improper use of the interstate commerce power and improper usurpation of legislative power by the administration.

## Agriculture and Government Regulation

As we have seen, the Federal Farm Board created in 1928 was incapable of stemming the fall in prices of agricultural products up to 1933. The board lacked an essential power, the ability to reduce agricultural supply. The intent of the Farm Board was to increase prices, and the primary intent of the Roosevelt administration in its agricultural policy once again was to increase prices.

The First Agricultural Act of 1933 aimed at reducing supplies and raising farm incomes by increasing prices. This was to be accomplished by use of acreage allotments by reducing the plantings of specific crops, by government payments to withdraw land from use, by government purchase and destruction of crops and animals, and by more efficient marketing of agricultural products. The program was to be financed from taxes on the processing of agricultural products. The public was to pay with higher prices and higher taxes.

Besides the obvious problems for the consumer of higher prices and higher taxes during a depression, other problems plagued the program. Output in 1933 was not much less than in 1932, because good weather, concentration on the most productive land, increased use of fertilizers, and violations of acreage restrictions maintained production levels. Increased domestic prices tended to increase agricultural imports and to decrease agricultural exports.

But parity prices increased from 55 in 1933 to 73 in 1936. **Parity** measures the purchasing power of agricultural products in terms of their purchasing power in a base period. At the same time, the base period was 1910 to 1914. A rise from 55 to 73 in parity meant that agricultural prices increased more rapidly than the prices of things farmers bought.

In *United States* v. *Butler* (1936), the First Agricultural Adjustment Act was declared unconstitutional as an improper use of the taxing power. The Soil Conservation and Domestic Allotment Act of 1936 was a stopgap measure that appropriated $500 million to get farmers to put land into sod for soil conservation purposes. Then, the Second Agricultural Adjustment Act (AAA) of 1938 set up the machinery that has endured with various modifications for over 35 years. The government aimed at parity pricing to increase the purchasing power of agricultural products. If two-thirds of the growers of a crop agreed, quotas would be set. A price would be set, and if prices dropped below that level farmers could sell to the government at the set price. If output went beyond quotas, acreage allotment would be decreased, reducing the land for future plantings.

The AAA of 1938 firmly implanted parity pricing and acreage controls in U.S. agriculture. Competition was replaced by the decisions of the U.S. Department of Agriculture. The consumers suffered, as they had to pay in two ways, higher prices and higher taxes.

Another area of legislative activity important to agriculture was credit. For decades, farmers had complained that their credit needs were neglected by the banking system. Acts such as the Farm Credit Act of 1933 and the various agricultural acts of 1934 concerned with mortgages brought the federal government directly into the area of agricultural credit.

## Banking and Finance

We already have seen that recurrent waves of bank panics from 1930 to 1933 were an important factor in deepening the depression. The supply of money (Table 18–5) dropped from $26.4 billion in 1929 to a low of $19.4 billion in 1933, forcing prices down (Table 18–4) from an index of 100 in 1929 to a low of 75 in 1933. In 1929, there was the great stock market crash in October. There followed a continued, jerky decline in stock prices that brought the *New York Times* industrial average of corporate stock prices from its high of 452 on September 3, 1929, to 58 on July 8, 1932. These experiences led people to advocate basic institutional changes. The Roosevelt administration moved quickly. Some unkind souls have murmured, though, that this seemed like closing the barn door after the horse was gone.

Immediately on taking office, Roosevelt declared a three-day bank holiday on March 9, 1933, closing the banks for a week. All banks were audited; half were allowed to reopen without supervision, one-fourth reopened under various degrees of supervision, and one-fourth were too shaky to reopen at all. This massive surgery restored the public's confidence in the banking system and stopped runs on banks and waves of currency withdrawals.

A number of acts were passed that changed the institutional structure of banking and credit. They included the Emergency Bank Act of 1933, the Bank Acts of 1933 and of 1935, the Gold Reserve Act of 1934, and the Home Owners Loan Acts of 1932 and 1933. The most important features of these acts were the following:

1. The Federal Deposit Insurance Corporation (FDIC) was created to insure deposits against bank failures. When depositors were assured that they would be able to recover their deposits if a bank failed, the main

reason for runs on banks was nullified. Confidence returned and currency flowed back into the banking system.

2. The structure of policymaking of the Federal Reserve was centralized as the powers of the board of governors were increased. No longer could individual Federal Reserve banks refuse to go along with board policy. The action unified Federal Reserve economic policymaking. This creation of a single monetary policy for the United States brings to mind the saying that "When they are right, they are very, very right; when they are wrong, they are horrid."

3. The power of the president to vary the gold content of the dollar was confirmed, and, with the Silver Purchase Act of 1934, the treasury increased purchases of silver and its use in the nation's supply of currency. Devaluation and increased use of silver were part of the administration's strategy to increase prices. This inflationary strategy was only partially successful.

4. The powers of the Reconstruction Finance Corporation (created under Hoover) were extended and increased. In addition to lending to banks, railroads, and power companies, the agency also began to lend to industrial companies.

5. The Hoover program of guaranteeing loans to homeowners was extended. These guarantees were taken over by the Federal Housing Administration (FHA). The effort was to stabilize the real estate market and reduce foreclosures on homes.

With the Sale of Securities Act of 1933 and the Securities and Exchange Commission (SEC) Act of 1934, the administration turned its attention to the stock exchanges. They were now to be regulated by the Securities and Exchange Commission and corporations were required to file with the SEC information concerning the securities they issued and were held liable for misinformation.

Similar reforms were made concerning the various commodity exchanges with the establishment of the Commodity Exchange Commission through the Commodity Exchange Act of 1936.

## Social Legislation

The Hoover administration refused to involve the federal government in direct relief to the unemployed. Instead, it put the entire burden of supporting the millions without jobs on private charitable agencies and state and local governments. The responsibility was too great for them to handle. With continued criticism and great reluctance, the New Deal early entered into providing federal relief to the massive numbers of destitutes in American society.

From 1933 to 1936, the Federal Emergency Relief Administration dispensed about $3 billion for direct relief. The Public Works Administration (PWA) set up under the NIRA in 1933, spent over $4 billion by 1941 to employ workers on public works projects. In 1935, the Works Projects Administration (WPA) was set up to coordinate public works programs. From 1935 to 1942, the WPA spent over $13 billion on public interest construction projects and employed at one time or another 8.5 million people. The most employed at any one time was 3.8 million people. The WPA did not solve the problem of unemployment, for this was not resolved until 1942, after the start of World War II.

The Civilian Conservation Corps was established in 1933 to provide employment for young men, who were taken out of the cities and employed on useful projects concerned with conservation in the parks and forests of the country. Hundreds of thousands of young men were helped in this way.

A weak start in the area of public housing was made with the Wagner-Stingall Housing Act of 1937. The aim was slum clearance and low-cost housing. But by 1940, only 150,000 homes had been built, which was a modest amount, especially in view of the president's comment that one-third of the American people were poorly housed.

The Fair Labor Standards Act of 1938 set a maximum work week standard of 40 hours per week by 1940, and set a standard for the minimum wage to increase from 25 cents to 40 cents per hour over seven years. Many categories of labor were excluded, however, including agricultural labor.

The most well known of the New Deal's social legislation was the Social Security Act of 1935. With it, the United States would finally follow the example of other developed nations, such as Germany and Great Britain, in providing its workers with a national retirement program. The retirement portion was constructed as a compulsory "insurance" program, with contributions from both the employee and the employer. The act also provided for unemployment "insurance" to be paid by federal taxes on payrolls. Criticisms of the program were many, including criticism of its actuarial unsoundness.

First, it did not immediately benefit—and perhaps it harmed—the recovery. While those benefits under the program that would increase purchasing power would be slow in coming, as it took time for people to qualify, the increase in taxes was immediate, and restricted disposable income as taxes were paid.

Second, coverage was restricted primarily to those in industry and commerce. It took many years of effort to expand coverage to the majority of the population.

Third, taxes to fund the program were highly regressive, falling more severely on the lower income groups. This introduced questions about equity in taxation that have not yet been resolved. (Although questions of equity must be answered not only with regard to the incidence of taxation but also with regard to the distribution of the benefits of government expenditures.)

Fourth, payments under the act, especially payments to retired persons, were very low. Many people found it hard to survive on Social Security payments alone.

## Organized Labor

Irving Bernstein,[2] in his excellent history of the labor movement in the 1930s, *Turbulent Years,* concluded, "The most important development that took place was the dramatic increase in the size of the labor movement. If one uses the National Bureau of Economic Research series, constructed by Leo Wolman and Leo Troy on conservative criteria, the membership of American unions (excluding Canadian members) rose from 2,805,000 in 1933 to 8,410,000 in 1941. This constituted an almost exact tripling in size. Perhaps even more significant, for the first time in the history of the nation unions enrolled a substantial fraction of those at work; by 1941, 23% of nonagricultural employment. Further, the prospect at the close of this period was that rapid growth, both in absolute numbers and in the share of employment, would continue for at least the duration of the war."

This expansion was accompanied by radical changes in the structure of the labor movement and in the national environment itself. Favorable public opinion concerning the problems of labor unions was mirrored by the revolution in labor legislation. Also, the principles of the American Federation of Labor as formulated by its founder, Samuel Gompers, were substantially altered.

Three prounion legislative acts reversed the basically antiunion legislative and court situation. The Norris-LaGuardia Act of 1932 was passed under the Hoover administration and rendered yellow-dog contracts unenforceable in the courts, seriously reducing the power of the courts to restrict union practice through injunctions. The courts now could not issue an injunction against union activities on the grounds that workers had signed contracts with the firm stating they would not join a union (a so-called yellow-dog contract). This reduced a serious limitation on union-organizing activities.

Section 7(a) of the 1933 NIRA, viewed by some union leaders as a charter of liberty for labor, stated that employees have the "right to organize and bargain collectively through representatives of their own choosing and shall be free from interference, restraint, or coercion of employers of labor, or their agents, in the designation of such representation or in self-organization." Labor representatives were to sit on the NRA boards of each industry, and the codes of each industry were to protect worker and union rights.

The third piece of legislation was the National Labor Relations Act of 1935, also known as the Wagner Act. It set up the National Labor Relations Board (NLRB), which was to enforce the act. The board was to draw up a list of fair employment practices, binding on both labor and management, and also was to oversee elections within firms to determine which collective bargaining organization would represent the workers. Finally, employers were forbidden to interfere with employees' rights to bargain collectively or to discriminate against union members as to tenure and employment and were required to bargain in good faith.

Although these laws were prolabor, it was the actions of the unions themselves that caused the expansion of the labor movement. First, the Wagner Act was not effective until April 1937. Charges of widespread violation of 7(a) and of the labor section of the NRA codes were frequently made. Insofar as this was true, it reduced the effectiveness of Section 7(a). Challenges to the NLRA were immediately made in the courts and the constitutionality of the act was finally upheld in April 1937. Only then could the board function.

Unions had broken out of their decline by April 1936 and by 1937 had increased their membership by 1.5 million. The point to keep in mind is that these acts only created a more favorable environment for membership growth; they were not the cause of the advances.

In 1933, union membership had reached its lowest point since 1920. Then, partly in response to Section 7(a), partly in response to the promises of the New Deal, new organizational drives were made. These were led by the three industrial unions in the AFL—The United Mine Workers under John L. Lewis, the Amalgamated Clothing Workers Union under Sidney Hillman, and the International Ladies Garment Workers Union under David Dubinsky. Their success in their own industries greatly strengthened the industrial union wing of the AFL. In 1935, these three industrial unions, along with a number of smaller ones, under the leadership of John L. Lewis, formed, first within the AFL, the Committee on Industrial Organization to organize labor on an industry basis.

They set up organizing committees in both the steel and auto industries. In 1937, violent strikes in the auto industry resulted in establishment of a union throughout the industry except for the Ford Motor Company. The violent opposition of Ford ended in 1941. In steel, the United States Steel Corporation reversed its historic antiunion policy, recognized the union, and signed a contract with it in 1937. Several important steel firms did not go along with U.S. Steel, and what was called "little steel" (such companies as Republic and Bethlehem) was not organized until 1942.

Conflict arose between the parent AFL and the committee. At the core of the conflict was craft versus industry unionism. The heart of the AFL was still the craft unions, such as the carpenters and the machinists. They saw the committee as a threat to growth in their membership and to their power in the AFL. The AFL executive committee ordered the Committee on Industrial Organization to dissolve and to place the newly organized members into their respective craft unions, not industrial unions. It refused to do so and the unions within the committee were expelled from the AFL. As a result, the expelled unions established a rival organization, the Congress of Industrial Organizations (CIO) in 1938.

With the arrival of the CIO, the AFL in its own defense launched an aggressive organizing effort. In the process, it came to realize that its craft orientation was a considerable hindrance, and the AFL also shifted to an industrial form of organization. While the craft unions remained a powerful factor in the AFL, the nearly 75-year conflict between craft versus industry was decided in favor of industrial unionism.

With the establishment of the CIO in 1938, the fear of Samuel Gompers about dual unionism (two unions in the same industry or craft) was realized. As Irving Bernstein[2] termed it, "civil war" broke out in the labor movement. The jurisdictional strike, one in which the workers strike to force the employer to recognize one union rather than another, occurred with increasing frequency after 1938. But this rivalry, as already noted, forced the AFL itself into active organizing. By 1941, the CIO was firmly established, but the AFL maintained its commanding lead in the labor movement. Although the CIO claimed 5 million members in 1941, Bernstein accepts Troy's[22] estimate of an actual membership of 2,654,000, while Troy's figure for the AFL was 5,179,000.

Political neutrality, another favored principle of Samuel Gompers, was undermined in the 1930s. Unions increasingly had an urban industrial base. Politically, Roosevelt made urban labor an important aspect of the Democratic coalition and the CIO became firmly committed to the Democratic Party. The AFL refused to endorse a presidential candidate until 1952.

## The New Deal: An Evaluation

As with most questions in economic history, an evaluation of the economic effects of the New Deal on American economic life is open to controversy and debate. But the following seems to be consistent with the preceding analysis.

The fiscal and monetary policy of the New Deal on the whole was expansive and may have contributed to the recovery from 1933 to 1939. The federal budget deficits in most years were somewhat larger than those during the last of the Hoover years. Also, increases in the supply of money stimulated increases in demand and thus output. The surpluses generated in state budgets caused total fiscal policy for all levels of government to be expansionary in only two of these years.

The fiscal and monetary effort was neither steady nor large enough, however, to achieve full employment. The reversal in both fiscal and monetary policy in 1936–1937 brought on the contraction of 1938. While the deficits were departures from historic practice, they were not revolutionary in nature, although they did provide precedent for future federal fiscal behavior.

The New Deal's policy on gold and international exchange insulated the domestic economy from the possible disruptions of changes in international demand for gold. Thus, monetary policy became more free to deal with domestic monetary policies. However, these actions accentuated international tendencies toward trade restrictions and a "beggar thy neighbor" policy that hampered recovery of international trade.

The inflationary aspects of the gold policy were only partially successful, with prices increasing more slowly than the devaluation of the dollar. Whether the price increases were beneficial to business enterprise through increased profit margins is an open question. But they did increase the burden on consumers, while the domestic purchasing power of the dollar fell.

Numerous changes were made in economic institutions. The Federal Reserve System was now a more centralized instrument of monetary policy. The establishment of the Federal Deposit Insurance Corporation, which insured deposits, met a serious deficiency in the banking system. Since now the likelihood of runs on banks, causing bank failures, was made more remote, the security of the banking system was substantially increased. The Securities and Exchange Commission was created to regulate securities exchanges and to provide rules for giving required information by issuers of securities.

The efforts to stimulate industry through the NIRA and its attempted establishment of industrial cooperation through association failed. The failure was not simply the declaration of unconstitutionality by the courts. Toward the end, the unwillingness of large firms, small firms, and labor unions to cooperate and share whatever revenue benefits accrued from cooperation eliminated much of the effectiveness of the act. The resulting increase in prices put an additional burden on the consumer. To the extent that the act was effective, its effects were to reduce competition and thereby reduce the competitive incentive to increase output.

The agricultural program, embodied in the Agricultural Adjustment Acts of 1933 and 1938, among other things, achieved moderate success in raising farm incomes. Even more important, the programs decisively interjected the federal government into increasing and persistent involvement in the most competitive industry of the economy. The decisions of the administration became a significant factor in determining the level of farm incomes. But the nature of this involvement produced a double burden on the general population: first, the high prices to the consumer originating from the price supports and, second, the taxes needed to fund the support program.

Social welfare programs, such as the WPA and the CCC, and federal financial support for state and local welfare programs provided incomes for the unemployed. The Hoover administration failed to meet the need for direct aid to victims of the economic disaster. Some people argue that even the New Deal programs were not large enough to eliminate unemployment and also that insufficient thought was given to the structure of the program. But the precedent of federal involvement in direct aid to the unemployed was established.

The Social Security program was initiated with the Social Security Act of 1935. The effect of Social Security on the depression was minimal, if not contractive. Recipients of Social Security during the period were few because of the need to qualify by working the necessary period of time and by the narrowness of the coverage. However, taxes were collected from present incomes, as people worked to obtain coverage.

Labor legislation, such as the Norris-LaGuardia Act of 1932, Section 7(a) of the NIRA of 1933, and the National Labor Relations Act of 1935, revolutionized the legislative position of organized labor. These acts reduced the use of the injunction and recognized the right of workers to organize, making it mandatory for management to bargain in good faith with unions. However, it introduced further monopoly power into the labor markets. Although this legislation was a substantial boon to union expansion, the renewed vigor of union organizing in the favorable public atmosphere of the depression was even more important in union expansion.

Some contemporaries and students of the period have charged that the New Deal was intent on destroying American capitalism. This does not appear to have been the intent nor was it the accomplishment of the New Deal. Although the federal government had participated significantly in the private market economy from its inception, its role increased both qualitatively and quantitatively in the 1930s, and the New Deal firmly established what has been called a **mixed-market economy.** Federal government expenditures and taxes rose to a level that made them a significant factor in the economy.

Federal regulation was expanded and became a decisive factor in a number of sectors of the economy. The legacy of the New Deal, whether one views it as a good or an ill or both, is the era of the mixed-market economy, the era of big government.

# Glossary

**"Beggar thy neighbor" policy**   A country's policy of international trade restrictions aimed at increased exports while decreasing imports.

**Current GNP**   Total value of annual output of final goods and services; it has not been adjusted for the effects of price changes and thus is not the best measure of the economy's performance.

**Full-employment budget**   The expenditures of the federal government budgeted to tax receipts that would have occurred if there were full employment.

**Mixed-market economy**   Government is an important partner in the market economy through a combination of expenditures and taxes and regulation.

**Open market operations**   The buying or selling of government securities by the Federal Reserve in the open market for the purpose of affecting the levels of reserves and thus the ability to lend of the commercial banking system. When the Fed buys securities, it increases bank reserves. When the Fed sells securities, it decreases bank reserves.

**Real GNP**   Total value of annual output of final goods and services that has been adjusted for changes in prices so that it measures only changes in output of goods and services. It is a better measure of economic performance than is current GNP.

**Rediscount rate**   The interest rate charged member banks by the Federal Reserve.

**Secondary demand**   Replacement demand for a product; for example, buying a second car to replace an original car.

## Questions

1. What were the causes of the Great Depression of 1929–1933? Distinguish between basic causes and aggravating factors.
2. In what ways did the stock market decline from 1929 to 1933 contribute to the economic contraction?
3. How did the banking panics of 1930 to 1933 affect the economy?
4. Evaluate the effects on the contraction of the Hoover administration's fiscal and monetary policies.
5. Was the depression caused by aggregate demand factors or by monetary factors?
6. Did Hoover help or hinder the international economy during 1929 to 1933?
7. What were the strengths and the weaknesses of Hoover's policy in regard to the depression?
8. What were the basic objectives of the New Deal?
9. Evaluate the Roosevelt administration's fiscal and monetary policies from 1933 to 1939.

10. Do you think that the fiscal and monetary policies of the Hoover and Roosevelt administrations were consistent or inconsistent with the recommendations of the "new economics"? Why?

11. Evaluate the institutional reforms of 1930–1939 in:
    a. Industry
    b. Agriculture
    c. Banking
    d. Social welfare

12. Do you believe that these reforms corrected abuses or weaknesses in those sectors?

13. Did these reforms contribute to economic recovery? How or how not?

14. Which groups "paid" for the reforms?

15. Which was more important in the renewed expansion of organized labor after 1933, favorable union legislation or renewed energy of the unions themselves?

16. What challenges to and changes were made in the original conception of unions established by Samuel Gompers in 1886?

17. Overall, do you think the Hoover administration was successful in restraining the contraction from 1929 to 1933? Why?

18. Overall, do you think the New Deal was successful in aiding the recovery of the economy from 1933 to 1939? Why?

## Suggested Readings

1. Bellush, Bernard. *The Failure of the NRA*. New York: Norton, 1975.

2. Bernstein, Irving. *Turbulent Years*. Boston: Houghton Mifflin, 1970.

3. Brown, E. Cary. "Fiscal Policies in the Thirties: A Reappraisal." *American Economic Review*, 46 (December 1956).

4. Brownlee, W. Elliot. *Dynamics of Ascent*. New York: Knopf, 1974.

5. Chandler, Lester V. *America's Greatest Depression, 1929–1941*. New York: Harper & Row, 1970.

6. Chandler, Lester V. *American Monetary Policy, 1928–1941*. New York: Harper & Row, 1971.

7. Friedman, Milton, and Schwartz, Anna J. *The Great Contraction, 1929–1933*. Princeton, N.J.: Princeton University Press, 1956.

8. Friedman, Milton, and Schwartz, Anna J. *A Monetary History of the United States, 1867–1960*. Princeton, N.J.: Princeton University Press, 1963.

9. Galbraith, John Kenneth. *The Great Crash, 1929*. Boston: Houghton Mifflin, 1954.

10. Gordon, Robert A. *Economic Instability and Growth: The American Record.* New York: Harper & Row, 1974.

11. Hansen, Alvin. *Fiscal Policy and Business Cycles.* New York: Norton, 1941.

12. Hawley, Ellis W. *The New Deal and the Problem of Monopoly: A Study in Economic Ambivalence.* Princeton, N.J.: Princeton University Press, 1966.

13. Keynes, John M. *The General Theory of Employment, Interest and Money.* New York: Harcourt Brace Jovanovich, 1936.

14. Mitchell, Broadus. *Depression Decade: From New Era Through New Deal, 1932–1940.* New York: Harper & Row, 1969.

15. Nash, Gerald D. "Herbert Hoover and the Origins of the Reconstruction Finance Corporation." *Mississippi Valley Historical Review,* 46 (December 1959).

16. Romasco, A. U. *The Poverty of Abundance: Hoover, the Nation, the Depression.* New York: Oxford University Press, 1965.

17. Rothbard, Murray. *America's Great Depression.* Kansas City, Kansas: Sheed and Ward, 1972.

18. Scheiber, Harry N., Vatter, Harold G., and Faulkner, Harold Underwood. *American Economic History.* New York: Harper & Row, 1976.

19. Schwartz, J. A. *The Interregnum of Despair: Hoover, Congress and the Depression.* Urbana: University of Illinois Press, 1970.

20. Sobel, Robert. *The Big Board: A History of the New York Stock Market.* New York: Free Press, 1965. Chap. 13.

21. Temin, Peter. *Did Monetary Forces Cause the Great Depression?* New York: Norton, 1976.

22. Troy, Leo. "Trade Union Membership 1897–1962." Occasional Paper 92. New York: National Bureau of Economic Research, 1965.

23. Warren, Harris G. *Herbert Hoover and the Great Depression.* New York: Oxford University Press, 1959.

24. Wolman, Leo. "Concentration of Union Membership." *Proceedings.* Industrial Relations Research Association, 1952.

# Chapter 19

## The 1940s and 1950s

The economic history of the 20 years from 1940 through 1959 falls conveniently into four periods. The war years from 1940 to 1945 witnessed the recovery of the American economy under the impact of expanded demand in a war economy. The economy continued its expansion in the immediate postwar period from 1946 to 1949. In those years, delayed demand from a depression and war-starved domestic economy was supplemented by the demand created by the reconstruction of war-ravaged Europe. The recovery from the mild recession of 1949 was accelerated by both military and consumer demand after the outbreak of the Korean conflict in 1951, and the economy expanded until 1954. There was a mild recession in 1954 at the conclusion of the Korean conflict, followed by a surge in the demand for consumer durables in 1955, and in 1956 and 1957 by an increased demand for producer durables. The sharp contraction in 1958 was followed by a quick but weak recovery in 1959.

These 20 years experienced the continuation of a number of factors. With the end of World War II, the large foreign investments typical of the period from 1900 to 1929 were resumed and by 1950, the multinational firm made its appearance. The expansion of unionization that commenced in the middle of the 1930s depression continued into the 1950s. The expansion of the federal government stimulated by the New Deal and furthered during World War II continued through the 1950s.

But there were also changes in economic patterns. After the war, urbanization slowed down as people took to the road and the flight to the suburbs became a flood. While the percentage of total employment in agriculture continued its historic decline, the percentage in manufacturing

also began to decline as the service industries became increasingly important. The pre-World War II period saw recurrent and severe contractions
of the economy such as the depressions of 1929–1933, 1921, and 1907.
After the war, the economy went through three *mild* recessions, in 1949,
1954, and 1958. The concern for unemployment characteristic of the
1930s was replaced by a concern for inflation as the postwar inflation of
1946 to 1949 continued through the 1950s.

# World War II, 1940-1945

## Prewar Years

War broke out in Europe in September 1939, and the recovery of the
American economy accelerated. Americans, remembering the inflation of
World War I, increased consumption demand in anticipation of price increases. Exports swelled from $3.1 billion in 1939 to $5.2 billion in 1941 as
the Allies increased purchases in the United States, and shipments under
Lend-Lease (the lending or leasing of material to the Allies) burgeoned
after January 1941. In addition, the federal government increased its own
expenditures, primarily on the military, from $6 million in 1940 to almost
$17 billion in 1941 (see Table 19–1).

   These increases in total demand generated multiplier effects as the
higher expenditures increased payrolls and purchasing power and further
raised consumer demand. In addition, the increased government and consumer demand stimulated a greater need for facilities and induced investment. The economy expanded, and GNP increased from $90.5 billion in
1939 to $124.5 billion in 1941. Because of depression-related high un-
employment and unused facilities, the consumer price index increased by
only 5% in 1940–1941 (see Table 19–1).

## The War Years, 1942-1945

The United States entered the war on December 7, 1941, and the economy
shifted onto a war footing. Federal government expenditures increased
sharply, growing from $17 billion in 1941 to $52 billion in 1942, $81
billion in 1943, $89 billion in 1944, and, as the war approached its end,
$74 billion in 1945. Under the pressure of war, nonmilitary expenditures
decreased from $3 billion in 1941 to $0.7 billion in 1945. As government
demand expanded, GNP grew from $124.5 billion in 1941 to $212 billion
in 1945.

   At the beginning of 1942, expansion was facilitated by a 10%
unemployment rate and by large amounts of excess plant and equipment.

Table 19-1. Economic Statistics 1940 to 1945 (billions of dollars).

| Year | GNP | Consumption | Gross Investment | Federal Expenditures for Goods and Services | |
|---|---|---|---|---|---|
| | | | | Military | Other |
| 1940 | 99.7 | 70.8 | 13.1 | 2.2 | 3.8 |
| 1941 | 124.5 | 80.6 | 17.9 | 13.8 | 3.1 |
| 1942 | 157.9 | 88.5 | 9.8 | 49.4 | 2.5 |
| 1943 | 191.6 | 99.3 | 5.7 | 79.7 | 1.4 |
| 1944 | 210.1 | 108.3 | 7.1 | 87.4 | 1.6 |
| 1945 | 211.9 | 119.7 | 10.6 | 73.5 | .7 |

| Year | Federal Deficit | Consumer Price Index (1957–1959 = 100) | Unemployment as % of Civilian labor force | National Debt |
|---|---|---|---|---|
| 1940 | − 2.7 | 48.8 | 14.6 | 50.7 |
| 1941 | − 4.8 | 51.3 | 9.9 | 57.5 |
| 1942 | − 19.4 | 56.8 | 4.7 | 79.2 |
| 1943 | − 53.8 | 60.3 | 1.9 | 142.6 |
| 1944 | − 46.1 | 61.3 | 1.2 | 204.1 |
| 1945 | − 45.0 | 62.7 | 1.9 | 260.1 |

*Source:* U.S. Department of Commerce, Bureau of the Census, *Historical Statistics of the United States, Colonial Times to 1970* (Washington, D.C.: U.S. Government Printing Office, 1975).

By September 1942, the economy had achieved full employment. The unemployment rate continued to decline, to a low of 1.2% in 1944. Resources continued to be shifted into war production. People worked overtime, and many who would normally not have been part of the labor force went to work for the war effort. The fabled "Rosie the Riveter" and many others like her who now participated in the labor force contributed substantially to the war effort.

The opportunity cost of the war soon became apparent. While consumption increased moderately, many forms of consumer goods were not produced; for example, the auto industry shifted completely to tanks, trucks, jeeps, and airplanes. Shortages in a wide variety of consumer goods quickly appeared by the end of 1942. Unessential forms of investment goods were sacrificed as these resources were shifted to war production. Gross investment fell from $18 billion in 1941 to a low of $5.7 billion in 1944.

Extensive planning efficiently mobilized the economy for the gigantic production effort. This planning was much more extensive than for World War I. Such agencies as the War Production Board and the Office of Emergency Management established a system of priorities for the wide

Wartime production, "Rosie the Riveter." (Photo no. 208-AA-352V-3 in the National Archives)

range of raw materials, semifinished goods, and transportation that, with reasonable efficiency, were channeled into war-related uses. Widespread support for the war contributed to the high levels of cooperation between management and labor. Moreover, strikes were illegal and uncommon.

With the shift of resources from civilian uses into the war effort, excess demand for consumption goods mounted. The increases in civilian purchasing power, as full employment returned, caused serious problems in allocating these short supplies of consumption goods (such as sugar, butter, gasoline, and tires) equitably and with a minimum of inflation.

Beginning in 1942, the Office of Price Administration (OPA) set prices, wages, and rents. It also set up a system of rationing for many of the basic civilian goods, including sugar, butter, tires, and gasoline. Most of the American people, in patriotic support of the war, cooperated with the rationing program. Although a black market for some goods appeared, especially in gasoline and tires, the quantitative importance of these illegal markets was probably small.

The government could have used taxation to reduce the growing purchasing power generated through the economic expansion. Although new taxes were added and receipts of taxes did grow, tax receipts accounted for only about 50% of the increased government expenditures. The other half reflected government deficits. Savings grew rapidly: People voluntarily restricted their consumption to help the war effort, found little available to buy, and were concerned with a possible return of unemployment after the war.

An important factor in the war against inflation was the sale of war bonds to individuals. These bond sales, while increasing the financial assets of the people, absorbed large amounts of purchasing power. A heroine of this war against inflation was Kate Smith, who, singing "God Bless America," encouraged the sale of millions of dollars in bonds.

On the whole, the effort to control inflation was a remarkable success. Prices increased by the moderate amount of about 4% per year during 1942 through 1945. This statistic understates the true impact of inflation, however, since it does not take into account the decreases in quality that undoubtedly took place. Still, all in all, inflation was moderate, probably due to the success of the program of price controls, rationing, and savings. These programs were largely successful because of the patriotic cooperation of the substantial portion of the American people. Obviously, this increase in savings was encouraged by the unavailability of consumer goods.

# The Postwar Economy, 1946–1949

## The Record

Much to the surprise of some economists, the conversion from a war economy, with government expenditures using as much as 50% of total output, was quick and was accomplished with little unemployment. Remembering the postwar depression of 1921 and the disastrous 1930s depression, many were concerned about a return to conditions of substantial unemployment. Instead, GNP rose from $212 billion in 1945 to over $257 billion in 1948, and unemployment remained below 4%. This expansion, however, was accompanied by a surge in prices as the consumer price index increased from 68 in 1945 to almost 84 in 1948. This was an increase of almost 24% in three years (see Table 19-2).

In late 1948, the expansion began to weaken, and the economy experienced its first postwar contraction. When compared to past experience (such as 1907, 1921, 1929–1933, and 1937–1938), this recession was mild indeed. The GNP declined from $257.6 billion in 1948 to only $256.5 billion in 1949, and unemployment increased to 5.9%. Prices decreased slightly. By the beginning of 1950, the economy was recovering.

Postwar production, meeting pent-up demand. (Photo no. 306-NT-769B-1 in the National Archives)

Table 19-2. Economic Statistics, 1946–1949 (billions of dollars).

| Year | GNP | Consumption | Gross Investment | Federal Expenditures for Goods and Services | |
| --- | --- | --- | --- | --- | --- |
| | | | | Military | Other |
| 1946 | 208.5 | 143.4 | 30.6 | 14.7 | 2.5 |
| 1947 | 231.3 | 160.7 | 34.0 | 9.1 | 3.5 |
| 1948 | 257.6 | 173.6 | 46.0 | 10.7 | 5.8 |
| 1949 | 256.5 | 176.8 | 35.7 | 13.3 | 6.8 |

| Year | Federal Deficit | Consumer Price Index 1957–1958 = 100) | Unemployment | Federal Debt | Net Exports |
| --- | --- | --- | --- | --- | --- |
| 1946 | − 18.2 | 68.0 | 3.9 | 271.0 | + 6.7 |
| 1947 | + 6.6 | 77.8 | 3.9 | 257.1 | + 10.1 |
| 1948 | + 8.9 | 83.8 | 3.8 | 252.0 | + 5.7 |
| 1949 | + 1.0 | 83.0 | 5.9 | 252.6 | + 5.3 |

*Source:* U.S. Department of Commerce, Bureau of the Census, *Historical Statistics of the United States, Colonial Times to 1970* (Washington, D.C.: U.S. Government Printing Office, 1975).

## The Causes of Expansion

The primary cause of the expansion was the surge in consumption and investment demand. Consumption demand, especially for durables, had been very low through 16 years of depression and war. By 1946, consumers held few durable goods, and the output of these goods seemed incapable of meeting the very large demand. Investment in plant and equipment had also been abnormally low during these years, and there were high levels of demand for new plant and equipment to replace that which had become technologically obsolete and also to increase capacity in the face of high levels of consumer demand.

The financing of this increased demand came from a variety of sources. Much was financed by the accumulation of liquid assets during the war in the form of savings and war bonds. Also, high profits accumulated during the war had substantially increased retained earnings of corporations, which were used for investment expansion. In addition, both consumer and business borrowings increased rapidly after the war. Finally, in 1946 Congress forced substantial tax cuts for both individuals and businesses past a reluctant President Truman.

Residential construction also revived and surged ahead as the housing shortage that had developed during the war became critical. Construction of housing for nondefense and nonmilitary purposes had ceased during the war. This, coupled with the low levels of construction during the 1930s, caused a severe shortage. An increase in population during the 1940s (the beginning of the so-called baby boom) had increased population by 19 million. The renewal of the shift to the suburbs started in the 1920s further increased the demand for housing. Residential construction had built almost 5 million new units by the end of 1950.

Most of this expansion was financed from borrowing and the liquid assets accumulated by individuals during the war. Also, the government contributed to this expansion. Under the G.I. Bill of 1944, the government guaranteed mortgages for veterans. In 1946 and again in the Housing Act of 1949, the federal government committed to building subsidized housing for low-income groups under the responsibility of the Federal Housing Authority.

An additional stimulus to aggregate demand came from increased exports as war-ravaged Europe and Asia relied on U.S. productive capacity to assist them until they could recover. Under the United Nations Relief and Rehabilitation Agency (UNRRA), primarily financed by the United States, supplies flowed into the devastated areas to provide for the hungry and the destitute. When the "cold war" between the Soviet Union and the United States began to intensify in 1949, U.S. aid became more directly politically motivated. The Marshall Plan was launched to strengthen the internal production capacity and financial structure of a number of European countries, to reduce the possibility of communist success. Eventually, under the plan, almost $9 billion was channeled into such countries as Greece, Italy, France, and West Germany. Most of these funds were used to buy exports from the United States.

While the U.S. government, learning from the reparation–war debt experience of the 1920s, used primarily governmental unilateral transfers or foreign aid to support desired foreign economies, after World War II private foreign investors from the United States were also active. In 1946, foreign investments began to increase, primarily in Europe, but also in the various less developed countries. Unlike the 1920s, these investments were primarily direct investments in productive capacity. The investments, especially those made in Europe, were increasingly made in manufacturing industries. In the less developed countries, investments in raw materials were still important, but more and more concentration was placed on processing materials and on manufacturing.

This process of foreign investment had begun before World War II. The steady increase in direct foreign investment in manufacturing and processing in time created **multinational firms.** These are firms with economic facilities for processing, manufacturing, and sales that are worldwide.

The development of multinational firms was, in large measure, a response to the growth of world markets. Improved communications lowered information costs; improved transportation, with the development of a worldwide system of air transportation, and technological development, especially of computers, increased economies of scale. These factors allowed firms to increase their size without incurring diseconomies of scale. However, they generated concern in part because the global nature of dispersion of facilities gives the firms such flexibility that no one country may be able to exercise control over their activities.

In summary, then, funds provided to other countries by U.S. government transfers, and foreign investment, and exports to the United States financed a U.S. export surplus in the amounts of $6.7 billion in 1946 and $5.3 billion in 1949. These net exports increased total demand in the United States and contributed to the expansion.

## Government Economic Policy

With the end of the war, the Republican-dominated Congress moved quickly to liquidate wartime spending, taxes, and controls. Government expenditures and taxes were cut substantially. Given the inflation that occurred, these cuts were not contractive enough despite the appearance of government surpluses in 1948 of $8.9 billion. Truman, concerned that inflation in 1946 would get out of hand, pushed for the extension of OPA and price controls. Congress, however, allowed the act to expire in 1946, thus removing federal controls over prices, wages, and rents. While government actions were not designed explicitly to counter business fluctuations, fiscal policy played a contractive role, although not enough to prevent inflation.

Congress passed the G.I. Bill in 1944, which gave veterans the right to $20 a week for 52 weeks after discharge; the right to a guaranteed mortgage loan on the purchase of a house; and the right to subsidy payments on attending an approved educational institution. The G.I. bill had many ramifications, but in terms of its effect on total demand, it was definitely expansionary.

In 1946, the Employment Act was passed. It created the Council of Economic Advisers to advise the president on economic matters and created the Joint Committee on the Economic Report of the President to give Congress a committee specializing in economic matters. Also, it stated that the federal government should work to achieve "maximum employment, production and purchasing power." This act committed the government to formulating and executing stabilization policies.

## The Union Movement

Unions continued to increase in membership, from 7.3 million in 1940 to 14.7 million in 1949. But after the war union pressures for higher wages and widespread strikes met a hostile public and Congress. The Taft-Hartley Act of 1947 was meant to restore balance to a situation seen as too favorable to unions. A number of provisions unfavorable to unions were included. These included prohibition of secondary boycotts, jurisdictional strikes, excessive union fees, featherbedding, and closed shops. Furthermore, unions were required to give 60 days' notice of intent to strike and required also to bargain in good faith for 30 days. The president could declare a strike a threat to the national interest and obtain a court injunction delaying the strike for 90 days. The honeymoon that the revitalized union movement had had with a sympathetic public and Congress in the 1930s was over.

## 1949 and Recession

Toward the end of 1948, the ability to supply began to catch up with the high levels of postwar demand. Demand began to level off in its growth rate. Inventories began to pile up, and induced investment began to slide as demand for expansion of facilities decreased. Investment dropped sharply from $46 billion in 1948 to $35.7 billion in 1949. Increases in consumption and government expenditure were not enough to offset this decline. GNP dropped slightly (by about $1 billion), and unemployment rose from 3.8% to 5.9%. Prices also dropped, by about 1 percent.

By the end of 1949, the economy was beginning to recover from this mild first recession after the war. Consumption and residential construction were still expanding, as were government expenditures for goods and services, especially military goods. Almost as if by accident, the tax cut in 1948 prior to the contraction sustained consumer purchasing power.

# The Korean Expansion, 1950-1954

## The Record

By the beginning of 1950, the economy was recovering from its first postwar recession. The outbreak of the Korean conflict in June of 1950 further accelerated this expansion, and the economy moved forward rapidly. GNP increased from $285 billion in 1950 to $365 billion in 1953. As a result of this expansion, unemployment fell from 5.3% to 2.9%. But also under the stimulus of expanding demand, prices rose from an index of 84 in 1950 to 93 in 1953 (see Table 19-3).

Table 19-3. Economic Statistics 1950 to 1954 (billions of dollars).

| Year | GNP | Consumption | Gross Investment | Government Expenditures | Federal Expenditures for Goods and Services | |
|------|-----|-------------|------------------|------------------------|-------------------|-------|
| | | | | | Military | Other |
| 1950 | 285 | 191 | 54 | 38 | 14 | 4 |
| 1951 | 328 | 206 | 59 | 60 | 34 | 4 |
| 1952 | 346 | 217 | 52 | 75 | 46 | 6 |
| 1953 | 365 | 230 | 53 | 82 | 49 | 8 |
| 1954 | 365 | 237 | 52 | 74 | 41 | 6 |

| Year | Federal Deficits | Consumer Prices (1957-1958 = 100) | Federal Debt | Net Exports | Unemployment |
|------|------------------|-----------------------------------|--------------|-------------|--------------|
| 1950 | − 2.2 | 84 | 256.9 | + 1.1 | 5.3 |
| 1951 | + 7.6 | 91 | 255.3 | + 3.0 | 3.3 |
| 1952 | 0.0 | 93 | 259.1 | + 2.6 | 3.0 |
| 1953 | − 5.3 | 93 | 266.0 | + 1.4 | 2.9 |
| 1954 | − 1.2 | 94 | 270.8 | + 2.5 | 5.5 |

Source: U.S. Department of Commerce, Bureau of the Census, Historical Statistics of the United States, Colonial Times to 1970 (Washington, D.C.: U.S. Government Printing Office, 1975).

But in 1953, the Korean War ended, and federal expenditures, especially military expenditures, declined. The economy entered its second postwar recession. This, too, was mild, although unemployment climbed to 5.5% in 1954.

## Causes of the Expansion

During the 1949 recession, consumer demand for durables and residential construction was still strong, because of the 1930s depression and a war-starved economy. Residential construction was stimulated as interest rates fell under the impact of general falling demand in 1949. The recovery began by the beginning of 1950.

After the Korean War broke out in June 1950, aggregate demand surged ahead. Part of the increase in consumption and investment demand was in anticipation of renewal of inflation and the reestablishment of war-time controls. A second surge in demand was prompted by increases in government expenditures for goods and services. On the federal level, an expanded military sector boosted expenditures from $14 billion in 1950 to $49 billion in 1953. State and local government expenditures also contributed to the expansion under the impact of continued shifts of population to suburbia and the increase in educational expenditures as the baby boom continued into the 1950s.

Given the elasticity of supply, this increase in demand was greater than the ability of the economy to fill it without increases in prices. Inflation returned in 1950. The government responded with controls over prices, but the legislation that gave the president the power to set prices was allowed to lapse in 1952.

## The 1954 Recession

With the end of the Korean War in 1953, federal expenditures, mostly in the area of military expenditures, were cut by $10 billion. This decrease should have caused a severe contraction, but because fiscal and monetary policy were used intelligently, it resulted in only a mild recession. As government expenditures were cut, taxes were also decreased, shifting demand from government to civilian sources. At the same time, the Federal Reserve engaged in an easy money policy, increasing bank reserves and reducing interest rates. An increasing supply of money and falling interest rates stimulated borrowing for consumption, investment, and state and local expenditures based on borrowing.

# Again Boom and Recession, 1955–1959

The economy was recovering by the end of 1954. Stimulated by a boom in demand for consumer durables, the economy surged ahead in 1955. Record highs were made in the production of autos as well as of other consumer durables. As this boom collapsed, the slack was taken up by expansion in producer durables. The economy continued to expand until late 1957. But inflation revived along with the expansion.

The low levels of demand for consumer durables and a declining level of investment demand toward the end of 1957 slowed down the expansion. Efforts of the Eisenhower administration to counter the persistent inflation triggered the third and most severe postwar recession, that of 1957–1958. The administration moved to reduce the deficit in the federal budget, and the Federal Reserve contracted the supply of money and raised interest rates. The economy contracted. The federal budget deficit increased to almost $13 billion in 1959. Unemployment increased to almost 7%, the highest rate since the beginning of 1942. But for the first time prices increased during a contraction. The economy recovered quickly and began to expand by the end of 1958 (see Table 19-4).

Table 19-4. Economic Statistics, 1955 to 1959 (billions of dollars).

| Year | GNP | Consumption | Gross Investment | Government Expenditures | Federal Expenditures for Goods and Services | |
|------|-----|-------------|------------------|-------------------------|------------------|-------|
| | | | | | Military | Other |
| 1955 | 398 | 254 | 67 | 75 | 39 | 6 |
| 1956 | 419 | 267 | 70 | 78 | 40 | 5 |
| 1957 | 441 | 281 | 68 | 86 | 44 | 5 |
| 1958 | 447 | 290 | 61 | 95 | 46 | 8 |
| 1959 | 484 | 311 | 75 | 97 | 46 | 8 |

| Year | Federal Deficits | Consumer Prices (1957–1958 = 100) | Federal Debt | Net Exports | Unemployment |
|------|------------------|-----------------------------------|--------------|-------------|--------------|
| 1955 | − 3.0 | 93 | 274.4 | + 2.9 | 4.4 |
| 1956 | + 4.1 | 94 | 272.8 | + 4.6 | 4.1 |
| 1957 | + 3.2 | 98 | 272.4 | + 6.3 | 4.3 |
| 1958 | − 2.9 | 102 | 279.7 | + 3.4 | 6.8 |
| 1959 | − 12.9 | 104 | 287.8 | + 1.2 | 5.5 |

*Source:* U.S. Department of Commerce, Bureau of the Census, *Historical Statistics of the United States, Colonial Times to 1970* (Washington, D.C.: U.S. Government Printing Office, 1975).

# What's New?

## Automatic Stabilizers

The three postwar recessions, in 1949, 1954, and 1958, were relatively mild, especially when compared to the economic disaster of the depressions of 1907, 1921, 1929–1933, and 1937–1938. One explanation for the relative mildness of these business fluctuations was the appearance of a number of **automatic stabilizers,** factors that tended to dampen business fluctuations without conscious decision-making. Two points must be kept in mind. First, these stabilizers were not created to function as stabilizers, and second, they were not strong enough to eliminate fluctuations.

One form of stabilizer was government expenditures in the form of transfer payments. Unemployment compensation, welfare payments, social security, veterans' payments, and business subsidies, especially to agriculture, tend to increase automatically during a contraction. The increase in expenditures enlarges purchasing power, countering the contraction. During a period of expansion with inflationary pressures, such expenditures inhibit the rate of increase, reducing the inflationary pressures.

The strength of the stabilizer has tended to increase as transfer payments have grown from 4% of personal income in 1940 to 6.6% in 1950, to 7.1% in 1960.

A second stabilizer was the federal progressive personal income tax. As unemployment develops with a contraction, personal income falls and also average effective tax rates. The effective overall tax rate falls, lessening the impact of the contraction on disposable income and consumption. During inflation, money incomes increase and incomes move into higher tax brackets, lessening the expansion of disposable income and consumption growth.

Federal income taxes increased in importance from 1940 to 1960. In 1940, federal income taxes were only 15% of federal tax receipts. In 1950, they were 38%, and they were 44% by 1960. Payment of federal income taxes averaged 1.4% of personal income in 1940 and 10% in 1960.

In 1929, government expenditures for goods and services were about 9% of GNP. By 1960, this had grown to about 25%. Because government expenditures are a much more stable component than investment, total demand became more stable and dampened business fluctuations.

In 1946, Congress passed the Employment Act, which committed the federal government to interfere in the economy to achieve an undefined acceptable level of employment and prices. By 1945, much of the business community had accepted the need for government involvement in maintaining employment and price stability. The Employment Act may have increased business confidence and increased the stability of investments by encouraging longer investment planning time, or what is called a **longer planning horizon.**

## Inflation

As World War II came to an end, many people were concerned about a possible revival of the righ unemployment rates of the 1930s. As an example of this concern, toward the end of the war the company making Pabst Blue Ribbon beer had sponsored an essay contest for economists on the question of how 50 million civilian jobs could be obtained after the war. This concern over unemployment quickly turned to one over persistent long-term inflation. The price index (1957–1958 = 100) was 48.8 in 1940, increasing to 84 in 1950 and to 104 by 1959. Prices over these 20 years rose by over 100%.

## The Military-Industrial Complex

President Eisenhower in 1961, during his last address to the people of the United States, warned about the dangers of what he called the *military-industrial complex,* or the cooperation between the defense department and a collection of major corporations that provide materials for the military. He was concerned that this combination of economic and political power would be difficult to control by the civilian political leadership.

Of course, military expenditures for goods and services reached a high point toward the end of the war in 1945, with $73.5 billion expended, comprising 34% of the GNP. These declined after the war until a rearmament program began with the start of the cold war in 1948. The Korean War in 1950 gave a further boost to military expenditures, which declined at its end in 1953. In 1955, military expenditures again increased. In 1959 such expenditures for goods and services stood at $46 billion, almost 10% of GNP.

It seems apparent that military expenditures comprised a substantial share of total federal expenditures for goods and services, and they were a significant share of total GNP. It also seems apparent that these expenditures played a role in business fluctuations, their increase aiding in the recovery from the recession of 1949 and their decrease impacting the contraction of 1954. However, it would be difficult to prove that military expenditures were the primary factor in causing the expansions and contractions of the U.S. economy from 1945 to 1959. These variations were the result of many factors, only one of them being variations in military expenditures.

## The Distribution of Income and Poverty

Table 19-5 shows that there was little change in the share of total income going to the lowest 40% of income receivers between 1941 and 1962. The middle income receivers (the third and fourth fifths) did increase their shares from the top fifth income receivers from 1941 to 1957. The word "poor" is defined here within the context of the United States experience and involves *relative* income shares. The poor fall within the lowest 40% of income receivers, although not all would be considered poor in an absolute sense. Income redistribution from the production of goods and services as indicated from Table 19–5 did not increase their relative shares. Income improvement, then, to those in poverty came from economic growth increasing total income generated, and from transfer payments for unemployment compensation, social security, and growing welfare systems.

John K. Galbraith,[5] in his best-seller *The Affluent Society* (1958), sounded one small note of concern that was to become much louder in the 1960s. He maintained that public needs, including income redistribution to the poor, had increasingly been neglected in people's concern with their own private consumption needs.

---

Table 19-5. Percentage of Income Received by U.S. Families and Individuals 1941 to 1962.

| Income bank | 1941 | 1947 | 1957 | 1962 |
|---|---|---|---|---|
| Lowest Fifth | 4 | 4 | 4 | 3 |
| Second Fifth | 10 | 11 | 11 | 11 |
| Third Fifth | 15 | 17 | 18 | 17 |
| Fourth Fifth | 22 | 24 | 25 | 25 |
| Highest Fifth | 49 | 46 | 43 | 44 |

*Source:* U.S. Department of Commerce, Bureau of the Census, *Historical Statistics of the United States, Colonial Times to 1957* (Washington, D.C.: U.S. Government Printing Office, 1960), p. 166; Herman P. Miller, *Income Distribution in the United States* (Washington, D.C.: U.S. Government Printing Office, 1966), p. 21.

---

## The Balance of Payments

From 1945 through the rest of the 1940s and 1950s, the United States experienced large deficits in the balance of payments (see the Review of Economic Concepts in Chapter 13). U.S. earnings of foreign exchange came primarily from two sources: the favorable balance of trade with exports exceeding imports and the flow of dividends, interest, and profits from U.S. foreign investments. This second source was a growing one, as U.S. residents continued to make foreign investments after the war.

However, these earnings were not high enough to provide the foreign exchange needed to finance other foreign transactions. The transactions were primarily in four categories. As peace returned, American tourists spent increasing amounts in other countries. Also, the United States became the "policeman" of the world, and significant sums were spent abroad to maintain U.S. military forces. For political and perhaps also for humanitarian reasons, the U.S. government provided large sums to rehabilitate and strengthen the economies of many countries. At first, under the Marshall Plan, these funds went primarily to war-ravaged developed economies of Europe and Japan, those that would provide allies against Russia in the cold war. Later in the 1950s, this aid went increasingly to less developed economies. Finally, with the end of the war, the location of American foreign investments changed. Such investments increasingly went to developed countries rather than underdeveloped countries and more into facilities for commodity production than into producing raw materials.

Since the demand for foreign exchange exceeded what our trade surplus could supply, a balance of payments deficit developed. To cover that deficit, nonresidents accumulated claims to U.S. dollars and a small but steady trickle of gold was exported.

For most of the period, this deficit, with its nonresident accumulation of dollars and gold, was desired and was a goal of government policy. At the end of the war, the economic future of the noncommunist European economies was very uncertain. Much of their physical capital had been destroyed. Financially, there were few monetary reserves. The accumulation of dollars and gold through the U.S. deficits solved this problem of lack of reserves and greatly strengthened these noncommunist economies.

However, by the mid-1950s, this **dollar gap** or shortage had been solved. The gap now became a surplus. But the U.S. economy did not seem to be able to reverse its deficit position in the balance of payments.

# A Summary

The economic expansion of the 1940s and 1950s was marred by only three mild contractions, in 1949, 1954, and (the most severe) in 1958. This 20-year period (even excluding the war years of 1941–1945) was one of longer-term increases in income and sustained employment that rivals if not exceeds that of 1897 to 1914 and the "prosperity years of 1922 to 1929.

High levels of consumption demand, fueled by the privations of the 1930s and the postponed demand of the war years 1941–1945 were led by demand for consumer durables. The move to the suburbs, the housing shortages caused by depression and war, and government subsidizing of middle-class housing through veteran benefits and FHA loan guarantees stimulated high levels of residential construction. Investment demand for construction of plant and for equipment was fueled by induced investment (the need for facilities to meet increased consumption demand), replacement investment (replacing worn-out and technologically obsolete plant and equipment, resulting from low levels of investment during the depression and war), and autonomous investment (technological changes occurring from 1945 to 1959). High levels of government expenditures from rearmament, highway construction, and income redistribution through increased transfer payments were significant additional sources of demand.

But there were persistent problems that continued to plague the economy. The concern about a possible return of massive unemployment after the war was replaced by 1959 with growing concern about inflation. The lowest 40% of income receivers did not increase their share of total cash income. The poor gained from economic growth and growing transfer payments, but the problem of poverty remained. A balance of payments deficit created after the war to strengthen noncommunist economies (the dollar gap) remained by the end of the 1950s after the dollar gap had been met.

Expansion continued into the 1960s and 1970s. But old problems remained, and new problems were to appear.

# Glossary

**Automatic stabilizers**   Factors in the economy that tend to dampen business fluctuation without conscious decision-making.

**Dollar gap**   Shortage in international reserves in western European countries and Japan that existed between 1945 and 1955.

**Longer planning horizon**   An increase in investment planning time.

**Multinational firm**   A firm with economic facilities for processing, manufacturing, and sales that are worldwide.

# Questions

1. What were the factors that caused the expansions of 1940–1948, 1950–1953, and 1955–1957?
2. What were the factors that caused the contractions of 1949, 1954, and 1958?
3. How did the automatic stabilizers contribute to the relatively mild contractions occurring from 1940 to 1959?
4. What were the problems that plagued the U.S. economy from 1940 to 1959?
5. Evaluate the performance of the U.S. economy from 1940 to 1959, stressing its strong points and its weaknesses.

# Suggested Readings

1. Bernstein, Irving. "The Growth of American Unions, 1945–60." *Labor History*, 2 (Spring 1961).
2. Blyth, C. A. *American Business Cycles, 1945–50.* London: Allen & Unwin, 1968.
3. Craf, John R. *A Survey of the American Economy 1940–1946.* New York: North River Press, 1947.

4. Friedman, Milton, and Schwartz, Anna J. *A Monetary History of the United States, 1867–1960*. Princeton, N.J.: Princeton University Press, 1963.

5. Galbraith, John Kenneth. *The Affluent Society*. Boston: Houghton Mifflin, 1958.

6. Gordon, Robert A. *Economic Instability and Growth: The American Record*. New York: Harper & Row, 1974.

7. Hamberg, Daniel. "The Recession of 1948–49 in the United States." *Economic Journal, 62* (March 1962).

8. Kolko, Gabriel. *Wealth and Power in America*. New York: Praeger, 1962.

9. Miller, Herman P. *Income Distribution in the United States*. Washington, D.C.: U.S. Government Printing Office, 1966.

10. Soltow, Leo. "Evidence of Income Inequity in the United States, 1866–1965." *Journal of Economic History* (June 1969).

11. Vatter, Harold G. *The U.S. Economy in the 1950s*. New York: Norton, 1963.

# Chapter 20

## The 1960s and the 1970s

Economic historians approach the analysis of recent events with a measure of caution and hesitancy. The reason is that we do not yet have an historical perspective on those events; there has not been time to discover and evaluate the data to determine new trends as opposed to continuations of historically observed patterns. As we approach the very recent economic history of the United States, therefore, we deal more with impressions, the outcome of which is as yet unknown.

In this last chapter, we will look at an overview of the record of the U.S. economy from 1960 to 1977. The primary emphasis in this review will be on the variations in output, employment, and prices; we shall attempt to offer some indications of the causes for such variations. The second half of the chapter will be concerned with some of the more important problems of the U.S. economy as we approach the 1980s.

## The Expansion of the 1960s

### Slow Growth and Low Inflation, 1960–1964

The decade opened with a mild recession in 1960 and 1961, the mildest of the four postwar recessions. Declines in investment and slow growth in consumption and government expenditures kept the advance of GNP in 1961 to $14 billion. In 1961, unemployment rose to almost 7%. Some economists have argued that the main cause of the recession was the extended strike in the steel industry in 1960.

The economy expanded more vigorously in 1962, but the rate of growth in real terms remained low, averaging less than 3 % per year for the years 1962 through 1964. This slow growth became more significant when compared to the two-digit real growth rates in such countries as West Germany and Japan and the more than 5 % rate in the Soviet Union. Also, this slow growth was mirrored in unemployment rates above 5 %, rates that many considered too high for the health of the economy. The one redeeming feature of this sluggishness was the low rate of inflation. The price index (1967 = 100) rose only from 89 in 1960 to 93 in 1964, or at the average rate of only a little more than 1 % per year (see Table 20-1).

Table 20-1. Economic Statistics, 1960–1969 (billions of dollars).

| Year | GNP | Consumption | Gross Investment | Federal Defense | Federal Other |
|---|---|---|---|---|---|
| 1960 | 504 | 325 | 75 | 45 | 9 |
| 1961 | 520 | 335 | 72 | 48 | 10 |
| 1962 | 560 | 355 | 83 | 52 | 12 |
| 1963 | 591 | 375 | 87 | 51 | 14 |
| 1964 | 632 | 401 | 94 | 50 | 15 |
| 1965 | 685 | 433 | 108 | 50 | 17 |
| 1966 | 750 | 466 | 121 | 61 | 17 |
| 1967 | 794 | 492 | 117 | 72 | 18 |
| 1968 | 864 | 536 | 126 | 78 | 21 |
| 1969 | 930 | 580 | 139 | 78 | 20 |

| Year | State and Local Expenditure | Government Transfer Payments | Federal Deficit | Consumer Price Index (1967 = 100) | Unemployment (Percent of Civilian Labor Force) |
|---|---|---|---|---|---|
| 1960 | 46 | 28.5 | + 0.3 | 89 | 5.5 |
| 1961 | 50 | 32.4 | − 3.4 | 90 | 6.7 |
| 1962 | 54 | 33.3 | − 7.1 | 91 | 5.5 |
| 1963 | 58 | 35.3 | − 4.8 | 92 | 5.7 |
| 1964 | 64 | 36.7 | − 5.9 | 93 | 5.2 |
| 1965 | 70 | 39.9 | − 1.6 | 95 | 4.5 |
| 1966 | 79 | 44.1 | − 3.8 | 97 | 3.8 |
| 1967 | 89 | 51.8 | − 8.7 | 100 | 3.8 |
| 1968 | 101 | 59.6 | − 25.2 | 104 | 3.6 |
| 1969 | 111 | 65.8 | + 3.2 | 110 | 3.5 |

*Source:* U.S. Department of Commerce, Bureau of the Census, *Historical Statistics of the United States, Colonial Times to 1970* (Washington, D.C.: U.S. Government Printing Office, 1975).

During this time, poverty was rediscovered. A spate of books and research reports were published revealing that at least 20% of the families in the United States received incomes below levels considered minimum for subsistence. What was even more worrisome was that a disproportionate number of the poor were concentrated among minorities, the aged, and families without male heads of households. Also, poverty had become more concentrated in urban areas. Perhaps the most prominent of the books on the subject was one that had a substantial impact on policymakers, Michael Harrington's *The Other America*.[3]

The balance of payments deficits that had begun to become serious in the second half of the 1950s continued. The efforts of the Kennedy and Johnson administrations to counter the deficits seemed to have little effect.

## Quickening Growth and Renewed Inflation, 1965-1969

Concern about slow growth, high unemployment, and poverty quickened; and after 1964, a series of programs was initiated in response to this concern. The Johnson administration consciously used "Keynesian" fiscal policy to stimulate the economy. In 1964, a three-year tax cut program was passed, with the largest cut to take effect in 1965. The seeming success of this fiscal policy substantially improved the reputation of the economics profession with politicians and the general public. Economists became the wise men of Washington, those who had the answers for the ills of the U.S. economy.

In 1964, the administration launched its "war on poverty" with a series of programs, the most important being the Economic Opportunity Act, which set up the Economic Opportunity Administration. The main thrust of the act was education and training of the poor in such programs as the Neighborhood Youth Corps, the Job Corps, and Vista. This war on poverty is considered by most to have been a failure because of incompetent administration, inadequate planning, and local political interference and manipulation. In 1973, the Economic Opportunity Administration was disbanded, and the remaining programs were shifted to other government departments. The government and the American people had lost the frontal assault in the war on poverty.

A final factor was the escalation of U.S. involvement in the Vietnam conflict in 1965 and 1966. U.S. troops in Vietnam rose to over 500,000, and defense expenditures increased. The Vietnam "conflict" became a full-scale war.

Under the impact of these three sources of increased expenditures and increased demand, economic growth quickened. Unemployment dropped in 1965 to 4.5% and by 1966, unemployment dropped to below 4%.

But this increased demand and low unemployment began to quicken inflation. In 1965, inflation had increased to 2% for the year. At the beginning of 1966, inflation began to increase faster, and the Federal Reserve instituted a tight money policy to counteract the rise in prices. President Johnson was vigorously opposed to this policy, declaring that we could have both "guns and butter" (referring to the U.S. involvement in Vietnam). The Fed was correct, however, in its policy, and inflation in 1966 averaged only 2%. But in 1967 inflation rose to 3% and in 1968 to 4%, and it reached 6% in 1969.

In 1968, Johnson tried Keynesian policy once again and obtained a 10% surcharge on federal income taxes (everyone had to add 10% to his or her income tax bill). This time the tax increase had little effect on reducing demand as people decreased their marginal propensity to save, paying most of the tax increase from their accumulated savings. It seemed the Keynesian economists were not always right in their policy recommendations.

With its increases in military expenditures, rising inflation, high incomes, the escalation in Vietnam increased imports relative to exports, especially after 1967. The balance of payments worsened and the administration decreased the convertibility of gold (limiting convertibility to foreign central banks), and pressures on the dollar caused an increase in the flow of gold out of the U.S. economy. This reduction in gold convertibility moved the U.S. economy further away from a convertible gold standard.

Although the 1960s experienced the longest sustained expansion of the U.S. economy in history (1961–1969), it also ended with serious problems. Inflation had returned and was rising, topping 6% in 1969. The balance of payments problem had remained and was deepening—it could not be ignored and was now a major problem. The war on poverty had collapsed.

The substantial increases in transfer payments, especially in the form of welfare and social security, were able only to prevent a decrease in the percentage of income going to the lowest 40% of income receivers (see Table 19-5). In addition, poverty became increasingly concentrated in urban areas, contributing to the crisis of the inner city. In part, urban financial problems, which were approaching crisis proportions, were caused by the influx of the poor and the flight of the middle class and industry to the suburbs.

The performance of economic policy recommended by the economics profession was mixed. The tax cut of 1965 and the tightening of credit by the Federal Reserve in 1966 were considered to have been successful on the whole. But the tax increase of 1968 was a failure in stabilizing unemployment and inflation.

Table 20-2. Economic Statistics, 1970–1977 (billions of dollars).

| Year | GNP | Consumption | Gross Investment | Government Expenditures Federal Defense | Federal Other |
|------|-----|-------------|------------------|-----------------------------------------|---------------|
| 1970 | 972 | 618 | 140 | 74 | 22 |
| 1971 | 1063 | 668 | 160 | 70 | 26 |
| 1972 | 1171 | 733 | 188 | 74 | 29 |
| 1973 | 1306 | 809 | 220 | 74 | 29 |
| 1974 | 1412 | 889 | 214 | 77 | 34 |
| 1975 | 1528 | 980 | 189 | 84 | 39 |
| 1976 | 1706 | 1094 | 243 | 87 | 43 |
| 1977 | 1890 | 1210 | 294 | 94 | 51 |

| Year | For Goods and Services State and Local | Government Transfer Payments | Federal Deficit | Consumer Price Index (1967 = 100) | Unemployment (Percent of Civilian Labor Force) |
|------|-----------------------------------------|------------------------------|-----------------|------------------------------------|--------------------------------------------------|
| 1970 | 123 | 75.9 | − 2.8 | 116.0 | 4.9 |
| 1971 | 137 | 89.9 | − 23.0 | 121.0 | 5.9 |
| 1972 | 151 | 99.4 | − 23.4 | 125.0 | 5.6 |
| 1973 | 167 | 113.5 | − 14.8 | 133.0 | 4.9 |
| 1974 | 192 | 134.9 | − 4.7 | 148.0 | 5.6 |
| 1975 | 215 | 169.8 | − 45.1 | 161.0 | 8.5 |
| 1976 | 231 | 184.7 | − 66.4 | 170.5 | 7.7 |
| 1977 | 250 | 197.8 | − 45.0 | 181.5 | 7.0 |

Source: Economic Report of the President, 1978 (Washington, D.C.: U.S. Government Printing Office, 1978).

# Instability in the 1970s

## The Recession of 1970–1971

The long-term expansion of the 1960s ended with the recession of 1970–1971. The rising inflation of 1969 eventually discouraged consumption and investment; the decline in investment after the extended expansion caused a fall in real GNP. Unemployment rose to 4.9% in 1970 and to almost 6% in 1971.

The experience of the 1958 recession was repeated, only worse. The rise in unemployment was accompanied by inflation. The price index increased from 110 (1967 = 100) in 1969 to 116 in 1970 and to 121 in 1971, a rise of 5% and 4%, respectively, per year.

Both the unemployment and inflation rates were unacceptable. But an effort to reduce one would require policies that would tend to increase the other. Some economists were beginning to talk of a "crisis in government policy." John Galbraith[1, 2] labeled the phenomenon of rising unemployment with inflation a "crisis in stabilization policy." Galbraith argued that functional finance fiscal policies and monetary policies based on "Keynesian" analysis could not deal with both conditions at the same time. Efforts to reduce unemployment would at the least prevent prices from falling. He called for mandatory price and wage controls to control inflation.

In early 1971, congress voted President Nixon the authority to impose wage and price controls. While some have argued that this was more a dare than a serious intention, if dare it was, Nixon accepted it. On August 15, 1971, Nixon issued what has been called his "New Economic Policy." This policy, indeed radical for its time, was to attack all three problems of the economy at once: unemployment, inflation, and the balance of payments deficits.

To deal with unemployment, he proposed a number of tax cuts especially aimed at stimulating investment. To combat inflation, he utilized the powers conferred on him by the recent legislation and imposed a 90-day wage and price freeze, to be followed by a series of phases with various degrees of controls. The controls would end with a voluntary program in late 1973 and 1974 when the enabling legislation expired. To attack the balance of payments deficits, he imposed a 10% increase in tariffs on imported automobiles and abandoned the gold standard completely by **floating the dollar** in the international exchange markets. The aim was to have market forces determine the exchange rates of the dollar. With a deficit, the dollar would **depreciate** (more dollars would be needed to buy a given amount of foreign exchange). As a result, the foreign price of U.S. exports would decrease while the domestic price of imports would increase. The resulting increase in exports and decrease in imports would help to alleviate the payments problem.

It is unclear whether Nixon's wage-price controls were a success or a failure; more research is needed. The controls have many critics. Some charge that they were unnecessary because the rate of growth of prices was beginning to decrease before August 15, 1971. Others have concluded that the administration of the controls was inadequate and influenced by pressure groups and that serious mistakes were made. There have been arguments that, as the controls were removed, prices and wages increased to "catch up" and that part of the inflation of 1973 and 1974 was caused by firms and unions trying to make up for postponed increases.

But the freeze and early controls may have broken the cycle of price increase expectations that lead to anticipatory demand and price increases. In effect, then, the freeze may have "cooled" the inflationary surge started in the late 1960s. Clearly, during the three months of Phase I, there was virtually no increase in consumer prices; and during Phase II, there was only a 3.4% price rise over a 17-month period.

## Expansion and Decline, 1972-1974

The economy resumed its expansion before the end of 1971. Unemployment fell only slowly with this advance, remaining at an average level of almost 5% in 1973. While the inflationary rate cooled in 1972, the rate began to increase toward the end of that year. A prime stimulant to the increase in the rate was the sharp rise in food prices, primarily the result of a billion-dollar purchase of wheat for immediate delivery by the Soviet Union, plus a disastrous loss of the anchovy catch off Peru, which increased the prices of feed grains and flour. The depreciation of the dollar by 10% in 1973 further increased foreign demand for the then relatively cheaper U.S. agricultural exports. Another stunning blow to world and U.S. inflation was the increase in crude oil prices by OPEC (Organization of Petroleum Exporting Countries) in late 1973.

As inflation accelerated in 1973, the Federal Reserve, under the direction of Arthur Burns, moved to severely restrict excess reserves in order to increase interest rates and to reduce lending. These monetary actions were designed to reduce aggregate demand and reduce prices. The Fed, however, proved unsuccessful in controlling prices at that time. This occurred in spite of increases in the prime bank rate to over 12% and, for a time, the drying up of excess reserves to such an extent that the *Wall Street Journal* wrote about the possibility of a liquidity crisis in the banking system.

Inflation continued to increase in 1974, but at the same time unemployment also began to increase, and real output began to decline. The recession of 1974 began. It was the most severe contraction the economy had faced since the 1930s. Real GNP declined by about 3%. Unemployment reached a high of 9.2% Consumer durables, especially automobiles, were hardest hit. Unemployment in the auto industry reached 25%. Aggravating the contraction and inflicting additional harm, though, was inflation, which topped 12% in 1974. The term applied to this situation was **stagflation**—high inflation and high unemployment occurring at the same time.

The balance of payments worsened as Europe and Japan shared in the contraction and as U.S. exports fell much more than imports. An unfavorable balance of trade occurred; for example, in 1974, imports exceeded exports by $5.4 billion.

## Recovery, 1975-1977

Under the impact of high unemployment and low levels of demand, as well as nonrepetition of the oil price increase of late 1973, the inflationary rate declined, reaching lows in some months of 1976 of 4 to 5%. Despite the recovery, unemployment rates fell only slowly, still averaging 8.5% in 1975. The rate remained above 6% at the end of 1977. While the economy was growing vigorously, the ghost of high unemployment and high inflation remained.

The unfavorable balance of trade reversed itself in 1975, with a $9 billion export balance as the inflation in Europe and Japan remained higher than that in the United States. In 1976 and 1977, the deficits in the balance of payments steadily increased as U.S. imports of oil, autos, consumer electronics, and steel increased.

# Conclusion

From the country's founding in 1783, the U.S. economy has shown an amazing record of growth. Starting with 13 states along the Atlantic and 3 million people, the country grew to span a continent, with over 220 million people. From an economy based primarily on agriculture and rural life, the United States became a complex industrial society with its people concentrated in urban-suburban pursuits. GNP in the late 1970s was on its way to $2 trillion. Although rising prices caused a substantial portion of that GNP growth, the record still is one of impressive achievement.

Nonetheless, serious problems remained. Some were old problems, some were new, and some were old ones with new twists.

## Economic Stabilization

Prior to the publication of John M. Keynes' *General Theory* in 1936, the view was widely accepted that the least government was the best government. Expenditures should be just large enough to cover necessary services and taxes should balance the expenditures. Considerable concern was felt about incurring any national debt. Monetary policy was primarily aimed at supporting the financial security of the banking system and maintaining a favorable balance of payments.

After the depression of the 1930s and publication of Keynes' *General Theory*, government policy changed to one of economic stabilization. Both fiscal policy (expenditure and tax) and monetary policy (supply of money and interest rate) were directed to counter unemployment and inflation. At times, government stabilization policy has been successful. The decrease in GNP during the recession of 1954, for example, was considerably less than the cut in military expenditures at the end of the Korean conflict. This was so because of an easy money policy (increasing the supply of money and decreasing the interest rate) and because of a cut in taxes (an expansionist fiscal policy). Other examples were the tax cuts of 1964, stimulating output, and the tight money policy of 1966, with its diminishing effect on the inflationary surge. Some failures were recorded, such as the abortive attempt to cool inflation through a tax increase in 1968.

Beginning with the recession of 1958 and again in the recession of

1970–1971, but most especially in the recession of 1974, a new situation appeared for economic stabilization policies. That situation was one of rising unemployment and rising prices at the same time (stagflation). Traditional fiscal and monetary policies could not deal with both at the same time, as policymakers tried to deal with one, policies were pursued that tended to aggravate the other. If unemployment and inflation are both at unacceptable levels (as, for example, when in 1974, unemployment was 9.2% and inflation was over 12%), the worsening of either one makes an already unacceptable level even more unacceptable. In addition, both inflation and unemployment have become more resistant to control.

There are a number of reasons why this has occurred. Some of the inflation may stem from foreign sources that are difficult to control. Examples are OPEC's 400% increase in oil prices at the end of 1973 and an increased foreign demand for U.S. agricultural products, again in 1973. Increased monopoly power (the ability to restrict supply) may increase prices higher than those justified by productivity or those which would exist under competitive conditions. Examples are cost-push inflation generated by unions (gains in wages higher than increases in productivity) and administered price inflation from firms that increase the price on the finished product by restricting supply. Unemployment may be caused by shifts in demand for different kinds of labor through changes in demand for products (anthracite coal to oil, for example), or changes in technology (such as automation eliminating need for unskilled labor). Other factors are inflation induced by the federal government through high deficits, increasing demand above the ability of the economy to supply at stable prices, and through increases in prices because of certain government regulation by such agencies as the Department of Agriculture and the Interstate Commerce Commission. These factors either are immune to the effects of variation in aggregate demand resulting from fiscal or monetary policy or are very resistant to such manipulation.

What is important to keep in mind is that stagflation creates a crisis in fiscal and monetary policy. Because of the newness of the problem, historical experience does not suggest how it may be resolved. At least two alternatives have long been urged. One alternative is widely associated with economist Milton Friedman. Called *monetarism*, it is based on the conclusion that variations in the supply of money are the most important factor in economic stabilization. Monetarists recommend that the supply of money be increased each year by a fixed percent, generally recommended at 4%. This increase in the supply of money would accommodate stable prices, and increases in productivity and the supply of labor. The monetary rule would stabilize growth in the supply of money and, hopefully, would force the market economy into more stable growth.

Another alternative is widely associated with John K. Galbraith. It is called an *incomes policy*, or wage and price controls. Such controls could break inflationary expectations and, with the cooperation of society, could provide controls over inflation while government policy dealt with unemployment.

Controversy will continue over the strengths and weaknesses of monetarist and incomes policies. Government stabilization policies have become more complex, difficult, and confused. Will government policy-makers and economists devise effective programs to lessen inflation and unemployment at acceptable rates of growth in the 1980s? Only time will tell.

## Balance of Payments Deficits

Deficits in the balance of payments had started at the end of the war as government aid was extended to a war-ravaged world. With the onset of the cold war, this aid was concentrated on bolstering allies in western and southern Europe by meeting their needs for dollars, aiding their economic recovery, and shoring up their weak financial reserves. However, when the dollar gap had been satisfied by 1956, the deficits continued.

By the 1970s, the deficit problem had become serious and persistent. As part of his new economic policy of August 1971, President Nixon abandoned an already greatly restricted gold standard and floated the dollar. Since then, the exchange rate of the dollar has either floated, determined by market demand, or has been stabilized by market activities of either the United States or foreign governments. The dollar depreciated at the end of 1971, again in April of 1973, and once again in 1978.

In terms of the balance of payments accounts itself, the major problems lie in the inability of the United States to earn enough in the merchandise or commodity account (exports versus imports), in receipts of dividends, profits, and interest from prior foreign investment, to provide foreign exchange for other transactions in the current account plus the steady debit balance in long-term capital. The situation worsened in the 1970s because of a tendency to increase imports relative to exports. In the decade of the 1960s, the balance between imports and exports was, for the decade, a credit balance of $40.8 billion. From 1970 to 1977, this had become a debit balance of $10.8 bilion.

Because of the inability to earn foreign exchange to pay for debit balances in both the current and long-term capital account, nonresidents have continued to accumulate short-term assets in the United States. These assets are concentrated in four groups: Japan, West Germany, holdings by OPEC countries, and claims to dollars held in Europe, so-called *Euro dollars*.

The increase in imports has been concentrated in two areas: oil imports of $34.6 billion in 1976, and manufactured and semimanufactured goods, principally from Japan and western Europe. A continual drain has been U.S. foreign investment, which amounted to $84.1 billion in the period from 1970 to 1976.

No one knows how long the United States can continue this deficit position or what measures will be taken to deal with it. What is very apparent is that the balance of payments situation can no longer be ignored. It has now become a problem of the first magnitude.

## Pollution, Resources, and Economic Growth

The economic growth of the United States has been accompanied by substantial disregard for the future supplies of many resources and a lack of concern for the effects of production and consumption on the environment within which we live. The virtual mining of the soil (continuous cropping without replaced losses in soil nutrients) in agriculture through most of the nineteenth century and the overcutting of many areas of timberland are prime examples of this disregard of future resources. Pollution of air, rivers, lakes, and oceans through consumption and industrial production are costs that have been largely ignored until recently.

Economic analysis does provide some justification for the wasteful use of natural resources. Labor in the nineteenth century was the scarce resource, land or timber the abundant one. The scarce resource, labor, would be conserved, while the abundant resource would be used in ways to conserve the scarce resource, labor. Also, as long as the environment could absorb the pollution and "clean itself," clean air and water were free goods, and the use of the environment as a free dumping ground for production and consumption waste could be tolerated. Therefore, the calls for conservation—for example, the conservation movement during the presidency of Theodore Roosevelt in the early twentieth century—went largely unheeded.

By the 1960s, the problems of pollution and scarcity of material resources could no longer be avoided. A rash of books, articles, and organizations concerned with pollution and scarce resources began to appear. Predictions were made that unless economic growth itself was curtailed pollution would intensify to the point of threatening human existence on this planet. The Club of Rome sponsored a study by Meadows and others,[7] called *The Limits of Economic Growth*, that predicted the exhaustion of nonreproducible resource such as oil by the year 2000 and resultant worldwide poverty if economic growth was not immediately curtailed.

Most economists have confidence that pollution can be controlled by government regulation or even by the market itself without reducing economic growth. Even the Club of Rome, in a more recent study, has revised its predictions in a more optimistic direction. Many people argue that economic growth is needed to provide the facilities to reduce pollution. Also, many economists maintain that (a) technological change caused by high prices of scarce resources will encourage new technology that conserves the scarce resource or new technology that substitutes new resources for the old; and/or (b) the functioning of the market, in which high prices for scarce resources reduce the quantity demanded of that resource, will encourage the use of lower-priced, more abundant resource substitutes. Either or both may solve the problem of reduced supplies of nonreproducible resources.

Beginning in the 1960s, a series of legislative acts at federal and state levels substantially expanded government responsibility in the area of pollution control. Included in these acts was the establishment of the federal Environmental Protection Agency (EPA) to coordinate these programs. Many criticisms have been made of the implementation of the program. Some critics feel that the program is too weak to deal substantively with reducing pollution. Other critics charge that the programs increase administrative red tape, increase costs of production to control pollution, and lose needed jobs in communities as facilities are either closed because of the higher cost of pollution control or because projects are refused permission to operate on environmental grounds.

The increase in oil prices and the oil boycott of 1973–1974 brought home the problem of resource supplies, but little seems to have been learned from the lesson and even less action taken. In the area of pollution control, U.S. society has not decided how much "clean air" it really wants. Nevertheless, these problems must eventually be resolved. Exactly how industrial societies will accommodate themselves to declining supplies of essential resources and resolve the conflicts of pollution control is yet to be seen.

## Poverty and the Urban Crisis

In 1963, President Johnson, with great fanfare, announced his war on poverty. By the end of his term in 1968, that war was well on its way to a finish, although not with a bang but with a fizzle. Finally, the breakup of the Economic Opportunity Administration in 1973 and the transfer of its few remaining programs to other agencies perhaps marked the official end of that war. At the beginning of the program, about 20% of all U.S. families and individuals were defined as living in poverty. By 1977, this had dropped to about 12%, due primarily to increases in the country's economic growth.

This poverty was still concentrated disproportionately among "disadvantaged" minorities (blacks, Native Americans, Chicanos, and Puerto Ricans), families headed by women, and the aged. Also, it was increasingly concentrated in urban areas. But, perhaps most disturbing of all, second-and third-generation welfare recipients were becoming increasingly common.

The optimism of the 1960s has substantially passed. The public increasingly feels that eliminating poverty is a hopeless task. No one seems satisfied with the existing welfare programs, and many have assessed these programs as not only failing to eliminate poverty, but perhaps as being an important factor in perpetuating it. Yet no one seems to be able to come up with an acceptable alternative.

One aspect of the poverty problem is the deepening financial crisis of U.S. cities. With the influx of the poor into urban areas, there has also been a move by the middle class out of the cities into the suburbs. Exactly how much the latter is influenced by the former is still hotly debated. In addition, many of the new industries being established have been sited in suburban areas, and smaller cities and suburban shopping centers have drawn shoppers away from urban stores.

These factors have pressed the cities financially in a variety of ways. First, the poor pay fewer total taxes (real estate, sales, and income taxes) than their more affluent, middle-class, retreating, former neighbors. In effect, the tax base decreases. In addition, the loss of industry and commerce has also reduced city revenues. On the other hand, the increase in low-income residents has tended to increase city expenditures for education, health, police and fire protection, and welfare.

Many recommendations have been made. They include the taking over by the state and/or federal government of functions such as hospitals and welfare. Larger governmental units could be formed to include urban-suburban areas. The state and/or federal government could transfer funds to cities for their use.

Although some of these recommendations have been implemented in part, the problem of the cities' financial solvency still remains. In 1974 and 1975, a number of cities (New York City and Newark, New Jersey, for example) came very close to bankruptcy, and Cleveland, Ohio, declared bankruptcy in 1978. Where might that occur again?

## The Federal Bureaucracy

The federal bureaucracy grew slowly in the nineteenth century, reaching 95,000 employees by 1900. In the next 30 years, however, growth quickened, reaching 565,000 employees by 1930. With the coming of the depression and the advent of the mixed economy (one with a substantial role for the federal government), the federal bureaucracy expanded at a rapid rate; to 996,000 employees in 1940, 1.93 million in 1950, 2.27 million in 1960, and 2.73 million in 1977.

This bureaucracy has entered most every phase of economic activity. There are departments dealing with agriculture, commerce, labor, housing, health, education, and welfare. There are the major regulatory agencies, such as the Interstate Commerce Commission, Federal Trade Commission, Securities and Exchange Commission, Food and Drug Administration, Federal Communications Commission, Environmental Protection Agency, and the Civil Aeronautics Board. One must not forget the Defense Department and, of course, the Internal Revenue Service. There is little that society does in the United States that is not in some way or another touched by the federal bureaucracy.

The purpose here is not to comment on the desirability of government bureaucracy but rather to ask a question that has grown out of our historical experience with that bureaucracy: Whose interests are served by the bureaucracy? And who controls the bureaucracy?

There are three possible areas of bureaucratic interest. First, the interest of the society as a whole may be the prime motivating factor. The bureaucracy may try to juggle the conflicting interests of the various segments of the society to come up with actions that are intended to in some way benefit the whole of society.

Second are the interests of the particular segments of the economy for which particular bureaucrats are responsible. The Department of Agriculture is concerned about the interests of farmers; the Department of Labor is concerned about labor's interests; and so on. Schultz and Dom[8] have called this the Balkanization of government. Each agency then becomes the spokesman for the particular group in its charge.

John K. Galbraith,[1, 2] in his books *The New Industrial State* (1966) and *Economics and the Public Purpose* (1973), has argued that the corporations and governments are really run by interlocking committees of experts. These technocrats are necessary because the problems and size of the activities are too complex for any but experts. An important point in his argument is that these experts operate on the basis of their own self-interest, which is to maintain control and expand that control. While there are disagreements with the specifics of Galbraith's theory, the question is very much open as to whether the bureaucracy is motivated by its own self-interests.

Serious questions have been raised about whether Congress and the president, who have the immediate "watchdog" function over this bureaucracy, can or even desire to control the federal bureaucracy. An even more pertinent question is "can the voting citizen adequately 'watchdog' the 'watchdogs'?"

And the ultimate question is "Can the bureaucracy (federal, state, or local) prove flexible enough to meet the problems at the end of the twentieth century?"

## Monopoly Power Revisited

In this history of the U.S. economy, we have touched on the development of monopoly power in the economy through the creation of large-scale business firms, unions, and big government. Since World War II, two additional forms of combination have appeared that have made more difficult and complex the problem of measuring the amount of monopoly power that exists and the means by which it is exercised in the marketplace. These forms are the conglomerate and the multinational firm.

Historically, large enterprises were formed through vertical and horizontal integration within the same industry. When it was formed, U.S. Steel included coal mines, coke works, iron mines, steel mills, and plants working the steel into different forms. This was an example of **vertical integration,** or one firm controlling the various stages of production in one industry. As it grew, General Motors absorbed automobile plants making different brands of cars. This is **horizontal integration,** or one firm controlling several plants at the same stage of production.

A **conglomerate** is a single organization that produces goods or services in a variety of different industries. LTV is a conglomerate that owns operating divisions in such diverse industries as electronics, aerospace, electrical wire, steel, stereo equipment, and meat packing. The conglomerate makes the problem of antitrust activity by the government more difficult since it creates the possibility of informal, noncompetitive arrangements between industries.

The multinational firm, as noted in an earlier chapter, is one that gains a significant portion of its assets in and income from facilities outside its home country. The operation of these firms is truly worldwide, not only because of worldwide marketing but also because they draw raw materials and semifinished products from a network of their facilities in many countries, and their manufacturing plants are also located in many different countries. Some examples of such firms based in the United States are Esso, Standard Oil, Ford, and General Motors. Based in foreign countries are Royal Dutch Shell, Mitsubushi, Nestle's, Krupp, and Volkswagen.

One problem that a number of observers are concerned about is the potential ability of multinationals to thwart any individual country's economic policies, either its economic stabilization or balance of payments policies. This might be done by shifting production between plants in different countries. The firms' planning involves plants in many countries, and that planning could well conflict with the planning of individual countries. Also, such firms hold large amounts of foreign exchange, and their shifting of these currencies from one country to another may destabilize exchange rates.

A number of factors have developed that may have increased the competitive environment of the U.S. economy. Many are factors that have reduced information and transaction costs. For example, widespread use of the automobile, as well as other transportation changes, have increased the substitutability of one firm's products for those of another. The current series of trade agreements between the United States and other nations have reduced tariff rates and thereby increased the substitutability of foreign products for domestic products, reducing the monopoly power of domestic producers.

## A Note of Optimism

The U.S. economy has gone through many changes in response to changing economic conditions. There is no doubt that changes will continue to occur, for economic development is a process of change. Change, therefore, is the one characteristic that historians can depend on. In the past, the U.S. economy has met these changes and has continued its long-term processes of intensive growth and development. There is no reason to presume that the changes in the future, at least in our lifetime, as well as continued long-term growth, will not also be accomplished.

# Glossary

**Conglomerate**   A single organization that produces goods or services in a variety of different industries.

**Depreciate**   To lessen in value. For example, a currency depreciates when it buys less of a foreign currency per unit of the domestic currency than previously.

**Floating the dollar**   A policy that allows the exchange rate of the dollar for foreign monies to fluctuate depending on supply and demand conditions without government interference.

**Horizontal integration**   The combining of two or more firms that produce at the same stage of production in the same industry, into one larger firm.

**Stagflation**   A condition of high unemployment and high inflation at the same time.

**Vertical integration**   The combining of two or more firms that produce at different stages of production in the same industry, into one larger firm.

# Questions

1. What were the significant features of U.S. economic fluctuations in the 1960–1964 period? The 1965–1969 period?
2. Do you think the accepted recommendations of certain advisory economists for economic stabilization in the 1960s were successful? Explain your conclusion.

3. What economic problems were present at the end of the 1960s?
4. Briefly describe the main characteristics of economic fluctuations in the 1970s.
5. What was Nixon's New Economic Policy? Was it "successful"?
6. In the recessions of 1970–1971 and 1974, there was much talk of a crisis of economic policy. What did this mean?
7. What are the major economic problems facing the United States as the economy approaches the 1980s?
8. Are you optimistic or pessimistic about the ability of the U.S. economy to continue its long-term expansion? Why?

## Suggested Readings

1. Galbraith, John K. *The New Industrial State.* 2nd ed. Boston: Houghton Mifflin, 1972.
2. Galbraith, John K. *Economics and the Public Purpose.* Boston: Houghton Mifflin, 1973.
3. Harrington, Michael. *The Other America.* New York: Macmillan, 1962.
4. Haveman, Robert H. *The Economics of the Public Sector.* New York: Wiley, 1976.
5. Jarret, Henry, ed. *Environmental Quality in a Growing Economy.* Baltimore: Johns Hopkins University Press, 1970.
6. Johnson, Arthur W. *The American Economy: An Historical Introduction to the Problems of the 1970s.* New York: Free Press, 1974.
7. Meadows, Donella H., et al, *The Limits to Growth.* New York: Universe, 1972.
8. Schultz, George, and Dom, Kenneth W. *Economic Policy Beyond the Headlines.* New York: Norton, 1977.
9. Ward, Barbara, and others, eds. *The Widening Gap: Development in the 1970s.* New York: Columbia University Press, 1971.
10. Will, Robert E., and Vatter, Harold, eds. *Poverty in Affluence.* 2nd ed. New York: Harcourt Brace Jovanovich, 1970.

# Glossary

**Absolute advantage**   The advantage that occurs when a nation or area is more efficient in producing a good or all goods than any other nation from which it might import that good or those goods.

**Accelerator principle**   The principle that as the rate of growth of consumer and industrial demand increases, the need for additional facilities increases and induced investment increases. These increases create a positive accelerator and the economy expands. The reverse occurs where the rate of growth of consumer demand declines.

**Aggregate production function**   The function showing the factors that determine changes in output.

**American System**   The term given to the system of standardized products, continuous production, and interchangeable parts begun in the early nineteenth century.

**Assembly-line production,** or **mass production**   A process depending on the standardization and thus interchangeability of parts and the development of a system or systems of flow of materials logically arranged so as to facilitate assembly of the product.

**Automatic stabilizers**   Factors in the economy that tend to dampen business fluctuation without conscious decision-making.

**Autonomous investment**   Investment determined by factors other than changes in income or consumption.

**Backward linkages**   Effects of input-output relationships or demand-supply stimuli from one economic activity to probable economic activities that existed in prior stages of production. For example, expansion of steel production through technological change increases the probability of developing coal and iron deposits.

**"Beggar thy neighbor" policy**  Policy of international trade restriction on the part of a country aimed at increasing exports relative to imports.

**Blacklist**  A list distributed to employers of workers considered "undesirable" for employment. Used against union members.

**Capital-labor ratio**  The number of dollars of capital (invested in machines, buildings, and so on) used per unit of labor.

**Classical view**  A view of economic development set forth in various forms during the late eighteenth and early to mid-nineteenth centuries by the classical economists, beginning with Adam Smith. Economic development is regarded as productivity growth, which is obtained through specialization and division of labor and capital, which in turn depend on the size of the market, the stock of capital, and economic institutions.

**Clearinghouse**  A means by which the notes of different banks are cleared through some central bank or institution.

**Company union**  A union whose membership consists only of the employees of a particular firm and that is dominated by that firm's officials.

**Competition**  The market form in which no buyer or seller is able to influence price by his or her own actions. Competition requires the following conditions: absence of collusion, flexible prices, and free entry and exit.

**Complementary industries**  Industries that serve a number of different industries, although they may have been created to service only one.

**Conglomerate**  The combining of firms that produce in different industries.

**Consolidation**  Forming one larger company out of a number of smaller companies.

**Constant returns to scale**  The return when long-run average costs are constant as scale (short-run average cost curves) increase.

**Construction companies**  Separately incorporated firms whose primary function was to raise financial capital and construct the railroads.

**Consumption function**  A function representing the various quantities that a society is willing and able to consume at different levels of income.

**Cost externalities**  Reductions in the average costs of a firm that result from actions taken outside of the firm.

**Craft unionism**  Union representation of workers by trade or craft rather than by industry.

**Credit**  All transactions in the balance of payments accounts that generate an immediate obligation for a nonresident to pay a resident. Or, all transactions that increase foreign demand for dollars or increase the supply of foreign monies in the foreign exchange market; for example, an export.

**Cross-sectional data**   Data that show the occurrence of a particular event in different activities at the same point in time or over the same span of time.

**Current account**   The sum of the balance of payments merchandise and invisible items accounts.

**Current GNP**   Total value of annual output of final goods and services; it includes the effects of price changes. It is not the best measure of economic performance of the economy.

**Data**   The records of economic events. In a broad sense, the word *data* refers to all events or happenings that are observed and recorded, not simply those that are quantified.

**Debit**   All transactions in the balance of payments accounts that generate an immediate obligation for a resident to pay a nonresident. Or, all transactions that increase foreign supply of dollars or increase the demand for foreign monies in the foreign exchange market; for example, an import.

**Decreasing returns to scale**   See **Diseconomies of scale.**

**Deficit in the balance of payments**   A deficit that results when a country is unable to obtain enough foreign exchange from its sale of goods and services or from long-term investment to pay for what its citizens purchase from other economies.

**Deposit multiplier**   The increase in money supply possible under a fractional reserve banking system given the reserve requirement and the amount of excess reserves in the banking system.

**Depreciate**   A currency depreciates when it buys less of a foreign currency per unit of the domestic currency.

**Derived demand**   Demand for a resource that is brought about by the demand for a product or service produced by that resource.

**Diseconomies of scale,** or **decreasing returns to scale**   The return when long-run average costs are increasing as scale (short-run average cost curves) increases.

**Dollar gap**   Shortage in international reserves in western European countries and Japan that existed between 1945 and 1955.

**Dual unionism**   More than one union existing for a single craft or industry.

**Economic determinism**   In the pure sense, the view that economic history is a progression of events in which people act almost exclusively on the basis of their economic self-interest or through adjusting to the changing economic reality.

**Economic development**   The long-term process through which per capita output grows and structural change occurs as well.

**Economic instability**   Variations in the level of economic activity, primarily variations in output, employment, and prices. It is considered a more appropriate term than *business cycles,* or *business fluctuations.*

**Economic institutions**   The organizational means through which economic decisions are made and implemented.

**Economic integration**   The tying together of product and resource markets in such a way that resources are allocated to their most efficient uses.

**Economic profit (rent)**   A payment to a factor of production greater than that necessary to bid for its use or greater than its opportunity costs.

**Economic rent**   See **Economic profit.**

**Economies of scale, or Increasing returns to scale**   The returns accruing as the long-run average cost curve slopes down as successive short-run average total cost curves, each showing a larger scale of operation, result in lower average costs.

**Elastic demand**   The relationship that exists when the quantity responds greatly to a given change in price, or when the percentage change in quantity demanded is greater than the percentage change in price, or when the elasticity coefficient is greater than 1.

**Elasticity coefficient**   A number indicating the degree of responsiveness of quantities to something else; as, for example, the price elasticity of demand represented by the following formula:

$$\frac{Q_1 - Q_2}{Q_1 + Q_2} \div \frac{P_1 - P_2}{P_1 + P_2}$$

$Q_1$ is beginning quantity, $Q_2$ is ending quantity, $P_1$ is beginning price, and $P_2$ is ending price. (Ignore the minus sign in the results.)

**Elasticity of demand**   The ratio is between the rate at which the quantity demanded of a product changes and its price changes.

**Elasticity of output**   The rate at which output increases as effective demand increases.

**Embargo of December 1807**   Based on an action of Congress, President Jefferson forbade the import or export of goods from and to Britain and France in retaliation for their seizure of U.S. commercial vessels from 1792 to 1807.

**Empty lands**   Those lands in which a new economy (rather than the evolution from an old economic order) evolves.

**Entrepot trade**   Trade that enters a country and then is transhipped to another country without being changed in form.

**Entrepreneurship**   The function of organizing resources in such a way that economic production occurs.

**Envelope curve**   The long-run average cost curve as it encloses or envelops an array of short-run average total cost curves, each representing a particular scale of operation.

**Equation of exchange**   A definitional relationship that shows that $MV = PQ$, where $M$ is the stock of money, $V$ is the income velocity of money, $P$ is the price level, and $Q$ is the number of final goods and services.

**Equilibrium price**   Also a market clearing price. The central price tendency of a market or the price that tends to eliminate both gluts and shortages.

**Extensive growth**   The growth that occurs as more resources are used to produce an output unchanged in composition or techniques of production.

**Favorable balance of trade**   When exports exceed imports or there is a credit balance in the merchandise account.

**Floating the dollar**   A policy that allowed the exchange rate of the dollar for foreign monies to fluctuate depending on supply and demand conditions without government interference.

**Forward linkages**   Effects of input-output relationships or demand-supply stimuli from one economic activity to probable economic activities closer to the ultimate user of the activity. For example, wheat production provides raw materials that could be used in flour milling.

**Fractional reserves**   In colonial times, refers to the need of a merchant bank to keep reserves in the form of gold or silver that are a fraction (less than 100%) of the currency in circulation. This is based on the principle that depositors will not come into the bank and demand gold or silver for the currency in an amount equal to total deposits.

**Full-employment budget**   The expenditures of the federal government, compared to taxes that would have been received if there had been full employment.

**Granger laws**   State laws passed in the 1870s and 1880s to regulate railroads.

**Gresham's law**   The rule that relatively overvalued money drives relatively undervalued money out of circulation.

**High-powered money**   The reserves of banks, consisting of gold, silver, coins, and certificates to specie, that could be readily loaned.

**Holding company**   A company formed for the purpose of buying stock in other companies and thereby controlling these other companies.

**Horizontal integration**   The combining of firms that produce at the same stage of production in the same industry.

**Human capital formation**   The investment in education that results in improved human skills and increased marginal physical productivity.

**Income elasticity of demand**   The rate at which the demand for a product changes in relation to the rate at which income changes.

**Increasing returns to scale**   See **Economies of scale.**

**Induced investment**   Investment induced or caused by changes in income and consumption. When the rate of increase in consumer demand is increasing, induced investment increases.

**Industrial union**   A union that draws its members from a specific industry rather than from a specific trade or craft.

**Inelastic demand**   The relationship that exists when the quantity demanded responds little to a given change in price, or when the percentage change in quantity demanded is less than the percentage change in price, or when the elasticity coefficient is less than 1.

**Information costs**   The costs to buyers and sellers of obtaining the price and technical information necessary to make rational choices.

**Innovation**   According to Schumpeter, innovation means new products, new processes, new machines, or even new markets that open up new opportunities for profits.

**Intensive growth**   The growth that involves increased productivity and involves a changed composition of output and techniques of production.

**Interlocking directorates**   Situations in which the same people appear on the boards of directors of a number of different corporations in the same industry; policies could then be more easily formulated in these several corporations that would eliminate competition and substitute cooperation.

**Internal and external economies of scale**   Lowered unit costs of production associated with larger-scale activity. Such lowered costs are internal if they result from increased scale by the individual firm; they are external if they result from actions taken outside of the individual firm.

**Interpretation**   The final product of economic history, the result of drawing historical conclusions by testing hypotheses within the framework of theory.

**Investment function**   A function representing the various quantities that the society is willing and able to invest at different levels of income.

**Invisible items account**   A major subaccount within the current account of the balance of payments. It contains primarily services such as expenditures by tourists; transportation; insurance fees; dividends, profits, and interest on foreign investments; and transfer payments.

**Land banks**   Established by a number of states in the 1780s, these banks issued paper currency backed only by loans on land.

**Law of demand**   The hypothesis that consumers will buy more of goods at (relatively) lower prices than at (relatively) higher prices.

**Law of diminishing returns**   Also known as the law of increasing opportunity cost. The idea that in reallocating resources to produce one good, a society must ultimately give up more and more of another good.

**Law of supply**   The hypothesis that firms will supply more of a good at (relatively) higher prices that at (relatively) lower prices.

**Leading sector theories**   Theories that hypothesize the existence of a sector or sectors of the economy that create effects on intensive growth and development through supply and demand effects that spread through the rest of the economy.

**Legal tender**   Money that according to law must be accepted in payment for all debts, public and private.

**Lockout**   The employer's equivalent of the strike. Occurs when the employer locks the door of the plant and does not allow workers to work.

**Longer planning horizon**   A longer investment planning time.

**Long-run time period**   A period of time long enough so that all factors of production used by the individual firm can vary, including plant size.

**Long-term capital account**   A balance of payments account containing all entries in the balance of payments concerning long-term investments (the purchase of stock or bonds or direct investments) by residents in other countries or nonresidents in this country.

**Macro model**   One concerned with economic activity on the level of the whole economy.

**Marginal factor cost**   The cost of hiring an additional unit of a resource.

**Marginal propensity to consume**   The percent or portion of any change in income that becomes personal consumption expenditure rather than savings or tax payments.

**Marginal propensity to import**   The amount of increased income spent on imported goods.

**Marginal revenue product**   The change in total revenue associated with hiring an additional unit of a resource. It is determined by multiplying the marginal physical product of the resource by the marginal revenue of the firm.

**Mass production**   See **Assembly-line production.**

**Mature debtor nation**   A nation that has a credit balance in the balance of payments merchandise account. This, in turn, provides the foreign exchange to pay for the debit balance in dividends, interest, and profits resulting from outflows of income earned by prior foreign investment in the nation's economy.

**Mercantilism**   A system of practical economic policy, dominant in the seventeenth and eighteenth centuries, giving rise to "managed" economies with extensive government involvement. Each government aimed to maximize the economic power of the nation by creating a favorable balance of trade resulting in an inflow of gold.

**Merchandise account**   A major subaccount within the current account of the balance of payments. It reflects the exports and imports of goods.

**Merchant banks of the 1780s**   Banks chartered by state governments with the power to issue currency backed by gold and silver. Their loans were primarily commercial.

**Micro model**   The analysis of the activities of the smaller units in the economy such as the individual market, or consumer, or firm.

**Mixed assemblies**   A local unit of organization in the Knights of Labor, consisting of union members from a variety of occupations.

**Mixed-market economy**   Combination of important federal expenditures and taxes in the economy and regulation of sections of the economy to make the federal government an important factor in the market economy.

**Model**   See **Theory.**

**Monocultural**   In reference to a region, monoculturalism refers to specialization in producing one or a very few basic commodities.

**Monopoly power**   The ability of a buyer to directly influence price by varying supply in the market.

**Multinational firm**   A firm with economic facilities for supply, processing, manufacturing, and sales that are worldwide.

**Multiplier effect**   A multiple change in income from any given change in aggregate demand. The size of the multiplier depends on the marginal propensity to consume or save.

**Navigation Acts**   A series of acts by which the British Parliament regulated trade during the colonial period. Among other regulations, the acts restricted trade within the empire to ships of the British Empire and enumerated exports that had to be shipped directly to Britain, regardless of their ultimate destination.

**Net creditor nation**   A nation that has more investment in other countries than foreigners have in that country.

**Net debtor nation**   A nation that has more investment by foreigners in its economy than its residents have in other countries.

**Nonintercourse Act of 1809**   Act of Congress that allowed trade with Britain or France if they stopped seizure of U.S. ships. In 1809, trade was allowed to resume with France.

**Normal profit**   A payment to entrepreneurship equal to its opportunity costs.

**Open door policy**   A policy advocated by the United States in the late nineteenth century to allow all countries to trade and invest through-out China.

**Open market operations**   The buying or selling of government securities by the Federal Reserve in the open market for the purpose of affecting reserves and thus the ability to lend of the commercial banking system. When the Fed buys securities, it increases bank reserves. When the Fed sells securities, it decreases reserves.

**Parity**   A measure to express the purchasing power of farm products. It compares an index of farm prices to an index of the prices of what farmers buy.

**Pooling**   Firms jointly deciding prices, shares of market, and other conditions of the market, as a method of reducing competition between firms.

**Precautionary motive for holding money**   Holding money for protection against unforeseen happenings that require spending.

**Price elasticity of demand**   A measure of the responsiveness of quantity demanded to changes in price along a given demand curve.

**Price elasticity of supply**   A measure of the responsiveness of quantity supplied to changes in price along a given supply curve.

**Primary boycott**   When a striking union urges people not to buy from the firm against which the union is striking.

**Primary demand**   The initial demand for a product stemming from those who had never before bought the product.

**Principle of comparative advantage**   The advantage that a nation or area derives from specializing in producing those goods in which it is relatively more efficient and importing from other nations the goods that they produce with relatively greater efficiency.

**Production function**   The input-output combinations of an economy, an industry, or a firm.

**Production function of the staple**   The function that shows the relationship between resource input and staple product output.

**Production possibilities curve**   A diagrammatic presentation of a production possibilities function.

**Production possibilities function**   A relationship that shows the various combinations of output that the full employment of a nation's resources (land, labor, capital, and entrepreneurship), using the best of current technology, can produce.

**Putting-out system of manufactures**   Home industries using materials supplied by merchant manufacturers. The merchant would then pick up these finished or semifinished products from the workers' homes and pay them.

**Quasi-rents** Payments to a resource owner due to the inelasticity of supply of that resource.

**Real GNP** Total value of annual output of final goods and services that has been adjusted for changes in prices so that it measures only changes in output of goods and services. It is a better measure of economic performance than is current GNP.

**Rediscount rate** The interest rate charged banks by the Federal Reserve for borrowing from the Fed.

**Reexports** Foreign imports that are exported again without any change in form.

**Regressive taxes** The tax rate decreases as taxable income increases.

**Reserve ratio** The ratio of bank reserves to deposits and notes; this reserve indicates the amount of specie that banks chose to or were forced to maintain in relation to their loans and note issue.

**Residentiary industries** Industries that provide goods and services needed by residents of a particular area.

**Safety valve theory** The assumption that in the nineteenth century the free or nearly free land on the frontier would provide an alternative to eastern industrial employment and would limit the ability of industrial employers to "exploit or oppress" the American working class.

**Scale of operation** A firm's operations when utilizing a particular size of plant or number of plants.

**Secondary boycott** When a striking union urges people not to buy from another firm that does business with the firm against which the union is striking.

**Secondary demand** Replacement demand for a product, or, for example, by those who bought a second car to replace an original car.

**Sharecropping** A system of tenancy in which the renter pays the landlord a certain percentage of his crop for the use of the land.

**Short-haul versus long-haul rates** Often discrimination in railroad rates occurred when rates for short hauls (distances) were either higher than for longer hauls or were higher per mile, giving a price advantage to those shipping over longer distances.

**Short-run time period** A period of time short enough such that at least one factor of production is fixed in amount for the individual firm. Often the limiting factor is fixed plant size; that is, fixed floor space.

**Social overhead capital** Forms of capital available for use or consumption by the public (such as roads, canals, railroads, and educational facilities).

**Speculative motive for holding money** Holding money in order to make investments when opportunities arise.

**Stagflation** A condition of high unemployment and high inflation at the same time.

**Subsidiary industries** Industries needed to allow another industry to function. In the leading sector of 1792–1815, foreign trade, shipbuilding and shipfitting were subsidiary.

**Substitution effect** The amount by which consumers tend to substitute a good when its price is falling, for other, now relatively more expensive goods (as implied by the law of demand).

**Supply** A schedule of the various quantities that sellers are willing and able to sell at various prices during a given time.

**Takeoff** In the economic development theory of Walt Rostow, the stage in which economic development becomes the normal and ongoing condition of society.

**Terms of trade** The ratio of export prices received to import prices paid (stated in the form of indices).

**Theory** A set of formal relationships between forces of factors, or a model, or an analogy to, or a simplification of, the complex reality of a period.

**Time series data** Data that show the occurrence of a particular kind of event at different points in time.

**Trade assembly** A local unit of organization in the Knights of Labor consisting only of union members from the same craft or occupation.

**Trade deficit** A deficit that occurs when imports exceed exports.

**Trade surplus** A surplus that occurs when exports exceed imports.

**Trade unionism** A philosophy of union organization in which the concentration is primarily on gaining benefits for union members in terms of increased wages, reduced hours of work, and other conditions of employment; avoids direct political involvement.

**Transactions costs** The costs of effecting exchanges between buyers and sellers.

**Transactions motive for holding money** Holding money to buy things between paydays.

**Trust** A form of business organization in which firms in an industry turn over their common stock to a trust company and receive in return trust certificates. As a result, the trust company controls each individual firm.

**Unilateral transfers** Funds transfers arising when nonresidents receive funds that they are not obligated, now or in the future, to pay back, either in money or goods and services. An example is an immigrant's savings of U.S. dollars that he takes with him when he moves back to his original homeland.

**Unit elastic demand** The condition that exists when quantity demanded changes proportionately with a given change in price; or the percentage change in quantity is equal to the percentage change in price; or the elasticity coefficient is equal to 1.

**Velocity of exchange** (V)  The number of times the supply of money changes hands in a given time period. The assumption, here, is that the spending of money was only for final goods and services.

**Vertical integration**  The combining of firms that produce at different stages of production within a single industry.

**Visible items of trade**  Commodities, such as tobacco, that can be exchanged in trade.

**Waltham Plan**  A system of integrating spinning and weaving equipment within the same plant; introduced in Waltham, Massachusetts.

**Weber Thesis**  The argument of Max Weber that Protestant theological ideas of the Reformation period influenced the behavior of people in ways that were beneficial to rapid economic development. Weber said that psychological conditioning was induced by the theological positions of religious leaders, especially Luther and Calvin.

**Yellow-dog contract**  A contract with an employer wherein a worker agrees not to join a union. Often used as the basis for a court injunction against a union's organizing activities.

**Young creditor nation**  A nation that has a credit balance in the balance of payments merchandise account that provides the foreign exchange to permit long-term capital investment in other countries; it has a debit balance in the long-term capital account.

**Young debtor nation**  A nation that has a debit balance in the balance of payments merchandise account, paid for by credit balances in the long-term capital account.

# Index